# A CRUEL ARITHMETIC
*Inside the Case Against Polygamy*

*For Truman Oler*

# A CRUEL ARITHMETIC

*Inside the Case Against Polygamy*

Craig Jones

A Cruel Arithmetic: Inside the Case Against Polygamy
© Irwin Law Inc., 2012

Published in 2012 by

Irwin Law Inc.
14 Duncan Street
Suite 206
Toronto, ON
M5H 3G8

www.irwinlaw.com

ISBN: 978-1-55221-297-4

Library and Archives Canada Cataloguing in Publication

Jones, Craig E. (Craig Elton), 1965–
A cruel arithmetic : inside the case against polygamy / Craig Jones.

Includes bibliographical references.
Issued also in electronic format.

ISBN 978-1-55221-297-4 (bound).—ISBN 978-1-55221-308-7 (pbk.)

1. Bigamy—Canada.  I. Title.

KE9062.J64 2012          345.71'0283          C2012-903470-3
KF9436.J64 2012

The publisher acknowledges the financial support of the Government of Canada through the Canada Book Fund for its publishing activities.

We acknowledge the assistance of the OMDC Book Fund, an initiative of Ontario Media Development Corporation.

Printed and bound in Canada.

1 2 3 4 5   16 15 14 13 12

# Contents

# Foreword

The polygamous community of Bountiful, British Columbia, had been a stain on the Canadian conscience for decades. It was known that men in the community, members of a fundamentalist offshoot of the Mormon sect, took several wives, and that many of these wives were underage. Yet, to the growing frustration of the British Columbians and of their government, no prosecution had ever been brought against them.

The reason: prosecutors within British Columbia's famously independent Crown prosecutors' office, known as the Criminal Justice Branch, feared Canada's 120-year-old law against polygamy was unconstitutional —a violation of the religious freedom, certainly, of those who claimed the practice as a part of their faith, and possibly of other rights. Not that this was a view restricted to the prosecutors. So long as it occurred between consenting adults, polygamy seemed to many observers a matter of personal choice. If there were specific allegations of exploitation or abuse, these could be addressed by means of other sections of the *Criminal Code*. But to make a crime of polygamy itself?

To some this was overbroad, an improper use of the criminal law to express societal disapproval. Others questioned whether even disapproval was warranted. Surely this was a relic of Victorian prudery or cultural chauvinism, or perhaps both; a blinkered prejudice in favour of Western ways and traditional values. Was polygamy, whether observed in the ultra-conservative lifestyle of the Bountiful colony, or the libertine adventures of urban freethinkers, unusual? Certainly. But where was the harm sufficient to justify overriding constitutional rights?

To be sure, you could find examples of abuse within polygamous relationships. But you could find examples of abusive monogamous relationships as well. As for one man, one woman, "till death do you part"— that train had left long ago. Was polygamy—multiple wives at the same time—all that different from the "serial monogamy"—a succession of wives at various times—practised by many men, some of them famous and admired? Not so long ago, same-sex marriage had seemed strange, even threatening; now it was the law. Was not multiple marriage simply another step along the road to greater tolerance?

The sight of one man with many wives might seem to suggest an imbalance of power and status, the stuff of retrograde male fantasies. But polygamy need not always take the form of polygyny: polyandry—one woman, many husbands—was also possible, along with various other combinations, homosexual and heterosexual. At that, polygamy arguably empowered women, bidding up their value in the marriage market while allowing them their choice of the most desirable mate, albeit on a shared basis. In an increasingly multicultural Canada, could the legal proscription of polygamy long survive?

These arguments admittedly did not reflect the majority view, whether among British Columbians or Canadians generally. Perhaps not entirely coincidentally, they also did not reflect the views of successive BC attorneys general. Lacking the general power to direct Crown prosecutors to take action against the Bountiful polygamists, they twice directed the appointment of outside prosecutors, only to see them, too, balk at the constitutional gate. When finally yet another special prosecutor was appointed, Bountiful's lawyers were ready. Here, they argued, was a clear case of abuse of process, of a government shopping around until it found the special prosecutor it wanted—that is, doing an end run around prosecutorial independence. And so that case failed, before it had begun.

Enter Craig Jones, then the supervising counsel of the constitutional law group in the Attorney General's office and the author of this absorbing memoir. It was Jones who was given responsibility for referring the question of the law's constitutionality to the courts as a way to break the impasse, and it was Jones who, as lead counsel, successfully argued the government's case in the trial that ensued. As intriguing as any case would be that, as Jones says, combines "crime, religion, politics, and sex," and as important as any case would be that establishes fundamental points of constitutional law, what makes the Polygamy Reference so fascinating (and historic) is that it was all new: both the process and the arguments were without precedent, at least in Canada.

There had been judicial references before, but never at the trial court level: a way of ensuring the reference could hear factual evidence of how polygamy was actually practised, in Bountiful and abroad, rather than merely consider abstruse constitutional principles. As for the arguments Jones was to present on the harms that legalized polygamy would entail, they were entirely novel: to a large extent, Jones and his team of young lawyers would be making them up even as the trial progressed.

I have a little bit of personal knowledge of this. I've known Craig for many years. We'd both had some involvement with the BC Civil Liberties Association, mine peripheral, his rather more substantive, as the organization's former president. As such, I knew Craig to take a broadly liberal or libertarian approach to questions of legal rights, and from our very general discussions of the polygamy issue beforehand, I suspect his personal views going into the reference were closer to those of the prosecutors in the Criminal Justice Branch than to the Attorney General's. In arguing the case for the law's constitutionality, he would be taking a professional rather than a personal position.

You can see a little of that, I think, in the questions he devised for the court to answer. Was Section 293 of the *Criminal Code*, the polygamy law, "consistent with the *Canadian Charter of Rights and Freedoms*"? On the other hand, might the law be interpreted to require that the polygamy in question "involved a minor, or occurred in a context of dependence, exploitation, abuse of authority, a gross imbalance of power, or undue influence"? By inviting the court to narrow the law's application, the second question hedged against the possibility of defeat on the first. Rather than require the court to answer yes or no on the constitutional question, it gave it a third option: it depends.

But somewhere in the course of researching and framing his arguments, Jones convinced himself the law was constitutional as it stood, without need of such qualifiers, as he later convinced the court, and as I predict he will convince many of you. The second question assumed, in line with the law's critics, that it was necessary to show specific harms to those involved in a polygamous marriage in order to justify its prohibition by the state. The epiphanal change in Jones's thinking was this: that the harm from polgyamy, in any society where it is widespread, is not just to those immediately involved in a polygamous relationship, but to society at large. Indeed, even if it did *no* harm to its direct participants, that broader societal harm would remain.

The arguments that would be advanced in support of this claim applied the insights of evolutionary psychology, and drew on groundbreaking empirical research from around the world, much of it commissioned especially for the case. As such, Jones's case was an explicit rebuke to the existing scholarship on polygamy, much of which he rightly scorns as tendentious, shoddy, or both, but even the best of which was typically steeped in the assumption that the harms at issue were to specific individuals. If it does nothing else, this book will convince you that, where polygamy is widespread, the harm is also.

The argument is as follows. At the level of the individual, theory and evidence point to a strong evolutionary bias in favour of polygamy. Men increase their odds of passing on their genetic code by mating with as many women as possible, while women, without the same opportunities for mass reproduction, must focus on improving the survival chances of each child by finding and keeping a partner for the long-term business of child-rearing. The success of such evolutionary strategies over millions of years has, it is argued, hard-wired such proclivities into our genes. Left unchecked, polygamy—or more specifically, polygyny—would be our natural state.

But: there is a second evolutionary imperative at work, at cross-purposes with the first. At the societal level, the same process of natural selection favours monogamy. Societies that repress the polygamous impulse have tended to thrive and prosper compared to those that do not; since the Greeks, the most advanced societies have been broadly monogamous. Yes, that implies we can make such judgments about societies. I haven't waded through the mountains of empirical research Jones's team assembled, comparing polygamous and non-polygamous societies across a broad range of indicators of social health, but it was sufficiently compelling to convince a judge.

Perhaps it would not have done so had Jones not backed up this statistical correlation with a plausible causal explanation, as simple as it is ineluctable. The institutionalization of polygamy invariably means an imbalance of marriageable females and males—a small number of the men monopolizing a large number of the women (the alternative, polyandry, is a theoretical curiosity). The "cruel arithmetic" of this situation has two immediate consequences. First, the shortage of women is met by increasing efforts to expand the supply, notably by lowering the age of marriageability. Second, the surplus of men gives rise to the sorts of pathologies observable wherever large numbers of unattached young men are found: crime, disorder, and so on.

But those are just the start. Whatever sexual "bargaining" power women might theoretically enjoy in polygamous societies by virtue of their relative scarcity is in practice overwhelmed by the more traditional sources of power—financial, institutional, physical—that are typically the preserve of men. The value women is not in themselves, but as marriage properties; it does not accrue to them, but to their husbands. As with any valuable property, it is the rich and the powerful who command the most, adding an element of class envy to the resentments of the unmarried males.

The survival of such societies—male-dominated, highly stratified —require strict regimentation: not only of women, but of society generally. That is true whether one is speaking of those countries in the Middle East and sub-Saharan Africa where polygamy is still prevalent, or of an isolated religious community like Bountiful. Indeed, Jones warns,

Bountiful, with its "child brides" and "lost boys," is a microcosm of the kind of society Canada would become if polygamy were legalized. As Jones told the court at the outset of the trial, "Bountiful did not create polygamy; polygamy created Bountiful."

This may be the most difficult part of the argument for some readers. I think the case is unanswerable that, *where polygamy is widespread*, the harm that results is societal and general, not individual and specific: it hurts monogamous families as much as polygamous, single people as much as married people. But would it become widespread in Canada, notwithstanding our traditions of equality and freedom, without criminal sanction? Jones argues forcefully that it could, but we are necessarily in the realm of speculation. Could one accept that it is potentially harmful, and still argue for less intrusive measures to combat it than the *Criminal Code*?

One posited source of its proliferation is immigration from polygamous societies. But if there is sufficient evidence of its harm to warrant criminalization, the same evidence would surely also justify disqualifying those who practise it from admission to the country. Similarly, if what distinguishes marriage from mere cohabitation is solemnization—if the "invocation of some external authority with (even notional) powers of enforcement is necessary to make polygamy 'take' and spread"—could not a society merely refuse to recognize polygamous marriages, thereby depriving them of the oxygen of legal and social approval, not to mention, tax benefits? Yes, that's discriminatory, but again, if criminal penalties are in order, milder measures must be as well.

But this, too, is speculation. Jones may be right that we can't risk it: that the harms from polygamy are so great, and the biological impulse to it so strong, that the door must not be opened even a crack. And while this book is, true to its title, an argument against polygamy, it is many other things as well: a diary of Jones's thoughts and feelings as the trial progressed; a portrait of the close-knit Vancouver legal community, with its many colourful characters; a layman's introduction to courtroom procedure and the practice of law.

There has never been a trial quite like the Polygamy Reference. As Jones suggests, there may never be one like it again. I feel much the same way about this book. Hugely informative, sharply argued, warmly recalled, it is every bit as extraordinary as the trial it recounts.

Andrew Coyne
July 2012

# Acknowledgments

British Columbia Attorney General Wally Oppal should get full credit for putting momentum behind the province's polygamy file after decades of uncertainty and inaction. His successors—Mike de Jong, Barry Penner, and Shirley Bond—each took a particular interest in the subsequent Polygamy Reference proceeding, and would have shouldered the blame had the whole enterprise collapsed in failure, so it is fair that they should claim a large measure of credit also for its success. Each had a personal hand in aspects of the case's progress. Successive Deputy Attorneys General Allan Seckel and David Loukidelis, and my immediate superior, Assistant Deputy Richard Fyfe, threw their support behind this untried and ambitious idea of a trial of the constitutional issues through a reference proceeding. Each showed enough faith in me and my team to trust us with virtually every aspect of the conduct of the litigation.

This book is partly memoir, and any such work, as Ben Franklin recognized, is in some measure an exercise of the ego. After all, we write these things in the conceit that something we have done is worth reading about at some length. That Franklin offered his disclaimer in the introduction to the autobiography of, to my mind, one of Western history's greatest figures and then went on to write the balance with such offhand humility and genial charm is remarkable. I am no Franklin. I'm sure that, whatever efforts I take to conceal it, my recollections of the polygamy case and its conduct will reveal an element of pride. I can only hope that it does so without obviously intruding on the story that follows.

With that disclaimer behind me, I should say right from the beginning that had the litigation, which is at the heart of this book, been left in my hands alone, it would have been a mess, or at the very least, a very different case from the one I describe here. I worked with some exceptionally dedicated and talented lawyers in the Legal Services branch of the Ministry of Attorney General, and it will be my privilege to introduce you to many of them as this story progresses. By not naming them here I avoid the difficulty of listing them, which would inevitably imply some sort of ranking (unless it were alphabetical, which would just be silly). In addition to the lawyers, though, who as I say you will meet, I need also to acknowledge Nancy Reimer, our team's paralegal, and Carol Brossard, Pamela Hull, and Kaley Isbister, legal secretaries extraordinaire, who handled the almost indescribable complexities of litigation with dozens of counsel, witnesses, and consultants from all over the world. My secretary (yes, we still do use that honourable appellation) at my Victoria office, Chris Lloyd, and Legal Office Manager Heidi Hynes kept the group together during my extended absence during the trial. My colleague Richard Butler relieved me of many managerial responsibilities in that period with no expectation of rank, recognition, or reward (and he received none of these, naturally). His incisive criticisms and editorial reviews of argument on this case, as on so many others, were invaluable. I should mention too the indefatigable John Nelson, then an articled student, who, among his many feats of endurance that year, dove repeatedly into government archives in Victoria and Ottawa and surfaced with innumerable pearls. There were many others who contributed off the corner of their desks. Working with them was constantly inspiring.

Some parts of the book closely follow the written submissions we made to the court. Because I was the principal author of those submissions, I have not been shy about adopting their language, at times almost verbatim. But I must acknowledge that those passages, as indeed our case as a whole, resulted from a collaborative effort of research and discussion, and Leah Greathead, Karen Horsman, and Sarah Bevan, in particular, made important editorial and textual contributions to many of the documents we produced.

The book itself came about with the encouragement of Jeff Miller, my long-time publisher at Irwin Law. Jeff recognized that this would be a bit of a departure from his firm's black-letter legal offerings, but was willing to give it a try. Pamela Erlichman provided copy editing services (and encouragement) through the final drafts, and Joe Henrich, who figures prominently in this book, reviewed some of the scientific passages to ensure my embarrassment would be limited.

And, as always, my wife, Amanda, and children, Daniel and Sadie, bore my lack of presence (physical, and often otherwise) with understanding and good cheer, both during the trial of the reference and in the writing of this book.

# Introduction

For hundreds of thousands, perhaps millions of years, human society was almost universally polygamous. That is, in any given community, at least some men could be expected to have several wives simultaneously.

We will never know who originally came up with the idea of monogamous marriage. I'm not referring here to the notion that a *particular* man should have only one wife—most marriages are monogamous even in polygamous societies. I'm speaking of monogamy as the idea that no man should be allowed to have *more* than one wife, and the further innovation that the community should have a role in ensuring that is so, through the imposition of rules, norms, mores, and, eventually, laws. Monogamy in this sense probably wasn't the result of a single philosophical epiphany, and it certainly did not result from theistic or prophetic revelation, but it does appear to have developed rather quickly and, in terms of human society, rather recently. The term "revolutionary" is apt as a description of this "socially imposed universal monogamy" (as one expert witness would later term it) whereby king and subject alike were limited to a single reproductive partner, at least in theory.

Monogamy appears to have begun in the early democracies in ancient Greece and spread through Rome's military and, later, religious dominance of Europe. It gathered momentum so that, although the majority of societies throughout history have been polygamous, this number is shrinking today to the point where societies with state-endorsed polygamy number only a handful. Around the world, even nations where the right of a man to have multiple wives has the deepest cultural and religious roots seem to be turning official backs on the practice; and if there is an international legal trend, it is one of, if not criminalizing, then at least of delegitimizing and discouraging polygamy. So it is curious that in the West, and most particularly in Canada and the United States, many have been urging that the laws should move in the opposite direction: these aspiring reformers suggest that, in the rights-based, diversity-respecting nations of the

1

twenty-first century, it is the legal enforcement of monogamy, rather than the practice of polygamy, that has run its historical course.

Opponents of polygamy in this country, on the other hand, from feminist activists to conservative adherents of traditional Western religions, maintain that it is inherently abusive and discriminates against women, that it's harmful to children and morally repugnant. Some even posit monogamy as a pillar of Western democratic and economic development and argue that decriminalization of the practice of polygamy would be a retrograde step on almost every level.

Polygamy's supporters (or perhaps it is better to call them defenders because most do not advocate the practice as much as attack the right of the state to prohibit it) counter that there is nothing objectionable about polygamy *per se*. It might be demeaning of women in some contexts; in others it might not (in fact, in one conceivable manifestation—multipartner male gay marriage—it wouldn't involve women at all). These commentators have argued, not unreasonably, that if there are abuses in any particular situation, we should deal with them as abuses rather than banning polygamy. Many of the harms associated with polygamy in North America, they further argue, are more the result of the criminalization of the practice than of polygamy itself. And as our understanding of the near-universality of polygamy across human societies has developed, psychologists, anthropologists, and historians have suggested that polygamy is at least as "natural" a human behaviour as monogamy. Why shouldn't the law, they ask, conform to our evolved preferences?

Some of those advocating a toleration of polygamy even say that it *enhances* female status and choice: they argue that women's value is increased in a scarce marriage market, not reduced. Why not let them take advantage of that, in a society where so many other advantages seem to accrue to men? And as for monogamy being a pillar of Western democratic development, that may or may not be so, but in Canada today we are too far advanced to quell individual liberty in service of some engineered utopia. The revolution in gay rights and same-sex marriage, they say, has shown us that moral panic and stereotyping can be overcome through simple accommodation of minority mate-preferences without rending the social fabric.

And of course, for some, polygamy is far beyond a matter of choice; it is a matter of religious imperative. So shouldn't we respect the free exercise of religion if it isn't hurting anybody?

The debate has suffered badly from being conducted based on an uneven smattering of facts: anecdotes of "good polygamy" sent piecemeal to combat the horror stories of polygamy's "victims" or "escapees." The arguments were built upon sand, bolstered by supposedly self-evident social truths: that prohibiting polygamy is the result of Judeo-Christian imperialism and (to use perhaps the most grotesque term from the banal shorthand of postmodernism) the "othering" of cultural and religious minorities or, on the other hand, that polygamy itself is inherently oppressive of women because it suggests an asymmetry of value of the genders.

In Canada in 2010 this engaging but rather theoretical philosophical and academic debate became an unprecedented legal battle. For the first time anywhere in the world, polygamy's champions—religious adherents, civil libertarians, and a court-appointed advocate known as the *amicus*—would bring forward all the available evidence and arguments to support decriminalization. Opposing them—defending the polygamy ban—would be government lawyers, women's rights advocates, and other groups determined to see that polygamy remained illegal. The forum was the BC Supreme Court, in a procedure known as a "trial court reference," the first one in Canadian history. The Chief Justice of the Court would hear and consider what he would later call "the most comprehensive judicial record on the subject ever produced."

I had the privilege to be lead counsel for the Attorney General of British Columbia in the case. This book is my take on the matter officially known as *Reference re: the Constitutionality of s. 293 of the Criminal Code of Canada*, but universally referred to in shorthand as the Polygamy Reference.

The written evidence in the Polygamy Reference filled a small library (quite literally—a separate room in the courthouse was set up to house it); the testimony played out over months in the winter of 2010–11. Expert social scientists, clinicians, theologians, and law professors were followed by a procession of those who had experienced polygamy firsthand. There were witnesses who testified anonymously and others who gave impromptu press conferences on the courthouse steps.

In this book I try to describe the issues in the context of the evidence and arguments put before the court. In that sense, this book is about polygamy and a fundamental clash of rights: the right of a society to declare it to be criminal behaviour versus the right of individuals to be free to arrange their most intimate personal affairs according to their conscience. The book is also, necessarily, a bit of a history, because the debate has to be put in its context: why is it that this extraordinary trial came to pass in Vancouver, British Columbia, on Canada's notoriously laid-back "Left Coast"? And, because I was a lawyer deeply involved in the litigation, this is also the courtroom memoir of a most fascinating and complex case, and a bit of the story of the people who brought the issue forward and argued it so thoroughly.

I hope here to be fair to the arguments made on the other side because I have a lot of sympathy for them; many of the positions articulated by the defenders of polygamy were ones that I would have made (and sometimes did) before reflection and research led me to reconsider. Like most Canadians I have a strong civil libertarian instinct: I want the state to justify any infringement on our freedoms. This book isn't an argument against the civil libertarian position, but it is, at least in large part, an explanation of why I and others who began from the same initial "default" position came to move beyond it.

As I write, it is not yet certain whether, or how, the question of the constitutionality of the polygamy law will make its way to the higher courts. It may well be that the final verdict on the constitutional questions is yet to come. A lawyer should always be careful about arguing his case in the public forum—we make our submissions in court, in case our role as advocate for our clients should become confused with our personal views. At the same time, lawyers also have an obligation to participate in the public conversation and help explain how courts approach legal matters. I hope that this book is not seen as an attempt to influence the final outcome of any future proceedings, but instead as a contribution to the public conversation around this fascinating topic.

I should say a word about my sources. All the documents quoted in this book are, one way or the other, in the public record. They may have been filed in court proceedings, reprinted in the *Gazette*, or published in the media or online. Because this book is meant to be, on some level, something of an "inside story" of the litigation, at times I have described some events or conversations that might otherwise be considered as confidential information related to the case. When I have done so, I have cleared the publication of these passages with my then-employer, the BC Ministry of Justice. I offer these anecdotes for context and colour, but I'm conscious that they may be suspected as self-servingly selective, and I would not discourage a reader from approaching them with that caution in mind, even though I was never asked to change or remove any of the text.

When it comes to what was said in court, my source is, of course, the trial transcript. We had the services of Charest Reporting throughout the hearing and arguments, and on most days it was the legendary Spencer Charest himself who did the transcriptions. Each evening, Charest would distribute to all participants via email a "rough draft" of the day's proceedings. An official, clean transcript would follow about a week or two later. But even with Charest at the keyboard, a court transcript is a fairly dry representation of spoken language, and so I have taken some very minor liberties with the official record. At times, I have italicized a word or phrase to more closely reflect the emphasis of the speaker. At other times, I have made adjustments to punctuation where my recollection or notes would reflect different phraseology. Finally, I have on rare occasions "cleaned up" the grammar to better reflect the meaning, for instance by removing "ums" or repeated words. These minor editorial changes, however, are exceptional, and the passages I quote from the transcripts are the best representations I can make of the word-for-word goings on in the courtroom.

The polygamy case was heard at a time when the practice of litigation is in transition. Economic pressures have meant that thorough airing of complex legal problems has been supplanted by summary trials on affidavit evidence. Trials are expensive and time-consuming, and as a consequence they are disappearing—fiscal reality dictates that almost every civil case will settle, and it is a common complaint that young litigators might get into court for only a few days each year, and often not even that. Recourse to the courts is an increasingly illusory ideal: many of history's defining civil cases likely wouldn't be litigated today. *Pro bono* work is still a feature of the professional life of the bar, but rarely involves taking cases to trial because of the high amount of court fees, expert expenses, and other "hard disbursements" of litigation that are now tacked on to the opportunity cost of lawyers' time. There are other aspects of modern practice that give rise to some nostalgia: written submissions are methodically stripped of their elegance as the "plain language" movement has become a watchword for the lowest common denominator of prose; oral advocacy and cross-examination are vanishing arts, preserved like an ancient language by a determined few almost more out of affection than for any expected effect. And fewer lawyers nowadays practise in both the criminal and civil courts, something that was once, in British Columbia, routine. This too is a pity, because a busy criminal law practice had always been the graduate school of trial skills.

In moments where the sense of the dramatic overcomes me, I wonder if the Polygamy Reference might be thought of one day as one of Canada's last great constitutional trials, where skilled counsel dueled for weeks and months over truly fundamental questions before an astute and respected judge. Certainly the issue was broadly fascinating: the case had crime, religion, politics, and sex. It highlighted longstanding debates over the innate differences between men and women, and indeed over the nature of innateness itself. It challenged us to think hard about what we mean by harm, what we mean by liberty and human agency, even what we mean when we say that one thing is caused by another, and how we can claim to know. There was cold, cutting-edge evidence from leading experts in several fields, but also wrenching testimony from personal witnesses.

I know I will never have another case remotely like it.

# PART 1
# Beginnings

## Courtroom 55

Courtroom 55 is quite possibly the largest in the province, with more than a hundred public seats; but even so, on that morning, 22 November 2010, it was packed almost to capacity. Lawyers, more than thirty of them, filled the front half of the room arranged behind three rows of desks in front of the bench. Even those arrangements were inadequate for the numbers, and counsel spilled over into the seats usually reserved for the jury and media. It was an ocean of black wool and silk, spattered with stacks of paper, binders of documents, and laptops rigged to produce transcripts of the proceedings that scrolled across the screens in real-time.

Just before ten o'clock, the room was humming with conversations, shuffling papers, and clacking keys, all of which fell silent when the clerk appeared from the judge's entrance and called the court to order. A compact, energetic man emerged briskly and took his seat behind the raised bench in front. This was Robert Bauman, newly appointed Chief Justice of the Supreme Court of British Columbia. In the weeks and months ahead, I would attempt to persuade Bauman that Canada's 120-year-old criminal prohibition on the practice of polygamy did not unjustifiably infringe rights of religious freedom and human liberty.[1]

Along with lawyers from the federal Department of Justice, my team and I had put together a case that we believed was unlike any that had been presented in a Canadian courtroom or, for that matter, anywhere else in the world. We had worked over months to develop a model of polygamy and its effects that would draw on research from fields as diverse as psychology, anthropology, political science, economics, and history. The expert evidence we would present would be supported—perhaps particularized is a better word—by the testimony of real people who had observed and experienced polygamy and its effects on the ground. All of this would be to a single end: to convince Chief Justice Bauman that the criminal prohibition—section 293 of the *Criminal Code of Canada*—was not a meaningless vestige of Victorian prudishness but instead an important, even foundational, law that continued to perform a crucial function in a modern democracy.

It's customary at the beginning of a case that counsel take turns introducing themselves to the court on the record. This is not usually a long process. As head of the Attorney General of British Columbia's team, I said my name, then those of the four colleagues who had accompanied me that morning. Then, one by one, the other lawyers stood, made their introductions, and sat. On and on it went. Finally, the last lawyer had taken her seat, and Bauman gazed out over the black sea. He said:

> Counsel, we're embarking upon a historic reference, and that has not been lost, I'm sure, on all the participants. I make one rule at the beginning and not with any intention of making light of any aspect of the proceedings, but from now on . . . no one can move. Just for the purpose of the court recording and my own sanity, I have to know where everyone is at all times, so I'd appreciate it if you'd stay where you are and we'll make a map.

Amid the gentle laughter this provoked, I took a moment to turn and look over the audience in the gallery. The fifth estate was there: Daphne Bramham from the *Vancouver Sun*, who had probably done more than anyone in her investigative articles and book *The Secret Lives of Saints* to bring the issue of polygamy in British Columbia to public attention and therefore, indirectly, to Courtroom 55; Keith Fraser from the *Province*, one of the few legal journalists who took the time to understand much of what he was reporting; and Sarah Galashan, a former acquaintance from my University of British Columbia school days, now a well-respected reporter with CTV news. Other journalists I recognized but did not know by name.

The other spectators were an assortment. I picked out Nancy Mareska of Stop Polygamy in Canada, and two of the Mackert sisters, Mary and Rena, now middle-aged survivors of an American polygamist community, whose videotaped evidence would be played at the trial. In the second row I spotted the cheerful, plump woman who would offer her testimony for the Canadian Polyamory Advocacy Association (CPAA), in an affidavit where she described her relationship with the two men with whom she lived. She would be quoted later that week in a newspaper, describing life with her male partners as "like going to bed between two heat-seeking missiles." To which she added, unnecessarily from my point of view, "and I'm the heat!" The rest of the seats held a handful of university students, a couple of graduate researchers, court-watchers, a gaggle of judicial clerks,[2] and then scores of others who likely had no excuse but curiosity.

There was no one in the gallery whom I could identify as coming from the Fundamentalist Church of Jesus Christ of Latter-day Saints (FLDS), the most prominent fundamentalist Mormon organization in Canada, based in the world-famous openly polygamist community of Bountiful in the British Columbia interior. I had been half-expecting the church to pack the room with Bountiful women in their wrist-to-ankle dresses and their hair piled into the trademark "wave." Fundamentalist Mormon polygamy, and its fashions, were enjoying a notoriety as a result of the wildly popular HBO series *Big Love*, one of several television programs set in the context of a polygamous family.[3] Or perhaps, I thought, there might be representatives from the other polygamous faction at Bountiful, the breakaway sect led by former FLDS bishop Winston Blackmore, who was himself boycotting the proceedings because the government had refused to bankroll his involvement. But if any of Blackmore's group were in attendance, I couldn't spot them.

In another indication of the degree of interest that had surrounded the trial, our first order of business that morning was to argue over whether the proceeding could be televised. The application had been brought by the CBC, who proposed a live "webstream" coupled with occasional manned television cameras. Most of the participants didn't oppose the idea, but the government of Canada objected, and Bauman ordered that, at least for the time being, cameras were not welcome. This came as a relief; the CBC's last-minute application had consumed a lot of my time and effort over the previous week because my office had agreed to work with Court Services and the network on technical details in case permission was granted. Now we could focus on more pressing matters.

The lawyers who were there that morning, and who would reappear throughout the trial,[4] represented a broad diversity of interests: As I've mentioned, the federal Department of Justice had their group (it was the constitutionality of a federal law that was under challenge), and I had mine for the provincial Attorney General. On the other side of the aisle, the main players were George Macintosh, QC,[5] the *amicus curiae*, and two junior partners from his firm, Tim Dickson and Ludmila Herbst. Macintosh and his team had been appointed by the court to lead the case opposing the polygamy ban (I'll describe the *amicus*'s role in more detail later). Immediately behind Macintosh sat Bob Wickett, who would be representing the FLDS and its bishop, James (Jim) Oler. Wickett would be assisted throughout the hearing by two solid juniors of his own, Matt Siren and Andrew Scarth.

The other counsel were there for organizations that had been granted the status of "interested persons"; this allowed them to make arguments, introduce evidence, and, with leave of the court, cross-examine witnesses.

Douglas Christie appeared for a group called the Canadian Association for Free Expression (CAFE). That group was known mainly as a defender of neo-Nazis targeted under Canada's hate-speech provisions enshrined in the *Criminal Code* and *Human Rights Act*s, as indeed was Christie himself. Depending on whom you listened to, Christie was either a principled defender of the underdog or a co-opted mouthpiece for racists and anti-Semites. Personally I have always found him to be courteous and straightforward as a lawyer (more than can be said for some with whom I've been forced to deal over the years), and I had no difficulty accepting his involvement, though I expected that his eventual submissions would be somewhat off the beaten track (and indeed they proved to be).

West Coast Women's Legal Education and Action Fund (usually abbreviated as West Coast LEAF[6] or simply WCL) was British Columbia's most prominent women's legal advocacy group and unsurprisingly had sent an impressive crew. But its three formidable lawyers (Janet Winteringham, Deanne Gaffar, and Kasari Govender), must have been a little uncomfortable on the same side as REAL Women Canada, a socially conservative "family values" organization represented by Jonathan Baker. Polygamy made strange bedfellows in more ways than one.

My one-time colleagues of the BC Civil Liberties Association (BCCLA) (prior to joining government I had served on the association's board of directors, including two terms as president) had come to argue alongside the FLDS that the polygamy law should be struck down. So had the CPAA, although both the BCCLA and CPAA were at pains to explain that they didn't agree with the FLDS's brand of patriarchal and reportedly abusive polygyny. Not *that kind of* polygamy. The BCCLA had retained Monique Pongracic-Speier, who was widely admired for her recent work for the plaintiffs in the Safe Injection Site case (Monique and her co-counsel had won a rather stunning series of victories against the federal government and were soon to win one more at the Supreme Court of Canada).

Allow me to digress for a moment into etymology because you may have noticed that I used a new, perhaps unfamiliar, term in the previous paragraph. "Polygyny" (from the Latin meaning "more than one female") is, as the name suggests, a relationship in which a husband has more than one wife. It is (and this will be important) overwhelmingly the most common form of polygamy, which itself technically means more than one spouse regardless of gender. The opposite of polygyny is "polyandry," meaning one woman with multiple husbands. For purposes of this book, I use the term "polygamy" as it is used in common conversation, that is to say, generally referring to polygyny. But when distinctions are important I will occasionally revert to the more precise terms. I hope this won't prove too distracting. The term "polyamory," incidentally, means "multiple loves"—technically the term embraces any form of multipartner relationships (polygynous, polyandrous, or same-sex). Polyamory as a philosophy is generally expressed in secular terms, and as a movement, is organized only in the loosest of ways. Just which of these activities (polygyny, polyandry, polyamory) had been captured by Canada's polygamy law would be hotly contested.

To return to my description of the participants and their lawyers, then, the aforementioned CPAA was represented by John Ince, the rather notorious leader of the Sex Party, author, adult store owner and vigorous sex activist (is there any other kind?). Ince was a lawyer-turned-businessman who did not otherwise practise law, though he proved completely adept at litigating on behalf of his "clients" and his cause. The polyamorists, as I mentioned earlier, supported the idea that there could be *some* law to prohibit polygamy, but that it could not include the secular, egalitarian multipartner relationships that their membership idealized.

Rounding out this list of the groups in support of the antipolygamy law were the Christian Legal Fellowship (with their Calgary-based counsel Gerry Chipeur), BC Teachers Federation (represented by in-house lawyer Robyn Trask), the Asper Centre for Human Rights, the Canadian Centre for the Rights of the Child (both these groups were represented by Brent Olthuis and Stephanie McHugh from Hunter Litigation Chambers, a prominent Vancouver litigation boutique, along with Cheryl Milne, a Toronto lawyer and professor of constitutional law), and Beyond Borders, another children's rights group (represented by the Winnipeg-based human rights lawyer David Matas).

After the Chief Justice's decision against televisation, we took a recess and then settled back into our chairs. We stood again as Bauman emerged from his chambers and resumed his seat. As the Chief Justice sat, so did everyone except me. The Attorney General of British Columbia had "carriage" of the reference case (which is to say we had the principal responsibility for presenting the case), and so I spoke first, introduced the issues, and gave an overview of the evidence my team would be presenting and the submissions we expected to make over the two or three months ahead. I said to Bauman:

> You are being asked to settle a question that for decades has been in vigorous dispute: whether Canada's polygamy's law conforms to the *Charter of Rights and Freedoms*. As you've heard, some prominent practitioners and legal academics have disagreed sharply in this question. Legally, this case is difficult. No one could argue otherwise. Procedurally, as I've explained, it's unprecedented.

The proceeding *was* unprecedented, and not only for the novelty of the multilevel evidentiary case that we were planning to present. The Polygamy Reference[7] would mark the first time that a Canadian trial court (as opposed to appellate) had heard a legal issue referred to it by the government through an Order of the Lieutenant Governor in Council. It was a case without "parties" in the ordinary sense, just the two interested governments, a team of lawyers presenting the opposing case, and a host of groups wishing to weigh in on the many issues. And although a number of courts in various countries had considered the constitutionality of their own polygamy provisions, they had done so without the benefit of the extraordinary factual record that this case would generate. How this all came to pass will be a significant part of the story that follows.

## Anachronisms

The Attorney General's offices on Hornby Street look out over the Vancouver Law Courts building, a massive concrete, glass, and steel-truss structure at Robson Square, dead in the centre of the city. It is often repeated that its architect, Arthur Erickson, envisioned the complex as a fifty-five-storey tower lying on its side,[8] with a rooftop garden of three city blocks, built long before the term "green roof" had any public currency. The Robson Square complex is deceptively massive, a building only 138 feet at its tallest point but one containing 1.3 million square feet of floor space. It is the home of the Provincial Court, the judges of which do much of the heavy lifting of the justice system, including small claims, minor criminal matters, and much of family law. At the southern end, and joined to the Provincial Court side by an overpass above Smithe Street, is the home of the superior courts of the province, the BC Supreme Court (where we would have our trial) and Court of Appeal.[9]

The part of the complex that houses the superior courts is a stepped concrete design, capped by a massive slanted glass roof supported by a steel spaceframe that covers about fifty thousand square feet of public space. The design incorporated three cascading waterfalls using over a hundred thousand gallons of water-cooling throughout—meant to be a natural air conditioning system. The Law Courts portion of the Robson Square complex has thirty-four modern courtrooms and one "heritage" courtroom imported in its entirety from the older traditional stone courthouse building. Erickson's complex is said to be leaky, oddly laid out, confusing to navigate,[10] and brilliant.

The old neoclassic Vancouver courthouse remains beside the Robson Square complex, fixed like a granite pupae shell disgorging a hard, angular insect. The older building, with its façade dominated by traditional Romanesque columns and a massive stone stairway, is now the Vancouver Art Gallery. The proximity was quite deliberate: Erickson, the master architect, wanted his development to span what he saw as the two pillars of civilization: the arts and the law.

The "new" courthouse is now already three decades old, but something about it suggests a state of permanent revolution, or at least innovation, with its startling angularity, open-air aspect, forests of greenery, and cascading pools. Lawyers and judges in quasi-medieval costume work their ancient trades in a decidedly forward-looking, even futuristic, setting.

The British Columbia courts have a reputation for litigation at the progressive edge, and it doesn't take much imagination to believe that the building, which was brought into use just before the modern Canadian Constitution of 1982, was built to midwife the birth of the *Charter* era itself. Aboriginal rights and gay rights, as we now know them throughout Canada, were born here. Equality under the *Charter* was first comprehensively defined here. The legendary lawyers who spearheaded these and other landmark assaults on the establishment—Berger, Storrow, Arvay, and countless others, could in 2010 still be occasionally spotted in the airy corridors or lunching at the Law Courts Inn, the facility's captive restaurant tucked away on the fourth floor. Still other local rights pioneers, like Vicky Gray and Lynn Smith, were now themselves Supreme Court justices.

Whatever it was about Vancouver that made it such fertile ground for rights-based litigation, in 2010 the city had not yet shown signs of relinquishing its status as the constitutional epicentre of Canada. But even for the "Left Coast," the case that began in Courtroom 55 that morning was noteworthy: should Canada's law against polygamy be struck down as unconstitutional?

We might add this 120-year-old prohibition to the list of anachronisms in the modern practice of law, like the flicking black gowns of the lawyers who would be arguing the issue. Gowns? Yes, perhaps I should take a few paragraphs to describe, for the benefit of Americans and others unfamiliar with the Canadian legal process, the Canadian lawyer's mode of dress. There will be a purpose to this digression, I promise.

Canadian barristers,[11] like their English forebears, wear a black robe (actually a sleeved gown) that reaches almost to the floor. If you haven't seen one, you wouldn't be far off conjuring an adult version of dinnertime attire in Harry Potter's Hogwarts. The gown is made of wool (called "stuff") or, in the case of lawyers who have been awarded the designation

"Queen's Counsel" or "QC," silk. The wool gowns are of a slightly more pleated and elaborate design than the silks, and have a sash that drapes over one shoulder. (I should caution you before I continue that the features of court wear and their origin are not all that well established, and what I relate here is, in significant part, a mix of hearsay and legend.) It is often said that this sash is actually a vestigial *purse*. In the earlier days of the English bar it was deemed unseemly for a lawyer to take a fee for his service, lest he prefer wealthier clients and causes (imagine that). So the idea was that clients could approach the lawyer from behind and drop money in the over-shoulder receptacle, without the lawyer knowing who was paying how much. The QC's gown, it is further alleged, lacks the purse because that rank, historically, was a paid appointment of the Crown (though this was apparently a bit of a ruse—no QC since Sir Francis Bacon, the first, had actually collected from Their Majesties). In any event, QCs once were privileged to sit "within the bar" of the court with the judge and therefore were beyond the reach of those clients who would sully the profession with the mercenary clink of coins.[12]

Beneath the gown is a "court jacket," also known as a "court coat," but also incorrectly called a vest. It is a close-fitting jacket without lapels, buttoned up the front to a V-opening, beneath which is a white wingtip-collared shirt, capped off with "tabs" (called "bands" in England), two hanging strips of cloth that form a capital "A" shape beneath the chin. If I can descend further from any documented certainty, the legend has it that these tabs were originally the means by which a gentleman might wipe powdered tobacco—"snuff"—from his nose, one tab for each nostril. If this is their true origin, they must not have stayed white for very long.

If you are interested in why English (and Canadian) lawyers wear black, that development is more easily verified—up to and including the reign of Charles II, lawyers showed up in court in all manners of outfits according to the fashion of the day and the changing whim of the courts and bar, often with varied (if generally subdued) colours and even fur or lace trim. When His Majesty expired in 1685, lawyers (who considered themselves servants of the royal courts no matter who they were actually representing) adopted black gowns in mourning, and simply never gave them up.[13]

Beneath the waist, lawyers generally wear grey trousers (the most correct are of a purpose-built striped type) and black shoes, although rebels have, in recent years, undermined both of these requirements, and skirts and even brown shoes are now common.[14]

And what of the eighteenth-century-style horsehair wigs that we might recognize from PBS's reruns of *Rumpole of the Bailey*? Fortunately these hideously expensive, unwashable, and often bug-ridden headpieces are things of the distant past. In British Columbia, a law was passed in 1905 forbidding them to be worn in the province's courtrooms.[15]

What is perhaps most striking about the court dress of Canadian lawyers is that it does not appear to be legally mandated. At least, I have tried without success to find any basis—in legislation, regulation, the rules of court, or other sources of law, for a requirement that lawyers be gowned. In British Columbia, it seems now to be referenced in a single practice directive from Chief Justice Brenner issued only in July 2009. Apparently concerned that the level of decorum in his courts was slipping (or at least was inconsistent), the Chief Justice set out the types of hearings at which counsel ought to gown in the Supreme Court—including civil trials, appeals from provincial court, and most criminal proceedings. Prior to this date, as I say, I'm not sure that there was any requirement beyond traditional imperative and the implied authority of the presiding judge, which is perhaps a very good lesson in the power of cultural norms to bind us to behaviour.

I promised before I descended into this sartorial side street that there was a purpose to the diversion. The easy metaphor is aesthetic: like gowning in a modern courtroom, the polygamy prohibition could also be viewed as an anachronism, a vestige of another age long before the modern, shiny *Charter of Rights*. The polygamy law has, as I hope to convince you, a fascinating history entwined with the early Mormon Church and First Nations practice at the dawn of Canada's imperial project in the West at the time of Confederation. But did the antipolygamy prohibition have a place in the modern firmament of criminal laws, as the almost medieval lawyers' robes persisted even in Erickson's ambitiously modern architecture? Did it serve any real purpose, any public or private good?

This leads me to a point which it is at least slightly deeper: we should be wary of simple explanations for traditions and rules and somewhat humble about our ability to deduce them. Consider the question: why does gowning persist in many Commonwealth courtrooms? Of all the various modes of legal dress tried over the centuries, this version "took" and has persevered with minor modifications for three hundred years. Why? There have been many arguments advanced in support of the traditional black gown. It may lend an air of dignity to the proceedings, reinforcing the gravity of the occasion in the minds of participants, including clients, witnesses, and onlookers. The gown also, I can attest, formalizes lawyers' own view of our role. Like Clark Kent's phone booth moment, putting on the gown defines our transition into officers of the court and thereby reinforces it in our minds. Then there is the austerity: like school uniforms, universal gowning subverts demonstrations of relative wealth and promotes social equality before the courts. Its deep history has also been lauded as contributing to the continuity of the law.

Those who do not believe that formal court dress should be retained would argue for different motivations for the rules and would also suggest other, negative, effects. They might say that there is no rational motivation, that, as herd animals, lawyers and judges are just mindlessly following convention. Gowns, they would argue, assist in the maintenance of the practice of law as a monopolistic cartel by reinforcing the barriers to public participation. The most cynical might emphasize that, like Latin maxims and arcane processes, priestly robes perpetuate the image of lawyer as possessor of mysterious knowledge. As for the benefits, these would be downplayed, and it would be suggested that they are outweighed by negatives.

Perhaps all of these, and more, factor in as causal bases for keeping traditional court attire. If we were to make a case for or against the retention of the gown, these might form the arrows in our argumentative quivers on either side. But the interesting thing to me is that no one would today support the use of the black gown by relying only on the basis of the reason for its original adoption. That is, it would be foolish to argue that robing in black must be preserved solely as a symbol of mourning for Charles II. So we might also hope that the question of whether we should retain the polygamy law on the books will also be a much, much broader discussion than might have been had on its adoption in 1890.

By 2010 it appeared that the big constitutional questions—the cases that challenged our deepest philosophical convictions—had been, if not settled, then at least thoroughly explored in the courts. The *Charter of Rights* was almost three decades old; by the twenty-first century, it seemed, *Charter* cases were less about fundamental issues and were concerned with defining the contours of rights laws, not their content. But the polygamy law, and the deep challenges it presented both constitutionally and philosophically, had been flying beneath the radar. For almost a century it was never prosecuted, and never challenged. Now all that had changed.

In my opening that November morning, I canvassed the various views on polygamy. Everyone had long observed that polygamy in practice, at least in Western nations, seems inextricably linked with insular and isolated religious groups, and accounts of polygamy are infused with stories of child brides and the institutionalized oppression of women and girls. On the other hand, if three people want to live together as consenting adults, why should that be the business of the state any more than homosexuality, sadomasochistic sex, or any other supposedly "immoral" behaviour that had long since been decriminalized is? Didn't Trudeau say in 1967 that "there's no place for the state in the bedrooms of the nation"? Wasn't he right? Surely if there were abuse in polygamy, we should target the abuse and leave the practice, *per se*, alone. And besides, the argument went, polygamy is actually quite natural for human beings; in the anthropological and historical record, monogamous societies are the exception, not the rule.

Against this view were some who said that polygamy, at least *polygyny* (remember, that is the form of polygamy where one man has more than one wife, rather than *polyandry*, which is the very rare opposite arrangement) is by its very nature so offensive to notions of women's equality that it could and should be banned on that basis alone.

The position that I would advance on behalf of the Attorney General was that polygamy did in fact involve a greater risk of harms to participants in polygamous marriages and their children. In the Attorney General's submission, though, that was probably not sufficient to justify its prohibition, because even if all that were true there could still be polygamous arrangements that were, in fact, harmless or beneficial to the participants. Our challenge would be to demonstrate, through evidence, that polygamy brought with it dangers to society that manifest *regardless of whether any individual instances were benign or harmful.*

The reference proceeding, I told the Chief Justice, was not about Bountiful or the FLDS *per se*. It was about polygamy, the practice. Polygamy, we would argue, was simply incompatible with a modern, rights-based democracy. It was inextricably linked with the oppression of women, the exploitation of girls, and the alienation of boys. This was so wherever it was practised, from Yemen to Texas to the interior of British Columbia, and it was so because *polygamy caused these things.*

It took me almost until noon on the second day to complete my opening. I described the 120-year history of the legal wrangling over polygamy in Canada and the evolution of the Attorney General's own position, which had effectively reversed since the prosecutorial authorities had loudly declared, in 1992, that the prohibition in section 293 of the *Criminal Code* was unconstitutional and should be rewritten.

The Polygamy Reference had, at last, got underway. As Churchill had said in a vastly more dramatic context, if we weren't at the end, or even at the beginning of the end, we were at least at the end of the beginning.

I'll resume my account of the trial itself much later in this book. For now, let me turn to providing the background story of how we all arrived at Courtroom 55 that November morning.

## A Deep and Profound Ambivalence

Polygamy's location in the psyche of the West at the first decade of the twenty-first century might be understatedly characterized as "complicated." However marginal in practice, the varieties of polygamy—multipartner conjugality—appeared to effortlessly capture the imagination of social philosophers and academics across the political spectrum. All seemed stricken with a form of paralysis—those who favoured criminalization nevertheless had little appetite for prosecution, and most who criticized the use of criminal sanction seemed reluctant to endorse any particular legislative reform. And through all this, it is striking how little that had been written on the subject of polygamy and its criminal sanction involved any original study or field research. It is difficult to understand how polygamy had escaped serious and sustained objective examination for so long.

In terms of its immediacy and presence in the minds of citizens and governments alike, what psychologists like to call "availability," the polygamy that mattered was that of fundamentalist Mormon communities in North America—that is, in the Mormon heartland of Utah and neighbouring Arizona, and its principal outposts in Texas, Mexico, and British Columbia. As I have mentioned and will describe far more fully later, the sole significant Canadian location was unofficially but universally known as Bountiful, a small community of about a thousand persons that had grown in the interior of British Columbia in the years since its founding at the end of the Second World War.

It was concern about Bountiful and discussion of a prosecution for polygamy there that gained some traction in the 1990s just as another elephant was lumbering into the room. This was the polygamy that is prevalent internationally, mainly in Islamic and tribal traditions (mostly African), which together, globally speaking, dwarfed the incidence of Mormon or other Western forms of multipartner marriage. Some feared that even in the West, polygamy—at least in its Islamic form—was resurgent along with fundamentalist Islam itself and the increasing adoption of Sharia law. And so discussions of polygamy increasingly took on the tenor of a clash of cultures more profound than the relatively marginal distinctions that separated fundamentalist Mormons from the rest of North American society.

Of course, when an activity is so closely associated with foreign cultures and religions, it is inevitable that its opponents will be suspected, and even accused, of being biased, even unconsciously. And perhaps, those whose opposition to polygamy rested on the idea that it was harmful were less vocal than they might have been for fear of being tarred with the most awful brush available among progressives: that of xenophobe, racist, bigot.

In any event, "progressive" thought on polygamy as the twentieth century drew to a close seemed to weigh heavily in favour of decriminalization. The Law Reform Commission of Canada recommended repeal of the prohibition in 1985, suggesting the law was "unnecessary and excessive."[16] The continued use of the criminal law to address the practice was again questioned in the Law Commission's report on "Close Personal Adult Relationships" in 2001.[17] Hardly surprisingly, all the discussion centred on whether polygamy could be seen as "harmful" enough to justify its absolute prohibition.

The BCCLA summarized well the prevailing liberal view that there was nothing inherently harmful about polygamy, recommending that other laws were adequate to the task of protecting against abusive polygamous (or monogamous) relationships:

> The BCCLA opposes the prohibition on polygamy on the grounds that all of the other alleged abusive and exploitive acts (child and spousal abuse) are clearly prohibited by existing, ordinary criminal provisions—provisions which the BCCLA believes should be vigorously applied, whether the relevant relationships are monogamous, bigamous, or polygamous. Mounting a fresh and additional attack on polygamous relations *per se* adds nothing to this equation beyond creating additional impediment to important human freedoms of association, conscience, expression, and religion.[18]

Martha Bailey and Amy Kaufman, in a book published in the United States on the eve of the reference case, offered a similar opinion:

> Those favouring retention of the criminal prohibition generally do so on the basis that polygamy is harmful to women and associated with gender inequality. We find more persuasive the arguments in support of decriminalization. Decriminalization does not indicate endorsement of the practice of polygamy or plural unions. Criminalization is not the most effective way of dealing with gender inequality in polygamous relationships. Other criminal provisions address the problems of child and spousal abuse.[19]

Bailey and Kaufman's 2010 review, one of the most comprehensive of its kind at the time, considered the "principles that should inform public policy" to include the harms associated with the practice. However, they had the same limited view of these harms as did the civil libertarians: they accepted that polygamy *could* cause harms to women and children of polygamous families, and its example could tend to denigrate ideas of gender equality,[20] but that it didn't necessarily do so, and that was really as far as they got.

At the time, both pro- and anti-criminalization advocates were making important, but questionable assumptions. The antipolygamy forces assumed that those harms that had been observed in polygamous relationships could be generalized into an assertion that polygamy was itself the cause of the harms, or at least that the practice carried an increased risk of harms. But both they and those who supported decriminalization premised all of their arguments on the idea that, if polygamy caused harm, it only did so to those involved in a polygamous household (usually this meant the wives, but the children were also recognized as potential victims). There was little or no accounting for the possibility of indirect or social harm beyond notional damages such as a diminution of the value of women's equality.[21] But at that time, hard facts of any kind regarding polygamy were hard to come by.

Granted, there had been some interesting work done in some foreign societies which attempted to compare the impacts of polygamous and monogamous unions where both existed side by side. Most significant perhaps was the ongoing work of Alean Al-Krenawi and his colleagues in the Middle East. But it was difficult to rely too heavily on studies of Bedouin Arabs given the vast differences in cultures and economies when compared to the developed West. Education or mental health outcomes may be worse for polygamist Bedouin wives and their children compared to their monogamist neighbours, but could you really extrapolate that as proof of harm from multipartner conjugality in Canada, with its economic security, universal health care, and relative gender equality?

When original "studies" in North America *were* conducted, they were hardly what one might consider "hard research" (we will later encounter a method of study with a subtly Orwellian designation, "qualitative research," which in extreme form seems not to resemble research at all). In the United States, the ethnographer William Jankowiak disappeared into FLDS communities and wrote of his observations in a series of journal articles for more than a decade; in Canada, Angela Campbell spent a few days in Bountiful interviewing those women who could be persuaded (or perhaps who had been ordered) to speak to her and generated a series of articles and opinions based on what she had been told.

Governments in Canada and the United States seemed extremely reluctant to use their powers of inquiry and investigation to develop any factual matrix on which to act, at least in part, it appears, because they didn't want to *have* to act should they uncover serious cause for concern. Politically and otherwise, there seemed to be little to be gained and much to be lost by taking a hard look at the polygamist communities in their midst. On the ground, workers from the health and education professions understood that they were dealing with insular and isolated communities—not just in Bountiful but also within immigrant populations where polygamy was practised. They did not want to jeopardize their access; perhaps a better way to put it is that they wanted to ensure that services were available to those in the community who needed them, and so they did not ask the difficult questions around, for instance, teen pregnancy. It was an approach not dissimilar to the "constructive engagement" urged by some as the best approach to dealing with troublesome and unpredictable foreign regimes. I'm in no position to judge whether it was the right approach when it came to Bountiful or similar places, but it does help to explain why, despite the contact, so little information of assistance to policymakers was learned over the years.

Some journalists did a splendid job of telling shocking stories in individual cases: Jon Krakauer's investigation of a particularly savage subsect of fundamentalist Mormons in Utah was published as *Under the Banner of Heaven: A Story of Violent Faith* and, like his other books, was widely sold and discussed. I have already mentioned Daphne Bramham's *The Secret Lives of Saints*, as close to a comprehensive history of Bountiful as had been produced. In addition, there had been at least a dozen book-length autobiographical accounts of fundamentalist Mormon polygamy, mostly written by those who considered themselves to have "survived" or "escaped" polygamy. Some of these, like Carolyn Jessop's *Escape*, became best-sellers.

Courts seemed no more eager to conduct a thorough investigation than academia or governments. It is striking (and indeed Chief Justice Bauman would later remark) how readily US judges appeared to accept the harms of polygamy without any evidence in support. The Utah Supreme Court in *State v Green* wrote:

> The practice of polygamy, in particular, often coincides with crimes targeting women and children. Crimes not unusually attendant to the practice of polygamy include incest, sexual assault, statutory rape, and failure to pay child support . . . [22]

Green's case was not a particularly difficult one—the defendant was a notorious fundamentalist Mormon polygamist who had married a succession of girls as young as thirteen (he had been the subject of a British documentary, *One Man, Six Wives, and Twenty-Nine Children*, a few years previously). But it put the problem nicely—to what extent could it be said that Green's transgressions arose from polygamy (or "bigamy" as the Utah law called it)? It did not go unnoticed that the Court's fairly categorical statement appeared derived less from evidence than free-association, perhaps a bit too liberal interpretation of Holmes's dictum that "the life of the law is not logic but experience." In the subsequent case of *State v Holm*, Chief Justice Durham complained (in dissent) that the comments in *Green* holding that certain crimes were "not unusually attendant to the practice of polygamy" were derived principally from a student law journal note that she found unconvincing. The Utah Chief Justice wrote:

> *Because the federal First Amendment analysis required only rational basis scrutiny, the court was content to reply on assertions in a student law review piece that polygamy was frequently related to other criminal conduct, together with two local cases, including the case of Green himself. Id. P 40 & n.14.* However, reviewing this assessment in light of the heightened scrutiny I believe is called for here, I cannot conclude that the restriction that the bigamy law places on the religious freedom of all those who, for religious reasons, live with more than one woman is necessary to further the state's interest in this regard. *Upon closer review, the Student Note is unconvincing. The State has provided no evidence of a causal relationship or even a strong correlation between the practice of polygamy, whether religiously motivated or not, and the offenses of "incest, sexual assault, statutory rape, and failure to pay child support," cited in Green, id. P. 40.* [emphasis added].[23]

Such doubts did not affect the Utah Attorney General Jan Graham, who also described statutory rape, incest, unlawful sexual conduct with a minor, child abuse, and cohabitant abuse as inherent in fundamentalist Mormon polygamy.[24]

But the evidence of harm to particular members of polygamous families, even if it were compelling, could never lead to a conclusion stronger than that polygamy carried with it *risks* of harm to persons involved. And even this would only be relevant if one could demonstrate that polygamy's horror stories were measurably worse than the hell experienced by many in "normal" dyadic family structures. This was a difficult proposition given the rates of spousal violence and child abuse throughout society, and the ethnographer Janet Bennion argued that abuses attributed to polygamy were *not* more frequent than in monogamy, at least in the families she encountered (her research focused on the Allred Group in Montana, but Bennion had also studied the LeBaron polygamous colony in Chihuahua, Mexico). The personality types who committed crimes in polygamy, Bennion said, would do so in a monogamous culture as well.[25]

Maura Strassberg, one of the more prolific of the US legal academics who concerned themselves with polygamy, concluded that only partial prohibition was justified given the harms as she understood them:

I conclude that modern Mormon fundamentalist polygyny consistently harms the liberty interests of teenage plural wives and should continue to be criminalized as long as it involves such teenage girls. The analysis of women who enter into polygyny as adults is more complicated. . . . I find it difficult to justify the criminalization of polygyny to protect adult women who choose to enter into such marriages for religious reasons.[26]

Strassberg had noted the coincidence of child brides and other harmful behaviour associated with polygamy, including the rigid patriarchy that controlled every aspect of economic and social life in polygamous Mormon communities, but expressed eventual confusion as to "precisely how polygyny produces such victimization."[27] Extensive surveys of polygamy laws, such as Cook and Kelly's report for the Department of Justice in 2006, focused on the harms to women that came necessarily from the inherent imbalance of a polygynous household (for instance, the power it gave men to control their wives through a threat to take another), but this was the extent of persuasive argument for *inherent* harms.

Protecting people from self-harm through paternalistic laws is not unheard of, but it is rare. We will have seatbelt and helmet laws, for instance, and restrictions on the consumption of dangerous foods and drugs. It is also not that unusual to have laws that criminalize the creation of unrealized risk to others—impaired driving is punishable whether or not there is an accident; unsafe firearm storage is another example of a crime that can be punished without any harm caused. But there are very few such paternalistic laws, or laws that prohibit no more than the creation of a risk, where the punishment exceeds a minor regulatory fine; polygamy, were it truly a paternalistic or risk-based law, would be one of the very few attracting serious criminal penalties.[28] Usually, those kinds of laws could be justified only if their breach was automatically harmful to other persons.

The uncertainty of the direction of causality of harm with polygamy was captured also by Shayna Sigman, who wrote:

The belief that polygyny causes gender discrimination or a low status of women in a given society is a classic example of the fallacy of *post hoc ergo propter hoc*. That polygyny can be found in societies that treat women poorly does not mean that the practice itself causes the gender inequality. Often, the true culprit of oppression merely lies in limitations on property rights for women, a practice that can be facilitated through polygamous life, but need not be.[29]

Sigman suggested reform efforts should address equality first, which would render polygamy's potential abuses less potent.

The dearth of a strong factual basis on which to base a criminal prohibition of polygamy was captured academically by Osgoode Hall's Susan Drummond in her article "Polygamy's Inscrutable Secular Mischief," the title of which really said it all. There, Drummond wrote:

> [I]t becomes extraordinarily difficult to state what the criminal conception of polygamy amounts to, apart from a mechanism to discipline and convict socially and politically marginalized groups.[30]

Here is where the academic literature takes its point of departure from negative assertion to positive. That is to say that the preceding passage, and indeed the conclusion suggested by Drummond's title, are mirror-opposites of the Utah Court's blasé assumptions of harms in *State v. Green*. Where the Utah Supreme Court seemed to require no evidence that polygamy was harmful, Drummond proceeds from the default position that it is not. And this then becomes the basis for a further (assumed) conclusion: if polygamy prohibitions could not be shown to be serving a valid secular purpose, they must be a method of targeting and punishing vulnerable minorities. One is led to suspect that Drummond was sufficiently attracted to this final conclusion (essentially that polygamy laws are tools of the powerful against the weak) that this might have coloured the facts that she considered when developing her major underlying premise (that polygamy is harmless). Granted, Drummond is a professor of law and was looking for harm only as it was expressed in the jurisprudence of polygamy prosecutions (scant as it is) and law journal articles. But at the same time that she demands that antipolygamy advocates produce hard evidence to support criminalization, she does not herself review the (even by then) considerable social science literature associating polygamy with harms.

Once the decriminalization advocates had accepted that there are no inherent harms to the practice, Drummond and her cohort tended to assume, as some will, that the lowest and most base motivations that can possibly be conjured to explain an opponent's position—in the case of polygamy it has been variously expressed as racism, sexism, xenophobia, simple unthinking prejudice, and disgust—must be the real ones. Bennion referred to concerns over polygamy's harms as myopic and media-driven.

This inclination in the "progressive" scholarship led to a mild form of historical revisionism. The generally even-handed Maura Strassberg (who did acknowledge at least a number of harms that she thought might actually inhere in at least some forms of polygamy) suggested that opposition to "the sexual excesses of Mormon polygyny" was the result of "Victorian prudery," which today should probably yield to "the late twentieth century attitude of sexual laissez-faire in which polygyny appears to many to be just another lifestyle choice made by consenting adults."[31] Even those

Canadian legal scholars who purported to trace the polygamy prohibition deeper still tended to look no further than the English Middle Ages. For instance, we have this assertion of religious targeting from Queen's University's Beverley Baines. After setting out what she anticipated the argument would be for the polygamy law's secular purpose, Baines said:

> However the history of the polygamy prohibition reveals a different objective. Whether that history is dated back to the 13th century in England when the church prohibited polygamy, or to the 1890s when the first *Criminal Code* prohibited polygamy in order to keep American Mormons out of Canada, the objective was religious.[32]

We will see that Baines was considerably off target in her understanding of the relevant history. Even Blackstone had recognized in the seventeenth century that the polygamy ban was of pre-Christian and nonreligious origin, and historians in recent decades generally trace its development to classical Greece. And far from attempting "to keep American Mormons out of Canada," the government in 1890 was actively encouraging their settlement in the West.

But you see my point: if you are convinced that the polygamy law was motivated by religious prejudice, then you would not be inclined to consider the evidence of its secular origins in ancient Greece and Rome. The conclusion drives the argument. Postmodernism often exhibits a love-hate relationship with legal functionalism. Postmodern scholars do tend to accept, on the one hand, that laws evolve in society according to their utility. But they are in the thrall of a fairly narrow view of which aspects of "society" the laws evolved to serve. Their tendency is to see *all* laws as furthering the interests of a narrow ruling class, and discount the possibility that many laws contributing to social order (basic property laws, for instance, or laws sharply restricting violence) have a much broader and more legitimate function. In any event, my main point here is that a full examination of the record (as was undertaken during the trial) would reveal a rather disappointing (to the law's opponents) lack of much in the way of sinister motives for the enactment of the polygamy prohibition.

I cannot blame the poor quality of the debate entirely on the decriminalization advocates. Absent a truly objective set of comparative data between polygamous and monogamous family structures or (more importantly in my view) societies, and lacking a comprehensive theory to explain (or even predict) polygamy's axiomatic or inherent harms, the scholarship of the antipolygamy side in the legal debate (the two most active voices in Canada were probably Stephen Kent and Nicolas Bala but there were others) consisted largely of gathering and categorizing anecdotal incidents or patterns of harm, an exercise barely more rigorous than that of their ideological opponents.

Bala, Campbell, Bailey, Kaufman, and others expressed something of a consensus in the 2005 report prepared for Status of Women Canada, that while there were harms *associated* with some forms of polygamy and while the practice was, as a result, risky, the facts could take us no further. Dealing with particular harms to women, for instance, the report says (at p 10):

> Throughout the literature discussing polygamous spousal relationships, it is quite commonly reported that the patriarchal nature of polygamy leads not only to women's subordination, but also their sexual, physical and emotional abuse at the hands of their husbands. . . . Nevertheless it must be recalled that spousal violence also characterizes too many monogamous relationships, and thus this difficulty is not unique to plural marriage situations. Having said this, where gender inequality lies at the core of a polygamous marriage it is arguable that there exists an increased risk of spousal violence.

> It would also be a mistake to believe that all polygamous marriages are abusive. . . . Certain anecdotes reveal genuine love and companionship among polygamous spouses and within their entire family unit, leaving us to question whether polygamy is intrinsically damaging to the spousal relationship.[33]

Hopefully you're beginning to appreciate one of the most fascinating aspects of the academic debate over polygamy: it was not a struggle between people who advocated for women's and children's rights against those who opposed them; it was not a typical debate of progressives against conservatives. Instead it was a dispute *among* feminists and rights advocates and progressives, because they could not agree on how best to advance these objectives. What did "progress" mean in this context? And there were similar schisms on the Right, with libertarians looking to punt the government from the bedrooms of the nation, and social conservatives urging preservation of monogamous marriage, which they perceived as a worthy Christian institution.

Perhaps the most ink was spilled in disagreement over how best to serve the interests of women, a recurring theme in the literature as it would also, much later, be during the trial. I will confess that I do not fully understand all the distinctions that feminists draw among themselves—"first wave," "second wave," and so forth, so I don't know if the different positions on polygamy can be attributed to these subgroups or not. But there is no question that many feminists active on the issue of polygamy, such as the University Women's Club in Vancouver (which sponsored forums and discussions on the topic and lobbied the BC government for action on Bountiful beginning in the 1980s and '90s), regarded polygamy as anathematic to women's equality. And yet you could also read a number of academic writers—from Maura Strassberg in the United States to others such as Lori Beaman in Canada—who would suggest that denying women the choice of a polygamous life might be as stultifying and frustrating of women's interests as forcing them to adopt it would be. Many others, such as Baines and Campbell, emphasized the harm done to some women by polygamy's prohibition and suggested that it outweighed any utility advanced by the law.

And indeed there was a more fundamental question about whether the law's objectives were worth accomplishing at all. The evolutionary psychologist Steven Pinker and the popular writer Robert Wright (to whom I will return later) pointed out that in socioeconomic theory, polygamy served women, overall, better than men. In a society where polygamy was an available option, many men would necessarily be deprived of the opportunity to marry and reproduce, whereas women would (assuming free choice) be able to choose between the complete attention of a single man or, perhaps, the partial devotion of a much better catch. Pinker referred to a pointed question posed by Laura Betzig: "Would you rather be the third wife of John F. Kennedy or the first wife of Bozo the Clown?"[34] In fact, went this libertarian argument, polygamy allowed women—polygamous and monogamous—to "move up the ladder" and marry more desirable men than they would get if monogamy were enforced. In a partially polygynous society, therefore, women would get both more desirable genetic partners and, on average, a higher level of economic contribution. Pinker concluded that, in a free society, "Laws enforcing monogamy would work to women's disadvantage." The real genetic losers of polygamy (and therefore the real beneficiaries of its prohibition), on this argument, were the men on the bottom rungs who would have no opportunity to marry at all (the key to—and fatal flaw in—this initially seductive argument is the idea of "free choice," because it turns out that one of polygamy's first inevitable social effects is the erosion of precisely this agency).

But whether or not you agree with the *social* theories of these evolutionary psychologists, it did appear that most scientists agreed that polygamy is a behaviour coded in all of our genes. This too did not sit very well with some, as we shall see.

The fact that the debate engaged its participants in fundamental questions around equality and liberalism meant that it ran the risk of being quite personal. I don't mean to suggest that the academic advocates or opponents of polygamy decriminalization resorted to *ad hominem* attacks or demonization of one another. They didn't. But the underlying suggestion on both sides was that the other was the hapless dupe of mendacious forces: that the pro-criminalization faction were writing in the service of arbitrary bigotry, though they might believe they were protecting the vulnerable; and that the decriminalization forces were unwittingly serving the interests of a malevolent and misogynistic patriarchy, even as they advanced their views (mostly) as ardent and sincere feminists. A nice example is the feminist critique penned by Michelle Chan in response to West Coast LEAF's position on the polygamy law (which was basically that it was all right to ban abusive patriarchal polygamy but not more innocent types). Chan complained:

> LEAF's position in support of the criminal prohibition continues to single out and stigmatize a practice associated with religious and cultural minorities. In doing this, LEAF privileges and constructs as normal a certain cultural and racialized distribution of power despite their concern for a nuanced response to polygamy. Ultimately, in supporting the Polygamy Provision, LEAF participates in dynamics of "Othering"; it positions those who engage in polygamous relationships as a cultural "Other," reinforcing the dichotomy between a civilized, Western "us" and a barbaric, non-Western "Them." In the process, the concerns of women in polygamous relationships, who may see their relationship with gender equality differently, are further marginalized.[35]

The conclusions that prosecuting polygamy was little more than an exercise in (albeit unconscious) bigotry was compounded by a certain tendency towards academic incestuousness in the progressive quarters. The decriminalization forces tended to collaborate and cite one another to the point where they had taller and taller castles on one another's sand. But by no means was this sin exclusive to the decriminalization advocates: we have seen how the Utah Supreme Court in *Holm* took its lead from its earlier decision in *Green*; and striking examples of spiralling mutually reinforcing citation can be easily found in the literature extolling polygamy's harms.

So I don't want to be too critical of Beaman, Campbell, Strassberg, Sigman, Baines, or Drummond at this point (I will be much more so later, at least with respect to the first two). What they were asking, at its root, is not unreasonable: that there must be some objectively verifiable harm attached to polygamy to justify its prohibition; that it was dangerous to permit the state to rely on anecdotal horror stories to justify the targeting of a practice that was closely identified with potentially vulnerable groups. I agreed with that idea, and I also agreed with Drummond's observation that one could look in vain for a principled articulation of objective harm in the cases that had been decided or the legal commentary as a whole.

If Chief Justice Durham's dissent in *Holm* is an indication of anything, it is that there had been a shift in the social burden of proof with respect to polygamy—people were decreasingly inclined to simply assume it was bad. This meshed with the requirement of the *Charter of Rights* that infringements on the liberty or religious practices of a citizen must be justified by the state on evidence, or at least on conclusions that might be reasonably inferred (that, in theory, the same requirement inhered in the US court's test of "strict scrutiny" was Durham's point in *Holm*). We had learned our lessons from the persecution of various minorities, and the message now being issued to the opponents of polygamy was to put up or shut up.

As I've tried to emphasize, the main difficulty with the polygamy debate as it developed, for instance, in the riposte between law professors Kent and Beaman, was that it viewed the harms of polygamy in traditional, narrow terms. Kent was able to marshal extensive evidence that some polygamous relationships were harmful to the wives and children; Beaman pointed out that there was no reason to believe that it was universally so. Neither confronted the further question of whether polygamy *per se* was harmful to others who may be completely distant from the relationship itself. This was a conceptual vacuum that hobbled all the evidence prior to the Polygamy Reference.

Beaman wrote in the abstract to her article "Who Decides?":

> Kent and I agree on several points: (1) no woman or girl should be forced to marry and/or have sexual relations against her will; (2) men who abuse women or children in the name of religion should not be protected under the guise of religious freedom; (3) women who report being abused in polygamous (or any) relationships should be taken seriously. Finally, and related to point two, a theological basis for the abusive behavior is not an automatic protection from sanction. Despite these agreements, there are significant points of departure between Kent and myself, including the characterization of polygamy as inherently abusive.[36]

You can see that the debate was focused around the legitimacy of the two types of harms that I described earlier: it was suggested that polygamy was a form of "self-harm" from which paternalistic protection was needed (for the wives), or that it created an *increased risk* of harm to the participants, for instance, by increasing the odds that children of polygamous families would be neglected or abused.

What wasn't really being discussed was the question of real but indirect harm, *social* harm. Under this argument, which would become the centrepiece of the Attorney General's eventual submissions, prohibiting polygamy was justifiable because the alternative, that is, permitting it, would cause serious adverse consequences throughout society—real consequences to real people—regardless of whether it was harmful to its participants in any particular manifestation. If small polygamous communities saw an increased incidence of serious social harms—the sexual exploitation of girls, for instance—it was not because polygamists were more inclined to exploit girls themselves (they might or might not be), but rather because a society where polygamy was practised is more likely to exploit girls. It was just more apparent in, for instance, Bountiful because the harm could not be externalized or diluted in the broader society. This distinction, between the harms of polygamous *relationships*, on the one hand, and the harms of a polygamous *society*, on the other, is essential to understanding the way the Polygamy Reference unfolded. And it is also key to understanding why the academic debate up to that point was so clearly missing the mark. What does it matter if the free choice of adults to marry multiple partners is unhealthy to them and their own children if their decision will necessarily lead to serious negative consequences to people elsewhere in society?

The criminal law can legitimately address itself to harms that are indirect, the result of "market effects," if I can put it that way. I can provide examples from diverse legal fields: in laws that regulate securities markets, we have prohibitions against "insider trading," that is, the buying and selling of shares by persons who have privileged knowledge of facts that give them an advantage over the general trading public. Now, insider trading is a crime whether or not the insider actually benefits from his knowledge, or to put it another way, it doesn't matter whether any person can be shown to have actually suffered harm as a result of the insider's trade. Criminalization is justified mainly because the proliferation of insider trading would necessarily reduce confidence in the integrity of the market. It can also be argued, of course, that insider trading does create an increased risk of immediate victims, not just social harms. This is an example where activities might be prohibited both on a "social harm" and "creation of risk" analysis.

Two more quick examples can be found in our child pornography and incest laws. We can prohibit the possession or distribution of child pornography even though it may cause no harm to anyone having contact with it, and even if there are no children harmed in its creation (for instance, if it is simply a drawing, painting, or fictional account of a child having sex). We are justified in prohibiting that because we believe it contributes to the market and thus increases demand for such material in a way that will lead to children being abused in the future, whether by the individuals involved or by others. And perhaps also because the harm is so heinous when set against the liberty interests of those who wish to deal in such material.

Even consenting adults are prohibited by incest laws from engaging in sex with a parent or sibling. This is so regardless of whether there is any harm in the relationship itself; indeed, it is possible to foresee a relationship that all participants would describe as completely positive. We could adopt a "risk of harm" analysis; that is, we could say that incestuous sex created an increased rate of birth defects (although, from what I understand of the literature on this point, this risk is usually overstated). But what then if we "tweak" the hypothetical and ask if incest should be legal between two consenting adults when effective birth control is used (or, if you insist that even that carries a risk, where one or both of them is sterile, or where the sex does not involve intercourse)? No, the better reason for prohibiting incest is because if it were permitted, if the legal sanction were removed, if the moral opprobrium relaxed, and if the practice of even consensual adult incest spread, then girls growing up will be viewed increasingly as potential sexual partners by their brothers and their fathers (incest is by far most common between a female and older male member of the household). Overall, throughout society, more girls will be sexually targeted in the home or groomed to be targeted at the moment of their legal majority.

Like the insider trading laws, you could also say that child pornography and incest prohibitions could be bolstered by the "creation of risk" analysis, and you would be right. I've already made reference to the idea that incest creates a risk of birth defects, which is why I "isolated" this variable in my hypothetical argument by removing the danger of a resulting pregnancy. Child pornography, it might similarly be argued, could be predicted to stoke the passions of a pedophile, thus increasing the risk of consequent harm to children if he acted out his fantasies. But as I have suggested, we are extremely wary of constraining liberties simply on the basis that they increase a risk, and the more such laws infringe on fundamental individual choices, the more wary we are, and that is the way it should be.

The academic debate over polygamy had revealed the danger of focusing on the risk of harm analysis alone. Risk in individuals is determined by finding harm in populations; they are two sides of the same coin. If you want to show, for instance, that children of a polygamous marriage are more likely to be neglected, then you will need to compare a large number of children from polygamous and monogamous marriages and see if there is more neglect in one or the other. In order to do this fairly, you will need a relatively large population and you will need to hold constant a number of potentially confounding variables (things that could correlate with both polygamy and neglect, such as cultural or religious inputs, economic factors, and so forth). In the North American context, with small populations that were insular and therefore difficult to study, there simply was no data, and so the risk-based argument proceeded from the point of view of warring anecdotes.

As a result, as the first years of the twenty-first century unfolded, a few things had become manifestly apparent. As Bailey and Kaufman put it, after over a century of dormancy, "the problem of polygamy is back."[37] And whichever way Canada's polygamy law came before a court, those wishing to maintain it would bear the burden of showing much more than simply "bad things happened in polygamy." They would have to show that bad things happened *as a result of the polygamy*—that harm inheres in the practice, not simply that it was coincident with it, at Bountiful or elsewhere. If they could not do it through a risk of harm analysis, they would have to find a new approach.

## Joseph Smith's "Peculiar Institution"

This book is not a history of Mormonism or the origins of polygamy in the early Mormon faith, a complicated topic and the subject of a number of excellent works that I could not hope even to summarize fairly. However, some basic facts are usefully recounted here to put the balance of the story and the issues in perspective.

The Mormon belief system, which would become institutionalized as the Church of Jesus Christ of Latter-day Saints, had been founded in 1830 by a young New England farmer and treasure-digger named Joseph Smith. It was through Smith's inspiration that polygamy's North American foothold was originally established, and it was his example that inspired its twentieth-century resurgence in the United States and Canada.

Smith claimed to have excavated some golden plates, and, with the assistance of an angel and some magic stones, he translated them and dictated *The Book of Mormon*, a further gospel of Christianity that purported to locate the second coming of Christ in pre-Columbian America and documented the establishment of a new "chosen people" on this continent. And although Smith certainly wasn't the only one of his day propounding a new religion (it seems to have actually been something of a cottage industry in the early decades of the United States), his strange stories, backed as they were with what appeared to be documentary evidence, took hold, and the young man found himself as the prophet of a burgeoning new, all-American faith.

Smith was a dynamic, extremely charismatic preacher and prophet, and a man whom many women apparently found attractive, a regard that was clearly shared by Smith. At some point he became either commanded or compelled (depending on whom you listen to) to seek wives in addition to his long-suffering Emma, which he began to do in 1841 when he fixed his gaze on the couple's seventeen-year-old servant.[38] In two-and-a-half years, Smith is thought to have amassed thirty wives, some of whom appear to have still been married to other men. Polygamy became an official, if still secret, part of Mormonism in 1843, when Smith had to break it to his wife. This he was able to do, fortuitously, with a commandment from God that he received and dictated himself:

> A commandment I give unto mine handmaid, Emma Smith . . . [that she] receive all those [wives] that have been given unto my servant Joseph. . . . But if [Emma] will not abide this commandment she shall be destroyed, saith the Lord; for I am the Lord thy God, and will destroy her if she abide not in my law.

In 1844 it was Smith himself who was destroyed, meeting his end at the hands of a mob that had descended on his Nauvoo jail cell (I have here skipped much of the narrative that is one of the most interesting stories of American history, but there are other and far better sources for an account of early Mormonism). But by then polygamy had established itself as a tenet of Mormonism despite the fact that the prophet had not openly advocated it. What followed were decades of turbulence as the Mormons were half led, half driven across the United States, finally populating the Utah Territory under the leadership of Smith's acolyte Brigham Young.

Young had even more wives than the dozens of Joseph Smith, in fact about fifty-six of them. Because Smith had never publicly taught polygamy, and because his widow Emma denied to the end that she had not been his only mate, it was widely believed in the late 1800s that the practice of Mormon plural marriage originated with Brigham Young, who announced it officially as LDS doctrine in 1852. The US government would not tolerate the practice of polygamy, though, and Smith's successors would engage in a running battle with the authorities.

Even before the 1878 decision of the US Supreme Court in *Reynolds v United States*,[39] polygamist Mormons had been under intense pressure and scrutiny in the Western Territories of the United States. *Reynolds* was the last legal straw for the mainstream LDS church, which quickly realized that it could not make peace with the United States and achieve its statehood ambitions, while remaining openly polygamous.

The *Morrill Anti-Bigamy Act* of 1862[40] criminalized the practice federally, and most importantly in the territories, which were until that point beyond the reach of state prohibitions. The sanctuary afforded by the territory of Utah was no longer. Yet the Mormons proved tenacious in their devotion to polygamy, and the struggle continued for another twenty-eight years, in which time the federal government expanded its laws, banning cohabitation and depriving polygamists and their sympathizers from holding office or sitting on juries. Finally, in 1887 Congress revoked the charter of the Church of Jesus Christ of Latter-day Saints, dissolving its corporate status and confiscating its property. In 1890 the LDS formally surrendered the fight and banned polygamy, and in 1894 Utah was admitted as a state on the condition that the practice be "forever prohibited."

But even as the LDS church moved away from polygamy, small groups of Mormons continued to embrace "the Principle" of plural marriage, both within and, increasingly, outside the LDS church itself. This included a small band that had established a foothold in Alberta in 1888 under the leadership of Charles Ora Card.

## The Law Against Bigamy

Most constitutional challenges to criminal laws are mounted against new legislation. Parliament seeks to change the law in a way that is offensive, and a lawsuit is brought to challenge it, or, more often, a criminal defendant hauled before the courts invokes his constitutional rights as defence. More rarely, a challenger seeks to overturn a law that is years, or even decades old. Almost never, though, is a constitutional challenge brought against prohibitions that have endured for centuries—perhaps millennia. When this happens, it is because the Constitution has evolved in a way that makes the existing law offensive today, even if it had not been a few years previously.

The law under challenge in the Polygamy Reference went back more than a hundred years, but its immediate forebears had originated many hundreds of years before. In the eighteenth century, the prototypical English legal scholar and jurist Sir William Blackstone identified multiple marriage as a capital crime that was included in Britain's antibigamy legislation dating from 1604.[41]

English laws came to colonial America with the first settlers, and remained the template for the nascent United States. Bigamy laws were in place in each of the states after the establishment of the union, but the advent of Mormonism in the nineteenth century quickly threw them into conflict with the idea of religious freedom and individual liberty, which were, at least in theory, foundational pillars of the new nation.

The provenance of the American ban on polygamy was described by the United States Supreme Court in the decision of *Reynolds*. The law under challenge in *Reynolds* was the 1862 Act of Congress, the *Morrill Anti-Bigamy Act*, which extended the prohibitions that were in place in each of the individual states into the United States territories where the Mormons had mostly settled. It read similarly to the British laws of old:

> Every person having a husband or wife living, who marries another, whether married or single, in a Territory, or other place over which the United States have exclusive jurisdiction, is guilty of bigamy, and shall be punished by a fine of not more than $500, and by imprisonment for a term of not more than five years.[42]

*Reynolds* represented the first sustained challenge to a federal law based on the Constitution's guarantee of the free exercise of religion. Therefore, in the course of its decision the Supreme Court was careful to emphasize that the precursors of the prohibition, while for a time enforced by the ecclesiastical courts in England, were essentially secular in its history:

> Polygamy has always been odious among the northern and western nations of Europe, and, until the establishment of the Mormon Church, was almost exclusively a feature of the life of Asiatic and of African people. At common law, the second marriage was always void . . . and from the earliest history of England, polygamy has been treated as an offence against society. After the establishment of the ecclesiastical courts, and until the time of James I, it was punished through the instrumentality of those tribunals not merely because ecclesiastical rights had been violated, but because upon the separation of the ecclesiastical courts from the civil the ecclesiastical were supposed to be the most appropriate for the trial of matrimonial causes and offences against the rights of marriage, just as they were for testamentary causes and the settlement of the estates of deceased persons.

> By the statute of 1 James I (c. 11), the offence, if committed in England or Wales, was made punishable in the civil courts, and the penalty was death. As this statute was limited in its operation to England and Wales, it was at a very early period reenacted, generally with some modifications, in all the colonies. In connection with the case we are now considering, it is a significant fact that, on the 8th of December, 1788, after the passage of the act establishing religious freedom, and after the convention of Virginia had recommended as an amendment to the Constitution of the United States the declaration in a bill of rights that

"all men have an equal, natural, and unalienable right to the free exercise of religion, according to the dictates of conscience," the legislature of that State substantially enacted the statute of James I, death penalty included, because, as recited in the preamble, "it hath been doubted whether bigamy or poligamy be punishable by the laws of this Commonwealth." . . . From that day to this, we think it may safely be said there never has been a time in any State of the Union when polygamy has not been an offence against society, cognizable by the civil courts and punishable with more or less severity. In the face of all this evidence, it is impossible to believe that the constitutional guaranty of religious freedom was intended to prohibit legislation in respect to this most important feature of social life [citations omitted].[43]

Critics of the *Reynolds* decision sometimes point to the first sentence of this passage, referring to polygamy as "a feature of the life of Asiatic and of African people," as proof of some racist or xenophobic inspiration in polygamy's opponents. But as I read it in context, the Court was not disparaging polygamy on racial or similar grounds (though I have no doubt that the judges shared the common prejudices of the day); it was simply explaining why, prior to Mormonism, it was not much of an issue in the United States or Europe, where it was considered "odious."[44] In fact, the principal concern of the *Reynolds* Court seems to have been focused on the role of marriage form in democratic structure:

Marriage, while from its very nature a sacred obligation, is nevertheless, in most civilized nations, a civil contract, and usually regulated by law. *Upon it society may be said to be built, and out of its fruits spring social relations and social obligations and duties with which government is necessarily required to deal. In fact, according as monogamous or polygamous marriages are allowed, do we find the principles on which the government of the people, to a greater or less extent, rests.* Professor Lieber says, polygamy leads to the patriarchal principle, and which, when applied to large communities, fetters the people in stationary despotism, while that principle cannot long exist in connection with monogamy. Chancellor Kent observes that this remark is equally striking and profound. . . . An exceptional colony of polygamists under an exceptional leadership may sometimes exist for a time without appearing to disturb the social condition of the people who surround it; but there cannot be a doubt that, unless restricted by some form of constitution, it is within the legitimate scope of the power of every civil government to determine whether polygamy or monogamy shall be the law of social life under its dominion [emphasis added; citations omitted].[45]

It is striking how closely the issues in 1878 resemble some of those that would be before the Court in the reference. The *Reynolds* Court was considering and rejecting the notion that polygamy should be upheld because it could be practiced "without appearing to disturb the social condition of the people who surround it," finding, on the evidence, that where polygamy runs its course it "leads to the patriarchal principle, and . . . fetters the people in stationary despotism." The Court clearly viewed polygamy as harmful to society even where it was not harmful in its individual manifestation, because it was, in the Court's view, incompatible with democratic government.

Later in this book I will describe the moribund fatalism of British Columbia's public lawyers in the first decades of the *Charter*, who concluded with little if any doubt that the polygamy law would be struck down on the altar of that document's new protections of religious freedom. I should say that the Canadians weren't alone in this concern. In a news conference on 23 July 1998, Utah's governor Mike Leavitt suggested that polygamy might be protected as the free exercise of religion under the US Constitution, arguing that these "hard-working, good people . . . have religious freedoms" that ought to be respected.[46] I have earlier described the emerging academic consensus at the turn of the last century to the effect that criminalizing polygamy could not be constitutionally sustained.

Obviously if we were to advance our argument against polygamy, its main thrust would be that we understand facts justifying the law today better than we did during this legal pessimism of the 1980s or '90s. In particular, any case against polygamy would be premised on arguments around harm. But there was another factor at play in the reluctance of authorities to act against polygamy in the United States and Canada between 1953 and the turn of the century, and it was only when this factor was reduced in influence that calls for action could gather momentum. I'm speaking of the paralyzing fear that prosecuting polygamy would be an unreasonably intolerant act.

Indeed, the Court in *Reynolds* appears to have been sensitive to arguments that the enforcement of the polygamy prohibition was an appeal to anti-Mormon "passion and prejudices" of the day.[47] The Court held that the prohibition was based on Congress's apprehension of the harms of polygamy, and it was not inappropriate to emphasize those "evils" to the jury:

> While every appeal by the court to the passions or the prejudices of a jury should be promptly rebuked, and while it is the imperative duty of a reviewing court to take care that wrong is not done in this way, we see no just cause for complaint in this case. Congress, in 1862 (12 Stat. 501), saw fit to make bigamy a crime in the Territories. *This was done*

*because of the evil consequences that were supposed to flow from plural mar-riages* [emphasis added].

The American courts' view of polygamy, incidentally, has not changed much in the intervening century. Sometime earlier I mentioned the recent decision of the Utah Supreme Court in *Holm*. Reviewing the history of Utah's bigamy prohibition (2006 UT 31), the majority of the Court in *Holm*, upholding the law against attack on the basis of religious liberty, wrote:

> Our State's commitment to monogamous unions is a recognition that decisions made by individuals as to how to structure even the most personal of relationships are capable of dramatically affecting public life.[48]

## The Mormons Arrive

Soon after the *Reynolds* decision in 1878 upheld the American antibigamy laws against constitutional challenge, some Mormons decided to settle in the Canadian West. They were led by Charles Ora Card, who a year previously had been directed by the president of the Latter-day Saints church in Utah to settle in Canada with forty families. The Mormons quickly established themselves as skilled farmers and built a community at Lee's Creek near Lethbridge, a settlement that later became known as Cardston, Alberta.

For hundreds, probably thousands of years previously, polygamy had been part of aboriginal life and culture in what had later come to be called the Northwest Territories and the Colony of British Columbia. But even with the consternation that the practice caused among Christian missionaries, Hudson's Bay Company representatives, and Indian Agents, no one had seen the necessity to actually criminalize the practice, preferring to use other tools of colonialism—religious entreaty, moral suasion, or (often) outright bribery—to discourage it. It was the arrival of Card's small delegation of immigrant Mormon farmers that put the issue squarely before the Canadian government.

By the time Card travelled to Ottawa to plead the Mormons' case, his small Canadian community had enjoyed its first season of farming. Canada had been welcoming of the industrious and capable Mormons, if warily, and Card was optimistic that the government of Canada might also provide a refuge for his followers' unusual lifestyle. After all, he reasoned, didn't Her Majesty have within her empire Muslims and Africans who believed that a man should, or at least could, have more than one wife at once? In a letter to the government, Card had written:

The comparatively few who need to seek rest and peace in Canada would not be a drop in the bucket compared with the millions of people who are protected in their faith and practice plural marriage under the Government of Great Britain.[49]

Sir John A Macdonald, the prime minister, welcomed Card's delegation but on the question of polygamy offered only disappointment. He later recounted the discussion:

Mr. Card and some others came to Ottawa. Some of them are British subjects by birth, one or two are Canadians by birth, and others were born in the United States. They said they wished to settle in Canada. They were informed what our law was, and they were told explicitly and distinctly that we were aware that the great cause of the antipathy towards them in the United States was the practice of polygamy, and they must understand that the people of Canada would be as firmly opposed to that practice as the people of the United States were. They said they were aware of that, but they wanted shelter from what they considered oppression. They were told—told by myself—that in any case where the practice was proved they would be prosecuted and punished with the utmost rigor of the law. They said they were quite willing to submit to the law. They attempted, of course, to argue their case, and they discussed the doctrines of Mormonism generally with me. I said to them: You must understand that there must be no mistake about it; there will be no leniency, there will be no looking over this practice, but as regards your general belief, that is a matter between yourselves and your conscience. We are glad to have you in this country so long as you obey the laws, we are glad to have respectable people. Her Majesty has a good many subjects who are Mohammedans, and if they came here we would be obliged to receive them; but whether they are Mohammedans or Mormons, when they come here they must obey the laws of Canada. I told them this, and they professed a sincere desire—I have no reason to doubt their sincerity—to submit themselves to the laws of Canada for the sake of the rest and equity that they thought they would get, instead of being surrounded by a turbulent crowd who were oppressing them in every way.[50]

However, after this 1888 meeting it was suspected that not all of Card's men had been convinced to abandon their multiple wives, and there was concern that the practice of plural marriage was in fact enjoying a renaissance among Western Indian nobility (some of whom were reported to convert to Mormonism out of a "taste" for its polygamous tradition).

The best histories of the early Canadian Mormon settlers indicate that they were true to their word that they would obey this country's laws, and only a handful are known to have married or lived polygamously in Canada in the nineteenth century. The more usual practice of the senior men, it appears, was to move only one of their wives to Canada, leaving the remainder in the United States, where the men might return for visits. There is no record of any violent confrontations between the Mormons and their Canadian hosts, and indeed from all that I have read, the local relations appeared generally cordial and cooperative. But the continued association of Mormonism with polygamy created concern across the country and remained something of a tinderbox awaiting a match.

Indeed in 1889 things did come to a head, as a result of the efforts of a single, troublesome Scot. Anthony Maitland Stenhouse was the son of a minor nobleman, and a recent immigrant to Canada. He made Vancouver Island his home and was soon a member of the British Columbia legislative assembly for Comox. Very little is known of his political achievements in office. Rather, Stenhouse is remembered in Canada for his inexplicable conversion to Mormonism (inexplicable because there were no Mormons within hundreds of miles of him). As if this weren't odd enough, Stenhouse, who doesn't appear to have been much of a risk-taker in other respects, resigned his position in the legislature, renounced his Anglican religion, and signed on with the Mormons in Southern Alberta, becoming a champion of polygamy in the territory until he returned to Britain in 1891.

It is interesting in light of subsequent arguments during the Polygamy Reference that, even in his day, Stenhouse felt obliged to defend polygamy in the context of its effects on women. Monogamy, Stenhouse wrote, "trammels a woman," while polygamy will "enlarge her scope."[51] In another letter he argued for the interests of women from a Darwinian perspective:

> It secures a husband for every woman that wants one . . . . Under a well ordered system of plural families, marriage would no longer be a lottery where ladies draw a blank, a fool or a husband, according to luck. They would no longer be daily insulted with the alternatives of a fool or none—and thus the law of natural selection, now so grossly outraged, would find its due accomplishment in the survival and perpetuation of the fittest family and the fittest race. It is true that some men would be wifeless, but these would mostly be men whose marriage and multiplication are a curse to the race.[52]

In the course of his research, Stenhouse had discovered what he thought was a "loophole" in Canada's criminal law: while bigamy appeared to be illegal, polygamy itself did not seem to be contrary to statute.[53] In 1886, the year Card's advance party had arrived in Canada to scout locations for settlement, Parliament had enacted a provision that read almost identically to the *English Acts* of 1828 and 1861:

> Every one who being married, marries any other person during the life of the former husband or wife, whether the second marriage takes place in Canada, or elsewhere, is guilty of felony, and liable to seven years' imprisonment.

But the "bigamy" law was still worded as it had been in 1604 England, when there was no state involvement in marriage, and most people became "married" simply by moving in together with or without much ceremony, religious or otherwise, and certainly without state sanction. In the intervening years, marriage had become a government-endowed institution, and indeed in Canada it had been the subject of careful constitutional assignment in 1867. Most bigamists were involved in a deception—they were trying to game the system and "legally" marry a second wife while they were still legally married to their first. Stenhouse's argument was that the Anglo-Canadian law barring subsequent marriages was directed at bigamy, which was premised on this deception, not polygamy, which was a consensual arrangement that, he believed, would be legally enforced in England as well as Canada.[54]

Stenhouse did not appear to acknowledge the decision in *Reynolds*, where essentially identical "bigamy" language had been applied to convict a Mormon polygamist. Moreover, he fixated on the statutes' requirement of *sequential* marriage, and proposed that even if that did capture most polygamy, it still did not apply if a man married two women at the same time. He wrote on 20 November 1889:

> There is one case of polygamy . . . whose bearing on the law . . . has [not] yet been ascertained. The case of the bridegroom with two brides is not an impossibility. Nor is it inconceivable that he might, as a bachelor, be duly wedded to both ladies at the same moment, neither of the wives preceding the other. In view of such a case the question arises . . . would the parties be liable to criminal prosecution?
>
> . . .
>
> As an undergraduate in matrimony, I propose to test the law as soon as I have found the ladies.[55]

Around the same time, the legendary Northwest Mounted Police (NWMP) officer Sam Steele reported to Ottawa that it was widely believed that the Mormons of Lee's Creek were practising polygamy in secret; he urged that the laws be changed along the American model (which by then had gone much further than the *Morrill Act* with the *Edmunds Act* in 1882 and *Edmunds-Tucker* legislation in 1887, progressively draconian attacks on the institutional power of the LDS church). However, Burgess, the deputy minister of the interior, apparently believed that the criminal law in Canada was then sufficient. He is quoted by Palmer as saying: "[I]f they are found to be guilty of infringing this law [marriage] they are liable to the pains and penalties upon conviction."[56]

It also does not appear that Card himself (who seems to have disapproved of Stenhouse's very public and provocative pro-polygamy campaign) had any doubts that Mormon polygamy was a crime under the existing law. After Burgess forwarded the NWMP allegations, he replied on 18 February 1890 that "the alleged crimes to which you refer, of polygamy and cohabitation, are not practiced either in or out of Cardston" and asked "that you will give our people a chance to prove their innocence."[57]

Historian Robert McCue, who has written the only biographical works on Stenhouse, takes up the story from there:

> Nor were the legislators in Ottawa prepared to take chances by treating [Stenhouse's] proposal [to publicly marry polygamously] as a joke. On 4 February 1890 Senator Macdonald, from Victoria, British Columbia, presented in the Canadian Senate a bill designed to remove any doubt as to whether bigamy laws applied to polygamy, and it specifically mentioned the "spiritual or plural marriages" of the Mormons . . . It was dropped from the agenda of the Senate on 4 March in favor of similar legislation introduced in the House of Commons on 7 February by Sir John Thompson, minister of justice . . . His bill covered a wider scope of offenses than the Macdonald proposal, which was largely adopted as section 8 of the proposed legislation . . . in explaining his intent, Thompson said:
>
>> Section 8 is intended to extend the prohibition of bigamy. It is to make a second marriage punishable . . . whether the marriage took place in Canada or elsewhere, or whether marriages takes [*sic*] place simultaneously or on the same day. In [the latter case] . . . the parties were not punishable under the present law. Section 9 deals with the practice of polygamy . . . which we are threatened with; and I think it will be much more prudent that legislation should be adopted at once in anticipation of the offence . . . rather than we should wait until it has been established in Canada (Debates 1890, 3162).[58]

*An Act respecting Offences relating to the Law of Marriage*, including what is now section 293 of the *Criminal Code*, was Parliament's response. McCue writes:

> This bill was passed by the Commons on 16 April 1890 and became law one month later on 16 May while Stenhouse was still [visiting] in Utah. . . . It left no doubt that polygamy was illegal in Canada and specifically prohibited the simultaneous multiple marriage scheme proposed by Mr. Stenhouse. . . . Every male person who, in Canada, simultaneously, or on the same day, marries more than one woman, is guilty of felony and liable to seven years' imprisonment.[59]

Stenhouse's role in shaping Canada's polygamy law was considerable. It is probably not an exaggeration to say that this otherwise unremarkable politician provided the impetus for the timing and in some respects the very language of the polygamy prohibition.

But if Stenhouse hoped that his agitation in favour of polygamy would win him a position of honour among the Cardston Mormons, he may have been mistaken. Card, as I said earlier, appeared to have been nervous about the attention that Stenhouse was bringing. We should remember that finding refuge in Canada was, for Card and others, a question of preserving their liberty, if not their very lives. Anything which jeopardized their sanctuary must have made them extremely uncomfortable indeed. And if Stenhouse was right and Canada did not have a law against polygamy when he arrived, it certainly did after he spent a year or so pressing that assertion.

So it is perhaps not entirely inexplicable that Stenhouse, having become Canada's leading champion of both Mormonism and polygamy, departed without fanfare for England in 1891 and seems to have had no connection with either for the rest of his life. His epitaph described him as "Anglican"; he never married, even once.

The original version of Canada's polygamy statute left no doubt in anyone's mind that it applied to the Mormon practice, because, in addition to "polygamy" and "conjugal union with more than one person at the same time," it also explicitly forbade "[w]hat among the persons commonly called Mormons is known as spiritual or plural marriage" (this provision would be deleted in 1954). But it would be incomplete to suggest that the law was aimed *solely* at the Mormons. Sarah Carter's excellent history *The Importance of Being Monogamous* documents the extent to which polygamy among Western First Nations peoples was also causing concern in Ottawa, and the *Debates of the Legislative Assembly* at the time the prohibition was enacted reveal that Parliament was also concerned the "Mohommedans" from elsewhere in the empire could not practice polygamy in Canada.

As originally enacted, the law was phrased this way:

5.(1) Everyone who practices, or, by the rites, ceremonies, forms, rules or customs of any denomination, sect or society, religious or secular, or by any form of contract, or by mere mutual consent, or by any other method whatsoever, and whether in a manner recognized by law as a binding form of marriage or not, agrees or consents to practice or enter into —

(a) Any form of polygamy; or,—

(b) Any kind of conjugal union with more than one person at the same time; or,—

(c) What among the persons commonly called Mormons is known as spiritual or plural marriage; or,—

(d) Who lives, cohabits, or agrees or consents to live or cohabit, in any kind of conjugal union with a person who is married to another, with a person who lives or cohabits with another or others in any kind of conjugal union; and—

(2). Every one who,—

(a) Celebrates, is a party to, or assists in any such rite or ceremony which purports to make binding or to sanction any of the sexual relationships mentioned in sub-section one of the section; or,—

(b) Procures, enforces, enables, is a party to, or assists in the compliance with, or carrying out of, any such form, rule or custom which so purports; or,—

(c) Procures, enforces, enables, is a party to, or assists in the execution of any such form of contract which so purports, or the giving any such consent which so purports,—

Is guilty of a misdemeanor, and liable to imprisonment for five years and to a fine of five hundred dollars[.]

The only nontrivial changes were made to the provision in 1954, when the *Criminal Code* was substantially overhauled and streamlined. The sections setting out the categories of polygamy were reduced to two, and as a result the operative provisions of section 293 currently read as follows:

293. (1) Every one who

(a) practises or enters into or in any manner agrees or consents to practise or enter into

(i) any form of polygamy, or

(ii) any kind of conjugal union with more than one person at the same time, whether or not it is by law recognized as a binding form of marriage, or

(b) celebrates, assists or is a party to a rite, ceremony, contract or consent that purports to sanction a relationship mentioned in subparagraph (a)(i) or (ii),

is guilty of an indictable offence and liable to imprisonment for a term not exceeding five years.

The three original provisions of the prohibition addressed themselves to three types of criminal conjugality: Mormon plural marriage, "any form of polygamy," and a conjugal union among more than two persons (there was a fourth category of "cohabiting" in a conjugal union, which was removed in 1954 presumably because it was completely redundant with the now section 293(1)(a)(ii)).

It seems clear from the history and context that the overlap among the provisions was deliberate. In the parliamentary debate of 1890, it was noted:

[I]t is right to observe that the difficulties which the United States has had to contend with in respect to the Mormons of Utah since the Brigham Young dispensation are serious and growing; and that from time to time earnest efforts have been made to overcome what seems to be an almost insuperable difficulty, owing to the extraordinary solidarity of these people and their determination to persist in and to conceal all legal evidence, at any rate, of their practices.[60]

The parliamentary debates also show a concern with the difficulty of capturing polygamy under then-existing law without proof of formalized marriage:

Sometimes they have witnesses, sometimes not; if they think any trouble may arise from a marriage, or that a woman is inclined to be a little perverse, they have no witnesses, neither do they give marriage certificates, and if occasion requires it, and it is to shield any of their polygamous brethren from being found out, they will positively swear that they did not perform any marriage at all, so that the women in this church have but a very poor outlook for being considered honorable wives.[61]

Obviously, the animating motivation behind the enactment of section 293 was the emerging threat posed by polygamist Mormon immigrants, but also, at the same time, Parliament sought to "cover off" the practice of polygamy by other groups. In the Senate, the leader of the house, Senator John Caldwell Abbott, indicated that the new provision was "mainly devoted to the prevention of an evil which seems likely to encroach upon us, that of Mormon polygamy, and it is devoted largely to provisions against that practice."[62] However, following this acknowledgment of the impetus for the new provision, Senator Abbott clarified that the purpose of the law was of broader reach, transcending the Mormon religion and culture:

> Of course the Bill is not directed against any particular religion or sect or Mormon more than anybody else; it is directed against polygamists. *In so far as Mormons are polygamists of course it attaches to them* [emphasis added].[63]

The original version of the statute was explicit: it referred to polygamous relationships under "any denomination, sect or society, religious or secular, or by any form of contract, or by mere mutual consent, or by any other method whatsoever."

Moreover, when the first iteration of the polygamy offence was introduced into the Senate in February 1890, it contained a qualification that it would not apply to "any Indian belonging to a tribe or band among whom polygamy is not contrary to law, nor to any person not a subject of Her Majesty, and not resident in Canada." However, one senator worried, "I think that is a very dangerous exception to make, because it may have the effect of exempting the very class to whom the Bill is intended to apply," and indeed the exception would be struck out.[64] The final version provided no exemptions to anyone.

It appears that no attempt was made to enforce the new law against the Mormon polygamists of Southern Alberta, who maintained a very low profile and in any event, as I have suggested, appear to have been meticulous in their adherence to their bargain with the government—that is, to bring only one wife to Canada and leave the remainders behind in the United States. The Cardston-based community grew through several generations, and by the early 1900s there were ten thousand Mormons in Southern Alberta.

The American LDS first renounced polygamy in the Manifesto of 1890, but continued the practice with a nod and a wink until 1904, when the Second Manifesto threatened the excommunication of anyone adopting or endorsing the practice. Over the coming decades, polygamy waned in the LDS, including among the very few Canadian Mormons who had continued it, and it virtually disappeared from the mainstream church; however, it continued among a handful of splinter groups, one of which formed a colony at Short Creek on the Arizona/Utah border, in the 1930s. Short Creek eventually became the twin cities of Hildale and Colorado

City, the former on the south side of the state boundary, and the latter on the north, and that community became the epicentre of Mormon polygamy and continues so until today.

## The Founding of Bountiful

Harold Blackmore was the young brother of John Horn Blackmore, a Cardston politician who served in Parliament as a Social Credit Member from 1945 to 1958. He had converted to the *idea* of polygamy in the 1940s and, like his brother, began to advocate a return to the practice. Unlike his brother, who remained monogamous, Harold decided to put his beliefs into practice: he took a second wife in 1947 (Florence, the sister of his legal wife, Gwen) and moved his new family from the Mormon enclave in southern Alberta to a sprawling property in Lister, virtually adjacent to the American border. This land would later become known as Bountiful.[65]

Harold Blackmore would later describe his conversion this way:

> When the Mormon Church started its bitter persecution of their own members who were teaching or living plural marriage, I spoke in defense of polygamy and was excommunicated for doing so. We have endured relentless persecution from them ever since.

> In December 1945, while on a researching trip to Salt Lake City, [I] met my wife's sister, Florence, in Idaho. She was very cool toward the things I had learned, was a thirty-year-old school teacher, of pioneer Mormon stock and had also been a missionary. We corresponded for a year and became convinced that plural marriage was right and that we should live it. We agreed to a common law relationship that would not be in violation of the anti-polygamy statutes.

> . . .

> We raised a family of seventeen children, eight from Gwen, five from Florence, and four adopted. We raised them in a forested area of British Columbia eight miles from town and had our own private school. Although I had a Bachelor of Science degree and was qualified in teaching and several other fields, prejudice and persecution was such that no employment could be had in those fields. We found that construction was the only occupation in which we could earn a living.

> We have built our family economy around home construction. Every member of our family has become a qualified builder. We develop our

own subdivisions, specialize in custom-built homes and are doing well. We have forty-six grandchildren so far and expect to involve all of them into our family economy.[66]

Judging by his writings on the topic, Blackmore had any number of reasons to advocate the spread of polygamy. He suggested it as a cure for divorce and single-parent families. He skirted the problem of mathematics by suggesting that there was a demographic surplus of women that needed to be accommodated (something that might have had particular resonance in the immediate postwar period):

> Every war condemns millions of women to lifelong singleness or widowhood. Life expectancy is greater for women than men and further contributes to this surplus.

Adding also that:

> Every male homosexual removes himself from the marriage market.[67]

He also embraced feminism, to this extent at least: he believed that, with women entering the workforce in unprecedented numbers, polygamy would "give women the necessary freedom and other needs while still maintaining a completely functioning family unit."[68] Later he wrote:

> [Male domination] is an area from which women are seeking liberation and God bless them for it. It is an old, false, sectarian, idea that a man as head of a house has a right to dictate policy, conduct and procedure, and that it is the duty of women and children to obey without question. Such tradition is of the lowest level of retaliation and oppression. It is true that someone, preferably the father, should preside, not dictate. One who presides at a meeting of equals does NOT make the decisions, nor does he dictate policy or procedure. His duty is to see that every person is given a full and impartial hearing and that all of those involved come to a mutual understanding.[69]

I would suggest that these views could be viewed as quite distinct from the oppressive patriarchy that dominated even mainstream religious households at that time, and you might even say that they represent fairly progressive views for a highly religious man in the immediate postwar period. So what went wrong as Blackmore's experiment grew from a handful of families into a community of hundreds?

Harold Blackmore didn't understand it, but he was releasing into his isolating incubator in the forested interior of British Columbia a behaviour coded within our DNA for millions of years. It proved to be a force that Harold Blackmore would not be able to control, and it would eventually drive him from the very community he created. Polygamy is a powerful, primitive force; it is always there: it breathes, it waits. And when it is released, it grows and consumes.

# PART 2
# On Human Nature

## The Devil Inside

What possessed Harold Blackmore and his wife to marry a third and adopt the polygamous lifestyle, enduring the excommunication and ostracization that would inevitably follow?

The simplistic explanation would be that Harold, Gwen, and Florence were led to polygamy through devotion to their religion. But let me suggest to you that such an explanation might be putting the cart before the horse. What if the religion simply provided an environment—a pretext—in which an unusual but natural human mating behaviour could become manifest? Fundamentalist Mormons did not invent polygamy; they simply, for a brief period of time, resurrected it in the middle of an overwhelmingly monogamous social environment. In this context it is interesting that almost every advocate of faith-based polygamy presents it as not only a religious imperative, but also in some way a natural human family structure. Is it? And if so, does it matter?

One of the riskier, or at least more controversial, aspects of the Attorney General's case in the reference would be our invocation of evolutionary principles to explain the phenomenon of *polygyny* and its establishment as the overwhelmingly dominant form of *polygamy*. Equally fascinating is the question of whether the competing mating model—monogamy—could also have evolved, and how. The overall theory of the Attorney General was a cultural and cognitive co-evolution—that is, the combination of evolved behaviours and social structures that succeeded or failed based on their ability to survive as genes or as ideas through the generations.

The starting point is the relatively new field of evolutionary psychology—the application of Darwinian principles to patterns of human behaviour, instead of simply to physical attributes. David Buss, a pioneer in the field of evolutionary psychology, explains it as "a hybrid discipline that draws insights from modern evolutionary theory, biology, cognitive

51

psychology, anthropology, economics, computer science, and paleoarchaeology." The gist of it is that behaviour has evolved through selection over deep evolutionary time, and that "[h]uman psychology consists of a large number of functionally specialized evolved mechanisms, each sensitive to particular forms of contextual input, that get combined, coordinated, and integrated with each other to produce manifest behavior."

That specific behaviours—not just more generalized cognitive systems—evolve in tandem with more physically apparent features is a fact we easily accept when we are discussing any other species. If a particular breed of finch feeds off insects plucked from holes in trees, it would be unsurprising that it has evolved both a long beak *and* a tendency to search for food in holes.

The difficulty comes with the application of evolutionary principles of behaviour in the context of human societies. Ideas of "human nature" are easily exploited in the service of all manner of prejudices to the point where suggestions that human behaviours are innate are almost automatically offensive because they suggest immutability and therefore a futility in the progressive will to alter behaviour through social change. Evolutionary psychology, then, is seen by many as a capitulation to human nature, a denial of free will, and a surrender of our responsibility to improve society. To look at it a slightly different way, our social order, from religions to behavioural norms to laws, is premised on our will to impose standards of behaviour on others, even where that behaviour has no effect on us. Humans are unique in that norm-enforcing characteristic. And those most inclined to design rules for others (with the best of intentions, of course) believe that their project is undermined by suggestions that there may be real, innate, and immutable barriers to social manipulation.

This is a particularly thorny idea where the suggestion is that there are evolved and more or less innate differences between different groups of people. Differences asserted to have evolved among the races, making some smarter or more creative or lazier than others seemed thoroughly debunked by Stephen Jay Gould in *The Mismeasure of Man*, only to resurface again in the debate that surrounded the publication in 1994 of Herrnstein and Murray's *The Bell Curve*.

The debate over the social implications of evolutionary theory followed very quickly in the wake of Darwin's *Beagle*. In the Victorian era and beyond, "natural selection" was cheerfully recruited by imperial apologists as not only explaining, but *justifying* the subjugation of the world by the most advanced few. The success of one group over another was deemed to be foreordained, *ipso facto* proof of genetic superiority. The theme will be immediately recognizable to students of the philosophies of Nietzsche or the rhetoric of Nazism.

I am not aware that any adherent of evolutionary psychology suggests that there are any significant genetically evolved behavioural differences among peoples (our racial and geographical divergence, it appears, has been too recent, and human interbreeding too frequent, to make much of a difference).[1] In fact, much of the research done in the field is dedicated to demonstrating just how *similar* people are across cultures and continents. But what is accepted as demonstrably true in evolutionary psychology is that people tend to behave predictably, based on certain factors: whether they are children or adults, where they fit in their families and social hierarchies, and, most controversially, whether they are male or female.

Setting aside for the moment evolutionary psychology's political implications, I think most people would, on reflection, admit that human beings engage in behaviour that is both innate and evolved. Few would balk if I were to suggest that it is perfectly reasonable and natural that I care more for my child's welfare than for yours. Granted, I might care *somewhat* for your child—I would probably pick him up if I saw him lying face down in a puddle, and I might advocate social programs to keep him fed and healthy (why I would do even that much is a question to which I will return). But I'm not likely going to feel the degree of love for your child that I feel for mine, and I'm certainly not inclined to pay your kid's way through college, except at gunpoint. The genes of an organism exhibiting such entirely undiscriminating behaviour could hardly be expected to survive against more genetically "selfish" peers.

The explanation of this preference from evolutionary psychology is simple: those behaviours that favour your genetic children over others, to the extent that they can be encoded biologically, will be more likely to be passed along to future generations. A set of genes encoding behaviour that does not distinguish in favour of its kin and act accordingly will be swept aside in the Darwinian struggle by those that do.

The counterargument is that these things are subject to human choice, and are thus malleable, and this is of course true. We can *choose* to be callous, in other words, or to be altruistic and generous. Consider adoptive parents, who decide to take on and support children in whom they have no direct genetic stake. Or communities where extended family groups care for children together. How does evolutionary psychology deal with that?

Evolutionary psychology would not lead us to conclude that we could never care for a nongenetic child. What it would predict is that, *on average*, people will care for their own children more, and that this should be apparent when we look at overall patterns of human behaviour. Cultural norms, education, and other environmental factors should heavily affect our behaviours, but nevertheless our evolved *tendencies* endure beneath the surface, where they are visible only as behavioural patterns in populations, rather than identifiable causes of any particular human's action.

So in studying "blended" families, we might assume that any individual stepparent will love a stepchild as much as a genetic child. In fact we all know step-parents who are incredibly devoted to their kids and whose child-rearing commitment is exemplary, and we also know genetic parents who are complete idiots with their offspring. But we're talking here about overall tendencies, behavioural *inclinations* that are only apparent when behaviour is viewed in the aggregate.

In the 1960s, William D Hamilton formalized the theory of *inclusive fitness*, an idea which suggested that we will tend to favour relatives who are most likely to pass down our genes. So I'll put some money towards my brother's children's education, but somewhat less than for my own children's, and I might even contribute to my cousin's kids, but less again. This insight led to a host of experiments demonstrating convincingly the expected pattern of preferences, reflected in data showing that fathers, for example, invested more heavily in their genetic children than in adopted children, which perhaps isn't shocking, but also that they tended to invest less to the extent that they had reason to be uncertain of a child's paternity, which is, you'll have to admit, highly suggestive.[2]

The evolved tendencies can be even more intriguing than that, and at times the research has been quite shocking. We have recently discovered, for instance, that a child is far more likely to be murdered by a stepparent than by a genetic parent. Not just a little bit more likely, *but forty to 100 times more likely.* A lack of genetic relatedness, in fact, appears to be the single greatest risk factors for violence in general and domestic violence in particular, and the risk goes up almost exactly in proportion to the degree of remoteness (regardless of the domestic arrangements—for instance, we are less likely to be violent towards a brother than a half-brother, and so on, whether we live with either, or both, or neither).[3] Nor can the effect simply be attributed to the violent propensities of the stepparent, because in the overwhelming majority of cases where stepchildren were abused, the same parent's genetic children were not.

Studies from Australia demonstrate the subtlety of these genetic preferences and their affect on behaviour. The "Cinderella effect," as it is called (after the stepfamily conflict in the fairy tale) is not limited to violence. A comprehensive review of accidental deaths revealed a staggering statistic: children who lived with a stepparent were fifteen times more likely to meet an accidental end than children who lived with both biological parents. Incredibly, this risk was eight times higher even than the rate of accidental death in the children of single-parent households. If a child lived in a household with no biological parents, the risk of accidental death skyrocketed further, to about thirty-eight times higher. When the study's authors looked at drowning in particular (a type of accidental death that is closely associated with failures of supervision), the figures were starker still: twenty-five times the risk for stepparent households, eighty-two times the risk for households with no genetic parent present.[4]

So genetically programmed behaviour lurks beneath the surface of human psychology, however wonderfully malleable it may be in other respects. And evolutionary psychology finds, not surprisingly, that behaviour most closely related to reproductive success tend also to be the most difficult to modify through socialization. The Cinderella effect has now been well documented among Xhosa students in South Africa and Hadza foragers in Tanzania, rural villagers in Trinidad, as well as through numerous studies in Canada and the United States.[5]

In postwar Israeli *kibbutzim*, for instance, an attempt was made to raise children entirely communally. The experiment was an abject failure: though high levels of cooperation in child-rearing were possible, it was simply impossible to overcome mothers' instincts to care for their own children above those of others, and many questioned whether the attempt to break the maternal bonds could be anything but harmful for the children.[6]

This is where it gets tricky, because you will notice that I just now referred to *mothers* and not *fathers*. Evolutionary psychologists would say that, because men and women (like males and females of any species), have defined *biological* roles and capabilities, the evolved *behaviours* of the genders would also be different from each other. And this is what gets us in a row over polygamy, because laws premised on stereotypes of gender roles are, from an equality rights perspective, deeply problematic.

But before we get into a political debate, let's try to develop some baseline expectations from a view of humans as naturally evolved organisms existing in a particular environment. Biologically, a woman may expect to be able to pass along her genes to twenty children (the historical and anthropological high-side "norm" is closer to twelve), because it is not simply biological investment that is required but a substantial amount of time and effort in nursing and child-rearing too. Men, on the other hand, are capable in theory of having hundreds or even thousands of children, providing that they can find a sufficient number of willing partners (or, as has been more the norm at various times, unwilling victims).

So evolutionary psychology would predict that genetic behavioural codes that accompany male biological features would favour different reproductive strategies than those which accompany female features. Because of the exponentially higher consequences of sex for women compared to men, we would expect to see women being far more discriminating about whom they have sex with, to prefer fewer partners than men do, and to favour long-term committed relationships in which the father invests heavily in the family over a series of casual sexual encounters.

And indeed these things do seem to hold true, both in our own culture and across the anthropological record. You can attribute this phenomenon to various social factors, but its cross-cultural robustness and sheer strength of predicted results suggests that there is something much deeper going on.

The evolutionary explanation is relatively straightforward: the environment in which we evolved imbued sex with reproductive consequences. Generally, the more sex, the more offspring. A casual sexual encounter is relatively low-risk and high gain for males, who would (modern laws notwithstanding) be able to walk away from the offspring and move on to the next encounter if they preferred. For women, on the other hand, a casual sexual encounter risks serious consequences for many months, and more likely for years as the child is born, nursed, and raised to self-sufficiency. Indeed, in much of the world pregnancy for a woman carries a significant risk of her death. So "coyness" (and I mean this in the biological sense of selectiveness) should be expected of women far more than of men. This should give men an imperative to seek ways to overcome natural female selectiveness and assert their own control over reproductive opportunity.

If all this strikes you as simplistic, then I haven't sufficiently explained it. The fact is that the more complex and adaptable the organism, the less predictable will be its behaviour, because evolution will furnish it with alternative behaviours to select, depending on the environment in which it finds itself and, depending on your views of free will and human agency, the conscious choices it makes. So the evolved behaviours of humans, even with respect to mating strategies, exist in a spectrum, as we all, I think, recognize. What we must accept if we take the findings of evolutionary psychology seriously is that the spectra are different for men and women, just as they are different for eighteen year olds when compared to forty year olds. Whatever the resulting behaviour, nature has left us with *tendencies* and *inclinations* that are, when viewed in the aggregate, measurably and reliably distinct. What I mean by this is that the distinctions are only really meaningful when discussed in populations, rather than individuals. Knowing that men, for genetic reasons, are more predisposed to sexual adventure than women does not allow us to predict what any particular man would do given a certain set of circumstances; however it does permit us to say that, taken as a whole, men will tend to seek more partners than women will.

# Why Polygamy?

This leads us to polygamy. Evolutionary psychologists consider that men have a palette of possible mating behaviours that extends between the extremes of limitless short-term casual encounters, on the one hand, and devoted monogamy on the other. A single partner and a small family permits a man to invest intensely in a few children, each of whom will, as a result of his presence and assistance, have a greater chance of surviving to reproductive age themselves. The opposite strategy is simply to mate as many times as possible and invest nothing further in each child, hoping that the advantage of sheer numbers will outweigh the increased mortality.

Polygamy is the middle ground, or perhaps, the best of both worlds, genetically speaking. If a man has the resources—time, money, perhaps the assistance of followers or slaves—he can have several wives and invest at near-optimal levels in a number of families. For men with the wealth to allow it, evolutionary psychology predicts that polygamy will be an extremely successful strategy, and as such, it will have been hardwired in us—not as destiny, but as an option to be employed where circumstances were favourable to it. Even if the children of polygamy are less likely to survive to reproductive age (due to the more thinly spread paternal investment), this disadvantage will be overcome through the sheer number of possible offspring.

Originally, this may not have been very often. In paleolithic societies, "vigilant egalitarianism" (an overriding need to "get along" with peers to foster alliances and cooperation) and environmental realities meant that men could rarely support more than one family; polygamists in these types of societies, some of which persist today in Africa and South America, tend to have two wives or, very rarely, three or four. Indeed such accommodations may have been practical necessity: higher death rates for men in wars or hunting accidents would mean that polygyny would not necessarily leave any men unmarriageable. Until very recently among the Inuit, for instance, it was not unusual (and may even have been expected) for the brother of a dead hunter to "adopt" the widow and her children as his own second family (that it should be the brother, of course, supports an inclusive fitness theory). But as the hunter-gatherer social structure gave way to static, complex civilizations in the age of agriculture, inequalities of wealth became profound. And when this happened, the genie of polygamy escaped the bottle of environmental restriction and took on corresponding ly epic proportions.

The anthropologist Laura Betzig studied six civilizations that had practised polygamy on different continents over four thousand years: Mesopotamia, Egypt, Aztec Mexico, Incan Peru, imperial India, and imperial China. What she found demonstrated unequivocally the power of polygamy, uncorked.

Bhupinder Singh, the Maharaja of Patiala, married 365 times and housed 332 women in his harem. Make what you will of the fact that he died, in 1938, at age forty-six. Kings of the Chou Dynasty kept dozens of wives and scores of concubines. The Chinese emperor Fei-ti was said to have kept six palaces housing more than ten thousand women. Lesser figures, such as princes, generals, and upper- and middle-class men were restricted to correspondingly lower numbers: hundreds, scores, a dozen, or a handful according to rank. The Incan king in Peru kept "houses of virgins" with at least fifteen hundred women at his beck and call. Around the world, wherever wealth grew, so did the vast inequality of its distribution, and with it, the even more profoundly unequal distribution of the most valuable thing of all, from an evolutionary perspective—reproductive opportunity.[7]

Why the insane numbers? It would seem that the inclination to polygamy, like our taste for fattening and sugary food, lacks much in the way of a restraint mechanism and for the same reason: we need fat and sugar to survive and pass on our genes, and they were scarce in the environment, so we became largely unrestrained consumers. This was not a problem when we could not obtain enough food to make us fat. Now we can easily, and obesity is epidemic. If men are genetically inclined to more wives, and if the usual restraints (environmental, social, economic) are removed, it is not surprising that many will indulge, and some with the resources to do so will become gluttons.

Is the polygamous strategy successful? On the macro scale, you may know that Genghis Khan was a notorious collector of wives and concubines, as were his sons. But even geneticists were shocked to discover that, as a result, Mr. Khan has *sixteen million* male descendants barely eight centuries later. Even when practised on a much more modest scale in societies where the inequality is not as extreme, polygamy proves itself a winning genetic strategy. A comprehensive survey of Mormon lineage in the late nineteenth century demonstrated quite unequivocally that polygamy was superior, from a genetic fitness point of view, to monogamy: polygamists had more surviving children (in absolute terms), who had more children, and so on.[8]

But here's where we encounter the first inherent difficulty with polygamy: yes, polygamists had more surviving children than monogamists, but monogamists' children were, individually, more likely to survive and thrive, because, to put it bluntly, they were more valuable to their fathers and received, *per capita*, more of the paternal investments in time, money, and attention. So polygamy improves the genetic odds of the men who practise it, but sacrifices children, who do worse, on average, where it is permitted. I'll return to this theme of paternal investment later, but introduce it now as the first fly in the ointment of polygamy's Darwinian justification. It presents us with the question that underlies all the others: do we want to live in a society that is genetically optimal, or something more social and more just? If the former, then we should logically embrace polygyny more than we do (I'll get to the subtle ways that we do embrace it later). If the latter, then we should invent a better, more just, more *socially* optimal alternative. And that's exactly what we did.

## Why Monogamy?

Given the strong selective advantage provided by polygnous mating behaviour, one might be forgiven for asking how monogamy became the dominant form of human relationships in Western Society. The answer may be found in two other evolutionary principles, working together: *group selection* and *cultural evolution*.

Group selection is the idea that genes persevere through generations if they belong to *groups* that successfully compete against other groups. It has long been a mystery, for instance, why we should be at all altruistic. Individual Darwinian selection would suggest that any organism that wastes resources (even energy) assisting nonrelatives would be swept aside by genes that were more selfish. The phenomenon of *social*, as opposed to simply *genetic*, cooperation is rare among living organisms. How could it evolve?

Consider the behaviour of some herd animals, such as bison or elephants, who travel in groups of varying degrees of genetic relatedness. Within these groups, the animals are competitive with one another, and selfish genes tend to prevail. However, when threatened with a predator, these animals might back themselves into a circle, their young in the middle, with the pointy bits bristling outward. It is not difficult to recognize this cooperative behaviour as evolved, and in a sense that goes beyond individually selfish genes: members of herds that were inclined to collective defence survived; those that were not perished. The genetic advantages of collective defence makes these animals "care" for nonrelatives in a way that appears—indeed that *is*—altruistic. But then, when the environment changes, when the predator moves on, the members of the herd revert to individual, perhaps even violent, competition among themselves.

And of course with humans, there are many levels of groups—we have our immediate family, then our "village" of people with whom we're most closely acquainted, up and up through tribe or clan to an entire society, nation, or culture. Natural selection will be operating on all of these groups as well as at the individual level, with the general rule being that the adaptation at a given level of hierarchy tends to be undermined by selection at the lower levels. Group selection, therefore, is a powerful force always in tension with the individual competition below it.

Human society could not have grown so complex, so specialized, so interdependent unless humans were capable of being the most socially cooperative species on the planet. Even social insects like ants, where cooperation is hardest-wired and so-called altruism most often identified, are generally incapable of cooperation beyond their close genetic relatives. Ants will stream out in paroxysms of suicidal sacrifice to defend their own queen, but would not be expected to come to the defence of adjacent colonies. This "altruism" is really "inclusive fitness"—selfish genes can propagate, not only through an individual but also through his or her sibling hosts, so such selfless behaviour in certain conditions is to be expected.

Altruistic cooperation is such a dominant feature of human interaction that we might consider it *the* defining characteristic of our species. We are human because we cooperate; we cooperate because we are human. Like the bison, the degree to which we favour selfish versus selfless behaviours will depend on the situation facing us. Yet our capacity for cooperation and social selflessness is fundamentally different in kind, and orders of magnitude greater in extent, than even our most closely related cousins, the chimpanzee and bonobo.

So far, I've only discussed how seemingly inconsistent behaviours, which I broadly categorize as selfish and selfless, could have simultaneously evolved and become encoded in our genes. This only goes partway, however, in accounting for the spread of *particular* cooperative behaviours. Genetic evolution—whether because of individual selection (including the effects of inclusive fitness) or group selection—operates maddeningly slowly, usually over thousands of generations.[9] *Genetically*, humans today are for all present purposes identical to our paleolithic ancestors. Yet our societies, our lives, are so different that an outside observer would be forgiven for concluding that we were a different species entirely. This change, over only ten or twenty thousand years, cannot be accounted for by genetic evolution. Instead, it is the result of another feature of Darwinian morphology that, while not unique to humans, is nevertheless of a different magnitude and kind in our species: *cultural* evolution.

Behaviours can be learned without language, simply as a result of imitation. Members of a group of apes, for instance, can learn to wash their food after the first ape discovers the practice. But humans have a capacity for communication on a different level entirely. Steven Pinker wrote in his groundbreaking 1994 book *The Language Instinct* that "[s]imply by making noises with our mouths, we can reliably cause precise new combinations of ideas to arise in each other's minds."[10] Thus behaviours can be spread ("do as I say") without the need for demonstration, and can even be advanced hypocritically ("not as I do"). Rules can be established, agreed to, shared, and enforced.

And the group with the best rules—the rules that best preserve members of the group and advance their survival and therefore their reproductive success—will outcompete its neighbours who have inferior rules. The rules (some call them memes) become the cognitive equivalent of selfish genes: like genes, memes operate through the process of variation, mutation, competition, and inheritance. And as humans spread over the planet with increased density (the total human population of the world by 1350—about 300 million—was small, but nevertheless fully 100 times what it had been thirty-five thousand years before, in pre-agricultural paleolithic times), groups came within more frequent contact and more frequent competition.

The sheer number of our behavioural modules has evolved alongside our unparalleled use of language to give us not only an extraordinary flexibility of our individual behaviour (this is not unique to humans), but also an ability to coordinate our choices with one another and compare notes within and between groups to develop strategies going forward. Like genetically evolved cooperative strategies, these cultural features of societies will also evolve as groups with the most successful cultures outperform those whose strategies are less apt to the environment. But unlike biological evolution, *social* or *cultural* evolution can happen incredibly rapidly, in a single generation or less. Thus we are not surprised when members of recently "discovered" paleolithic cultures can so readily be assimilated into "modern" Western societies (when we permit them to). We are incredibly flexible and fluid in our ability to conform to ideas that spread and evolve among us.

What does this mean? Given the strong individual selection advantages of polygyny, the fact that monogamy became the dominant cultural mating behaviour and marriage practice of the West suggests that it had substantial advantages over the status quo, at least within the context of the societies in which it developed (essentially, Western nations). Indeed the continuing spread of the monogamous form in the face of our evolved preference against it suggests that it may be in fact *vital* to the modern Western societies in which it evolved. Were it possible to accommodate a significant degree of polygyny in a competitive modern Western democracy, then monogamy simply could not have triumphed as it has.

This is the essence underpinning the "cognitive-cultural co-evolution" argument against polygamy: it must be harmful to success because the most successful societies have consistently suppressed it. It is an argument in need of evidence, of course, because the same thing might be said of a number of behaviours that we now regard as socially harmless. But most of these are false examples: true, Western nations historically forbade gay marriage (and even homosexual mating behaviour), but the West is hardly unique in its mistreatment of gays and lesbians. If gay marriage, like polygamy, were a feature found primarily in societies we view as less socially advanced, then this might give us pause in joining that movement. In fact the opposite is true. For all kinds of reasons, the modern embrace of gays and lesbians by the mainstream appears to have had nothing but positive effects.

No, polygamy is a behaviour that is uniquely tied with societies marked by profound social and, in particular, gender inequality, as we will see. And monogamy has grown in tandem with the democratic West that, while hardly perfect in its own evolution, is nevertheless embraced as the best (or at least, as Churchill famously argued, the least bad) of currently foreseeable human societies.

Progressive legal thinkers who so vociferously reject evolutionary psychology have less difficulty with the idea of *cultural* Darwinism: the principle that the best, most apt norms, mores, and laws will prevail supports their idea that we should focus our attention on improving the rules rather than dwelling on whatever vestigial behavioural tendencies remain from our prehistoric past. There may be a lingering concern among them that the idea of "success-seeking" societies are driven by "wrong" goals; that is, it may be true that improving gender equality has made societies more competitive because the increased utilization of women's economic capital has improved wealth-generation overall, but does that mean that efforts in that direction should stop if increased equality no longer improves a society's Darwinian competitiveness? Or is equality, is social justice, a goal itself, and one more worthy? An interesting, fundamental question, certainly, but perhaps it is one left for another day.

The pressing question, and the source of the criticism from some feminists of the argument I make here, was why it was necessary to establish the innateness of polygamy. If polygamy did indeed correlate (and apparently cause) the host of social harms we attribute to it, why does it matter if it is an evolved behaviour or one governed entirely by social design?

I viewed this question as important to our ability to support and justify the polygamy prohibition. We expected the law's challengers to argue that polygamy would never spread in the population, given the nature of Canadian society. So the question of innateness of the inclination was relevant.

We also expected them to suggest that there was reason to believe that, if polygamy were decriminalized, it would be manifest equally as polygyny and polyandry, thus negating the problems associated with the unequal distribution of marriage opportunity and blunting an argument that women would necessarily disproportionately suffer from the inequality inherent in polygyny. In short, we would be assisted to the extent that we could show (1) that polygamy would increase if the law permitted it to, and (2) that it would manifest significantly more often as polygyny rather than polyandry. It may not have been strictly, logically *necessary*. But the evolutionary view of polygyny as a human tendency would provide important corroboration of the other components of the argument we would eventually make.

## Wars Over—and Against—Women

Evolutionary psychology would eventually have one other contribution to make to our theory of the polygamy case, and it was related to the fate of "lost boys." This prediction was a simple matter of numbers. In a polygynous society, the fact that some men get more than one wife means that others, and perhaps many others, get none. What are the implications?

We all know from a lifetime of observation that men are much more violent than women. What is less well known is that single men, and in particular young single men of lower social status, are the most predictably violent of all. Steven Pinker, Harvard's polymathic cognitive scientist and linguist, summarizes the evolutionary psychology underpinning this behaviour:

> [R]eproductive success varies enormously among males, and the fiercest competition can be at the bottom, among males whose prospects teeter between zero and nonzero. Men attract women by their wealth and status, so if a man doesn't have them and has no way of getting them he is on a one-way road to genetic nothingness. As with birds that venture into dangerous territories when they are near starvation, and hockey coaches that pull the goalie for an extra skater when they are a goal down with a minute to play, an unmarried man without a future should be willing to take any risk. As Bob Dylan pointed out, "When you got nothing, you got nothing to lose."[11]

As studies on the topic began to be done, the results appeared to support the predictions of the evolutionary hypothesis. Wright summarized some of the science that, even in 1997, supported the idea of the "pacifying" effect of marriage on violent men:

Fortunately, male violence can be dampened by circumstance. And one circumstance is a mate. We would expect womanless men to compete with special ferocity, and they do. An unmarried man between twenty-four and thirty-five years of age is about three times as likely to murder another male as is a married man the same age. Some of the difference no doubt reflects the kinds of men that do and don't get married to begin with, but Martin Daly and Margo Wilson have argued cogently that a good part of the difference may lie in "the pacifying effect of marriage."[12]

You might be forgiven for thinking it a bit farfetched to declare marriage as an answer to violent crime, but perhaps it is not. Several writers on the history of the Middle Eastern conflict recount the story of how Fatah, the Palestinian parent organization that had spawned the ultra-violent Black September terrorist group, went about disbanding the smaller organization in the 1970s. Instead of simply assassinating the most radical young members, Fatah instead held a party in Beirut and introduced them to attractive young women. These young heroes of the movement were further incentivized with jobs and apartments, and cash bonuses for the birth of children. The result was remarkable as the die-hard terrorists became dedicated family men. From time to time the PLO would test them by asking them to undertake risky overseas missions. To a man, the former domestic terrorists, now husbands and fathers, declined. Marriage, as a prophylactic to risk-taking and violence, works—we call it "settling down" for a reason.[13]

Returning to polygamy, we can understand why Pinker would predict a violent society: "Under polygyny, men vie for extraordinary Darwinian stakes—many wives versus none—and the competition is literally cut-throat."[14]

And in fact, the only actual studies done on the subject (to that point) did seem to support the correlation. In 2007 Miller and Kanazawa reported:

> across all societies, polygyny makes men violent, increasing crimes such as murder and rape, even after controlling for such obvious factors as economic development, economic inequality, population density, the level of democracy, and political factors . . . [15]

If we wished to be harshly cynical, we could view much of the behaviour of humans throughout history through the lens of an evolved psychology. When we do, it appears that the male capacity for violence—organized as well as individual—in service of reproductive opportunity is virtually unlimited. "Many homicides and most tribal wars are directly or indirectly

64

about competition for women," observes Pinker.[16] He would find support from Homer's wistful Achilles, summarizing his "heroic" career by saying, "I have spent many sleepless nights and bloody days in battle, fighting men for their women." Other studies have demonstrated convincing evidence that young men in diverse cultures—from the Yanomamo tribe to Colorado street gangs, band together and engage in violence to improve their chances of reproductive success.[17] In keeping with the predictions of evolutionary psychology, there has never been an occasion, as near as anyone can tell, of women banding together in significant numbers to kill anyone (for any reason).

Achilles' confession raises an interesting point that goes somewhat beyond individual psychology and into the realm of evolved *group* behaviour. As I've said, "group selection" theory holds that human societies are organized and develop rules in ways that maximize the group's success in competition with others. This is also apparent in a group's willingness to use organized violence to maximize genetic "fitness."

So it is of some interest that the harnessing of male violence in the service of a group's reproductive opportunity is also a theme throughout history. And it isn't just the amount, but the *focus* of violence that can trace roots to evolutionary advantage; so inevitably campaigns where one group seeks to eradicate another often involve the systematic murder of males coupled with campaigns of rape against women and girls. This may be noticed in the earliest accounts of genocide in the Old Testament right up until the most recent Balkan conflict, with its mass slaughter of men and boys overlain with campaigns of rape and forced prostitution directed at women and girls.

There are a number of stories in the Bible where God instructs his followers to commit genocide against other peoples for all manner of sins (usually just happening to be in the wrong Promised Land at the wrong time), but is the best example for present purposes is probably the campaign against the Midianites. In the biblical account, on God's orders, the Israelites kill all the Midianite men and take women and children captive. This angers God, who issues a further edict:

> Now therefore kill every male among the little ones, and kill every woman that hath known man by lying with him. But all the women children, that have not known a man by lying with him, keep alive for yourselves.[18]

Set aside your natural horror at this direction, for a moment, and consider its undeniable genetic logic and sophistication. It rejects the crude evolutionary advantage provided by a simple male/female "gendercide"[19] in favour of something more nuanced: by preserving only the virgin "women children" to take as wives, concubines, or sex slaves (remember that this was a polygynous age), the Israelites' God was introducing a further level of evolutionary security by an assurance of "paternity certainty": none of the conquerors' newly acquired "partners" would be giving birth to children of their deceased husbands.

In other words, this particular religious instruction could not have been better crafted to pass along genes if it had been designed for that very purpose. And the point I'm trying to make is that *it was*. We make social rules, particularly with respect to differential treatment of the genders, and then we excuse them as having some greater authority, preferably religious or moral. But by more than just happy coincidence they serve what Richard Dawkins famously dubbed the "selfish gene."[20]

So this can get you thinking in a couple of ways that are relevant to polygamy. First, you have the prediction that a polygamous society will have a lot more violence and crime in it from the unmarried males. This will, in and of itself, probably mean some repressive institutions provide control.

But second, you might also predict that institutions would arise that used prevalent male power—including male violence or the threat of it—to control reproductive opportunities for both men and women. Individual polygynists, particularly "hyperpolygynists," have often been observed to be despots, and the more wives, usually the more despotic. But the evolved psychology of humans would also suggest that a polygynous society must itself be more despotic to preserve the practice and maintain order.

These ideas, which were at the beginning only seeds of thoughts, would play out through the evidence at the polygamy trial where they were tested by science with quite breathtaking results. For all kinds of reasons, we would find, Wright summarized it well when he said: "A polygynous nation, in which large numbers of low-income men remain mateless, is not the kind of country many of us would want to live in."[21]

## Lyin' and Tiger and Newt (Oh My!)

Immediately after observing the effects of polygny on criminality and saying we wouldn't want to live in a polygynous nation, Wright launched into the following observation:

> Unfortunately, this is the sort of country we already live in. The United States is no longer a nation of institutionalized monogamy. It is a nation of serial monogamy. And serial monogamy in some ways amounts to polygyny. Johnny Carson, like many wealthy, high-status males, spent

his career monopolizing long stretches of the reproductive years of a series of young women. Somewhere out there is a man who wanted a family and a beautiful wife and, if it hadn't been for Johnny Carson, would have married one of these women.[22]

I would hear this argument both in court and out throughout the reference. Were we *really* a monogamous society? Didn't we let rich men cheat, have mistresses, divorce, and remarry? All the time, we have endured reports of scoundrels behaving badly in the media, and these too have added to the public discourse around polygamy, or at least around human mating strategies and nonmonogamous behaviour. Perhaps the most notorious episode ongoing at the time of the reference involved revelations about the private life of the revered figure of champion golfer Tiger Woods.

Beginning in December 2009, it was revealed that Woods's carefully crafted image of devoted husband and family man may have been, at the least, incomplete. In a series of progressively bad "tell all" interviews, a number of women began to "confess," and it quickly became apparent that Woods had been carrying on affairs lasting months or, in at least a couple of cases, years, with a host of women from waitresses to porn stars. Inevitably the Woods camp announced that he suffered from "sex addiction" (poor thing) and he withdrew from the pro tour as his marriage publically disintegrated.

On the spectrum of male human mating behaviours, Woods strategy would be located somewhere between the middle and towards the extreme—he seemed to favour a large number of liaisons that were conducted nonexclusively and with little investment in each. However, Woods also had a wife and children who were the main beneficiaries of his parental investment potential (a potential realized even after separation—Elin Nordegren reportedly received $100 million in their divorce settlement).

Even if all Woods's alleged liaisons were real, we still could not consider him as the most extreme example of the "wild oats" strategy. Gene Simmons, who parlayed his role as gargoyle-cum-bassist in the rock band KISS into a thoroughly perplexing success in "reality TV," has claimed to have slept with 4,600 women in his life. Wilt "the Stilt" Chamberlain, a legend of basketball (and then some), boasted in his autobiography to 20,000 liaisons at the time of writing (1992). Sometimes it appeared that, at least among the American entertainment elite, comedian Chris Rock was correct when he supposedly said "a man is only as faithful as his options."

Newt Gingrich would also be familiar as a data point in an anthropological study of human polygamous behaviour. The former House Speaker and one-time candidate for the Republican presidential nomination has adopted what evolutionary psychologists call "*de facto* polygamy," though in relatively mild form. He has been married three times, to successively younger women. In each of his remarriages, there was, shall we say, an *overlap* period during which he was carrying on a secret affair (the second affair, with his now-wife Callista Bisek, apparently lasted six years before it was discovered, or admitted). His current wife is twenty-three years younger than he is.

All of this is so predictable as to be almost tiresome, and Gingrich's trail of two abandoned wives hardly compares to, for instance, Johnny Carson's tally of six. What is interesting for present purposes is not that Gingrich, without a doubt a "high-status male" in anthropological terms (one with a greater choice among the various mating strategies), selected a biologically optimal (but still legal) approach and became a *de facto* polygamist. As I say, that is rather to be expected. What is interesting is the role that social norms appear to play in controlling this kind of behaviour. The Republican base, though perhaps not thrilled with the candidate's history of infidelity, appeared comfortable enough to support him for president, or at least not to oppose him on that basis. But when, on 19 January 2012, his second wife gave an interview in which she reported that, when his six-year affair came to light, Gingrich proposed an "open marriage" whereby he could carry on both relationships simultaneously, the Gingrich camp immediately recognized it as a potentially fatal crisis, and the candidate survived only by declaring that the story was false. The American voters, it appeared, could stomach all kinds of bad behaviour, but they would not tolerate a relaxation of the socially imposed authority of dyadic exclusivity. You could have a mistress, the message seemed to be, but you could not all agree that you could have a mistress—you had to endure the costs imposed on the behaviour. It was the *openness* of the proposed open marriage that offended more than the secrecy of the affair.[23] Marriage norms could be ignored and the transgression forgiven, but they could not be *altered*. Is that simple hypocrisy, or is it something much deeper?

Some have argued that our acceptance of nonmonogamous mating behaviour, through "serial monogamy," cheating, or hypersexual behaviour, does render the polygamy prohibition both useless and hypocritical. But there is another way of looking at it. If the overall unconscious purpose of this evolved set of rules is to reduce the inequality produced by one man monopolizing the reproductive capacities of a number of women, our present set of rules does seem to accomplish this. Yes, it is true that some men have sex with hundreds or thousands of women over their lifetime. But they cannot, like the despotic Moulay Ismail the Bloodthirsty,[24] keep them locked away to ensure paternity certainty, and with respect to any of the women "accessed" by, say Chamberlain, the odds are that their children were fathered by someone else. And while it is true that Gingrich's strategy has permitted him to dominate portions of the reproductive years of three women, that number pales in comparison to the dozens of wives often attached to leaders in fundamental Mormonism, and even they are not extreme examples of polygamous acquisition. The fact is that forcing Gingrich, at times one of the most powerful men in the country and the possessor of considerable personal wealth, to adopt serial monogamy over open polygyny may have reduced his acquisition of brides by a factor of ten.

The wealth is, of course, another factor in this (I admit somewhat digressive) discussion. The wealth disparity among polygamists in hunter-gatherer culture would be minimal, and in fact the differences among men would probably be manifest more in their life skills than in acquired wealth or property. Today, men in the marriage market could have possessions worth virtually nothing, on one hand, or billions of dollars on the other. So the fact that our current system forces serious consequences on a "*de facto* polygamous man" reduces this competitive advantage. Woods, as phenomenally wealthy as he is, could not endure too many $100 million divorces. So Wright is correct to observe that we have loosened the leash on polygynous behaviour through the advent of serial monogamy. But we nevertheless impose costs upon it. Similarly, men will be drawn to extramarital liaisons, but these too carry costs, in terms of social opprobrium if no other. And so perhaps, the polygamy law is there to fill a gap by imposing costs on the kind of polygyny that would otherwise be dangerously inexpensive, that is polygyny conducted in an environment that is isolated from mainstream social norms and free of any obligations of support.

If this view is correct, then the limited way that polygamy is practised within the law in modern society (serial monogamy, mistresses, affairs, and so on) probably generates a certain level of violence in society already. Our tolerance of the practices may represent an unconscious social compromise of the sort we make all the time. Benjamin Franklin once said that we should not trade a little liberty for a little security, but we do the opposite quite frequently. We endure risks and social harms to a certain level in society to preserve our freedoms—of speech, economic activity, and so forth. Reasonable people can disagree on whether the compromise is appropriately struck, but it cannot be right to suggest that, because we endure *some* harm in exchange for a degree of liberty, that we should permit unfettered liberty even if it would lead to increased harm.

# PART 3
# All Roads Lead to Bountiful

## The Persistent Polygamists of Lister

So let me return to the story of Harold Blackmore and Bountiful in the years after the Second World War, at which point he took the leash off what I say was his evolved preference for polygyny. By the 1950s, Harold had became the patriarch of a small polygamist community as more followers were convinced to move there and adopt the polygamist family structure, referred to in fundamentalist Mormon doctrine simply as The Principle. His founding family was joined by those of Eldon Palmer, Dalmon Oler, and Ray Blackmore, who was Harold's nephew (John Horn Blackmore's son) but was around the same age. Each was by then a polygamist. Later they were joined by the Bartons and McKinleys, and then others still.

The Bountiful group aligned themselves with the main fundamentalist Mormon group in the United States, which was run by its own prophet Joseph Musser and made its home base in Short Creek, Arizona. In time, Musser would be replaced by LeRoy Johnson, then by Rulon Jeffs, and finally by his son Warren Jeffs.

No sooner had the founding families of Bountiful established themselves and formalized their contact with their Southern counterparts, that the Short Creek polygamist community in the United States came under the government's most determined attack. In 1953, the town was raided by Arizona authorities and many of its men arrested. Hundreds of children were seized by the state.

This hardline approach, though, backfired. *Life* magazine ran sympathetic pictorials that painted the polygamists as harmless, simple folk whose only crime was being different. And they weren't even that different: patriarchal families were hardly radical in the United States of the 1950s, and the men, like Mormons everywhere, had short hair and conservative clothes. The Short Creek persecution (for many viewed it as

71

just that) seemed to mirror the paranoid pursuit of Communists in the same period, and there was widespread outrage from the Left, but also from the Right, who saw the raid as the nanny state run amok. And as I've said, the men of Short Creek, aside from their peculiar marriage beliefs, on other levels seemed exemplary—clean-cut, hard-working, deeply religious, and intensely American (when the raid began, the men of the community were gathered around the flagpole, singing patriotic songs as they awaited arrest). Despite the fact that the raid revealed unequivocal evidence of serious problems (and in particular child brides), the families were reunited and the state slinked off, beaten and humbled. Short Creek was left alone to grow and nurture its "peculiar institution," and the 1955 events set a tone that endured from decades to come. The raid became a significant episode in the persecution mythology of the polygamists, and would be held up, even in 2010, as the archetype of heavy-handed and inept state response. For governments, or at least for politicians, it was a cautionary tale whose lesson was clear: as painful as inaction on polygamy was, taking strong measures could be far worse still.

The ties between Short Creek and the Lister enclave that would become Bountiful were strong. There was an old "rumrunners' road" that led from the Bountiful property across the American border, and entire families could move back and forth at will. At least in those early years, niceties of borders and customs did not need to be observed.

But the bucolic excitement of the early settlement came up against some hard realities soon enough. It is one thing to establish a polygamist colony through migration, but it another thing to sustain it through the generations. When the polygamous pioneers arrived, they brought with them their own unnatural gender balance, with several women for each man. But they tended to have children in equal numbers of males and females, and as their children grew up and looked to marriage, the difficulties of the mathematics would play themselves out as Bountiful increasingly fell under the influence of the strict and conservative American wing of the church, which became, over time, if anything more oppressive as time went on.

As his community grew, Harold Blackmore came to bridle under the authority of the FLDS (as the Short Creek church came to be called) and its autocratic rulers. He was over time squeezed out of the Lister community and ordered by the church to move to Short Creek to supervise construction in 1964. Depending on whom you listen to, Blackmore was either persuaded to sign the BC properties over to the FLDS's trust, the United Effort Plan, or he had them stripped from him against his will. In any event, by 1968, Blackmore, who remained devout in his fundamental beliefs, had become so disenchanted by what he perceived to be the hypocritical and abusive ways of the prophet and "priesthood men" that he left the church altogether, moving his two wives and remaining children to Hurricane, Utah, not far away from Short Creek but clearly away from the church. He would remain both a bitter critic of the FLDS, and a staunch supporter of polygamy, until his death in 2000.

It's difficult to write—or even read—about Harold Blackmore without a measure of sympathy for a figure whose life was, on some levels, tragic. As I type this, I have before me an article from 23 January 1977, a UPI piece printed in the Dubuque, Iowa, *Telegraph Herald*. It describes Blackmore's appeal to the Utah Board of Education to launch an investigation into Short Creek's schools. Blackmore, it says, "charged . . . that 14-year-old girls are ordered to marry 60-year-old cult leaders and that the school is used to 'brainwash' youngsters."

But after the Short Creek fiasco, nobody wanted to know. The Bountiful community continued to grow as an FLDS outpost, with its own "bishop" and ministers but otherwise directed by the US-based prophet and his fawning courtiers.

Harold Blackmore was replaced after his ouster by his nephew Ray Blackmore, who became a prominent businessman in the area, operating a number of companies related to the local logging economy. Ray Blackmore was designated the FLDS's bishop, and upon his demise in the 1980s he would be ousted in favour of his charismatic son, Winston, who would be bishop until 2002, when he would be replaced by James Marion "Jim" Oler, who was holding that position when the Polygamy Reference began.

This is how, a hundred years after Smith's martyrdom, and decades after it had seemed to have been entirely eradicated from the Mormon Church itself, polygamy took root among a handful of adherents in South Central British Columbia, and grew in time into a community of a thousand souls.

## A Prolonged Paralysis

But by the 1980s, concerns were increasingly heard about the odd little community in Lister, and the frequency and specificity of the allegations increased over time. There were stories of child brides being traded across the border, of strange teachings and scary prophets. Daphne Bramham, the tenacious investigative journalist and columnist at the *Vancouver Sun*, began a decade of investigation that would make Bountiful and the government's inaction, a cause *célèbre* and a high-profile public issue, to many a politician's chagrin. Parties and governments came and went, but Bramham was there goading them.

Even Bramham did not convince everyone, and public opinion during this period seemed divided along roughly the same lines as were drawn in the academic debate I described earlier. To some Bountiful was just a quirky anachronism, its existence an example (albeit rather extreme) of the tolerant mosaic that was Canadian cultural diversity. To many others it was a kind of walled-off Disneyland for perverts and child-abusers. "A bunch of old men breeding girls for sex" opined a well-respected (and normally very reserved) former appeals judge with whom I was having lunch one day. He was not alone in this view, and demands that the government should do something about Bountiful erupted again and again.

But many had concluded, by that point, that a successful prosecution was doubtful, including the chief law officer of the British Columbia Crown.

Canada's new Constitution arrived in 1982, along with the *Canadian Charter of Rights and Freedoms*. In response to the renewed police interest in Bountiful, the BC Attorney General sought advice from some of its top lawyers on whether the polygamy prohibition could be enforced. One by one, a number of counsel from the Legal Services Branch, and a respected former judge consulted for his opinion, expressed their views that the law was a violation of religious freedom, and one that could not be justified under the *Charter*. This led a representative of the Attorney General's Criminal Justice Branch (CJB) to publicly announce, in 1992, that the law was unconstitutional and could not be prosecuted.

It was an extraordinary step to take, one that was probably unprecedented.[1] Newspapers in the United States as well as Canada warily noted that fundamentalist Mormons in Canada had apparently won the legal right to practise polygamy. Constitutional law professor Grant Huscroft wrote: "It seems highly likely that the decision of the Attorney General for British Columbia is correct. But there are many problems inherent in a decision to refuse to enforce a law."[2] Huscroft went on to argue that the Attorney General could not, constitutionally, declare his refusal to enforce a presumptively legitimate Act of Parliament:

> I think that the purported power to refuse to enforce a law is an inappropriate response to a perceived *Charter* violation. More important, it should be considered unconstitutional in its own right. A refusal to enforce validly enacted legislation appears similar in effect to a purported decision to suspend a law, and that has been unconstitutional since the Bill of Rights, 1688. Is it any less subversive of the Constitution if the reason for suspension of the law is the Attorney General's interpretation of individual rights under the *Charter*?[3]

Lawyers with the federal government in Ottawa were almost unbelieving of the hubris of the provincial revolt. Under the Canadian Constitution (unlike the US Constitution) "criminal law" is a federal responsibility, and the *Criminal Code* was supposed to set out a single law for the entire country. But the "administration of justice" was the constitutional responsibility of the provinces, so it was up to the provincial government to enforce the federal law. But what happened when a province determined that the federal law was invalid? As it turned out, stalemate.

Bob Edwards, then the Deputy Attorney General of British Columbia, forwarded the provincial government's legal opinions to his federal counterpart on 13 October 1992 and asked for the Canadian government's view on the matter. The federal government studied the law and Deputy Minister of Justice John Tait came to a different opinion: in a series of letters addressed to Edwards's successor Brian Neal, Tait communicated his department's conclusion that the law would probably withstand *Charter* scrutiny. Section 293, Tait wrote, "does not involve a clear cut case of a *Charter* breach, and, indeed . . . there is a reasonably good chance that the legislation would be upheld in litigation."

The province was persistent. Neal replied:

We have considered the grounds for your conclusion with interest . . .

Section 293 criminalizes a "status" and fails to distinguish between harmful and non-harmful (i.e., consensual) polygamous unions. The breadth of the section thus extends to criminalize a practice which is central to sincerely held religious beliefs even when the practice is not harmful. In our view, it is clear that such a provision would be found to violate s. 2(a).

. . .

In all of these circumstances, surely the better part of wisdom, and indeed of the public interest, is to take a proactive rather than reactive approach by amending section 293 and taking control of the legislative agenda now rather than to litigate and rely on the courts to lead us to the reforms required.

The federal government, in its turn, refused to budge.

This process was repeated again in 2001 when former Chief Justice Allan McEachern was asked by the provincial Attorney General to provide his opinion as to the constitutional validity of section 293. In his view also, section 293 was likely in conflict with the religious freedom guarantee in section 2(a) of the *Charter* and would be struck down if challenged in the course of a prosecution.

This time, it was an exasperated Geoff Plant, the Attorney General himself who, the following year, petitioned the federal government to change the law to make it conform with the *Charter*, perhaps by restricting its application to "bad" polygamy—that is where minors were involved, or where there were signs of abuse or exploitation. He wrote to the federal minister on 5 March 2002:

> There are serious ethical and legal issues that would arise should the [provincial] Criminal Justice Branch proceed with charges notwith-standing the fact that authoritive [*sic*] legal opinions have been obtained suggesting that there is an insuperable legal obstacle that would constitute a fatal flaw to a prosecution in such a case.
>
> . . .
>
> I respectfully ask you to encourage your officials to give this issue their immediate attention in order to undertake such legislative reform as is necessary to ensure that the *Criminal Code* contains constitutionally sound provisions that better respond to the inappropriate use of a power imbalance within a community designed to encourage young women to enter into sexual relationships through a form of marriage.

Yet the federal government had become, if anything, even more convinced that the law was good on its face and firmly refused to revisit the issue in a letter from Minister Cauchon sent 16 July 2002:

> The Department of Justice Canada will not undertake to review the offence of polygamy in section 293 of the *Code* at this time. In fact, repealing the prohibition of polygamy in the *Criminal Code* may violate the equality rights of women in Canada, and could also affect Canada's international commitments.

Not only was the federal government prepared to support a prosecution of Bountiful polygamists, but it was also now actually urging it:

> The situation in Bountiful community requires immediate attention. The Department of Justice Canada encourages British Columbia to address all alleged offences committed in the Bountiful community, including the offence of polygamy. Should section 293 of the *Code* be constitutionally challenged, the Department of Justice Canada will support British Columbia in upholding the constitutionality of the section.

Around that same time, there was the turmoil in Bountiful after the death of FLDS prophet Rulon Jeffs and the ascendence of his son, Warren. Warren Jeffs, a gaunt and scary sociopath with ultraconservative (even for a fundamentalist) views, was not the favourite of Bountiful's garrulous and (relatively speaking) easygoing bishop, Winston Blackmore. In the power struggle that followed, Blackmore was pushed aside and Jeffs's man, James Oler, was appointed as bishop in his place. Blackmore was excommunicated from the FLDS but many in the community remained loyal to him (not least the ten dozen members of his immediate family). As a result, Bountiful was divided into two roughly equal factions of about 500 each; half were loyal to Blackmore, and half to Warren Jeffs through Oler.

As might be expected, Blackmore's side of "the Split," as it became known, was the more liberal. Many of Blackmore's women dressed in modern Western clothes, wore makeup, and interacted easily with the surrounding community. Blackmore gave interviews to the media, and appeared on *Larry King Live* with his "live and let live" message on polygamy. Many in the media loved his "aw, shucks" demeanour and didn't press Blackmore on the messy facts underlying even his relatively benign form of fundamentalist Mormon polygamy (the wives he had taken as young as fifteen, for instance). Some of the members of Blackmore's congregation organized a Bountiful women's roundtable to discuss polygamy and their experiences with it. Oler's side, like the man himself, remained closed and inaccessible.

The Split caused severe difficulties for the residents of Bountiful. None of them owned their homes; since Harold Blackmore was duped into signing them over, the Bountiful properties were held in a US-based United Effort Plan, and now that the effort was far less united, nobody was sure where they stood (this situation would become even more complicated after authorities in the United States took over the trust). Then, of course, there were the schools: after the Split, Blackmore established Mormon Hills Elementary school as an alternative to the FLDS-run Bountiful Elementary and Secondary School (BESS). As in a civil war, families were divided from one another and even among themselves as the Jeffs loyalists were forbidden to speak to those on the Blackmore side.

These events, and the emerging public profile of Blackmore's followers (who had gone, in the view of some, from closeted criminals to become open scofflaws), led to increased calls for something to be done about Bountiful.

## Oppal's Crusade

Wally Oppal likes to tell a story that pokes fun at the naivety he displayed when he first came to office in 2005. As Oppal tells it, he sat in his first session of the legislature, the Liberals' star candidate turned cabinet minister, staring down the opposition during Question Period. Before long, a question came addressed to the Attorney General, and Oppal rose to give what he considered to be a thorough and informative answer. When he resumed his seat, Oppal says, a colleague leaned towards him and said, "Nobody really expects you to do that, you know." A moment later, another colleague leaned forward and added conspiratorially, "It's called *Question* Period, not *Answer* Period." That story tells a bit about Oppal. He has had his share of critics over the years, but few will deny that his approach to problems was refreshingly direct, even guileless.

I arrived in Oppal's Ministry of Attorney General almost exactly a year after Oppal himself. We had been acquainted for years before I'd become the head of his constitutional law group, and he had always greeted me warmly by name. I wasn't alone in this, of course, because Oppal's accessibility was a notorious feature of his character, as were his facility with names and his natural ability to make any interlocutor feel both at ease and the subject of his full attention. He was extremely approachable, and most in the legal community and in the media knew that if you wanted a private audience with the Attorney General he could be found at the Caffé Artigiano on Hornby Street, where he'd be happy to hold forth on almost any topic over coffee. This naturally drove his government minders and public affairs people, who jealously guarded their traditional role as the Attorney General's public interface, to distraction. Wally Oppal was an unguided missile, and the press loved it. Those of us tasked with implementing his decisions, however, sometimes had to scramble in response to "instructions" broadcast in the morning newspapers.

Oppal had been a powerful public presence in British Columbia long before he entered politics. He had been a prosecutor, a justice of the Supreme Court and, later, the Court of Appeal. He had conducted a public inquiry into policing in British Columbia and was not shy about taking public stands on controversial issues (Oppal tells another self-effacing joke in the form of a riddle: "What is the most dangerous place on earth?" he will ask. "The space between Wally Oppal and a microphone.")

One of the issues that Oppal took on in a very public way was Bountiful. After Oppal's arrival as Attorney General in 2005, the moribund police investigation gathered steam, and RCMP officers, led by Sergeant Terry Jacklin and Constable Shelley Livingstone, forwarded their first report on their investigation to Crown counsel on 29 September 2006. They recommended that charges be brought against Blackmore and Oler, the two competing bishops of the Bountiful community who had "married" a succession of teenaged girls from their churches. The crimes alleged were polygamy and the sexual exploitation of a number of girls.

However, in British Columbia, unlike almost every other province and territory in Canada, the decision on whether or not to press charges is not left to the police, but is rather made by Crown counsel, who consider the police recommendations, review the investigators' report, and then make a decision based on two criteria: First, is there a substantial likelihood of conviction? And second, is prosecution in the public interest?

When the RCMP's Bountiful recommendations reached the prosecutors, four senior Crown counsel, including Bob Gillen, the Assistant Deputy Attorney General (ADAG) in charge of the CJB, determined that the CJB would not approve charges. The Crown counsel reported both that there was insufficient likelihood of conviction and that it was contrary to the public interest to proceed, both with respect to polygamy, and also on the child exploitation charges.

This decision appeared outrageous and wrongheaded to many, not least Wally Oppal. Anyone who talked to the Attorney General in 2006 or 2007 (and many in the media did) would know that he was convinced that what was going on in Bountiful was bad, and that it needed to be dealt with. So it surprised no one when in May 2007 Oppal directed Gillen to appoint someone to revisit the question of charges against polygamists at Bountiful.

Gillen was known for digging in his heels to protect and advance the idea of the CJB as a separate entity within the Attorney General's ministry, and he enjoyed the loyalty of prosecutors in the field for his unflagging support of their independence. At the same time as Bountiful began to work its way again through CJB's world, Gillen was also fighting off attempts to have prosecutors called as witnesses in a public inquiry (the Frank Paul case) and a coroner's inquest (the Lee Inquest in Victoria), so it wouldn't have been surprising if the independence of prosecutorial decision-making was on his mind when Oppal's marching orders came down.

One distinctive feature of the Canadian system of justice is that the Attorney General has a number of different, and occasionally conflicting, roles. He's the prosecutor of criminal cases and "guardian of the public interest" before the courts, but he's also a member of cabinet and a politician. So a special prosecutor, a member of the private bar, is appointed to make charge-approval decisions, and to conduct prosecutions, in cases where it would be either inappropriate or unseemly to have it done by full-time employees of the government and ministry.

So it happened that Gillen, openly wary of the appearance of political intrusion into the Bountiful file, decided to appoint Richard (Rick) Peck, one of Canada's leading criminal defence counsel and an occasional *ad hoc* prosecutor, to act as an independent special prosecutor under the *Crown Counsel Act*, and determine whether charges should be laid.

Peck's report[4] issued on 25 July 2007 found that there was insufficient basis to proceed on any charges except polygamy, and that charges under that section could not proceed because of the constitutional uncertainty surrounding the provision. He recommended instead that the government call a constitutional reference to decide the question:

> A prosecution would likely face a number of obstacles, resulting in a cumbersome and time-consuming process. The constitutional issue might not be heard for some time after charges are laid, as other aspects of the trial process, such as disclosure issues or various defence motions, might take precedence. Given the unique history of this matter, including the lengthy passage of time since the first expression of police interest in Bountiful, and the existence of prior Crown opinions regarding the constitutionality of s. 293, these motions might be particularly lengthy and complex. They could result in the constitutional issue never being determined at trial.

Peck thought a reference would provide "an authoritative and expeditious judicial resolution of the legal controversy surrounding polygamy." He wrote:

> In my view, a reference to the BC Court of Appeal—with a probable further appeal to the Supreme Court of Canada—is the preferable approach to take. My view is that the public interest will best be served by an authoritative and expeditious judicial resolution of the legal controversy surrounding polygamy. The legality of polygamy in Canada has for too long been characterized by uncertainty. The integrity of the legal system suffers from such an impasse, and an authoritative statement from the courts is necessary in order to resolve it.

Finding that "a clear statement from the courts would be desirable" concerning the constitutional validity of section 293, Peck concluded:

> If the law is upheld, members of the Bountiful community will have fair notice that their practice of polygamy must cease. If they, in turn, persist in the practice, a prosecution could be initiated at the Crown's discretion, substantially free of the procedural obstacles which now exist.

A "reference" is a different type of proceeding. Under the *Constitutional Question Act*, the government is given the power to ask any question of a court, and the court answers the question as if it were issuing a judgment in a case. References are infrequent and usually used to settle difficult but dry questions surrounding provincial or federal jurisdiction when a controversy had erupted but was not yet the subject of litigation. Essentially, a reference question is the government asking a court to give its opinion on an issue, almost always a constitutional issue. Can the government expropriate a particular area of ocean floor? Can Newfoundland rip up the Churchill Falls power-sharing agreement with Quebec? Can Quebec secede from Confederation? The opinion isn't binding, technically, but historically reference decisions have enjoyed the same practical force as any other judgments.

I should say as something of an aside that not everyone thinks that courts should be in the business of holding forth in the abstract. The United States Constitution, through its separation of powers and restriction of federal courts to "cases and controversies," does not permit the judiciary to provide legal opinions to the executive. And in England, an early legal question referred to the judges of the King's Court by His Majesty Charles I in 1636 led to revolution.[5] Somewhat less spectacularly, Canada's 1996 decision to refer the question of Quebec's secession to the Supreme Court of Canada had annoyed Quebec; the province decided to simply not show up for the case, and dismissed the reference as illegitimate. Only after the Supreme Court held that Canada must negotiate secession if Quebecers should vote for it did Quebec do a partial about-face and hold it up as authoritative and binding (at least upon Canada).

But it wasn't any constitutional objection that inclined the British Columbia government against using the reference power to decide the polygamy question, it was Oppal's belief that it was simply better to proceed with a prosecution, where clear evidence of an abusive context could be brought. About a month after Peck's report was delivered on 6 September 2007, he wrote the ADAG, expressing his exasperation at the lack of charges, and issued a directive to the ADAG to retain another highly respected senior criminal lawyer, Leonard (Len) Doust, "to review Mr. Peck's analysis, including the history and other factors he considered in coming to a conclusion that a prosecution was less preferable than a reference."

Disappointingly for Oppal, on 20 March 2008 Doust confirmed the findings and recommendations of Peck and concluded that "given both practical considerations and concerns about fairness, a reference rather than a prosecution is the most appropriate way to proceed at this time."

Stymied again and privately fuming, Oppal went off to consider his options.

## Yearning for Zion

While British Columbia appeared to dither, Texas was being, well, *Texas*.

In 2003, Warren Jeffs, the fugitive leader of the FLDS, had decided that what his followers needed was a new home away from the prying eyes that continued to probe their traditional stomping grounds in Utah and Arizona. Through a shell corporation, the FLDS purchased

1700 acres near Eldorado, Texas, built an impressive new temple there, and by 2004 established a vanguard community of about 700 residents in what is usually referred to as the Yearning For Zion compound, or YFZ for short. The FLDS apparently intended that YFZ would be the new capital of the church's empire, believed to be tens of thousands strong across the United States.

Along with the first transplanted residents of YFZ from the FLDS town of Hildale/Colorado City (the former Short Creek that straddled the Arizona/Utah border) came stories of lost boys and child brides that had dogged the FLDS for decades. The Texas authorities took notice of this worrisome new outpost, and when a desperate call came from a female on a cell phone claiming to be a pregnant sixteen-year-old rape victim, they swooped in, seized most of the children (more than 400 in all), and executed search warrants that began to turn up a trove of deeply disturbing documentary evidence.

The phone tip, as it turned out, was a prank call by a mentally ill woman who wasn't even in Texas. But the raid and the search warrants executed were nevertheless upheld as valid. The seized documents (everything from church records to girls' diaries), and later DNA tests, revealed evidence of underage "celestial marriage" involving girls as young as twelve. In the ensuing investigation by child protection authorities, out of perhaps 300 adult residents of YFZ, 124 perpetrators of child abuse or neglect were identified. Grand juries indicted a dozen men for sexual assault of children, and lead prosecutor Eric Nichols began picking them off, one by one. If they didn't plead guilty, they were tried, and soon Nichols was batting 1000 and sentences of up to seventy-five years in prison were imposed. If you're going to rape a child, the message went, don't do it in Texas. By the time the polygamy trial began in British Columbia, seven of the twelve accused had been convicted; the remaining five charges, including those against Jeffs himself, were still being pursued.

The Texas raid was big news all over the world. Utah and Arizona had looked the other way in the years since the disastrous (from a PR standpoint, anyway) 1953 raid on the FLDS at Short Creek, when a sympathetic press (particularly *Life* magazine) virtually forced the authorities to back off their polygamy crackdown.

But Texas, at least, was serious. The YFZ raid took place just two weeks after Doust's ambivalent report on Bountiful was issued; the different approaches of Texas and British Columbia were stark and the media immediately refocused on the paralysis of authorities here. It was even reported that some of the seized children in Texas were in fact from Bountiful.

In truth, comparisons between YFZ and Bountiful were somewhat unfair. Despite the police investigations in British Columbia, there had been no complaints of the type that allowed the Texas authorities to act so decisively, even if that had been the wisest course (and many commentators believed that it was an unnecessarily heavy-handed approach). Still, Oppal appeared embarrassed that his people were not doing more to bring about prosecutions here, and some who knew of the types of evidence available to Peck and Doust (such as the *Sun*'s Daphne Bramham) were perplexed that charges had not been laid, if not for polygamy, then at least for child exploitation.


## The Scarborough Imam

And it must be said that Bountiful was not the only place in Canada where polygamy was an increasing concern in the spring and summer of 2008. I had described earlier the issue of polygamy among Canada's immigrant population of Africans and Muslims as an elephant in the room; in 2008 it became the subject of more open and urgent discussion.

Emboldened by the impotence of the polygamy law in the West, some among Canada's Muslim population had begun to take second, or perhaps third, wives. In May, even as the YFZ controversy was at its peak in the United States, a series of exposés in the *Toronto Star* revealed that a single imam in Scarborough had performed dozens of plural marriage ceremonies, openly declaring his *Charter* right to do so.

The circumstances as reported were sad and outrageous. The *Star* described the plight of Safa Rigby, mother of five, who had been in Egypt when she received a call informing her that her husband back in Canada had taken another wife. Ali Hindy, the Toronto imam who had claimed to have officiated at more than thirty polygamous marriages, arrogantly defended polygamy and even the practice of keeping the new wife secret from the first for a period of time:

> "This is in our religion and nobody can force us to do anything against our religion," he said. "If the laws of the country conflict with Islamic law, if one goes against the other, then I am going to follow Islamic law, simple as that."

Nor were Canadian Muslims the only ones to be taking up polygamy with one eye on the law. Reports from the United States noted the increasing popularity of the practice among American Muslim blacks, many of whose forebears had been in the New World since the days of slavery. And some nonpolygamous Mormons who began to discuss a return to the practice if its criminalization were overturned.

The laws certainly seemed to be playing a role in guiding behaviour. In India, there had been a wave of wealthy, successful, and prominent Hindus (lawyers, a high government official, even a Bollywood star) who had converted to Islam in order to marry a second time (Indian law permitted polygamy for Muslims but not Hindus). The practice had become sufficiently worrisome that the Indian Law Reform Commission had been tasked with producing a report recommending changes to close the religious polygamy loophole.

For Western nations grappling with renewed concern over polygamy, the greatest cautionary tale may have been France. That country introduced a family reunification policy permitting immigration by members of polygamous families in response to postwar labour shortages. A review of the literature reveals the catastrophic consequences as the numbers of polygamists in France swelled to hundreds of thousands. The research indicated that the situation for polygamist immigrants in France was dire indeed: often worse, in fact, than in their home countries. The French government reversed direction in 1993, but the damage was already done and the harms persist almost two decades later. The French example suggested that decriminalization of polygamy should be approached with great caution.

## Inside the Ministry

The British Columbia Ministry of Attorney General (as it was then known—it has since combined with the Ministry of Public Safety and Solicitor General to become the "Ministry of Justice") was populated by lawyers, most of whom were, and are, divided between two main organizations or "branches." CJB is the provincial prosecution service tasked with enforcing the laws of British Columbia and the criminal law of Canada, through charges pressed in the Provincial Court and Supreme Court of British Columbia. CJB's prosecutors operate, for obvious reasons, quite independently of government and usually even of the Attorney General him- or herself.

The ministry was led by the Attorney General, but practically speaking the person in charge day-to-day was the Deputy Attorney General, or DAG, who oversaw both the semi-independent prosecutorial branch (CJB) and my professional home, the Legal Services Branch, as well as a number of other elements of the ministry, each of whom was headed up by an Assistant Deputy, or ADAG. During the Blackmore prosecution the DAG was Allan Seckel; by the time of the polygamy trial Seckel had been replaced by David Loukidelis, who had come to the ministry after ten successful years as British Columbia's pioneering Information and Privacy Commissioner.

The second largest element of the Attorney General's potentate is Legal Services Branch (LSB), which was in turn broken down into a dozen groups, each with a particular area of specialization. It has, for instance, a Health Services Group, which provides solicitor's advice to the Ministry of Health and others who provide health services throughout the province. My group, Constitutional & Administrative Law (Con Admin), was found within the Barristers Division of LSB, along with Civil Litigation and Aboriginal Litigation groups. Con Admin has a rather unique role in the ministry; unlike most other groups, its lawyers do not generally have "clients" elsewhere in government to whom their time is notionally "billed." Instead, our lawyers' work is mostly what is called "core": it is done directly for the Attorney General. And because the work we do—litigating issues around the limits of legislative or executive authority—is often of central interest to both government and politicians, our connection with the directing minds of the ministry and the government is necessarily quite direct.

The constitutional side of Con Admin's practice mostly involved defending the government against allegations that its legislation or actions had offended either the *Charter of Rights* or the *Constitution Act, 1867*. Administrative law, despite its deceptively mundane name, was similarly concerned with defending allegations that the government had, in any instance, behaved unlawfully.

Some of British Columbia's top public law specialists in private practice had cut their teeth with Con Admin. Joe Arvay and Frank Falzon, both prominent Queen's Counsel, were two who had gone onto become leading practitioners in constitutional and administrative law, respectively. The late ERA (Bob) Edwards had graduated from the group to become the DAG and then one of British Columbia's best known and respected judges. Harvey Groberman and Lisa Mrozinsky were two other excellent jurists who had come up through the Attorney General's Con Admin Group. Some of our senior lawyers who had stayed in place had developed reputations as prominent experts in a number of fields.

## George Copley's Idea

George Copley was one of Con Admin's senior barristers who, for his own reasons, had stayed put for his entire legal career. He had been group supervisor before I was hired to replace him, and for a transition period his appointment was extended beyond the then-mandatory retirement age of sixty-five, first for one year, then for another.

While the leadership of the group was in this transition stage, the legislature abolished mandatory retirement in the civil service. Now with the option to stay in place, Copley decided to stick around and just litigate. Relieved of the administrative duties that he didn't particularly enjoy, he took on some of our thorniest cases, such as the Basi/Virk prosecution, the Harmonized Sales Tax litigation, a number of nasty labour cases, and the proceedings brought by private medical clinics challenging the province's single-payer universal health-care system. He had an encyclopedic knowledge of the caselaw, and a vast experience with the practicalities of constitutional litigation, so I turned to him often for his thoughts, and it is to him that the idea of a trial court reference has to be credited.[6]

It was a few days after Doust's 2008 report (endorsing the earlier recommendations of Peck) was submitted to the Attorney General, and I was sitting in Copley's Victoria office, seeking his counsel on the Bountiful problem, wondering aloud what Con Admin could contribute, if anything. The issue was in limbo—the prosecutors would not prosecute, deferring to a reference. The government would not commit to a reference, because the Attorney General wanted to see a prosecution.

To that point, the idea of a reference had been discounted because such proceedings lack the kind of evidentiary base that a trial provides. References are customarily made to the Court of Appeal or the Supreme Court of Canada, and so are generally fairly arid affairs, with lots of legal argument but not a lot of real-world relevance and almost no evidence of "adjudicative facts."[7] Most people who'd read Peck's and Doust's opinions in favour of a reference seemed to think that if the polygamy law was going to survive, a court would need to hear evidence from real people about the effects of "polygamy in practice." A reference to the Court of Appeal wouldn't cut it.

The insistence on airing the constitutional issues through a prosecution was more than just a theoretical disappointment to me. I felt confident that I could make the case that a reference, if one were made, should be handled by the lawyers of my group rather than being sent to CJB or to outside *ad hoc* counsel. The issues at large in polygamy were fundamental, striking to the very heart of constitutional law and straying deeply into philosophy. Moreover, having read even the small amount I had about polygamy and Bountiful to that point, I was aligned with those who felt keen frustration that we were, through inaction, consigning generations of girls to a kind of bleak servitude. I was very keen to be part of it.

So when I drifted into Copley's office that day it was mostly to vent my frustration at being kept on the sidelines. We both knew the idea of a reference hadn't gained any traction because everyone believed you'd need the evidence of a real trial, and so a prosecution was the only way to go.

Many people who knew Copley quite well nevertheless weren't aware that he had, like me, come relatively late to the profession. Unlike me, however, he had a good reason—he had been a research physicist at the University of British Columbia (UBC) before going to law school. To this background I attributed Copley's very methodical and analytical approach, as well as his donnish patience with more junior counsel.

"Of course," mused Copley that afternoon, "the *Constitutional Question Act* does provide for references either to the Court of Appeal or the BC Supreme Court . . ."

This was a crucial observation. If we wanted to have evidence, we could go to the Supreme Court—the trial court—with a reference instead of the Court of Appeal. That decision could then be appealed, but with the benefit of a full factual foundation. It would have many advantages of an adjudication in the context of a criminal prosecution, but with few of the downsides.

The difficulty was that no one knew what a trial court reference looked like because, even though Copley was quite correct, and it is explicitly permitted in the statute, no one had actually done one, anywhere in Canada, ever. In most cases, why would you? It would be better to get a more influential decision from the Court of Appeal than to slog through an extended "trial." But in this case, a "trial" was exactly what was needed.

As I mentioned earlier, in April 2008 the question of Bountiful was front and centre again. The YFZ raid in Texas had occurred on April 3; Oppal was immediately pressed by the media to announce British Columbia's intentions. Within a week he began to publicly muse about appointing another special prosecutor because he wanted a "more aggressive approach, which means you lay the charge and let the defence worry about the constitutionality issue. That's normally the way things are done."[8]

I sensed that Deputy Attorney General Allan Seckel, on the other hand, was open to innovative alternatives to a criminal prosecution in the wake of Peck's and Doust's reports. Some were concerned, as Peck had been, that a prosecution would be unfair, given the Attorney General's previous announcements that there was no valid law against polygamy; others believed that prosecutors might face lawsuits for malicious prosecution if they initiated proceedings in light of the peculiar history. Seckel and I discussed the idea of an application being brought by the Attorney General in his *parens patriae* role for an injunction, a topic that I'd written about for the *Canadian Bar Review* a couple of years before. In the course of that conversation I mentioned Copley's observation that a reference to the trial court was also an option.

Seckel was sufficiently intrigued that he invited me to explain what I thought a trial court reference would look like and turn my mind to the questions we might ask. He thought that an essential feature of the reference would be to appoint someone to argue the other side, sometimes called an *amicus curiae*, or "friend of the court." Throughout April, a few of us in LSB began to plan tentatively for a reference, in case the Attorney General could resist the tide against prosecution.

But, judging from his public comments, Oppal was still interested in the criminal process, and was telling anyone who'd listen that he wanted a prosecution but was being stymied by the prosecutors. He suggested to the press that he could order CJB prosecutors to take the case, but he would rather work with a prosecutor who did not believe the case was doomed to failure. He wanted a true believer.

Within weeks, the Attorney General pushed the question of Bountiful forward again. Oppal wrote another "gazetted" letter to Gillen on May 28, recounting the history and going further, with quite an extraordinary statement of discord between the Attorney General and his CJB chief:

> It is my opinion that the Criminal Justice Branch is mistaken in its belief that s. 293 of the *Criminal Code of Canada* is unconstitutional. Both Mr. Doust and Mr. Peck believe s. 293 to be constitutionally valid legislation. A valid criminal law is and should be enforced. To do so is appropriate and is not unfair.

> Therefore, pursuant to Section 5 of the *Crown Counsel Act*, this letter is my directive to you to retain the legal services of Mr. Terrance Robertson to conduct a charge assessment of the most recent police investigation into polygamy in the Community of Bountiful. He is to apply the Criminal Justice Branch charge approval policy as it relates to Section 293 of the *Criminal Code of Canada* and any other *Code* provisions. The policy requires first, a determination of whether there is a substantial likelihood of conviction based on the available evidence, and if so, whether it is in the public interest to proceed with a prosecution. If he concludes that charges should be approved, he is to conduct the prosecution and any appeals which may arise from those proceedings.

> As you may designate him to be either Crown Counsel pursuant to Section 4 (1) of the *Crown Counsel Act* or as Special Prosecutor pursuant to Section 7 of the *Crown Counsel Act*, I leave that designation selection for your determination.

So a third senior independent lawyer, Terry Robertson, was named by Oppal to conduct a review of the charging decision in the Bountiful case.

Disappointed, I shelved the idea of a reference as Con Admin was again relegated to the role of spectator.

Robertson, acting as a special prosecutor, approved charges of polygamy against Winston Blackmore and James Oler; these polygamist leaders of the two competing "congregations" at Bountiful were arrested on 7 January 2009 and released after turning over their passports and signing a recognizance. The prosecution looked as if it were underway.

## Arvay's End Run

As I recounted earlier, by the late 2000s Blackmore was a successful local businessman with somewhere around twenty-five wives. He had been the FLDS's bishop in Bountiful since the mid-1980s, and had enjoyed a close relationship with Rulon Jeffs, the US-based prophet of the church's ten thousand or so adherents. With Rulon Jeffs's demise and his replacement by his somewhat more sinister son Warren, Blackmore had fallen out of favour, and was replaced by James Oler as the FLDS's man in Canada—the Split referred to earlier in this chapter. Oler was also a polygamist, but perhaps lacking both Blackmore's business acumen or charisma, he had amassed only five wives by his mid-forties. Blackmore was excommunicated by Jeffs, but took the loyalty of about half of Bountiful's residents with him. So since the Split of 2002, the two communities had lived side by side in Bountiful, with separate schools and a lingering, bitter dispute over the fate of the community's commonly held real property.

Blackmore and Oler couldn't have been a less likely pair as codefendants. Blackmore was larger than life, gregarious, and outgoing. He had charmed the pants off Larry King on CNN (King, who had himself married seven younger women—albeit sequentially rather than simultaneously—likely recognized something of a kindred spirit and at times in the interview, seemed openly *admiring* of Blackmore), and Blackmore sometimes would take reporters for a drive in his pickup if he wanted to chat. *National Geographic* came to Bountiful and shot a documentary and magazine spread with the Blackmore side of the Split. Oler, on the other hand, avoided the media like the plague, and was rarely photographed. Many had viewed Blackmore as a liberal force within the FLDS; he had disavowed marrying teenaged girls a few years back (granted, after he'd married as many as nine of them), and wasn't as strict with his followers as Oler was reputed to be. "Oler's the creepy side of the FLDS," a lawyer who'd studied the community warned me. Oler was Warren Jeffs's man in Canada.

The police had amassed evidence indicating that, as minister and later bishop of the church, Blackmore had wed four fifteen year olds, a sixteen year old, and two seventeen year olds. Oler had married a seventeen year old and a fifteen year old after he'd taken over the post of bishop. Even if there couldn't be sexual exploitation charges, it looked like the two were caught cold on polygamy, if the law would withstand a constitutional challenge.

Blackmore and Oler "lawyered up" and lawyered up well. Oler's lawyer was Bob Wickett, a senior litigator who will return later in this story as counsel for the FLDS during the trial of the reference. And Joe Arvay appeared for Winston Blackmore.

Arvay is probably the most gifted and experienced constitutional lawyer in the country. Our professional lives had been, and still were, inextricably intertwined. He had been my lawyer in the aftermath of the 1997 APEC debacle; I was his co-conspirator in the early days of the Safe Injection Site litigation, and later, as counsel for the government of British Columbia, would be his ally in the Court of Appeal and the Supreme Court of Canada in that case. We had clashed monumentally in the *Election Act* challenge of *BCTF v AGBC* in 2008 (a challenge to third-party electoral spending limits) and would again in the Court of Appeal in 2010. I had beaten him in the trial of the *Arkinstall* "grow op searches" case;[9] he had achieved a resounding reversal in the Court of Appeal.[10] There weren't many significant constitutional cases in British Columbia in which one or the other of us wasn't somehow involved (and increasingly, we were both there), and I valued the fact that we could slug it out in court one day and then candidly discuss our views on the issues over dinner the next. He was the model of a progressive constitutional lawyer, and I am always flattered whenever someone remarks on the similarity of our career paths (Arvay too did a Master's at Harvard, flirted with academia, spent a number of years doing constitutional law at the ministry, and was appointed Queen's Counsel at a relatively young age). I permit myself to be at least intrigued by the coincidence that Arvay and I actually share the same birthday.

Arvay had by that time appeared more than forty times before the Supreme Court of Canada (he himself has kept no exact count), and he would be taking the lead for both accused during the initial constitutional phase of the proceeding. His first move had nothing to do with Blackmore's rights of religious freedom, and indeed had nothing to do with polygamy at all: not one used to playing a defensive role, Arvay turned to bring his guns to bear and unleashed a broadside that would change the direction of the polygamy litigation away from a headlong rush to prosecution.

It was Wally Oppal's own enthusiasm for the prosecution that brought it to an abrupt end. Arvay defended his client by attacking the decision to prosecute, filing an abuse of process application in the criminal case before Madam Justice Sunni Stromberg-Stein. Arvay said that the *Crown Counsel Act* provided that decisions of a special prosecutor were "final." This, he said, prevented Oppal from doing exactly what he fairly obviously had done—appointing a succession of prosecutors to consider and reconsider charges until he found someone willing to prosecute. Stromberg-Stein said that Arvay's objection really was to the appointment of Robertson as a second special prosecutor, and this was a matter for a judicial review proceeding, not an abuse application under the Criminal Rules. She told him to go away and reframe his objection under the *Judicial Review Procedure Act*, and come back in September to have the matter heard.

Not only would Arvay's maneuver quickly send the question of polygamy on its eventual path towards a constitutional reference, but it also marked my formal entry to the case as counsel. Until this point, Copley had been representing the LSB side of the Attorney General in the Blackmore/Oler prosecution, dealing mostly with Arvay and Bob Wickett's *Rowbotham* funding application.[11] Copley, for the Attorney General, had remained strategically mute in the face of the abuse of process application, leaving the argument up to Robertson as the special prosecutor, but it was clear that sitting on the sidelines was no longer possible. In a petition for judicial review, the Attorney General himself would be the respondent. The Attorney General would have to be defended, and that was the job of LSB and the Con Admin group, not CJB or its proxy, the special prosecutor.

But Copley had a problem: he was about to leave on an extended walking tour of England and would not be around to conduct the new proceeding. He wrote to me in July and asked if I would take it over.

And so, almost by accident, or at least by default, I became the Attorney General's counsel on the Bountiful file, with a little over a month to prepare for the judicial review. It wasn't the reference I had lobbied for; in fact it wasn't even a constitutional case at that point. But it was a great brief nonetheless, and I was determined to give it my all. I enlisted the help of Sarah Bevan and we prepared our case.

A recent hire, Bevan was a six-year call who had previously been a research lawyer at Hunter Litigation Chambers, one of the city's most respected litigation boutiques. She was a former Court of Appeal clerk and, in the words of her former boss (by then Supreme Court Justice) David Harris, "a beautiful writer." She remains one of the smartest and most thorough lawyers I've ever met. But even Bevan couldn't save my hide (or Wally Oppal's) in the Blackmore case. Whatever fine legal arguments we were able to come up with, it just didn't look very good. Oppal had made no bones about the fact that he disagreed with Peck and Doust, and that this was the reason he had appointed Robertson. We could make no convincing argument that anything had changed since Peck's report; the former Attorney General's enthusiasm for a conviction was palpable, and his repeated trips to the well of prosecutors certainly looked like the kind of pressure that the special prosecutor system was designed to discourage, even if, on our argument, it wasn't actually prohibited. And Arvay, an artist and showman in the courtroom, would doubtless take considerable enjoyment in reading to the Court every press statement Oppal had made on the topic.

We had heard that, at the abuse of process hearing before Stromberg-Stein, the judge seemed sympathetic to the defendants' position that Oppal had overstepped the bounds of propriety. The fact that she had referred the matter to be reheard as a judicial review suggested that she was expecting to grant relief. What could we do? The facts were the facts. By the end of the hearing of the judicial review held on September 3–4, the new Attorney General (Mike de Jong—Oppal had been narrowly defeated in the May 2009 election) understood that Stromberg-Stein appeared not to be persuaded by our submissions and that we should expect a negative decision.

It took Justice Stromberg-Stein less than three weeks to render her sharply worded judgment. The 2007 decision of Peck not to prosecute was deemed "final"; the prosecution under Robertson was quashed; and Blackmore and Oler were free to carry on with their unusual lives.

Oppal was, I think, personally and professionally offended by the decision, and liking him as I did, I felt badly that I had been unsuccessful in defending the lawfulness of his actions, which nobody doubted had been taken in good faith. Though he was by then out of government and no longer my boss, Oppal was still very friendly when we met, and he practically poked his finger through my rib cage when we next ran into each other on Hornby Street (outside the Caffè Artigiano, naturally). "You have to appeal," he said. "It's outrageous!"

# PART 4
# A Case for the Trial Court

## The Green Light

What now? An appeal of the *Blackmore* decision was possible and had, I thought, a reasonable chance of success. Our argument, that the special prosecutor provisions were not designed to *prevent* interference by the Attorney General, but only to ensure that it was overt and transparent, was (I still believed) the better interpretation of the *Crown Counsel Act*. But good law rarely stacks up to bad facts, and the unique circumstances that led up to the prosecution had, fairly or not, a whiff of impropriety about them. At the very least, the sheer persistence of Oppal in going after Blackmore and Oler left many people, including, I suspected, many judges, uneasy. This was particularly so, I thought at the time, because the charges were for polygamy *simpliciter*—there were no allegations of sexual exploitation or other criminal abuse, and many saw the use of the section as overreactive and disproportionate.[1]

In any event, an appeal of Stromberg-Stein's decision would have taken time, might have gone to the Supreme Court of Canada, and after years and hundreds of thousands if not millions of dollars, would have settled nothing except that the prosecution could restart. The constitutional issue would still be waiting for adjudication, and then more years, and more expense, as that matter worked its way up the appellate ladder. The concern over money was not incidental; in recent years, the government has increasingly found itself in situations where it has been forced to provide funding for defence counsel in complex criminal cases, through *Rowbotham* or other routes;[2] once the genie was uncorked, prosecution for even relatively minor offences was often ending up costing the taxpayer millions, while the legal aid budget for criminal defendants and abused wives in divorce proceedings was mercilessly slashed. Arvay had already made applications for special funding in the *Blackmore* case, and it appeared that the government would be, one way or the other, on the hook for his substantial legal fees once the prosecution resumed.

But the train wreck of the criminal case meant that the idea of a trial court reference began to gain traction again. The difficulties of a prosecution were by now clear. The new Attorney General, Mike de Jong, was not as personally invested in prosecuting as was Oppal, and he was quickly proving himself to be a smart man who read everything put in front of him and was decisive when circumstances required it. The economic downturn had imposed tight fiscal restraints across government, and the idea that a cumbersome and expensive prosecution, using excellent but high-priced outside talent, might be replaced by a more efficient process using in-house lawyers, likely weighed on the decision too. We could build on some of the groundwork already done (and connections made) by the stymied special prosecutor Terry Robertson and his associate Kat Kinch, and we could be ready to go, I felt, in months rather than years.

I was convinced that a trial court reference would be faster, cheaper, and, because it could deal more globally with the polygamy law not just at Bountiful, *better* than a renewed prosecution. I didn't really believe that the government wanted to start throwing people in jail for practising polygamy; they simply wanted some certainty around a law that could be used to head off religious exploitation, but which had been, for twenty-seven years, unenforceable. I believed that Attorney General de Jong had become interested in the plan, and he made time in his schedule on a number of occasions to discuss the various options with me and the DAG and ADAG.

Like most decisions in the Attorney General's ministry, the DAG's support was crucial. Allan Seckel had been brought in as deputy under Geoff Plant, who'd introduced him to the legislature as the best lawyer in British Columbia. This was not hyperbole. Seckel had the kind of quick intellect and intensity of focus that scared the living daylights out of many people. He had parlayed his love for basketball into an athletic scholarship at Simon Fraser University, where he'd earned a commerce degree. But it wasn't Seckel's basketball chops that stood out in university, it was his phenomenally quick mind. He went on to become gold medallist at the University of Victoria law school, capping his academic career at Cambridge with a Master's degree in law. Plant knew Seckel's talents well because they had been partners at one of Vancouver's largest blue-chip law firms, Russell & DuMoulin (now Fasken Martineau DuMoulin LLP), before Plant had left for politics.

Yet Seckel, who had become supportive of the idea of a trial court reference, suddenly vanished from the Attorney General's ministry. On October 5, he was appointed deputy minister to premier Gordon Campbell and head of the BC Public Service to replace Jessica MacDonald, who was leaving government. Granted, Seckel hadn't gone far, and would eventually be replaced by the redoubtable David Loukidelis, whom I had also known and admired for years. But in the meantime we had an interim DAG, Jerry McHale, whom I liked but didn't really know, and an Attorney General with whom I also had only a passing acquaintance. Would the reference still go ahead?

As it turned out I needn't have worried. Seckel would surely continue to have some influence in the ministry; it would be a foolish interim deputy who didn't consult Seckel extensively during the transition, and McHale, a delightful and clever man who got the job on an interim basis because he so clearly didn't want it permanently, was definitely no fool. In any event, the decision to press ahead with the constitutional reference would ultimately be that of Premier Gordon Campbell and his cabinet, so Seckel, though far less accessible to me, was far from out of the loop in his new position.

I had developed some proposed reference questions after consulting with Copley and looking over various precedents from appellate court cases. Some were convoluted and others simple; in the end, the Attorney General himself weighed in on the questions (de Jong had a good instinct for putting law in common language), and two basic questions were agreed on:

(1) Is section 293 of the *Criminal Code of Canada* consistent with the *Canadian Charter of Rights and Freedoms*? If not, in what particular or particulars and to what extent?

(2) What are the necessary elements of the offence in section 293 of the *Criminal Code of Canada*? Without limiting this question, does section 293 require that the polygamy or conjugal union in question involved a minor, or occurred in a context of dependence, exploitation, abuse of authority, a gross imbalance of power, or undue influence?

The first question needs little explanation. The second might at first appear perplexing. It arose from the historical concern of the Attorney General that it might be impossible to find evidence to support the prohibition of polygamy *per se*, and that the *Criminal Code* provision could only be saved if it were interpreted to apply only to "bad polygamy" and not "good polygamy." As our case would develop, the second question began to fade toward irrelevance, as we became increasingly convinced that, on the evidence, there was no such thing as "harmless" polygamy.

But concerns about actually proving the case were not at that moment the most pressing. Mid-October was consumed with preparations for the launch of the reference, which everyone anticipated would be widely noted, given the history. Extensive briefing had to be done, not just of the politicians who would be answering questions, but also of officials from the Public Affairs Bureau, who would be in charge of communications. Most of the stress arose from the intricacy of the timing. We had to carefully coordinate the signing and deposit of the Order-in-Council (OIC) in Victoria, the announcement of the reference by the Attorney General, and the filing of the documents in the Vancouver court registry. The government of Canada would also be announcing its participation. Ideally it should all happen on the same day.

In the end it went smoothly enough. Attorney General de Jong announced the reference on 22 October 2009 in his Victoria office at the provincial Parliament building; the OIC had been signed and deposited that morning, and preparations had been made for filing with the Court in the afternoon. I would attend de Jong's press conference in case I was needed and then fly back to Vancouver to oversee the filing, which was not straightforward on account of the novelty of the project. True to form, de Jong did a very good job rolling out the decision at the press conference and explaining the process. Because he had been so closely involved in the decision making around the reference, he handled the questions deftly and I was not required at all.

I was relieved as I walked back from the Parliament building towards the Harbour Air float-plane terminal for the thirty-five-minute flight to downtown Vancouver, but I also could not escape the unsettling feeling that this could turn out to be a catastrophically quixotic exercise. I had pushed for the idea of a trial court reference for two years, and much wiser minds like Seckel, my boss Richard Fyfe, and the Attorney General himself had bought in. They were relying on me to ensure that this initiative didn't suffer the same fate as the abortive Blackmore/Oler prosecution. This case, which we had pushed like a rollercoaster car to the starting position at the top of the rails, was now moving, and it would quickly gather momentum. I had never had conduct of a trial as lengthy or complex as this one was expected to be. There was no precedent to guide us, no experienced hand with ready advice. Every hour of every day, my mind roiled with thoughts of the number and variety of things that could pull us off the rails.

## The Early Stages

On the day the reference was launched, Canada's Attorney General Rob Nicholson announced that the federal government would fully participate in the proceeding. His 22 October 2009 press release read:

> The practice of polygamy has no place in modern Canadian society. The Government of Canada firmly believes that the *Criminal Code* prohibition against polygamy is consistent with Canadian values as well as compliant with the *Canadian Charter of Rights and Freedoms*. We strongly believe that this prohibition created by Canada's elected representatives should be upheld.
>
> . . .
>
> The Government of Canada welcomes British Columbia's decision to refer this case to the Supreme Court of British Columbia. I am pleased to say that the Government of Canada will be an active party in the reference and defend the constitutionality of the *Criminal Code* prohibition on polygamy.

The federal government had a particular interest in the polygamy law, beyond any utility it might have as a criminal prohibition *per se*. The fact is that, regardless of whether any Canadian is ever prosecuted as a polygamist, having section 293 on the books permits federal immigration authorities to refuse entry to polygamist families. The biggest danger posed by section 293's possible demise wasn't that fundamentalist Mormonism would spread, or that many mainstream Canadians would flock to the practice; the problems attendant with the practice of polygamy would come in through immigration and would take root first in Canada's Muslim and African communities, where the challenges in dealing with issues of women's equality, for instance, were already acute. The federal government also had a concern with its international obligations, which committed it to support women's equality and to oppose polygamy as part of that effort.

I soon became acquainted with the federal government team. It was headed by Deborah Strachan, a senior lawyer with depth of experience in both criminal and civil cases and with a particular interest in cases with international implications. Keith Reimer was second in command, fresh from a key role overseeing some of the federal government's interests in the Vancouver 2010 Olympics. They had three others who would be "gowning up" in the course of the hearing: Craig Cameron had been called to the bar on the same day as me, 21 May 1999; Robert Danay, an Oxford grad, and BJ Wray were very well-regarded juniors. A frequent presence in the gallery was another Department of Justice (DOJ) lawyer, Joanne Klineberg, the Ottawa-based policy wonk (she'll love reading that description) whose team had been working on the polygamy issue at the federal level for over a decade. As I mentioned, the federal government had, over the years, suffered from none of the province's ambivalence; their law was fine, thank you very much, and now they were going to pull out the stops to prove it. Having struggled upstream with so much of the weight of the reference since its inception, the province was pleased to have a well-resourced and committed ally in the fight.

If we were going to keep the case on a firm trajectory, we were going to have to move quickly to establish two things: an aggressive pretrial schedule and a process for an appropriately adversarial adjudication. I fully expected that Joe Arvay would want to be there for his client Winston Blackmore. In fact, I anticipated that Blackmore would expect to be the principal antagonist against the government, and that Arvay would seamlessly shift his application for *Rowbotham* funding in the criminal case to an application for "advance special costs" in the reference proceeding. I had embraced Seckel's early expressed view that it would be better to have an *amicus curiae* arguing the "contra" position against the Attorneys General. We would encourage the Court to avoid a narrow focus on Bountiful and its bishops *per se*, and deal with the constitutional question of polygamy in the broadest possible context. We wanted a wide and diverse representation of intervenors to appear, from religious practitioners of polygamy to activist groups opposed, but we wanted their participation to be limited compared to the Attorneys General and the *amicus*. If this became the Winston Blackmore Show, I feared, most of the advantages of dealing comprehensively with polygamy outside the context of a criminal prosecution would be lost, and the reference would be viewed as simply another step in the effort to prosecute the leaders of Bountiful. It would also be, I expected, very expensive.[3]

So from the beginning of the planning for the reference, we were prepared to move quickly in establishing a path congruent with our ambitions for the case. While the OIC was being prepared, my assistant contacted the Supreme Court Registry for advice on how it should be filed, keeping in mind that neither we nor the Court had any precedent to which we could refer. The registrar responded that the Chief Justice had advised that it should be filed as a requisition, attaching the OIC and reference questions; so this was done the same day as the reference was announced.

Along with the filing of the requisition and its accompanying documents, I sent a letter asking the Chief Justice for the immediate appointment of a trial and case management judge, and for an early hearing to appoint an *amicus* and provide notice to potential intervenors in the case.

Now we waited. Would Bauman embrace this reference as an important matter or would we wait months for the appointment of a case management judge?

Case management judges are assigned to complex cases early on in the process. Their role is to be proactive with the parties in streamlining the litigation. They will usually hear any preliminary applications, set schedules for exchange of materials, and browbeat and cajole lawyers who often have somewhat liberal views of expedience into maintaining some level of efficiency. My own goal for the reference was to have it concluded at the trial level within two years of its October 2009 filing. Given the usual path of multiparty complex litigation, this was very ambitious. But my experience had been that without firm goals and deadlines, the horizon for large cases could stretch out indefinitely, particularly when any party might have an interest in the matter not being adjudicated at all. I didn't want anything like that fate to befall the polygamy reference, but given the number of anticipated participants, it easily could have been bogged down. A weak or inattentive case management judge can make the difference between an efficient resolution in a complex case and an unmitigated gong show. So it was a very uncomfortable couple of weeks waiting for the Chief Justice's response to my letter of request.

Finally, on November 9 we received a memorandum from Chief Justice Bauman announcing that he was appointing *himself* as the judge to hear the reference and scheduling an immediate conference with counsel for just one week hence.

This was very good news indeed. Bauman had been a trial judge for more than a decade before being elevated to the Court of Appeal; he was there only for a short time before his surprise return to the trial court as the Chief Justice after the well-liked Don Brenner had announced his unexpected early retirement. As a judge, Bauman had solidified a reputation as a pragmatist with a genial manner but a no-nonsense approach. He was seen neither as a hide-bound conservative nor as a crusading judicial reformer. He was also regarded as smart and as an exceptionally clear judicial writer, which we thought bode well for our case. Nothing about polygamy was simple; none of the answers straightforward. We needed a thinker who could communicate his decisions beyond the legal community and into the public discourse, and now, clearly, we had one, and (a point that should not be minimized given the unprecedented nature of the proceeding) one with the authority of the office of the Chief Justice to keep things moving along.

Bauman and I had been acquainted during the brief period some thirteen years before when we had both been at Bull, Housser & Tupper, me as an articled student and he as a core partner specializing in municipal law. I don't recall ever having worked with him directly, but he had always remembered me and greeted me by name on the street or at social functions, which was flattering for a young lawyer in a big city. People who think that personal connections like this translate into advantage in the courtroom are certainly going to find themselves disappointed. But the fact that Bauman knew something about me and, I hoped, had some measure of respect for my work might, I thought, mean that he would not dismiss lightly the Attorney General's suggestions for mapping out how the reference process might unfold.

Bauman's memo set down a Case Management Conference for November 17, just over a week away. Predictably, Arvay was concerned that the appointment of an *amicus* would cast the die and his client Mr Blackmore would be shut out of the front-row seats. He wrote to the Chief Justice on the 12th:

> Please advise the Chief Justice that contrary to what is noted in the Requisition this matter is opposed. It will also be our position at this first case management conference that no matters of substance be decided as we have not even obtained a notice of motion yet and we need time to consider our response when we do receive it.

Even before the litigation was announced, I had begun to receive calls from a number of Vancouver's leading lawyers who expressed interest in the role of *amicus* if the government decided on the reference option. The decision was not mine, or even the Attorney General's, to make: an *amicus* is appointed by the Court itself. But nevertheless we would be expected to come to the Court with the name of a person we believed would do a good job, and who had agreed to take on the role. So from the beginning of the reference idea there had been considerable discussion about who should play this crucial role.

The eventual choice, George Macintosh, was by now in his sixties and solidly established in the very highest ranks of Vancouver litigation counsel. In one of the many coincidences surrounding the reference, he and I shared a strange history. In law school I had been arrested during the notorious 1997 APEC protests; when the incident had become the subject of a public inquiry under the aegis of the RCMP Public Complaints Commission, Macintosh had been counsel for some of the RCMP officers involved. I was a complainant and a witness at the hearing, so it came to pass that my first taste of cross-examination had not been as the lawyer in control of the questioning, but rather in the witness box myself with Macintosh grilling me (by further odd coincidence, my counsel at the APEC hearing was none other than Arvay).

Despite our earlier adversarial interaction, though, Macintosh was on my list of lawyers whom I, as a student of litigation style and skill, would try to watch perform in court whenever I could. Over time, my admiration for his legal abilities and his "off-the-field" cordiality had worn down any inclination I had to hold a grudge, and Macintosh and I had become more pleasantly acquainted. When I joined the government as head of Con Admin in 2006, his was one of the first calls I received, inviting me out for a lunch where he was generous with his thoughts and advice on a number of topics that were on my mind at the time.

Anybody's list of Vancouver's best lawyers in 2010 would have had Macintosh somewhere near the top. And, just as crucially, I felt confident that Macintosh would not only be an excellent adversary to the governments in the reference, but also that he would take seriously the responsibility to cooperate in bringing the matter before the Court in a timely and efficient way. I was very pleased when he agreed to allow the Attorney General to put his name forward to the Court.

So on November 17 we made our case for the appointment of Macintosh as *amicus* and for a system to notify the approximately one hundred persons and groups that we had identified as potentially interested in appearing at the proceeding. Arvay, for Winston Blackmore, and Wickett, who represented bishop James Oler and the FLDS, appeared to oppose the appointment of Macintosh, and in fact argued that the reference had been improperly initiated through the simple filing of a requisition; they said that it should have been brought by the more elaborate process of petition, with their clients served as respondents.[4]

The Chief Justice's first decisions as case management judge would, I expected, determine the course we would take. We had a vision of the reference procedure as a quasi-adversarial contest between the *amicus* and the Attorneys General, with the limited participation of other parties to assist in shaping the issues and evidence. Arvay and Wickett, viewing things through the lenses of their clients' interests, would see it as *R v Blackmore and Oler* continued. Which one, if either, would the Chief Justice adopt?

To my profound relief, Bauman took only two weeks to issue a judgment in which he roundly disposed of Arvay's objections, appointed Macintosh as *amicus*, and embraced our proposals for the invitation of intervenors (called "Interested Persons" under the Act). In so doing he offered a nice summary of what the case was, and wasn't, about:

> [45] A reference is a process by which a government is able to receive an advisory opinion from the court on a question of law outside the framework of adversarial litigation. As the Supreme Court of Canada explained in *Reference re Secession of Quebec*, at para. 25, a court hearing

a reference performs a function that differs from its usual adjudicative role:

> In the context of a reference, the Court, rather than acting in its traditional adjudicative function, is acting in an advisory capacity. The very fact that the Court may be asked hypothetical questions in a reference, such as the constitutionality of proposed legislation, engages the Court in an exercise it would never entertain in the context of litigation. No matter how closely the procedure on a reference may mirror the litigation process, a reference does not engage the Court in a disposition of rights. For the same reason, the Court may deal on a reference with issues that might otherwise be considered not yet "ripe" for decision.

[46] I acknowledge that this reference comes to court with a certain history, as was outlined earlier. I acknowledge, as well, that the opinion this Court ultimately renders on the reference questions will be of significance to Mr. Blackmore and Mr. Oler. Nevertheless, as the Supreme Court has stated, a reference does not engage the Court in a disposition of rights. It is not ordinary litigation.[5]

Macintosh's mandate as *amicus*, Bauman held, would be:

> (a) To advance any argument he considers appropriate in support of the answer "no" to question (1) of the reference, and to participate fully in the hearing of this matter to that end and for the purposes of appeal;
>
> (b) To advance any argument he considers appropriate regarding question (2), particularly arguments in opposition to, or distinct from, those advanced by the AG BC or AG Canada;
>
> (c) To make or respond to any motions or arguments he considers appropriate and consistent with (a) and (b) or as directed by the Court.

This was not the end of Arvay; he brought a subsequent application for Blackmore to be added to the case as a full party and for full government funding of his fees, but with the *amicus* already in place it was a difficult case to make, and Bauman would in due course reject any special status or funding for the bishop of Bountiful.[6] In the wake of the Court's denial, Blackmore and Arvay announced that the bishop would take no further role in the reference. Oler and the FLDS, however, stayed on, represented by Wickett.

At the time I thought that the FLDS's choice of counsel was peculiar. No question, Wickett was a well-regarded and experienced litigator in British Columbia. He was the managing partner at the respected mid-sized business firm of MacKenzie Fujisawa, which counted among its lawyers Thomas Braidwood, the former Court of Appeal judge who had gone onto fame as commissioner of the Taser inquiries. But although Wickett had a strong background in administrative, resource, and aboriginal litigation, he wasn't well known by the handful of lawyers who made constitutional law their specialty. Apparently, he had the reference brief because of the trust he had built with his clients over years of representing them in thorny matters arising from the Bountiful "Split" of 2002.

As the case progressed, though, I came to see the wisdom in his selection. Wickett's client, the FLDS, suffered from a public perception as a creepy cult of child molesters. Their prophet Warren Jeffs was in jail for participating in the rape of a young girl whom he'd married off to a salivating minion even as she cried in protest. Jeffs would soon be extradited to Texas and charged with several further counts, arising from his own "marriages" to teen and preteen girls. A number of other church leaders were either in prison or facing prosecution for similar charges arising from evidence uncovered at YFZ. One would expect the FLDS to have either a scrappy pit bull or a smooth, slick shyster for a lawyer. Wickett was neither: he was calm, reasonable, and disarmingly personable. He also exhibited an uncommon trait among litigators in that he was *creative*. Wickett would turn out to be a formidable adversary in the months to come, and I learned that I shouldn't be lulled by his friendly and easygoing manner.

It was Arvay's departure from the scene that gave me the most personal disappointment. I had been determined before the Court that he should not be allowed to take over the role of official opposition to the Attorneys General in the reference, and I could not agree that he, among all those opposed to section 293, should receive a million dollars to make his client's case. I had fought hard, in other words, against his plan for full-funded participation. But I'd hoped he and his client wouldn't withdraw altogether, and not only because I would have loved to face down Blackmore on the witness stand, where the "aw-shucks" evasions that had won over Larry King would, I was convinced, quickly wither in the face of questions that had to be answered.

No, I would miss Arvay because I knew his legal arguments would be second to none, and I wished that he would keep his hat in the ring at least to the point of making a submission at the hearing. But his client appeared adamant: it was all or nothing, and so Arvay would take no further part in the reference proceeding.

Blackmore's attempt to secure funding did provide something of a foreshadowing of what we would learn about the dark side of Bountiful life. Blackmore went to great lengths to communicate, through his own blog, through pet journalists and credulous interviewers like Larry King, an image of a sincere and devoted family man, not a cult leader. But in his affidavit in support of his funding application, Blackmore declared that, if he decided not to participate, he would see to it that no one else would be allowed "access" to any member of his "congregation." *Access?*

In accordance with Bauman's November order, our office had sent out notices to more than one hundred persons and groups, including even the embassies of some foreign countries where polygamy was either legal or common. The notices set out the constitutional questions, explained the reference process, and invited the recipients to appear and apply for standing as participants. Soon, the responses came in; the applications were made and decided in February 2010. As we had hoped, every group applying for status was granted it.

So the cast of participants was fixed. Opposing the law alongside the *amicus* were the CPAA, the Canadian Association for Freedom of Speech, James Oler and the FLDS, and my erstwhile colleagues at the BCCLA. Supporting the criminalization of polygamy was a somewhat larger assembly of human rights and women's rights groups and antipolygamist activists of various stripes. In all there were fifteen persons and organizations granted the right to participate in the proceedings.

To form the core of our "polygamy team," I managed to secure several of the best lawyers from the Con Admin group. Sarah Bevan, who had worked with me on the Blackmore case, would stay on board through the reference. Leah Greathead signed on with great enthusiasm and would have a strong leadership role on the file. Greathead set about convincing me that our team was light in real trial skills (Con Admin lawyers tend to do appellate work, of one sort or another, so we lack practice in developing and presenting live witnesses, or cross-examinations, for instance), and she persuaded me to recruit Karen Horsman and Eva Ross from the Attorney General's Civil Litigation Group. I didn't know Ross at all, but I was very pleased to have Horsman onboard—she was clearly among the best litigators in government, or, I have come to believe, anywhere. These three women would focus on gathering eyewitness evidence of polygamy as it was practised by the fundamentalist Mormons of that community and its American counterparts. Jean Walters, another of our group's more experienced counsel, would not appear in court but did bring to bear her particular talent for navigating the information bunnyholes of government and would eventually assist in cajoling recalcitrant bureaucrats into crafting helpful and informative affidavits. Freya Zaltz, a recent hire who had been a star student with the ministry, took on the job of finding witnesses who could testify regarding the practice of polygamy in the Muslim community. Freya would later be our trial coordinator, scheduling witnesses and overseeing our technical requirements, in addition to her role on the legal side.

## To Bountiful, via Damascus

So the field was prepared and the antagonists were assembling. Procedurally, we had achieved all we could have hoped. But the deeper question was, did we have a case?

In the early stages, we had no reason to be particularly confident, especially in light of the opinions prepared for the Attorney General historically.[7] As I recounted earlier, prior to 2007 all of these, including those from two respected former judges and the top government constitutional solicitor, had held that section 293 of the *Criminal Code* violated religious freedom and that the infringement was not justifiable under section 1. As I recounted earlier, the weight of academic commentary supported this view.

So when our little team took on the constitutional reference, riding the polygamy law down to a controlled defeat seemed like the best possible outcome, and one with which I wasn't particularly uncomfortable. Like the many experts who provided the opinions to the Attorney General before 2007, my initial view was that a polygamy law could not legitimately capture anything but harmful polygamous relationships, and I saw "harmful" in that context as meaning "immediately harmful." At the very least, it would have to be redrafted or, perhaps at best, radically "read down" by the courts, in order to remain on the constitutional side of the line.[8] If that were true, it was Canada's problem, not ours, and so the reference could serve a legitimate purpose of prompting them into action. British Columbia's priority, going back to the 1980s, was to know whether we had a valid law in our toolkit; if not, we needed a court to tell the feds to redraft it.

Nevertheless, in recent years (since Oppal's tenure as Attorney General) the Attorney General's position had shifted from disavowing the law to supporting it, and eventually to prosecuting under it. So it was clear that the position the government, albeit pessimistically advanced, would be in support of continued criminalization if a legitimate argument could be advanced. But what argument did we have to make?

Everyone seemed to agree that there was something creepy and weird about Bountiful, where a fifty-year-old man could marry a teenaged girl as his fourth (or twenty-fourth) wife. No one believed that the girl, raised in a polygamist church, taught by polygamist teachers, and often married without even meeting her groom until hours before the ceremony, could be consenting in any meaningful way to the marriage. But good, liberal Canadians seemed just as convinced that a straight, gay, or lesbian threesome, all freely consenting adults, should be able to live together forever if they so chose, and raise their families in peace.

I've described the rather empty academic debate earlier. The anticriminalization advocates said that opposition to polygamy was, at its heart, irrational. Like the resistance to gay marriage, they argued, it was premised on moral panic instead of any real threat of harm. Enforcing monogamy was like enforcing heterosexuality, premised at heart, on the "ick" factor. Authors repeatedly pointed out anecdotal stories of apparently happy, consensual, and otherwise harmless polygamous families. On the other side, most people couldn't really articulate why they opposed polygamy, they just did. And in support of that opposition, they tended to simply assemble a horrible parade of stories, with the expectation that the huge weight of negative narratives from polygamy's "survivors" and their supporters would overwhelm criticisms that they had no *objective* case to make that polygamy itself was the cause of the harms they described.

But if there was a better case to be made, I wanted to make it. I understood that our only counterweight to the religious and other liberties asserted by polygamy's defenders would be proof of harm. The Supreme Court of Canada had held in the past that specific harm was not necessary to support *every* criminal prosecution. However, I believed that if we wanted to override very important rights such as the religious freedoms of fundamentalist Mormons, Muslims, and others, we would have to go further than just showing a speculative apprehension of harm.

The readings that I had done on cultural evolution though, had given me a new perspective and something approaching optimism that we would in fact be able to demonstrate the harms of polygamy. Behind all the arguments was one simple fact: the polygamy law had endured as society had evolved, not unlike the tradition of lawyers' gowns that I described much earlier. Perhaps it had been selected for survival not because we were all unthinking sheep or bigoted imperialists, but because the prohibition of polygamy averted some real harms and provided some real benefits. But what were these harms and benefits, and how could they be proved?

I already knew what I described earlier, that a number of writers, including Pinker and Wright, had proposed that the pool of unmarried, low-status males created by polygamy's mathematics would become a social problem of their own, and I hoped that we might be able to introduce some evidence of harms in societies where similar antisocial and criminal demographics have been created by gender imbalances. But this still seemed somewhat tenuous, and it didn't lead to any "grand unifying theory" of polygamy's harms. I wasn't confident that the courts would uphold such an intrusive law simply out of fear that sexually frustrated men would get in more bar fights. More worrisome still was where the argument led (at least, where it led Wright): monogamy was a good deal for men (particularly if they were allowed a little polygyny on the side), but a bad deal for women. If we were to make a sympathetic case of harm, it would have to be because polygamy itself hurt vulnerable people in society.

The most vulnerable of all the potential victims of polygamy were, of course, children, and in particular girls. I felt confident that I could show the court a remarkable coincidence, one that had struck me as I read about polygamy around the world, and that was this: all of the polygamous societies seemed to marry young. Well, the *girls* seemed to marry young, and often to much older men. From Israel's Bedouin Arabs to Bountiful, from ancient First Nations practice to YFZ in Texas, polygamy and "child brides" seemed inseparable.

But coincidence wasn't enough. I was going to have to convince a judge, who probably began from the same civil libertarian position as I did, that the harms we associated with polygamy were actually *caused* by polygamy. Because otherwise, this ran up against the standard retort: "If child brides are the problem, that's separate from polygamy. Ban child brides if you like, but let the polygamists be."

I can remember precisely when my view of polygamy and the prospects for upholding the law changed, quite literally overnight. Daphne Bramham's *The Secret Lives of Saints*, a book about the polygamists of Bountiful, focused on child brides and "lost boys." Bramham had a striking turn of phrase, "polygamy's cruel arithmetic," which she used to describe the imperative in religious communities to somehow dispose of "excess" males to thin the competitive pool for women and girls. I was rereading Bramham's book when I had one of those moments where I might actually have slapped a palm to my forehead in a dawn of comprehension.

My epiphany, such as it was, was this: assuming that polygamy equalled polygyny, it was not only lost boys who resulted from the cruel arithmetic, *it was also child brides.* If you allow some men in society more than one wife, you create a demand, overall, for more women than the existing pool of prospective brides will satisfy. Where do these women come from? There are really only two options. One method to get more women into the available pool is to import them from outside the community—some ancient Greek city states, for instance, supplemented universal monogamy with sex-slaves brought in from overseas, permitting every man to still have at least one partner, but allowing several for the wealthiest. The other way is to recruit from the ranks of younger and younger girls. And if you adopt this tactic (as you have to if the Greek solution is not available), then the more polygamy you have, the younger you have to go.

In retrospect this seems so ridiculously obvious, yet at the time I vividly recall it as being a moment little short of Damascene. If this insight were correct, it would mean that as polygamy increased in any society, girls would be targeted at a younger age as sexual partners. Polygamy would lead to younger marriage (for girls but not men), and the preparation or promising of girls for marriage (and perhaps promising into marriage) even before that. It explained the phenomenon of child brides at Bountiful perfectly.

This potentially answered another conundrum. As I've said, it had been observed in a lot of societies where polygamy was practised that girls married young. But they married young in both polygamous or monogamous marriages. So the decriminalization advocates held this up as proof that it wasn't polygamy that caused the child-bride problem, but rather the peculiar cultures where it was practised. But if the cruel arithmetic explanation was correct, the causation was precisely the reverse—polygamy caused the earlier targeting of girls, which caused a culture to develop normalizing the practice of child marriage in any society where polygamy flourished.

In the same way, decrying the marriage practices of Bountiful as some sort of culture of "pedophilia" which could be separately addressed missed the point, because the men of Bountiful weren't really pedophiles, clinically speaking (well, *most* of them weren't). By and large, they weren't marrying fifteen year olds because they preferred them to adult women; there just weren't enough adult women to go around—their practices had adapted to their environment.

So you could say that, all this time, we had been looking in the wrong place for polygamy's harms: the question was not (or at least, not only) whether a polygamous relationship was a worse place to be than a monogamous one; it was whether a more polygamous *society* was necessarily a worse place to be.

The academic debate had, as near as I could tell, completely missed the point. Almost no scholarship connected the child-bride problem with polygamy's mathematics, and when the connection was made it led mostly to fairly nonsensical conclusions. For example, the American law professor Maura Strassberg in her 2003 article "The Challenge of Post-Modern Polygamy: Considering Polyamory" recognized that in polygynous societies, "women are ordinarily married off quite young to much older husbands,"[9] but curiously focused on the *men's* age. She had written:

Since most polygamous societies are relatively gender balanced, polygyny is made possible by postponing the age of male marriage.[10]

This was seen to be negative for young men, who suffered from having to wait for a bride. Strassberg's analysis in this respect relied heavily on a book by William Blum on polygyny in African tribal societies. Blum had written:

> If the men marry for the first time later than the women for the first time, and there is an equal ratio of males to females, then the population will always have an excess of marriageable females.[11]

Really, an *excess*? It seemed obvious to me that, regardless of the age of men at first marriage in polygamy, the fact of a gender-balanced society would *ipso facto* lead to a *shortage* of women. How could it be otherwise?[12]

One academic commentator, Shayna Sigman, did acknowledge the "empirical reality" that, in polygynous societies, "the average age that women marry is younger than it is for monogamous societies."[13] Sigman recognized this might be, in at least some cases, "a coping mechanism for demographics,"[14] and even speculated that, as a consequence, "abuse, rape, and kidnapping of adolescent girls may be made worse or more likely within the context of polygamy."[15] However, Sigman's concern in this regard was limited to the conclusion that "both the age gap for marriage and the slightly younger female average age upon marriage present a problem *when they result in minors being placed in polygamous marriages*."[16]

You can see where the reasoning here goes off the rails. The "coping mechanism" will lead to child brides, abuse, rape, and kidnapping, that's true, but the effect is felt *throughout* society—in the monogamous mainstream as well as in the polygamous "context." The harm certainly isn't only in polygamous marriages. So Sigman's main idea, that "the criminalization of polygamy and history surrounding enforcement" prevented the state from being able to investigate and enforce criminal laws against the sexual exploitation of minors was really quite irrelevant, even if it were true.

Again and again, the discussion circled back to the fact that academic writers seemed to consider only harm arising in polygamous marriages, not polygamous societies. The focus was entirely on how to accommodate polygamous unions while minimizing or addressing possible harms to co-wives and children. The commentators concluded that banning polygamy was unconstitutional because the law could be written to apply only to "bad" polygamy, or the state could simply scrutinize polygamous marriages looking for abuse and crimes. But the "cruel arithmetic" effect on the targeting of girls, like the increased criminality of men in a polygynous society, would be felt everywhere, and this was so even if every polygynous marriage was harmless, egalitarian, and restricted to fully consenting adults.

## Polygamy and Patriarchy

And other things followed from the "cruel arithmetic." The shortage of women would increase their value as a reproductive resource, and men and women both would struggle to exert control over that commodity. To the extent that men controlled the social institutions affecting women's availability for marriage, women would be commodified not for their own benefit, but for that of those men. Because men in polygamous societies needed to recruit girls, they needed to make them compliant, obedient, and accepting of the otherwise rather odious idea of marriage to much older men. So control over women and girls would be a crucial element of any polygynous system.

Harold Blackmore, the disillusioned founder of Bountiful, never understood what would be demonstrated during the trial—that it was polygamy itself, not some perversion of his faith, that led to the "brainwashing" and sexual exploitation of young girls. Or perhaps a better way of putting it was that the perversion of faith was, like many of the tenets of that faith, *caused* by his beloved practice of polygamy. As I said earlier, Johnson's and Jeffs's followers weren't marrying fourteen year olds because they were evil (though at least some clearly were); they were marrying little girls because they had run out of women. They weren't controlling girls and women with increasingly repressive measures because their religion compelled them to; they were doing it because women had become a scarce resource and a valuable commodity in the community, and men would exploit whatever power they had—religious, economic, and if necessary physical—to retain control over them. This being the case, Harold Blackmore's simultaneous defence of The Principle and criticism of the abuses could not possibly succeed: polygamy could not endure through the generations *without* abuse.

Another economic consequence of the gender imbalance created by polygamy is probably not independently verifiable, but provides further some explanation for the close connection between polygamy and patriarchy. This occurred to me during the debate in England and the Commonwealth over the demise of the Crown; for the first time, the rulers of England will be the eldest child of the monarch, of either sex. From time immemorial, kingdoms have tended to pass from the king to the firstborn son. This pattern for the transfer of wealth is imitated throughout the nobility and indeed as far down the social food chain as there is any wealth to transfer. The general rule seems to be that wealth is transferred

110

to the male progeny; only if there is no male issue would we expect to see a daughter inherit the family fortune.

Why would this be? Many feminists would say that it simply represents an affinity effect—men are men, and so they favour other men. But this is dissatisfying on many levels. There is no real reason for men to assist other men, particularly if their interest is in power or status maintenance. As with women, in fact, we would expect to see more intrasexual competition than intersexual. Also, if affinity were really at issue, then we would expect to see a different hierarchy of preference—if there are no male offspring, then why wouldn't the wealth go to nephews, cousins, or even strangers before it went to daughters? No, patterns of wealth transfer can be more elegantly explained on a different basis.

Consider the genetic advantage in investing in male children in a non-monogamous world. As long as humans don't always form lifelong sexually-exclusive pair-bonds, a male heir is more likely to pass along genes than a female heir. In an ordinary polygynous society, a successful man might expect to have dozens, if not hundreds of children in his life; a successful woman would have no more than twelve. So it makes sense, in a society where polygyny is a realistic option, for parents (not just fathers) to invest more heavily in boys than in girls. This is particularly so with respect to the transfer of material wealth, because throughout history, the wealthier men would be expected to have the most wives, mistresses, concubines, and opportunistic sex, so the advantage of maleness is compounded, with a corresponding deficit to girls.

And of course, it is not only material wealth transfer that would favour boys—every type of scarce resource, from educational effort to attention to health, would be kept from girls in favour of boys.

The more monogamous a society, the more muted this effect. Today in North America, it is very unlikely for a man to have more children than a woman is capable of (although because of the limited "*de facto* polygamy" of serial marriage, mistresses, and so forth, we can still expect men who have children to have, on average, more offspring than women who have children). We have numerous laws and social rules, such as spousal and child support laws (as well as restrictions on multiple partners), that have the effect of limiting male reproductive potential quite sharply. This being the case, we can expect parental investment per child to improve (and of course it does), but we can also expect the parental investment in girls to approach parity with the investment in boys. And, by and large, it seems to be so.

Now, economists will say that, depending on the details of the marriage "market," the increased value of women will generate what is called "brideprice"—a fee (monetary or not) that is paid to the parents of girls in exchange for a bride. That this might offset the economic incentives to invest in boys, though, is hardly reassuring, because brideprice is not collected by the bride, but rather by her family (particularly her father), and as such it simply formalizes her commodification.

So girls in a polygynous society will be truly in a bad way: under-educated, less healthy, the sexual targets of much older men, bartered as commodities among families in the community, without inheritance or control of their own marriage and reproductive prospects, and so forth.

In this way, the entire system of the FLDS—its indoctrination and grooming of girls, expulsion of boys, mismatched marriage, every-thing—could most usefully be viewed as a system evolved in the service of polygamy's simple economics. In this sense, as I would later say in my arguments to the Court, "Bountiful didn't create polygamy, *polygamy created Bountiful.*" And of course the same could be said about the most oppressive Muslim societies and African cultures in which polygamy thrives.

We can address each of these symptoms with separate laws, of course. We can mandate equal education and health benefits, inheritance, and criminalize the sexual exploitation and trafficking of girls (and we do all these things). But looking at it through the lens of evolved psychology allows us the advantage of seeing that these *are* symptoms, they are *effects*, and that until and unless we attack the root cause, then the disadvantages to girls will appear, opportunistically and invisibly, out of sight and out of mind, working their subtle harm. Only if we can change the environment and the reward structure for favouring boys over girls can we really ensure a shot at equality.

My immediate problem with this expanded "cruel arithmetic" theory, though, was that I could find no support for it in academic writing. Tentatively, I began to bounce it off colleagues, friends, and family. Did it seem plausible? My interlocutors played devil's advocate and we argued each aspect of the concept. At the end of the day, people had to concede that it made sense. The best counterarguments seemed to be two: first, that the mathematical effects would only be measurable in small, closed communities like Bountiful, and would be swamped in the larger populations; and second, that all aspects of the theory presumed that polygamy "uncorked" would be manifest as polygyny, rather than polyandry. If Canadians were equally inclined to either arrangement, then no shortage of women or excess unmarriageable males would be created.

And of course our most significant hurdle would be proving any of this in court. Yes we had the nice examples of Bountiful and the other FLDS communities, but they were so singular that we could expect the argument could be made that they said little or nothing about polygamy *per se*. At the time, as I said, I could find no academic in any discipline that had explicitly linked the problem of child brides with the cruel arithmetic. It was already February, and we were racing towards a trial beginning that November, and our expert evidence was due in advance, by midsummer. Could we find academics to follow up on these ideas and see if they had merit? Could an expert do the tremendous amount of work necessary in the few months allotted?

## The Problem of Proof

Since the earliest *Charter* cases, it was recognized that it was not possible to fairly adjudicate complex questions surrounding the justification of the infringement of rights without a full factual record.[17] This is why *Charter* claims have rarely been the focus of appellate references,[18] and the opportunity to produce evidence was the reason that we had gone to the trial court in the first place, as the Attorney General had confirmed in his press release announcing the reference on 22 October 2009:

> Pursuing a reference through B.C. Supreme Court gives us the option to introduce evidence and witnesses, which will put a human face on polygamy in contrast to the more abstract nature of a reference to B.C. Court of Appeal.

In the reference trial our challenge would be to present to the court proof that there are a number of harms that arise from polygamy, which, individually and taken together, are significant and substantial.

How do you go about proving that polygamy causes harm? Unlike with other offences, the harm of polygamy may or may not be apparent at the scene of the crime. It may be true, in an econometric sense, that every plural wife will result in either a child bride or an unmarriageable boy, but you will never know who they are: you can't draw an Aristotelian line between wrongdoer and victim.

We needed to show all the harms that were associated with polygamous relationships and families—mainly, harms to the women and children involved. We needed to show that these harms were prevalent, over and above their "background" in a monogamous society, so that the court could conclude that, even if polygamy was not *necessarily* harmful in its every manifestation, it nevertheless, in itself, carried increased *risks*. Beyond this, we needed to demonstrate that polygamy, whether or not it was harmful (or even risky) to its participants over and above monogamy, was *ipso facto* harmful to society, principally through the consequences of its mathematics, which would lead to a more violent and repressive society, and one in which girls would be sexually targeted at an increasingly young age.

Most importantly to my mind was to present to the Court a single, comprehensive theory of polygamy that explained why causation of all the harms we posited was not only a reasonable hypothesis, but in fact the inevitable explanation.

The evidence would be of two main categories, consisting of expert testimony and personal evidence: polygamy in theory and polygamy in practice. The expert evidence would demonstrate that polygyny was remarkably persistent in human societies, and polyandry was not, and why. We would then show what science predicted would happen in societies where the wealthiest and most powerful men were allowed to take a plurality of wives.

Our experts would then test this hypothesis against the evidence from around the world. If we were right, a society's degree of polygyny should correlate with everything from youth of brides to increased crime, even where all other appropriate controls were applied. There are two main categories of polygamy research: intracultural, where polygamist populations in a particular society (for instance, the Bedouin Arabs) are compared to their nonpolygamous neighbours; and cross-cultural, where entire societies or countries are compared to one another, having been classified according to the degree to which polygyny is present there. Each has its advantages and disadvantages. Intracultural studies permit for control of most variables—the polygamists and monogamists live in the same environment, attend the same schools, and so on, but they only measure harms within the two types of relationships; that is, if the monogamist group suffers harm *because* of the polygamous group, it not only would not be apparent in an intracultural study, but it might actually make the harm appear less than it is. Cross-cultural studies allow the harm to be demonstrated *throughout* a society, but they are open to the criticism that the societies compared are so different that you couldn't say whether polygamy actually caused the measured harms or whether it was something else.

How can we reliably draw conclusions as to causation? Social scientists can use regression analysis, controlling for appropriate confounding factors, to make more confident predictions about causative "direction" between two statistically linked variables, or among several. As the evidence developed, it appeared certain that we could say that, internationally at least, polygamy was causally related to a number of measurable harms.

We expected the main objection to this line of evidence to be that the international studies did not apply in the Canadian context. That, in other words, just because polygamy drives down the age of marriage in Africa or Asia, it would not necessarily do so here. This might be because our notions of equality would prevent polygyny from taking off if it were decriminalized, or it might be because the few who would take it up would be as likely to be polyandrous as polygynous.

A scientist might also consider the plausibility of the causal hypothesis when making assessments of the strength of evidence of cause and effect. Dr Shackelford (an expert witness for the *amicus*) in his evidence would use the example of ice cream sales, which statistically correlate with the number of drownings. We should not, he would caution, take from this that drowning causes ice cream sales (though grieving family members might seek solace in Häagen-Dazs), or that ice cream makes people drown (though it might, through those cramps our mothers warned us about). Far more likely is the hypothesis that hot summer weather causes an increase in both ice cream sales *and* drowning (as more people swim and go boating).

For the scientist, the plausible hypothesis can be tested by holding the proposed confounder constant and rechecking the correlation. If controlling for weather makes the relationship between drowning and ice cream disappear, causation can be fairly reliably asserted (though it is still possible to argue that some other factor causes good weather *and* ice cream sales *and* drowning).

If, after weather is taken into account, there is still a significant connection between ice cream sales and drowning, then something else needs to be considered. And so on. Causal certainty is virtually impossible in science, which must always hold out the possibility of an alternative explanation. But in law, the trier of fact must at some point take an off-ramp in assessing causation. We do this through the application of the balance of probabilities analysis, which invites us to choose the most likely among the various explanations offered for causation.

There is a prominent place in the process, in other words, for a common-sense assessment of the various causal explanations. So, in part, we would rely on the plausibility—or as I have put it, the inevitability—of our analysis. Simple mathematics dictated the theory that polygamy would drive down the age of marriage for girls. There didn't seem to be any competing theory to explain a correlation between polygamy and child brides. There is no reason to believe that very young girls simply prefer polygnists as husbands, and in fact it does not even seem that *polygynists* prefer young girls, at least not much (these alternatives can be discounted to the extent that monogamists also marry younger in polygynous societies). On the other side of the ledger, there is a hypothesis that a shortage of marriage-age women, coupled with men's evolved inclination to seek younger, rather than older, women as brides will combine to force the age of women's first marriage down when polygyny is permitted. Some argue that polygyny further exacerbates the problem because a system of marrying girls to older men is also an institutional control mechanism (institutions of inequity are also correlated with polygyny and hypothesized as one of the effects of women's commodification in a scarce market).

Of course it is still *possible* that there is some mysterious third factor that causes *both* child brides and polygyny. However nobody in the course of the reference was ever able to propose one that has withstood analysis, as we shall see.

Ideally, of course, a hypothesis would be tested by a controlled experiment. One would take two otherwise similar groups, and randomly assign one to marry polygamously, and the other monogamously. All other things being the same, you would then have your answer if the harms were manifest in the polygamous group. Obviously such a controlled experiment wouldn't be possible (never mind ethical) in modern North America.

This is where the fundamentalist Mormons enter the equation. Imagine if, over a century ago, we took a group of North Americans from among the mainstream population, and infused among them a belief that polygamy was permissible—even desirable. Over the course of a hundred years, would we watch as they change into a partially polygynous subsociety? Would a shortage of women mean that girls are married off at progressively younger ages? Would excess boys prove to be unmanageable, and would they be, one way or the other, removed from the community? Would this group develop systems of indoctrination that prepare girls for early marriage, and impose sharp control mechanisms over every aspect of sexual behaviour in society?

The FLDS was our controlled experiment, our petri dish of polygamy. We would be able to show that, after a century of development, it was not unusual in Bountiful and other FLDS communities for fifteen year olds to be wed to much older men; marriages to girls as young as twelve are repeatedly recorded. "Lost boys" litter the surrounding areas, adrift from family and community. Opportunity for reproduction is directly correlated with social status: the bishop, a wealthy businessman, has dozens of wives; lesser but still-powerful figures have a handful; men deemed worthy of marriage but with insufficient wealth to support polygamy have one. Senior men in the community decide who will marry, and when; premarital sex—even social contact between boys and girls—is sharply discouraged; once a "match" is made and a bride assigned, she relinquishes all control over her reproductive options.

The experts would show the theory of harm—to women, children, and society at large, from polygamy. The Bountiful evidence would show polygamy in practice.

I would like to say that the way the "convergent" evidence from the experts and individuals emerged was the result of a single prescient legal strategy, but in fact it was the result of a clash between two very different ideas of what our case should actually be about. Greathead and Horsman, especially, shared the belief that the key would be in the presentation of the personal stories of polygamy's "survivors." I felt just as strongly that this sort of evidence should *not* be the focus of our case, because it did not prove that polygamy caused the harm, and all the horror stories in the world could be undermined by the inevitable "good polygamy" testimony from the other side. So I believed it would be the "high level" experts who would carry the day.

Certainly Greathead's views could not be taken lightly. In my six years with the Con Admin group, I had come to recognize her as one of our most capable *Charter* litigators, especially when questions of equality were at issue. She had come to government after a stint in Arvay's firm, and just prior to the reference case had won so many trials and appeals that I had taken to calling her "Streak." With Horsman, a very experienced trial lawyer, in support, she made a compelling argument for emphasizing the eyewitness accounts of polygamy in practice.

Nevertheless, when I agreed that they should go off to the United States and begin collecting evidence of polygamy's harms from the men and women who had abandoned the FLDS and other fundamentalist Mormon communities, it was not with the expectation that they would come back with evidence that would form an absolutely crucial backbone of the case. Similarly, I like to think that Greathead, Horsman, and Ross did not foresee how the expert evidence that we were able to compile would turn out to be compelling. I believe our fundamental tension in the early days made the case so much better in the end: each of us worked to impress the other with the quality of what we were able to produce, because we each knew that if our own contributions flagged, the vision of the other would come to dominate.

## The Summer Exchange

### *First Steps and "Video Affidavits"*

In Canadian constitutional law, most *Charter* challenges proceed through two main analytical stages. In the first stage, the challenger bears the burden of demonstrating that a government law or activity has infringed upon constitutional rights. If they succeed, then the burden shifts in the second stage to the government—the law can still be saved if the infringement is said to be "demonstrably justified" by the standards of "a free and democratic society."

To facilitate an orderly hearing, Macintosh and I agreed early that we would explore a kind of hybrid proceeding. There would be a trial, with live evidence, but this would be preceded by an exchange of almost all the evidence in affidavit form. We would decide, after all the affidavits were exchanged, which of the witnesses should be heard at trial. Canada agreed to the arrangement, and a schedule for the exchange was worked out and approved by the Court. The challengers (mainly the *amicus*, the FLDS, and the CPAA) would provide their evidence on *Charter* breach in May. We would respond to this evidence, and also provide our evidence on justification, about a month later. Then, after a longer pause, the challengers would respond to our justification evidence.

This process was orderly but meant a lot of intense work for our lawyers, because virtually all of our affidavits had to be prepared within a very few weeks of receiving the first salvo from the other side. Essentially, all of our evidence had to be ready to go all at once, and soon. We were operating very much "on the fly," with the theory of our case developing as the experts began to submit their reports and the eyewitness evidence was gathered, assessed, and categorized.

Fortunately, Greathead's plan to locate and interview eyewitnesses in Utah, Arizona, and Texas, as well as the BC Interior, began to show immediate promise—clearly there were a great many potential witnesses. The difficulty was getting them to open up. Polygamy was a sensational issue and many were already jaded by the fickle attention of the media and authorities. In many cases too, the potential witnesses had family members who were still living in the polygamist communities, and they feared being cut off from contact with them, and perhaps worse forms of reprisal still. Greathead's strategy was to make an initial, low-pressure contact with a potential witness, and gradually build trust through subsequent communication. A second trip would then be planned to actually get the witness's evidence in a way that could be presented to the Court. And by the end of their adventures in Canada and the United States, Greathead, Horsman, and Ross would have stories that would have, by all accounts, made a compelling documentary.

The lawyers' trips took them to decrepit Southern jailhouses and remote rural shacks. They caught up with one of their witnesses, a "lost boy" who was now a long-distance trucker, after midnight in a shopping mall and conducted an interview then and there. The way Greathead recounted it, some of the scenes were reminiscent of the "compound" setting in *Big Love* (that HBO series about a polygamist that I mentioned earlier) with occasional appearances by the banjo-duelling inbreds of *Deliverance*. But the witnesses they had found were brilliant.

It was Greathead and Horsman who came up with the idea of the "video affidavit." Greathead had returned from an early, exploratory trip to the Bountiful area with a view that, if the Chief Justice could only have been in the back of the car, our case would be over and we would win. But Bountiful was hundreds of miles away from the Vancouver courthouse. How could we make the reality, in a sense, real, when we expected that all the evidence would go in first in the form of affidavits and only later be augmented with selected live testimony? Greathead's solution was to videotape interview with each of the "survivors" we could gather and then attach the recording to an affidavit in which the deponent swears to the accuracy of the video and the information there. This would allow the witnesses to "speak" to the court "in person," rather than through the dry device of the written word. It was a superb idea, and by the time the "team" was done, we had more than a dozen video affidavits shot and ready.

Greathead and Horsman's trips also led to some very important contacts with leaders of the antipolygamy effort in the United States, who provided some excellent evidence in the affidavit exchange and would become even more valuable as the trial progressed. Roger Hoole, for instance, an American lawyer who was working with a number of lost boys in their civil suit against the FLDS, came to be a bottomless well of evidence and potential witnesses, and even managed to secure for us a very rare copy of the FLDS's book of teachings, *In Truth and Light*.

Greathead had also returned from her initial trips extremely impressed by the Texas authorities who were prosecuting cases of child rape and polygamy in the aftermath of the YFZ raid. Eric Nichols was the lead prosecutor in Texas and he provided a comprehensive affidavit setting out information on the legal proceedings that had arisen in the wake of the YFZ raid. Hoole and Nichols, between them, ensured that we were "plugged in" to the community of US officials and activists who had been struggling against the FLDS and other polygamous groups for years. Nichols, and his colleagues in the Texas Rangers (who had overseen the YFZ raid and were custodians of the evidence seized there), would later play a pivotal role in assisting us to demonstrate the extent and nature of the child trafficking between Bountiful and the American FLDS communities.

While Greathead, Horsman, and Ross were flying all over hell's half acre, I focused on developing and assembling our expert evidence. I knew I had three main areas of high-level expertise for which I would need academic authority. First, I needed an evolutionary psychologist to demonstrate why polygamy happened, and why it tended to manifest overwhelmingly as polygyny, rather than polyandry. Second, I needed an anthropologist to describe its prevalence throughout the anthropological record. Finally, I needed a skilled researcher to conduct a literature review on the harms of polygamy. And, if I could possibly pull it off, I needed someone familiar with statistics to conduct some original research into correlations with polygamy's harms.

## The Expert Evidence Takes Shape

Joe Henrich is UBC's Canada Research Chair in Culture, Cognition, and Co-Evolution, a world-renowned anthropologist whose studies in comparative moral development and other areas of inquiry have shaken up the fields related to the evolution of cultural systems. An American originally from Philadelphia, Henrich was drawn to Canada as part of the last decade's "brain gain." In his early forties, he is a leading light in the growing field of evolutionary psychology as it relates to the development of cultures and social rules and norms.

Henrich is a committed interdisciplinarian, and is probably the only anthropologist in North America who holds tenure in both psychology and economics. Initially, though, it was his background in evolutionary psychology that led me to contact him. I needed someone to explain to the court why, practically speaking, polygamy would mean polygyny. If it didn't—that is, if legal polygamy would manifest equally as polyandry—then all the arguments based on mathematics would be moot; the numbers would cancel one another out and there would be no need for a polygamous society to recruit young girls, expel boys, or repress and control women.

I wrote to Henrich in March, explaining this idea of the harm, as I rather crudely understood it at the time:

> An aspect of our defence of criminalizing polygamy will be demonstrating that, in practice, polygamy means polygyny. We need to explain why multiple wives are apparently a near-universal phenomenon (or at least aspiration) of human cultures while multiple husbands are not. I have read some persuasive popular writing on this topic by evolutionary psychologists Robert Wright and Steven Pinker. I expect my argument to include that polygyny appears to be "hard-wired" into the human species, rather than arising simply as the result of patriarchal socialization or norms. I then expect to argue that, in a society with equal numbers of men and women, polygyny will inevitably create two types of social harm: first, a pressure to recruit younger and younger brides to feed the demand; and second, to the extent that the demand cannot be satisfied, a cohort of unmarriageable young men with the associated social problems (much interesting literature out of India and China lately).

Henrich was intrigued enough that he didn't rebuff me out of hand. He said that he did not normally do consulting because it took time away from his true passions, his teaching and long-term field research in Fiji and South America. "However," he allowed, "this is sufficiently interesting to consider." As we spoke further, Henrich emphasized that he wasn't interested in being a hired gun; he considered it unethical to do anything but conduct research and report his findings whatever they were. I said that's exactly what we wanted. Given that, he asked, would we agree that he could publish the results of any work he did for the case? This is something that you'd probably never agree to in ordinary litigation, but, and this may sound strange, I was confident that the facts we found would support the theory, because I had become convinced that it was right. And in any event, I took seriously the Attorney General's obligation in this case to put all relevant information before the court. We could not hide away Henrich's results, whatever they would be. If there really wasn't any harm in polygamy, I had told my colleagues, then we needn't preserve section 293. The point here wasn't just to win. If someone was going to make the argument that the law should be supported simply out of deference to Parliament or because there was some vague *apprehension* that polygamy might be harmful, let it be the federal government. It was, after all, their law. British Columbia would be there to prove harm, and would concede that if we could not convince the court of the damage inevitable from the spread of polygamy, we would fail, and we should fail.

In short order we had arranged Henrich's retainer.

I had searched out Henrich only because we needed someone to cover the evolutionary psychology part of the theory; however, as I reflected on his qualifications and read some of what he had written on the biological and social evolution of human behaviours, it became apparent that he could do much more. I gave Henrich the broadest possible brief: What do the sciences tell us, I asked, about the harms of polygamy? What can we predict if the practice were increased? Is there anything to the cruel arithmetic argument? How could we possibly prove it? Henrich pondered this, and said he had some ideas. He and his wife set off to work (Dr Natalie Henrich, I had learned, is herself an accomplished anthropologist with a Master's in Public Health from Harvard, and so we were pleased to have Henrich use her as his research assistant).

As the Henrichs periodically reported back on their progress, the case in support of section 293 began to look hopeful. Henrich's report would explain the evolved psychology of "human mating behaviour," including polygyny, and contrast this with "marriage behaviour," a culturally determined phenomenon. And of the harms of polygyny? Here too Henrich was putting together an impressive set of data. Using cross-cultural studies that controlled for potentially confounding cofactors, Henrich built on the work of economists and anthropologists to show that the degree of polygyny in a culture—any culture—correlated strongly with youth of brides, with age disparity between bride and groom, with control and abuse in domestic situations, and ultimately with a degraded status of women. The literature, when looked at as a whole, was quite extraordinary, and if the authors hadn't used it to ask the most helpful questions, Henrich called them up and asked for their raw data so he could look at it himself.

Henrich's work also shed light on the endgame of the lost boys phenomenon. Isolated polygamist communities such as Bountiful could get away with simply ejecting "surplus" boys and men who would then be absorbed into the larger community. However, if polygamy is more widespread throughout a society, the results could be more sinister still. Even a small imbalance in the numbers of young men and women created a cohort of men who were, as Pinker put it, genetically desperate and willing to engage in increasingly risky antisocial behaviour to secure reproductive prospects that come with wealth or status, or, more directly, to take reproductive opportunities by force through the domination and rape of women and girls. Henrich pointed to studies from China showing that official one-child policies had led parents to select boys over girls and had created small imbalances that translated into massive increases in crime rates.

I had read in the newspaper about the crime rates in China, so I was impressed but still a little wary of drawing conclusions. "How can you be sure that crime rates weren't going up anyway?" I wondered. Henrich explained, as he later would so effectively at trial, that different provinces in China introduced the one-child policy in different years. And in each province, the crime rate spiked fifteen or sixteen years after the policy was implemented, as the mismatched generation with surplus males reached the most dangerous years of late adolescence and early adulthood. The coincidence was so strong, he said, that we could infer not only correlation but causation. This was precisely the kind of science that we needed.

In addition to Henrich and the "personal experience" witnesses, we began to gather evidence from a number of other sources. Walter Scheidel, the chair of the Classics Department at Stanford University, signed on to provide an expert's overview of the history of polygamy (or, more accurately, of monogamy, the far more recent and localized phenomenon). Dr Lawrence Beall, a counselling psychologist with decades of experience dealing with the "survivors" of the FLDS in the United States, was engaged. Beall had testified in over forty US court cases, and had been retained as a prospective expert by Robertson's prosecution team. The federal government's own team produced three experts of their own, on cross-cultural studies, history, and religion.

One of our "allied participants" in the reference was a small organization called Stop Polygamy in Canada. It was run on a shoestring by a woman named Nancy Mareska, and I had initially regarded them as inconsequential to the reference. In February, after the procedure of the reference was determined, Mareska had contacted me for assistance filling out the necessary paperwork to appear as an "Interested Person." It was obvious that she could use the help of a lawyer, and I eventually put her onto Brian Samuels.

Mareska had persuaded Samuels to take on the case, and it turned out to be a very fruitful retainer. Samuels was an extremely smart Vancouver lawyer who had built his career in the specialized field of engineering litigation but had recently developed a taste for *pro bono* constitutional work. Samuels and Kieran Bridge, his co-counsel, were fresh from a series of victories culminating in the Supreme Court of Canada's landmark decision of *Ward v Vancouver (City)*, in which they had established the leading precedent for money damages awards in *Charter* cases (thus giving rise to a new cottage industry in suing the government). In the Polygamy Reference, Samuels and his colleagues would exploit the massive Rolodex and boundless energy of their activist client and produce witnesses and a compelling legal argument against polygamy. Their contribution, like that of the Hunter Litigation Chambers team representing the Asper Centre and the Centre for the Rights of the Child, would be beyond anything I initially expected.

## The Tapestry Connection

As part of their efforts in the United States, Greathead, Horsman, and Ross had established connections with activists from Tapestry Against Polygamy. They obtained an affidavit from Andrea Moore-Emmett, a journalist and student of polygamy, and the author of *God's Brothel*, one of the best-sellers among the many American books on fundamentalist Mormon polygamy.[19]

Moore-Emmett's evidence was particularly useful because her study of polygamy was not focused exclusively on the FLDS, the largest and most notorious of the US-based fundamentalist Mormon groups. In fact, she described in her affidavit a number of other, more or less famous, organizations:

i) the Apostolic United Brethren (AUB) which is centered in Bluff-dale, Utah, but also has settlements in Montana, Nevada, and Mexico;

ii) The Fundamentalist Church of Jesus Christ of Latter-day Saints (FLDS) which has settlements in the twin cities of Hildale, Utah, and Colorado City, Arizona, British Columbia, and Mexico. The FLDS also has splinter groups such as the Second Ward which formed a group not far from Colorado City in a community that became known as Centennial Park;

iii) The True and Living Church of Jesus Christ of Saints of the Last Days (TLC) of Mormon town of Manti, Utah, led by Jim Harmston;

iv) The Church of the First Born of the Fullness of Times head-quartered in Colonia LeBaron in Chihuahua, Mexico, led by Joel LeBaron;

v) The Church of the Lamb of God led by Fred Collier with members in Hanna, Utah, and Mexico;

vi) The Latter-day Church of Christ, also known as the Kingston Group, led by Paul Kingston based in Salt Lake City, Utah, with members in Utah, Idaho, and Nevada;

vii) The Church of Jesus Christ of the United Order led by Luis Gonzales with members in Sacramento, California, and in a community in Jackson County, Missouri, under the leadership of Floren LeBaron;

viii) The Righteous Branch led by Gerald Peterson Jr. in Paiquin, Utah;

ix) The Church of Jesus Christ led by Roger Billings in Jackson County, Missouri; and

x) The Patriarchal Hierarchy led by Tom Green at Green Haven, a row of trailers on Utah's West Desert.

What was particularly useful for our purposes was what Moore-Emmett described as the "common traits" of all these groups, summarized at paragraph 11 of her affidavit. This summary helped us "bridge" the individual evidence of those who had left polygamy, on the one hand, with the expert evidence that would have predicted these same outcomes:

- Systems of indoctrination, formal and informal, are used to prepare young girls and women for polygamous marriage, including marriage to much older men.
- The family structures are intensely patriarchal and inherently unequal between the men and women. There is an extraordinarily high degree of control exerted by men both within the families (by the father/husband) and the community generally (by men in leadership positions).
- Polygamous wives find it very difficult to leave their marriages. This is so for a number of reasons. They often have a large number of children, having been told by their husbands and religious leaders that they must have as many children as possible. People growing up in polygamist communities are taught not to trust the outside world. A woman who leaves the community becomes part of the outside community that is evil and cannot be trusted. Some women are forced to leave their children behind. If a woman is able to leave she, in many cases, must give up all ties with her family. Once she leaves she is not welcome back in the community to visit family. The woman is "dead" to her family. In some cases the women must give up all that they have ever known and experienced in life. Often the religious indoctrination and religious authority has made it impossible for the women to exercise true choice. These women often have no job skills, no education and no preparation for independent living. The blood atonement belief (one must pay for one's sin with death) held by many polygamist groups means that some women live in hiding in fear of death.
- Boys and young men are frequently forced from the communities in a variety of ways, apparently to reduce competition for girls and women among the group's men. The boys often have little education and find it difficult to cope in the outside world. They often become involved in drugs, alcohol, or prostitution.
- Girls are "married" at unusually young ages, sometimes between fourteen and sixteen years old, and they usually become pregnant shortly after marriage.
- The trading of girls for marriage purposes takes place between families and communities. This occurs over state and national boundaries.
- There is often a significant age gap of many years, even decades, between the men and women in polygamous marriages.
- In some polygamist groups girls are forced to marry a close relative (incest) sometimes causing genetic diseases and birth defects.

Laura Chapman is a social worker practising in Colorado who was also formerly a counsellor with Tapestry Against Polygamy. She was raised in a FLDS community, in a family with five mothers and thirty-one siblings.

She described her own observations growing up in that environment (such as her seventeen-year-old sister being married off to FLDS prophet Leroy Johnson, then seventy years old, and herself being married to a man she had barely met).

As with Moore-Emmett's evidence, Chapman's went beyond a survivor's tale because, like many who had turned their back on fundamentalist Mormon polygamy, she had made something of a study of the practice. And so her affidavit also usefully described many of the commonalities she had observed among the approximately twenty polygamous sects throughout North America. She related:

> Young women are often sent away from their childhood communities or convinced to marry within other polygamist communities. For this reason, I have relatives in almost all of the above-mentioned groups. For example, two of my former sister-in-laws were married to Warren Jeffs, my great-uncle Rulon Allred (once leader of the Allred group) was murdered by Ervil LeBaron a polygamist leader in Mexico (who later died awaiting trial for a number of murders). My Aunt Charlotte married Ervil LeBaron's brother Verlan LeBaron. Verlan's life as well as my grandmother's life, was threatened by Ervil LeBaron. Tom Green, an independent polygamist was charged with child rape and bigamy in the States. Tom Green's child bride, Linda Kunz, is my first cousin. The Kingston sect's mid-wife delivered my children in home births. My niece Samantha is the third-wife of Gerald Palmer, a man in Bountiful, British Columbia.

Chapman's affidavit listed many of the same harms as common throughout the Mormon communities with which she was familiar: child brides, arranged marriages, lost boys, an oppressive, cloistered environment, and little opportunity for education.

With the gathering of evidence underway, I began to rough out our constitutional argument with the assistance of Bevan and the UBC law professor Robin Elliot. Elliot and I had worked closely together years before during the tobacco litigation, and much of the written work in the constitutional trial and appeals in that case had been the result of this collaboration under the direction of the senior lawyers Tom Berger, Dan Webster, and Elliott Myers. I loved to collaborate with Elliot, partly because his extremely ordered approach to constitutional analysis was in tension with my own style, which tended to be more stream-of-consciousness. Elliot had spent a couple of years as legal officer at the Supreme Court of Canada and had a very advanced view of jurisprudence and a wise regard for judicial pragmatism. This level of actual litigation experience is rare among constitutional academics, and it made him a valued associate counsel at Heenan Blaikie, a Canadian law firm that aggressively recruited Canada's top constitutional minds. Prior to the reference, Elliot had worked with Terry Robertson and Kat Kinch of Harper Grey LLP, the lawyers who had been leading the aborted prosecution of Winston Blackmore and James Oler. He knew the file and the issues and had already given them a lot of thought, so we retained him as an *ad hoc* advisor, to complement our own efforts in preparing our case. In this case, combined with the contributions of Greathead, Bevan, and others, our resulting arguments would be, I thought, much better than the sum of our individual contributions.

## Evidence of Muslim Polygamy

One area where our evidence-gathering efforts had met with frustration was that of polygamy in the Muslim community. The difficulty here was that the practice was diffuse throughout many different immigrant and ethnic groups. It seemed to be generally practised in isolation, and had not yet hit a critical mass where polygamists had formed a group of their own.

Freya Zaltz had been asked to oversee this particularly difficult aspect of our case. She made contact with a number of people who knew something about polygamy in the Islamic communities (mostly in Ontario), but their evidence would be generally weak and indirect. There were, as of yet, no escapees from Canadian Muslim polygamy as there had been from Bountiful and the FLDS, or at least if there had been they were not inclined to come forward, perhaps on account of their shaky and uncertain immigration status (polygamist wives and their children, it would appear, were often brought into the country on false pretences).

Freya did obtain an affidavit from Dr Mohammad Fadel, an assistant professor and the Canada Research Chair in the Law and Economics of Islamic Law at the University of Toronto's Faculty of Law. Fadel explained Muslim theology and law with respect to the practice of polygamy. Fadel's affidavit was answered, or perhaps complemented by, that of the *amicus*'s expert Dr Anver Emon, an associate professor at the University of Toronto's Faculty of Law.

The other affidavit speaking to polygamy among Canadian Muslims was that of Alia Hogben, executive director of the Canadian Council of Muslim Women. Hogben reported contacts with polygamous wives who were, one way or the other, in crisis. Several reported that their husbands' second marriage was undertaken without their knowledge and consent, and there were other indicia of abusive domestic arrangements. But Hogben's affidavit was not even an informal survey; it gave no indication of the prevalence of polygamy or the incidence of its associated harms. All it accomplished was a confirmation that polygamy existed in the Muslim community, and that some adherents, including Hogben, considered it to be problematic.

After some discussion, the parties agreed that we would mutually "stand down" with respect to *live* evidence of Muslim polygamy—that is, we would rely on the affidavit evidence and not call upon any of the witnesses to testify. Several participants had put in affidavits on the nature of the practice in various Islamic traditions and communities. But no Islamic groups had elected to participate in the reference, and despite enormous efforts, at least on our part, no one had been able to come up with witnesses who had lived in an Islamic polygamous household and were willing to talk about it. In any event, the Islamic case for polygamy as a religious imperative was far weaker than the fundamentalist Mormons', because Islam, at best, only tolerated the practice, whereas the FLDS and similar groups believed that it was a practice mandated by God and required for an adherent to reach the highest level of exaltation in the afterlife.

Because I won't be discussing this aspect of the case in the course of the trial proceedings, however, I should take a few moments to summarize some of the evidence with respect to polygamy in Islam, because it is the most prevalent form of the practice on the global level, and therefore the greatest concern with respect to present and future immigrant populations in Canada.[20]

Polygamy in Islam dates from the faith's foundation, and was practised by the prophet Muhammad himself. It is expressly permitted by the Koran, albeit with certain limitations. It is not an obligatory element of Islam, however, and the actual incidence of polygyny varies across cultures and countries.

The primary legal basis for permitting Islamic polygyny is found in Sura 4, verse 3 of the Koran, which reads: "And if ye fear that ye shall not be able to deal justly with the orphans, marry women of your choice, two or three, or four." However, there is then Koran 4:129, which says: "You will never be able to be just among women even if you tried." There is considerable disagreement about the meaning of the two provisions. Does the Koranic text contain a general permission to take up to four wives? It appears so,[21] but some scholars, including Fadel, argued that, although permitted, "the simultaneous marriage of a male to more than one female is religiously disfavoured with respect to the man."

Modern nations with significant Muslim populations take different approaches to the practice of polygamy. Some, such as Tunisia and Turkey, have adopted Western-style legal prohibitions. In other countries polygamy is permitted for Muslims, but with some conditions. Pakistan provides a board of inquiry procedure to approve a proposed polygamous union; Egypt has requirements for notice to, and consent of, existing wives. In the Philippines and India, Muslims are permitted additional wives but others are not.

Still other predominantly Muslim countries have little or no restrictions on the practice, and some might be said to actually encourage it. Saudi Arabia, which holds the Koran and nunna (the practices of the prophet Muhammad) as the supreme law, is perhaps the most well-known example. There, an entire legal structure has developed to facilitate men's acquisition of subsequent wives and to disincentivize and punish women who would wish to leave polygamous unions.

We did have *some* particular evidence with respect to the practice among North American Muslims. As our designated Islam specialist, Zaltz secured an affidavit from Dr Dena Hassouneh, an associate professor with the Oregon Health & Sciences University School of Nursing. Hassouneh has studied and treated the mental health impacts on women in marginalized populations, including the study of the impacts of abuse on American Muslim women.[22] Hassouneh's report contained a review of literature on polygamy in Muslim families that identified a number of harms mirroring those found in fundamentalist Mormon communities: patterns of emotional and psychiatric problems, particularly among senior wives; higher incidence of domestic violence; poorer psychiatric, social, and academic outcomes in children; and problems associated with reduced paternal investment of time and resources in children, and jealousy and competition among co-wives.

Samuels and his team, representing Stop Polygamy in Canada, contributed another clinician's affidavit, this one from Dr Susan Stickevers, Chief of Physical Medicine and Rehabilitation Service at the Department of Veteran Affairs Medical Center in Northport, New York, and also the Residency Program Director and Assistant Clinical Professor of Physical Medicine and Rehabilitation at the State University of New York at Stony Brook. Stickevers is a medical doctor who, in her pain medicine practice, treated a number of Muslim women who were in polygamous relationships. She too offered a literature review that she conducted as part of a study group on the effect of polygamy on women and the family. In her affidavit she listed a number of harms associated with polygamy which she said were consistent with her observations of polygamous marriage from the field:

- higher rates of depression in senior wives;
- higher rates of anxiety in senior wives;
- higher rates of psychiatric hospitalization and outpatient psychiatric treatment for wives;

- higher rates of marital dissatisfaction for wives;
- lower levels of self-esteem observed in wives;
- higher levels of somatization observed in wives; and
- lower levels of academic achievement and more difficulty with mental health and social adjustment in the children of polygamous families.

There was nothing particularly compelling about the literature reviews offered by Hassouneh and Stickevers. It was taken as given that we could show an association between polygamy and the harms they described. The true value of these clinicians' testimony was to demonstrate that, when you came at the problem of polygamy from the Islamic perspective, the harms of polygamy looked very much the same as they did at Bountiful. In the context of the larger case, this reinforced the point of what we would call "convergence"—the idea that, when you viewed all the evidence together, an undeniable pattern to polygamy's harms emerged, one whose eerie uniformity suggested far more than simple coincidence.

For instance, after introducing the harms of polygamy revealed by her literature review, Stickevers then compared these findings to her experience treating women of Muslim polygamous relationships in New York. She noted that she had observed many of these same phenomena in those patients, and deposed in her affidavit that:

> [Seventeen] out of 18 (94%) of my polygamous female patients scored for high levels of depression, somatization, and anxiety on psychometric testing. This is significantly higher than the prevalence of depression and anxiety I observed in my monogamously married female patients.

Stickevers also noted that 94 percent of her patients' polygamous marriages were nonconsensual, and said that "many Muslim polygamous marriages in NYC come about as a result of coercion."

Despite the potential of the Muslim evidence to reinforce that from the fundamentalist Mormon communities, de-emphasizing the evidence of Islamic polygamy seemed like the right thing to do in the context of the reference, notwithstanding its prevalence, because it was less relevant to the constitutional issues before the Court. Whatever could be said of its theological status, it was clear that polygamy was not near as central to the Islamic faith as it was to fundamentalist Mormons; it could not be suggested, in other words, that the Mormons' claim should fail but the Muslims' should succeed. Similarly, while a court's balancing of "salutary and deleterious effects" under section 1 of the *Charter* might consider the extent of the infringement on the practitioners of all faiths, nothing we had seen suggested that the impact could be greater on Muslims, again because, unlike fundamentalist Mormons, few Muslims claimed to be religiously *compelled* to have more than one wife.

Clearly it would be the fundamentalist Mormons who had both the strongest case on religious freedom and also showed most obviously examples of the harms that we said were caused by polygamy. I wanted to be able to draw a direct line between the predictions of experts like Henrich and their manifestation in the petri dish communities of the FLDS, and so from my point of view, it made sense to focus the live evidence portion of the trial on exploring those communities in the greatest depth.

## The Afghan Millionaire

If we needed a graphic reminder of the possibility of polygamous immigration, it would be provided by another notorious court case involving an Afghan millionaire and a tragedy on the Rideau Canal in Kingston, Ontario. In June 2009 the bodies of three teenaged sisters, Zainab, Sahar, and Geeti Shafia, were discovered along with that of a woman, Rona Amir Mohammad, fifty, in a black Nissan with a broken left taillight submerged at the Kingston Mills locks on the canal. All four had apparently drowned.

Corresponding areas of damage led the police to conclude that the car had been pushed into the river by the Lexus SUV belonging to the girl's father, Mohammad Shafia. Shafia, then fifty-eight, was a wealthy businessman who had immigrated to Canada from Afghanistan via Dubai. His wife, Tooba Mohammad Yahya, forty-one, and their son, Hamed Mohammad Shafia, twenty, were charged with first-degree murder in the deaths.

This would, of course, have been a grotesque crime in any circumstances. But the circumstances of the Shafia murders bear some special scrutiny here, because as the story unfolded it became apparent that the deceased woman, Rona Amir Mohammad, who had immigrated to Canada as the teenagers' aunt, was in fact Mohammad Shafia's first wife: the principal accused was the millionaire patriarch of a polygamous family.

As the facts of the case were revealed in the media, it became quite clear that the Shafia clan exhibited all the elements of an abusive patriarchal despotism. The theory of the Crown's case was that Mr Shafia had exploded into homicidal rage at the continuing "humiliation" triggered by his inability to control what he saw as licentiousness in his daughters, who wished to dress in the Western manner and date boys of their choosing. The allegations were that Shafia's second wife (the girls' biological mother) and their son obediently assisted in the "honour killings."

So many elements of the Shafia family seemed to personify harms that had been associated with polygamy, and indeed they seemed to present a vicious caricature of the archetype: a high-status man who had married a somewhat younger woman as his first wife and a considerably younger one as his second (Shafia would have been thirty-eight when his first child was born; his wife would have been twenty-one). The patriarch exhibited an obsessive control over his wives and female children, particularly regarding the girls' social opportunities. There was conflict between the "sister wives," to put it mildly. He enlisted his son as a proto-despot, and exerted a level of control over his much younger second wife apparently sufficient to permit her recruitment into a murder plot against her older sister wife and her own daughters. This all seemed to fit an exquisitely familiar pattern, *in extremis*.

As the *R v Shafia* matter progressed on a track more or less parallel to the Polygamy Reference, it provided a useful reminder, not only that abusive polygamous families could be found in Canada outside the context of Bountiful and the FLDS, but that the *pattern* of abuse was eerily similar. The *Shafia* case was never mentioned in the course of the Polygamy Reference but informed part of the social context and emphasized the extent to which the harms of this secret practice might be going unknown and unaddressed elsewhere in the country.[23]

## The Polyamorists' Evidence

The other group that was heard primarily through affidavits and counsel, rather than through live evidence, was the polyamorist group, represented in the reference by John Ince and the CPAA.

Since the beginning, the ambition of the CPAA was to distinguish polyamory, which they practised, from patriarchal polygamy, which they agreed could legitimately be banned. So one of their challenges was attempting to define what polyamory was. As part of the voluminous Brandeis Brief in the case (see later in this chapter), the CPAA had introduced a number of books and articles documenting the phenomenon of contemporary sexual nonexclusivity, including *Understanding Non-Monogamies* by Meg Barker and Darren Langdridge; *Polyamory in the Twenty-First Century: Love and Intimacy with Multiple Partners* by Deborah Anapol; *The Ethical Slut: A Practical Guide to Polyamory, Open Relationships and Other Adventures*, 2d ed, by Dossie Easton and Janet W Hardy; and *Opening Up: A Guide to Creating and Sustaining Open Relationships* by Tristan Taormino.[24]

It was clear that, while the term "polyamory" literally simply refers to the loving of more than one partner at a time (in which case many of us are probably polyamorists at some point in our lives), the polyamorists themselves identified with a more concise idea, though still one difficult to define with real specificity. Strassberg attempted a definition in her article "The Challenge of Post-Modern Polygamy: Considering Polyamory" (at 439–41):[25]

> Contemporary practitioners have coined the names "polyamory" and "polyfidelity" to describe a wide range of partner arrangements that vary as to the number of people involved, the sexes of those involved, the sexualities of those involved, the level of commitment of those involved, and the kinds of relationships pursued.
>
> Imaged as a form of commitment which is flexible and responsive to the needs and interests of the individuals involved, rather than a rigid institution imposed in cookie cutter fashion on everyone, this new polygamy reflects postmodern critiques of patriarchy, gender, heterosexuality and genetic parenthood. Such a "postmodern polygamy" might occasionally look like traditional patriarchal polygamy, but it differs in important ways. For example, it could as easily encompass one woman with several male partners as it could one man with multiple female partners. It also includes the expanded possibilities created by same-sex or bi-sexual relationships, neither of which is contemplated by traditional polygamy.

No one knows for sure how many polyamorous relationships there are in North America, but some estimates put the figure so high that it might exceed even the most optimistic estimates of fundamentalist Mormon and Islamic polygamy combined (which generally put those numbers, in total, as several hundred thousand). A 2009 *Newsweek* article cited estimates of the number of openly polyamorous families in the United States as exceeding half a million;[26] more speculative figures cited by Anapol put the figure of polyamorists as high as 10 million. Now, one might be suspicious of this figure in that it would include men who simply *wanted* more than one partner at a time (even if, like the "Bachelor Polygamist" Anthony Maitland Stenhouse, they could not actually persuade women to give effect to this ambition); if this is the case, the number might not appear quite so surprising, and it emphasized the difficulty of defining polygamy and polyamory, and the question of where other forms of sexual nonexclusivity fit in to the definitional spectrum, if at all.

I was always concerned about the challenge from the polyamorists, because they generally described a form of relationship, as near as I could gather, that didn't display the same harms that we associated with polygamy, or at least if it did, it wasn't as obvious as it was in other contexts. The problem of the hypothetical "Commercial Drive threesome," as I came to refer to it, became a difficulty which I returned again and again.

Of course, a central question in the discussion would be whether polygamy, if permitted, would manifest as polygyny rather than polyandry. Civil libertarians and some others suggested that Canada's relatively advanced state of gender equality would prevent its spread in its old, patriarchal form, and therefore the "cruel arithmetic" would not necessarily apply. The polyamorists put a slightly more nuanced spin on this, and suggested that if multipartner conjugality were only permitted in contexts of true equality, it would be harmless and even beneficial for women.

In any event, it was not entirely surprising that when the other side's evidence arrived, the five affidavits Ince produced from the polyamory community were focused on polyandrous relationships, where more than one man was sharing the affections of a single woman.

What the affidavits of John Bashinski, Karen Ann Detillieux, Zoe Duff, Forrest Maridas, and Sarah White demonstrated convincingly was that there were at least a few Canadians living lives of multipartner conjugality in ways that bore no resemblance to the patriarchal polygamy in its Islamic or fundamentalist Mormon forms. But despite the fact that they were obviously selected because they depicted relationships with women at the "centre" and were therefore not contributing to even notional female inequality, the CPAA's witnesses didn't reassure me that polyandry would be a common form of polygamy should the restraints be removed.

In fact, many of the relationships in the polyamorists' affidavits would be recognizable to anthropologists studying the phenomenon. The research indicates that polyandry can occur where it is mandated in an environment of scarce resources and limited reproductive opportunities for the men involved. The fact that, where it has been documented elsewhere it is almost always a temporary solution to immediate environmental pressures seemed also consistent with the evidence—and so it was suggestive that, at the time the affidavits were drafted, none of the polyandrous relationships they described had persisted for more than two or three years.

We could, of course, have called the polyamory witnesses for cross-examination, perhaps with a view to demonstrating characteristics of their relationships that would fit them in with anthropological or psychological expectations and place them as "outliers" in the polygamy spectrum. But what would be the point? It would appear like a mean thing to do to people who were being quite courageous in offering their evidence (and indeed it would have been), and at the end of the day, the truly egalitarian, "harmless" polyamorist was someone who we had to deal with, even as a reasonable hypothetical. We decided to simply accept their evidence as given.

There was one interesting wrinkle in the evidence of the CPAA. In addition to direct evidence from their affiants, the polyamorist group introduced the results of a web-based survey that they conducted from 7 April to 7 May 2010, specifically for use in the proceeding. Somewhat surprisingly, the CPAA's survey required respondents to confirm their belief in the principle of gender equality. In other words, the group was pre-screening out of their results anyone in patriarchal polygynous households.

Even with this (perhaps sharply) skewed sample, therefore, it was enlightening that, when multipartner conjugality manifests as either polygyny or polyandry, there were more than three polygynous relationships for every polyandrous one. This didn't really prove anything—the survey was small, the sample was self-selected, and the facts unverified. But nevertheless, the results were intriguing and consistent, or as we had begun to say "convergent," with the totality of the evidence. It appeared that the human inclination to polygyny was bubbling up and asserting itself even among those Canadians who seemed most committed to ideas of gender equality and progressive liberal values.

In any event, it was my hope that the polyamorists' evidence would be of only peripheral interest at the end of the day, because our position was that such relationships were not "marriages" or "conjugal unions" so as to be captured by the polygamy law.

This might seem like an arbitrary distinction—that is, drawing a line between three adults living together, on the one hand, and three adults living together in a "marriage" on the other—but I didn't believe it so. There may be harms that attached to some "polyamorous" relationships that weren't marriages. But in my view, there was something about marriage, about the invocation of some external authority with (even notional) powers of enforcement, that permitted polygamy "take" and spread. As long as polyamorists steered clear of plating their practice with the purported endorsement of a state, or a god, or a vigilant enforcing community, their way would remain isolated and any harms would be essentially localized. At least that was something I was willing to accept as a working hypothesis. Who knows, if polyamory really does take off, and if it caused the same problems as polygamy, perhaps the law would have to be changed to accommodate that new reality. But line drawing, as we would urge the Court, is Parliament's business, and when dealing with a spectrum of risks and harms the line has to be drawn somewhere. Why set a speed limit at 80 km/h instead of 70, or 90? Why make the criminal threshold for drinking drivers .08, when .07 is not much less dangerous and .09 not much more so?

## The Brandeis Brief

Prior to his appointment to the United States Supreme Court, the famous American lawyer and jurist Louis D Brandeis was counsel in a case that involved a challenge to state legislation setting a limit on the maximum hours that women could be made to work.[27] Rather than provide evidence through witnesses or attached to a sworn affidavit, Brandeis appended to his submissions a number of documents with social science data on the employment conditions of working women. This device became known as a Brandeis Brief and since then has become a principal method of proof of "legislative facts" in constitutional cases in the United States and, less often and more controversially, in Canada.

In the Polygamy Reference, the Attorney General submitted scores of articles and other documents as its Brandeis Brief. We attempted to include the bulk of the significant articles and books from the social sciences and legal academia concerning polygamy and related issues. These were supplemented by many more from Canada, the *amicus*, the CPAA, and others, and they formed a foundational reference library upon which the courts, the participants, and the general public could draw for information.[28]

In the end, I'm not sure how much utility there was in the Brandeis Brief materials, because much of the literature on polygamy was also cited within (and sometimes attached to) reports of the experts, and even some lay witnesses referred to or appended their own books on the subject. The judge would not be short of reading material.

## The Bountiful Demographics

Not long after the schedule for evidence exchange had been set, I had asked Wickett to provide me with a rough census of the Bountiful community, so that we might assess how the mathematics of polygamy played out on the ground. Obviously, Wickett's information was limited to the Oler side of the Split, and was based on a rough head count rather than formal census data. Nevertheless, the demographic breakdown Wickett eventually provided to us was interesting (I am reproducing here the table as it appeared in his e-mail to me):

| | |
|---|---|
| Married persons | 115 |
| Unmarried persons 18 or older | 55 (22 females and 33 males) |
| 17 year olds (all unmarried) | 8 (7 females and 1 male) |
| 16 year olds (all unmarried) | 14 (9 females and 5 males) |

Married persons living in monogamy 60

Married persons living in polygamy 55

Of those in polygamy; family of 3 27

Of those in polygamy; family of 4 16

Of those in polygamy; family 5 or more 12

The largest polygamist family is a family of 6.

There are 8 single mothers, 1 single father and 4 unmarried widows.

We didn't expect to find any direct evidence of children being married, as we understood that the practice of underage marriage had been halted several years previously (and indeed it was far from certain that *any* FLDS marriages had occurred since Warren Jeffs's capture and imprisonment), and so we expected that any "child brides" in the community would now be adults. Nevertheless, Henrich crunched the numbers, and made some observations.

Henrich noted that the percentage of men who are polygynous is 33 percent, making the Bountiful FLDS a "highly polygynous" community by global and historical standards. He said that, of the 147 ethnographically and historically known polygynous societies that have been sufficiently quantified by anthropologists in the Standard Cross-Cultural Sample, Bountiful is at the 83rd percentile. This means that only 17 percent of the 147 independent human communities for which there is sufficient anthropological data have a higher percentage of polygynously marrying males.

Most interesting, though, was the imbalance between the numbers of men and women. Henrich wrote in a supplementary report:

> Thirty percent of the adult men appear to be missing, or alternatively females have entered the community from elsewhere at a greater rate than males. This expected imbalance can even be observed among 16 and 17 year olds, where there are 2.7 times as many females as males. Despite the gender imbalance, 34% of men age 18 and up are unmarried while only 5.8% of women over 18 are unmarried.

The fact that Bountiful FLDS showed both sides of the "cruel arithmetic"—both an excess of unmarried men *and* an overall gender imbalance (suggestive of the expulsion of men and boys, or the recruitment of females from either outside the community or from among children) was expected, but nevertheless compelling. It was a small but important window on polygamy in practice, and it provided a demographic backdrop against which the individual evidence that would emerge—of child brides, lost boys, and human trafficking—would play out.

# PART 5
# Trial Diary

## Opening the Case

The trial of the Polygamy Reference began, incredibly, on schedule, the day the Chief Justice had set: Monday, 22 November 2010. I recounted at the beginning of this book that, on that morning, Bauman heard and rejected an application by the CBC to video-broadcast the proceedings. The balance of the week would be consumed with opening statements, led off by the Attorneys General and their allies.

The crowd in Courtroom 55 would thin as the days progressed (trials are never quite as exciting as we are led to believe), but the level of public interest nevertheless remained very high, and details of the opening statements were reported in all the major media from local papers to the BBC.

My opening was by far the longest, because the Attorney General had "carriage" of the reference and I needed to explain the legal basis for the proceeding and a bit of the historical background of the case. Bevan thought that we needed to confront head on the Attorney General's reversal of position on the constitutionality of section 293. I had taken her advice, and walked the Court through the evolution of thought on the subject since the Attorney General had announced in 1992 that the law could not withstand *Charter* scrutiny. It was an opportunity to show that, although we might start from the civil libertarian position and hive off "good" from "bad" polygamy, the simple fact of the social harms forced us to reconsider and rethink. This was an important point to make: Macintosh, the *amicus*, was expected to counter our social harm evidence by saying that we developed it just for this reference, that it was in fact an afterthought. We had to show that we didn't have a position in need of evidence; we had a position that had been mandated by the evidence we had developed. So, after outlining the Attorney General's 1992 and 2002 statements that the law was unconstitutional, I said:

Yet before you now, the Attorney will be arguing that the section is constitutionally sound, and that in fact resort to redrafting, reading down or reading in is not necessary. This represents—and there is no way to minimize this—a wholesale reversal of the Attorney's 1992 position. The Court may legitimately ask: why has this come about?

There is no doubt that one reason is the evolution of *Charter* jurisprudence, and in particular the notion that the *Charter* is a document that does more than ensure the rights of citizens against the state, but balances important competing rights of various groups in the equation. That's one reason.

But far more important in the analysis is the evolution of the Attorney's understanding of the harms associated with polygamy.

The opening statement set out the framework of our case and focused on the question of polygamy's harms and how we expected to prove them. In the Attorney General's theory, polygamy would inevitably lead to the earlier sexualization of young girls and other social problems. There were a number of important themes that I wanted to leave in Bauman's mind as we went through the evidence.

In any litigation, one side or the other has the advantage of inertia (or, to look at it more dynamically, of momentum). As wedded as we are to the idea of the judge as impartial arbiter, and as much as any judge struggles to be open minded and fair, a lawyer would be foolish to ignore the starting, or default, position of the Court. The law assigns various burdens of proof to different issues, but there is an unwritten, overall burden, based on the judge's basic views. Is the judge starting from the position that the polygamy law is "bad," or that it is "good"? Who will bear the burden of shifting him from the default stance?

Judges are by nature conservative, for good reasons. The natural inclination is to not make a decision that will have far-reaching and unknown ramifications. So among the first things I said when my argument had begun was this:

> The challengers urge the court to make Canada the only Western nation to decriminalize polygamy.

I paused and then repeated this sentence for emphasis, and then moved on to describe the challenge and our position. I summarized the central issues as three: purpose, harm, and interpretation, but focused the bulk of my opening submissions on what we expected to show of harm. In our view, the harms from polygamy were universal, and Bountiful served as a useful exemplar of what would happen if polygamy were to take off in a given society. Because, I said, the things we saw at Bountiful—the tight constraints on girls and women, the sexual targeting of adolescents, the lost boy phenomenon—were not just random associations with polygamy; they were the consequences of it. I said:

> The Court will hear from the challengers that, if there are problems at Bountiful, they are problems arising from the insular, rigid, patriarchal, inegalitarian and isolated community. They will even suggest that criminalization itself causes, or at least exacerbates, these inclinations. They will say we don't need to worry about harmful polygamy taking root elsewhere in Canada because it only arises in this kind of environment, and how many Bountifuls can there be? But this misses the point.

As a matter of logic, science, and as a historical fact, one conclusion clearly emerges:

Bountiful did not create polygamy; *polygamy created Bountiful*.

Deb Strachan opened Canada's submissions after me. She spent some time explaining Canada's interpretation of section 293, an interpretation which I thought was strained but from which Canada simply could not be moved. In their view, "polygamy" in the first subsection of 293 meant only multiple marriages that were legal where they originated, while "conjugal union" in the second subsection referred to marriage-like relationships but nevertheless ones that still required a ceremony or formalization of some sort. By their definition, the Mormons of 1890, Blackmore and Oler, and many, if not most, of the Muslim men with more than one wife were not practising polygamy under the *Criminal Code*. I could not see how the definition could be sustained, even on the wording of the *Code* itself, which seemed to make clear that the sanction applied regardless of whether there had been any rite or ceremony, and regardless of whether the polygamy or conjugal union was recognized by law. But I had by then learned that Canada's system of litigation supervision was so cumbersome (each position taken had to be approved by the legal team, two committees, and sometimes by officials at the top of the justice department and government) that, at this late stage, resistance, as they say on *Star Trek*, would be futile.

After our "allied" participants had each given their brief openings, the *amicus* began his, making the argument we had been anticipating— the argument that, were we in his position, we would have made. This was followed by those Interested Persons (IPs) aligned against section 293. By noon Thursday, we were done the openings.

The media coverage that week was extensive. As is usual for a government lawyer, I declined to give any interviews, and the Attorney General was saying little through his spokespeople. Even so, the opening statements were widely reported in the *Sun, Province, Globe and Mail,* and by multimedia organizations from the CBC to BBC. My name and photograph, along with those of other lawyers involved, appeared in a number of stories. The *Sun* even had "bio" pages on me, Strachan, and Macintosh. Mine had information culled from my CV and (it seems) from my Facebook page. The photos show me dour, tired, and awkward, and I resolved to avoid posing for pictures in the future.

All this coverage meant that everywhere I went people wanted to talk about the case and give their thoughts on the correct outcome. This was actually very helpful to me; I learned to summarize our arguments and our responses to the various immediate objections, more concisely. It was as if every reception, dinner, or lunch I attended gave me an opportunity to rehearse some aspect of our case. My wife just rolled her eyes at my resurgent public presence, such as it was; she'd been around the block before with high-profile, prolonged litigation. "Here we go again," she said in late October. "See you in February."

# Round One: December 2010

## *The Ground Rules*

The shape of the proceeding had been determined through a series of pre-trial conferences and hearings. It would look something like a trial: the lawyers would be gowned, and each party would present its case. However, we wouldn't do so in the traditional way, with one side presenting all its witnesses and then the other. Rather, it was modelled more closely on a public inquiry, with witnesses being scheduled according mainly to their subject area and, within some rough categories, their availability. Almost all of them were from out of town, and many were from out of the country. Zaltz took charge of scheduling them all in the two-and-a-half-month window the Chief Justice had designated.

We did propose that the witnesses appear in two broad phases: in the first, which would consume the month before Christmas, the focus would be on expert evidence; in the second, we would have live examinations of lay witnesses who had had personal experience with polygamy. We planned to play the video affidavits (of those witnesses we had decided not to call to testify live) throughout the hearing, as openings in the schedule permitted. To permit counsel and the Chief Justice to attend to other matters over the long period of trial, we aimed for four days of trial each week.

As I mentioned earlier, each witness, whether expert or lay, was expected to put in his or her evidence through an affidavit, and then a subset of these witnesses would be called to testify, either because the participant putting them forward thought they would be more effective in person, or because there was a need of another participant to cross-examine them. This idea was Macintosh's, put forward in the expectation that it would both focus the evidence and shorten the hearings. It proved to be a very effective plan, and provided a lot of flexibility for some "horse trading" among the participants in the interest of expediency, without sacrificing the evidentiary record.

## Angela Campbell

The first witness to appear was presented by the *amicus* as an expert: Angela Campbell. You may recall Campbell as the law professor who had done "field research" in Bountiful and had emerged since 2005 as Canada's leading academic expert on the community.

Campbell had authored one of four parts of a Status of Women Canada report on polygamy in 2005. In the course of her research and writing, she had become concerned, she said, that too little attention was being paid to the actual experiences of women with polygamy, particularly at Bountiful. Her overall point was that women's lives in the polygamous sect weren't either all that bad or all that different.

Since 2005, Campbell had spent a few days in Bountiful doing interviews and focus group sessions with a handful of women, all but one of them on the Blackmore side of the Split. She also had ongoing correspondence with members of this group. With this small and almost certainly unrepresentative sample she employed what she called "qualitative research" to extrapolate conclusions about what "the women of Bountiful" thought of their lot in life. Her conclusions were essentially that the polygamist wives of Bountiful were surprisingly modern, empowered, free, and happy. But she went much further and also made a number of conclusions that seemed overreaching given the shallowness of her inquiry. She suggested, for instance, that the lost boys phenomenon was unsupported, that teen marriage, while it may have occurred "historically," was a thing of the past, and so on. It appeared that she was saying all that she could to suggest that Bountiful wasn't bad, just different, and that it was our own ignorance and prejudice that led us to condemn the polygamy practised there. Her writings were music to the ears of the FLDS and *amicus*, and we weren't surprised when, in the first exchange of evidence in the summer, Campbell's affidavit was among those proffered.

It was hard to take Campbell's findings too seriously. How is a law professor in any better position to make ethnographic conclusions than anyone else with a few days' exposure to the community? We wrote to the *amicus* before the trial and asked exactly in what field Campbell was an "expert." The answer came:

> We intend to qualify her as a witness entitled to give opinion evidence, as a legal scholar and qualitative researcher, addressing the interface between the practice of polygamy and the legal prohibition against polygamy, with emphasis on the polygamous communities in Bountiful, BC.

It seemed clear that, as ethnographic fieldwork, Campbell's effort was lightweight and superficial; most anthropologists or others engaged in ethnography would spend months or years in a community before they could pretend to speak confidently about the beliefs or practices there. What could anyone really learn in twelve days?

Under gentle cross-examination by Samuels and Greathead, it became apparent that Campbell had spent even less time in Bountiful than the twelve days that she initially described; two days of her first five-day trip, she confirmed, had been spent in travel from the East, and activities outside Bountiful. Moreover, she freely admitted that she hadn't asked the most basic questions that would ensure the representativeness of her sample. And even though the transcripts of her interviews had been produced to us in anonymous, redacted form (with the originals held under seal by the court), it seemed quite plain from the information revealed that a least half of her study participants were wives of one man, Winston Blackmore. Samuels suggested, and Campbell accepted, that Bountiful was a patriarchal community with "a reputation for deception," but also that she hadn't asked any of the women whether their husbands or senior males in the community had put them up to speaking to her (because she thought that would be "insulting" to them). She offered views about various harms related to polygamy, such as the lost boys, while noting that she had asked no questions on the point. In all, it seemed that Campbell was far more interested in learning about the negative effects of prohibition than exploring any negative effects of polygamy itself.

When Samuels and Greathead were done, Craig Cameron, for the Attorney General of Canada, took a turn, disputing that Campbell was even a qualified "legal scholar." He said:

> My Lord, I don't know that you would have anyone who would be able to reliably or consistently tell you the ambit of what a legal scholar is or is not an expert in, other than something that relates in some manner to the law.

Bauman clearly had thought this had gone on long enough, and offered his own definition of "legal scholar": "How about anybody who went to Harvard?"

I couldn't resist piping up from where I sat in the jury box: I had the same degree as Campbell did, having finished at Harvard a year after her. "I'll agree with that," I said. Cameron looked back at me and grinned: "I'll take no position."

Despite these questions around her method and expertise, Campbell was qualified as an expert. It was clear by this point that the Chief Justice was of the view that a liberal position on admissibility of evidence would be taken and that any frailties in Campbell's evidence would go to weight. Fair enough. It was now time to question Campbell on the merits of her observations and conclusions.

When I took over the cross-examination of Campbell on the second day, I wanted to move away from the criticism of her methods and get her views on some of the important aspects of the case.

In fact Campbell had some serious gaps in her knowledge. She had sworn in her affidavit that the "allegations of systemic child abuse" at YFZ had been "unfounded," something she confirmed under cross-examination as her own opinion; she revealed that she was completely unaware that seven men from YFZ had by then been convicted of child rape (in fact she contested that from the stand, insisting that there had been no convictions for anything but bigamy); she was vaguely aware of "ongoing allegations," but that was it.

The 2008 raid of the YFZ compound is something of a crucible in FLDS lore. The characterization of the raid as a heavy-handed over-reaction of the state authorities is, along with the Short Creek raid of 1953, a pillar of the Church's persecution myth. So was the denial of any systematic child abuse at YFZ. The fact that the myth was so readily and uncritically accepted by the scholarly advocates of decriminalization was deeply disturbing. It was almost like holocaust denial among some revisionist historians. Why hadn't these people done their homework? Does "qualitative research" mean you just ignore the facts?

But I wanted to go fairly gingerly with Campbell because I thought she could be useful to us and there was no sense in completely undermining her credibility. Despite the obvious weaknesses in her work, she was an honest and forthcoming witness and had thought carefully for a number of years about the harms associated with polygamy, so I believed she could offer some things of value even if her characterization of the views of the women of Bountiful and her understanding of the facts of recent history were to be treated with caution.

One of the challenges facing us in the reference was our proposed introduction of some objective *quantitative* evidence regarding Bountiful. We had received, late in the day, birth registration records from BC Vital Statistics that showed at least eighty-two births to teen mothers from Bountiful, many of whom came to Canada from the polygamist communities run by the FLDS in the United States (we knew this because the mother's place of birth was listed on the records). We had also developed a comprehensive analysis of the bleak educational outcomes for the students of Bountiful's two schools, Bountiful Elementary and Secondary School (BESS) and Mormon Hills. But we were now in the middle of trial, and expected the introduction of this evidence to be contentious. It would help, I thought, if the *amicus*'s own expert would agree that the admission of such evidence would be of assistance to the Court.

I asked Campbell to agree with me about some of the major harms that had been associated with polygamy, such as child brides, lost boys, inequality of women and girls, and so on. She agreed that these things had been noted in the literature as correlated with polygamy. Then I suggested that it would be very useful to have data from Vital Statistics (in the form of birth registration records) or the Ministry of Education (tracking dropout rates, graduation figures, and postsecondary education statistics). She agreed that these would be very useful in assessing the harms associated with polygamy in Bountiful. With that endorsement in hand, I moved on.

Part of the *amicus*'s argument was that the criminalization of polygamy simply drove groups like the FLDS to be more insular and isolated. So I was struck when Campbell described under direct examination that, in recent years, the criminal prohibition had been increasingly on people's minds at Bountiful, that some women reported not even knowing in their early years that polygamy was illegal. Now, she suggested, the criminal law was weighing more heavily on the residents' minds, and guiding their behaviour. So on cross-examination I had Campbell take us through a brief history of Bountiful and the FLDS, and she accepted that, after its 1947 founding, Bountiful had been insular to the point where its residents had been instructed not to speak with outsiders. She then acknowledged that this was no longer the case, and that, at least since the Split of 2002, insularity had *decreased*. So I put it plainly to her on cross-examination, asking her to agree with me that insularity had actually diminished, not increased, with awareness of the criminal prohibition. She did. In fact, she admitted that, while she believed that the practice of underage marriage had virtually ceased on the Blackmore side of the Split since 2002, she had no reason to believe that plural marriage had not also stopped, and that she was not aware of *any* polygamous wedding at Bountiful since 2002.

Finally I asked Campbell to consider Henrich's assertion that child brides were an inevitable consequence of the mathematics of polygamy. She admitted that she had never considered the possibility in her previous work, but, with a little prompting, accepted all the principal points of Henrich's analysis.

Q The argument with respect to child brides is that the—is that polygamy requires more women than men and that in order to increase the market of available women there is an inevitable downward pressure on the age at which girls are targeted for sexual relationships with men.

A M'mm-hmm.

Q You understand the theory?

A Yeah.

Q My question?

A The theory being that, just to clarify, the theory being that in order for polygamy to work out, numbers have to be unequal and the ages of wives have to sink?

Q Right. Now, if you had that theory?

A M'mm-hmm.

Q And if you had information that cross-culturally around the world, using appropriate analyses, polygamy in society correlated with the youth of brides, would you consider that to be associated with polygamy, that should be of concern?

A I would.

Q You would. And this would be a concern, wouldn't it, regardless of whether all of the polygamists married thirty year olds?

A I'm not sure how that would be as much of a concern. If individuals were adults who consent, so there you're talking about specific incidents rather than statistical trends.

Q The theory is both polygamists and monogamists draw from the same available spouses.

A Yeah.

Q Because some men have more than one spouse the pool has to be increased with younger and younger girls both for polygamists and monogamists; would you agree to that?

A The age thing. Why younger and younger?

Q If you need to increase the pool where else would you go?

A Right. So the pool increases by virtue of having this greater number of available adolescent girls?

Q Right.

A Okay.

Q So to get back to the question, that would be true?

A M'mm-hmm.

Q Whether or not the polygamists themselves were marrying of-age girls or underage girls?

A Does the concern subsist even if this happens—with polygamy the marriages happen at the age of thirty?

Q Exactly.

A Yes.

Q Have you ever considered that harm as part of your weighing in the balance the harms of polygamy versus the prohibition?

A No.

Q You have considered, though, the other end of the mathematical problem, which is the unmarried or unmarriageable males—the lost boys in the Bountiful context—you have read about that?

A Yes.

Q And you've thought about that?

A Yes.

Q Are you aware of the literature in the international social sciences that suggests that a gender imbalance, particularly among young people, is correlated and, in fact—let me ask it this way, correlated with increased antisocial behaviour and crime?

A No.

Q You're not aware of the studies with respect to the outcomes of the one-child policy in China, for instance?

She shook her head again. I continued:

Q  You haven't been following that. If it was true that a gender imbalance of unmarried young people in favour of males—unmarried males—was correlated with increases in antisocial behaviour and crime, you would agree that that would be a concern with respect to polygamy because it creates that?

A  If it's shown it creates the imbalance and if it's shown that it leads to these adverse outcomes you've named, then that would be a concern to be reckoned with.

Cross-examination almost never yields the Perry Mason "aha!" moments from television and the movies. But that isn't the purpose, at least not with expert witnesses. As with Campbell, if your case is correct and the witness honest, you—and the judge—can only benefit if you engage the expert in a conversation and allow her to make your points for you, or at least agree with them. This was as close to a Perry Mason moment as I could hope to get.

Eliciting helpful information from the other side's experts is important because judges have a natural difficulty deciding points where expert opinion diverges. The very fact that expert opinion is allowed on a given subject means that the court has decided it needs the assistance of persons more knowledgeable than it is; therefore, it's a conundrum if the experts tell you very different things. So, as a lawyer, if you can make a point while saying "and both sides' experts agree that . . ." you are in a much better position.

And Campbell had connected some important dots. She accepted the plausibility of our theory on its central points; she had acknowledged that the harms that would flow would be significant matters "to be reckoned with," and she confirmed that she had never considered the questions previously in her research. This last point was important because Campbell was simply at the vanguard of academics who agitated for decriminalization, and it was all but an admission that, when they had done so they were weighing an incomplete set of harms.

So by the end of Campbell's cross-examination I was feeling very good about our case. Our most novel and vulnerable assertions had been at least conditionally accepted and even embraced, in theory, by the other side's principal expert. I had the feeling, that Wednesday afternoon, that Campbell had handed us momentum.

## Lawrence Beall

The next witness in that second week was one of our experts, Dr Lawrence Beall. Beall was a clinical psychologist from Utah with an expertise in post-trauma counselling. Among his more than 4,500 patients had been a number of escapees from American fundamentalist polygamous communities, whom he termed "survivors." Beall had testified in over forty American cases related to polygamous communities, including five high-profile prosecutions of FLDS leaders. Our team of Greathead, Horsman, and Ross had learned about him in their research on the American cases and had made contact when they visited Utah to gather video affidavits. I had a few concerns about Beall in the early days, having never met him. Would he come across as too much of a crusader or advocate? Would he be defensive, appear shifty or unconvincing on the stand? I wasn't very reassured when I saw some of Beall's writing, which I found to be difficult. Greathead and Horsman, however, assured me that Beall was going to be good, so his affidavit, sworn in Utah and couriered to us in Vancouver, was filed with the Court in July.

To put it mildly, I needn't have worried about Greathead and Horsman's judgment in recruiting Beall. No question, he had strong feelings about what he had learned about the FLDS, its "sexual grooming" of young women, and expulsion of young men. He described the Church's "caste system" whereby a few privileged families accumulated wealth and wives at the expense of the majority and the common symptoms he observed in the victims he treated, including a presentation that he described as "robotic." But far from being a wild-eyed antipolygamy activist, under direct examination by Horsman, who displayed very good instincts for when to switch into and out of "leading" questions, Beall presented what he had learned about polygamy in practice in a way that was calm, matter of fact, and devastating.

So far, so good. But how would he hold up under cross-examination?

Again, I needn't have worried. Efforts by Wickett for the FLDS to cross-examine Beall just seemed to make things worse for them. Beall was questioned about his own religious beliefs (Beall is Mormon). This took us all by surprise. In fact, Horsman and Greathead had assured Beall that, while American lawyers might have tried to make some hay by invoking his personal religious beliefs, that sort of thing just wouldn't wash in a Canadian courtroom. And as predicted, that line of questioning went nowhere fast.

Wickett also tried to suggest to Beall that he used the discredited technique of hypnosis to "recover" fictional memories of abuse from his patients. Wickett based his questioning on an account from the popular literature (*Lost Boy* by Brent Jeffs) in support. As it turned out, Beall had never treated Jeffs (it seems that Jeffs got the name wrong in his book). And as to the suggestion that Beall's data was tainted by hypnosis? This was the exchange:

Q Did you use—did you utilize hypnosis on any of your patients?

A No.

Aha. Here Wickett may have thought that he'd heard a dishonest answer. So it was time to build up the tension.

Q And I'll come back to this in just a moment. The recovery of memory through hypnosis is a very controversial area. Correct?

A I don't even consider it controversial. I think it is unethical.

By this point, Wickett must have been thinking that something was awry—could Beall just have admitted that one of his practices was *unethical*? Nevertheless, he pressed on:

Q And it's your evidence that you didn't hypnotize any of your patients?

A No, I do not—I'm adamantly against it and I've even taught on the unethical nature of retrieving memories through hypnosis. I do not do that.

Maybe thinking he had Beall cornered (but no doubt perplexed by Beall's answers which seemed just too easy), Wickett confronted Beall with Jeffs's statement that he had recovered his memories of abuse in the course of a couple of hypnosis sessions with a "Dr Larry Beale." Beall said that he'd seen Jeffs's video (it was among the Attorney General of BC's video affidavits that Beall had reviewed in preparation for the trial). So Wickett phrased his question so as to presuppose that client confidentiality would prevent Beall from answering it.

Q He's a witness in this case and in his book he speaks about his treatment by you. You know what, Doctor, I'm not even going to ask you because I expect you're going to tell me that even if it's in the book you don't want to be talking about one of your patients?

A That's not my answer.

Q I'm sorry?

A I did not treat him.

Q You did not treat him?

A I did not.

It is a popularly stated "rule" of cross-examination that you don't ask a question to which you don't know the answer. For reasons probably already apparent, I personally don't think that's a very good rule, at least with respect to experts and other witnesses you expect will answer forthrightly. But the above exchange between Wickett and Beall reveals that, even if you *think* you know the answer, you could be wrong, and one can't put too much stock in the answer you expect to get.[1]

At another point in the cross-examination, Wickett challenged Beall to admit that he wouldn't provide his clinical records to the Court. It seemed that the FLDS wanted to make Beall's evidence appear unfair and unreliable, because Beall summarized his findings with respect to the women he had treated without revealing their identities or clinical records. This would be a bit of an ironic position for the Church to take, given that they had argued that some of their own witnesses should be anonymous and testify behind a screen. In any event, it seemed to be where they were heading. Beall phrased his responses slowly and carefully, and the answer was so good that it was almost as if Wickett had strapped on a suicide-bomber's vest and invited Beall to pull the cord:

A   No, if those [the patients' clinical records] were requested they would not be produced.

Q   Even if ordered by the Court?

Wickett was a good trial lawyer, and he understood that one of the most powerful techniques of cross-examination is to align the judge against the witness, rather than taking on the role of antagonist himself. So, for instance, if one wishes to challenge a witness on a fact, it is often better to say "Are you seriously telling his Lordship that . . ." instead of "Are you seriously telling me that . . ." This is not so much to curry favour with the judge as much as to impress on the witness that his evidence is for the court, not simply for the sake of argument. I have noticed this technique among the best trial lawyers, and if there are confrontations required in my own cross-examinations it is a method I am quick to employ. In his present question, Wickett seemed to be using a variation on this idea.

Beall began his response by saying: "If I may?" He had established this as his polite way of signalling that he was going to answer the question with more than a yes or no, that it required some fuller explanation. He then paused and pursed his lips before continuing:

> When these women came to work with me . . . *they were very afraid.* Some of them . . . *feared for their lives.* I had to guarantee to them I would protect their privacy, and under no conditions would I disclose them, *and I will keep that promise.*

The answer was chilling. Beall would rather go to jail than expose his patients to harm—possibly even murder—at the hands of members of the FLDS, Wickett's own client. Could anyone hearing that doubt that Beall was convinced the threat was real? This moved the project of dismantling the FLDS out of the realm of just good policy, and suggested that it may be a matter of life and death.

What do you say to an answer like that? Wickett, deciding that discretion was the better part of valour, opted for retreat:

Q Okay. Thank you, that's a very straightforward and honest answer.

Day three to us, and the week was over. We had the momentum, but there was much to do. The next week would see some "high-level" expert testimony—Drs Grossbard and Wu. This would then culminate with testimony from Henrich, upon whose analysis almost every aspect of our social harm case depended. If Henrich survived, if the Court accepted what he had to say, I believed our case for the social harms of polygamy would be almost unassailable.

## Shoshanna Grossbard and Zheng Wu

Shoshanna Grossbard is a professor of economics at the State University of San Diego. She had been studying the political and family economics of polygamy for thirty years and developed strong views on its effects on women around the world. She was put forward by the Christian Legal Fellowship, an intervening group represented by the noted Alberta lawyer Gerry Chipeur, whom I knew from my early days representing a group of Catholic UBC students in a free-speech case as someone with a commitment to religious causes before the courts.

Grossbard's affidavit set out many of the harms "associated" with polygamy, but could not go the step further and establish a real causal link:

G. Concluding Assessment

(a) In the cultures and societies worldwide that have embraced it, polygamy is associated with undesirable economic, societal, physical, and emotional factors related to women's wellbeing. The natural economic consequence of polygamy is increased market value for women, though the women themselves do not realize the economic benefit of their greater value. Rather, women tend to be treated more like commodities in polygamous societies, and their freedom to manage their own economic circumstance and destiny is reduced. This loss of control by women in polygamous civilizations is seen in the early and arranged marriages, which are so prevalent, along with the practice of paying a brideprice. Easy exits from marriage by the way of simple divorce proceedings add to women's undesirable circumstances observed in polygamous societies. The physical and emotional distress associated with the polygamy way of life is no less devastating.

. . .

(d)  It has not been proven scientifically that the association observed between polygamy and any of the undesirable individual social features mentioned above is caused by the institution of polygamy. Nevertheless, the list of undesirable social features is so long that it is hard to escape the conclusion that some of these results are caused by the institution of polygamy. If only part of the undesirable results mentioned above will follow from the legalization of polygamy in Canada, it is sufficient reason to strongly oppose a legalized polygamy that may cause significant harm to women, children, and the men who love them. Furthermore, men may suffer undesirable consequences as increased competition for women may increase the number of involuntarily unmarried men.

Because her affidavit really didn't break any new ground, and in particular it didn't establish any caused harms, I hadn't expected much from her testimony, despite her impressive credentials and experience in the field. And at first she was as I expected. Just as her affidavit had been brief and rather superficial, her direct evidence might be described as mechanical. But under cross-examination, Grossbard seemed to come alive, and every question from Tim Dickson, Macintosh's junior co-counsel, became an opportunity for her to show her depth of knowledge and the sincerity and authority of her conclusions that polygamy caused a variety of harms, to its participants and more generally.

Grossbard revealed that she had come to her views against polygamy only with great reluctance. She had begun decades before, she explained, from the typical "free market" position of the Chicago School, which held that polygamy could be good for women because it increased their value and permitted them more choice of arrangements. Over time and with intense study, she had come to realize that women could never "capture" their increased value in polygamous societies because men would exploit all the institutions that they controlled to commodify and "profit" from the women's enhanced position.

Grossbard made a number of points that no one else did. Most revealing to me was her assertion that, as a political economist, you could measure polygamy's offensiveness to women's interests by the amount of investment women around the world committed to eradicating it. She gave as examples the nineteenth-century American suffragettes, who made eschewing polygamy a condition of membership for Utah (that is, Mormon) women, all the way to the just-released report of the Quebec Status of Women organization. If polygamy did not harm women and if there was no reason to fear its spread if decriminalized, Grossbard reasoned, why was this prominent organization dedicating its resources, and 150 pages, to dire warnings of the practice? Not a bad point.

Grossbard was followed by Dr Zheng Wu, a demographer and expert on marriage patterns in Canada. Wu had prepared two reports for the *amicus* citing a host of statistics revealing rates of marriage, cohabitation, and so on. His main theme seemed to be that marriage was waning, cohabitation gaining, and that it all evolved over time. I confess that for the life of me I hadn't been able to comprehend the relevance of Wu's affidavits until I read the *amicus*'s opening statement. There, he said (at para 45):

> Within the Canadian population, polygamy is statistically almost non-existent. The pool of unmarried men that already exists in Canada is many times greater than the populations of all the polygamous communities in Canada combined. Any "pool of unmarried men" that might realistically be created through polygamy is statistically meaningless.

But Wu had not provided evidence on these points. I worried that Macintosh was going to wait until final arguments, and then try to use Wu's data for the proposition that the impact on society of decriminalization would be small, absorbed by the already large pool of single folks in Canada. It was a tricky strategy—he didn't have any evidence really on that point, and hadn't put forward an expert. He was just going to try to connect the dots when summing it all up. Wu would say "two" and "two," and I expected that Macintosh would say "four" (or perhaps, "five" or "six").

My suspicions that this was the tactic seemed confirmed the night before Wu's testimony, when the *amicus* sent us a two-page spreadsheet listing the numbers of single men and women in Canada, broken down by age. The figures showed that, in every age category from adolescence to retirement age, single men outnumbered single women by a significant margin. In other words, there was already a pool of excess unmarried men, hundreds of thousands of them. How could a little polygamy hurt?

To head Macintosh off at the pass, I decided to simply put the question directly to Wu, who had already established himself as an honest, neutral, and sincere expert witness. I read him the *amicus*'s paragraph 45, and then just asked him whether he could offer evidence to support what Macintosh was saying. Sentence by sentence, Wu carefully confirmed that he had no evidence to support the *amicus*'s contention.

In any event, Wu's document indicating that there was *already* an imbalance in the gender ratios of single men and women in the Canadian population did not, to my mind, assist the *amicus*, and in fact did the opposite: it meant that there could be *no* absorption effect, as there might be if there were a greater number of women, which Henrich would point out when the document was put to him in examination in chief.

The next morning I bumped into Don Brenner, the former Chief Justice of the Supreme Court and now a very busy legal consultant and mediator. Brenner often took an interest in my cases, and stopped by my table in Glass City, the Hornby Street café we both frequented for breakfast. I brought him up to speed on that week's evidence, and that I felt the experts from the other side had ended up as our witnesses. "Always nice when you can do that," he said.

"Well, if they're honest and I'm right, they'll say so," I suggested.

"Right," said Brenner, and wished me luck.

## The Survivors' Videos

On Day 10, we started playing Greathead's video affidavits, which she, Horsman, and Ross had gathered from witnesses in BC and throughout the Western United States. They would be the first "personal" evidence heard by the Court, and we led off with one of the most emotionally wrenching stories, that of Rowena (Rena) Mackert, a now middle-aged survivor of the FLDS community at Short Creek, where she had been subject to horrendous sexual abuse from the age of three. Mackert's pedophilic father had been one of the men arrested in the 1953 Short Creek raid. Thanks to the intervention of *Life* magazine, which held him up as a victim of an overreactive state, Rena and her sixteen sisters had been returned to their predatory father by apologetic bureaucrats.

Our point in putting in so many of the survivors' stories was to show, again and again, how the harms predicted and described by the experts in fairly dry, academic terms played out "on the ground" in a polygamous community. It was one thing to hear Henrich talk about "diminished paternal investment in offspring." It was quite another to hear Sarah Hammon describe her upbringing in a house with thirty siblings and a father who didn't know her name or which of his nineteen wives was her mother. Or to hear Mary Mackert describe the frustration of watching the loneliness of her own children in their father's absence.

Similar points could be, and were, made with respect to all the other harms invoked by the experts. Child brides were not simply a phenomenon of Muslim countries and sub-Saharan Africa, according to Susie Barlow, who had married her fifty-one-year-old husband at sixteen, or

Carolyn Jessop, married at eighteen to a man of fifty. Mackert recalled the circumstances of being married to an older stepbrother:

Q  Can you tell us about your marriage, how it came about and how you found out about it?

A  Okay. My father's fourth wife he married when I was 13 and she had a son that was 16. John and I hated each other. It was very clear. Everyone knew. At 3 o'clock in the morning on a Saturday morning—Sunday morning, actually. Saturday night was priesthood meeting for the men. And father got home from it and hours later my mother and he came to my bedroom, woke me up and told me that Uncle Leroy—Leroy Johnson had had a revelation and that I was getting married. I sat there stunned. I didn't want to get married. I just wanted out.

Q  How old were you?

A  I was 17. My father—my mother asked don't you want to know who you're supposed to marry, or who you're marrying, and I kind of looked in disbelief, you know, I really didn't want to know. Told me John, and John who, and I'm running down the list of all the Johns that I know and my father said Swaney and it was like a knife was stabbed through my heart. There was no love lost between the two of us. I was really headstrong and he was too.

I didn't get any sleep that night. The next day everyone went to church and I stayed home with John's mother and she rummaged through material to find something to make a wedding dress, and she and I spent Sunday afternoon and Monday morning making my wedding dress. . . . John got home from church probably about 5 o'clock in the afternoon, so I had been up for about 14 hours. And father called everyone down to the living room and told them that we were getting married. We got married the next afternoon.

Sometimes the "convergence" between the high-level expert evidence and the personal testimony was explicit. Sarah Hammon had obviously been thinking about polygamy's cruel arithmetic for a lot longer than I had, and the transcript of her video affidavit neatly described the results:

A  Any time you have a closed society living in polygamy you're going to go through these phases of lost boys and child brides. It's going to have to happen in order to maintain polygamy. You either go towards monogamy or you go through these phases, and I don't see it how it goes any other way. Because if one man has three wives there's two men who have none, and that's just what is going to happen. And, you know, girls and boys of the age that they start developing normal healthy relationships at 15, 16, 17 years old and start learning to relate to each other, the boys you know they can't—it's hands off because this girl might belong—potentially belong to a 50-year-old man, and the girls the same thing. I can't be friends with him because I might get placed with somebody else and that is just going to break my heart. They never—not only are they told not to do it but they just—they never can anyway because it's just impossible to develop those relationships because they know they're a dead end.

Q  And what happens with the boys, the ones that—that can't get wives?

A  They end up—you know, I have a theory that even before they know—even before they become a lost boy as a group, lost boys as a group, that they have this sense already there is not going to be a partner for me. There will be no partner for me. This guy has five wives, this guy has seven, this guy has eleven.

Q  And can they exist in your community without a partner?

A  What normal man would want to? No, there's not an excess of single men in the community. They have to leave, and how devastating. And that's another thing that so many people think the women are the victims, but there's victims everywhere. There's a mesh of victims of this because the men have been taught since they were little boys that in order to go to heaven they have to have three wives. So here is a man that is damned just because of bad math.

Q  Right. Right.

A  How heartbreaking. How heartbreaking for these guys, you know, they have done nothing wrong except for believe this thing that their parents, the people that they trust most, have taught them. And they're going to hell because of bad math. It's wrong.

As I said, our idea was to play video affidavits to fill gaps in the schedule of live witnesses, rather than all at once in a block, and I think this was a very useful device, because it never let the proceedings get too remote from the stories of the real people who had lived through the harms about which the experts were debating. If ever the discussion felt as if it was becoming too dry and academic, then the videotaped voices of Mary, Rena, and Howard Mackert, Carolyn Jessop, Sarah Hammon, Susie Barlow, Brent Jeffs, Teresa Wall, Paula Barrett, Richard Ream, Don Fisher, and Jorjina Broadbent were there, ready to refocus the attention of the court from the war in the air back to the carnage in the trenches.

## *Joe Henrich*

Joe Henrich's comprehensive evidence was uncontroverted by any expert on the other side (unless you count Dr Shackelford's brief retort that "bad things happen in monogamy too"), and so I knew that if it were presented well and was not undermined through cross-examination, that part of the case was effectively over.

I spent almost half an hour going through Henrich's CV prior to the beginning of his testimony. I wanted to impress upon the Court, after Campbell and before Lori Beaman, Henrich's credentials in interdisciplinary work. Henrich had a PhD in anthropology, but also held tenure in the departments of psychology and economics. He was a Tier 1 Canada Research Chair in Culture, Cognition, and Evolution; he had published in most of the prestigious journals in all three of his fields, as well as others such as *Biology* and *Nature,* and he had been a reviewer of articles for virtually every leading publication in general science and the fields of his specialization. Henrich had received an early-career scholar's award from the US president at the White House, and more recently the Killam Prize in research from UBC. He had lectured in Stockholm and at Oxford. He was, his eighteen-page CV demonstrated, a very serious scholar.

He was also an experienced field researcher, having gone on dozens of trips to work on anthropological and economic projects involving indigenous communities in South America and Fiji. Each trip had lasted between one and nine months. This was good background, given that Campbell's controversial Bountiful work had involved spending parts of only twelve days in the community. I asked Henrich to explain why a researcher would need to spend so long living with his subjects; I needed to show Bauman what real science looked like.

Disarmingly, Henrich didn't actually look like a scientist at all. His bright green eyes and athletic physique had led at least one secretary in my office to dub him "Doctor Dreamy." But I couldn't have hoped for a better witness on the stand. He was clear, articulate, and everything he said was backed with bulletproof research work.

If you want to understand the Attorney General's case against polygamy, you need to come to grips with the evidence of Henrich. Many of the witnesses testified, anecdotally but persuasively, of the harms that were associated with polygamy. Dr McDermott, the government of Canada's main witness, would go further to show the extent to which those same harms were statistically correlated with polygamy, cross-culturally. The strength of the association strongly suggested causation, but did not prove it nor did it suggest a plausible causal mechanism. But Henrich went beyond simply showing the correlation, and laid out a comprehensive theory of how polygamy actually *caused* those harms. If this causal relationship were accepted by the Court I was convinced, then we would have substantially won our case.

I described earlier my contact with Henrich and our discussions regarding the scope of his retainer. After I had engaged his services, Henrich and his wife Natalie went off to review all the available literature in the sciences and social sciences, and over the course of four months produced a report entitled "Polygyny in Cross-Cultural Perspective: Theory and Implications." The report was nothing short of a comprehensive theory of polygamy and the most likely method by which it causes the harms with which it is so frequently associated. It was the entire theory of our case, built from the ground up with solid science.

Henrich used his multidisciplinary expertise to brilliant effect, developing a theoretical model of why human psychology favours polygyny and how the consequential effects of polygyny are the necessary by-products of a polygynous social structure. He then used a number of different methods to test all aspects of the theory. Henrich's eventual conclusions, expressed at page 2 of his overview, were that:

- A nontrivial increase in the incidence of polygyny, which is quite plausible if polygyny were legalized given what we know about both male and female mating preferences, would result in increased crime and antisocial behaviour by the pool of unmarried males it would create.

- Greater degrees of polygyny drive down the age of first marriage for (all) females on average, and increase the age gap between husbands and wives. This generally leads to females marrying before age eighteen, or being "promised" in marriage prior to age eighteen.

- Greater degrees of polygyny are associated with increased inequality between the sexes, and the relationship may be causal as men seek more control over women when women become scarce.

- Polygynous men invest less in their offspring both because they have more offspring and because they continue to invest in seeking additional wives. This implies that, on average, children in a more polygynous society will receive less parental investment.

- Greater degrees of polygynous marriage may reduce national wealth (GDP) per capita both because of the manner in which male efforts are shifted to obtaining more wives and because of the increase in female fertility.

Henrich's findings flowed from two aspects of our evolved psychology. First, Henrich demonstrated what I described earlier: that both men and women are inclined to adopt polygyny as a mating strategy, albeit for different reasons. He spent some time placing human mating strategy in the context of the spectrum of animal (and particularly primate) behaviour, and then wrote in his report (at p 3):

> First, like other animals, human males and females have different mating strategies rooted in the nature of primate sexual reproduction. Females are limited in their direct reproduction to the number offspring they can rear to maturity in their lifetimes, and are necessarily committed to high levels of investment, at least in the form of providing the egg, gestation, and lactation. In contrast, with little investment (sperm and a small effort), males can potentially have thousands of offspring that they can decide to invest in, or not, based on the costs of obtaining mates vs. the impact of additional investment in their offspring. Because human offspring benefit from the investment of both parents (at least in ancestral human societies) females seek to form pair-bonds with those males who are best able to invest in their offspring (males possessing high social status, wealth and valued skills). A female does not generally benefit from establishing simultaneous pair-bonds with multiple males because (1) she can only have one pregnancy at a time (so lots of sex with different males does not increase her reproductive success); (2) this brings males into conflict (sexual jealousy); and (3) this creates confusion regarding male paternity (and greater paternity confidence increases paternal investment). In contrast, males benefit both from pursuing additional pair-bonds with different females at the same time, and from additional extra-pair copulations (short-term sexual relationships).

Henrich's second foundational point was that humans have also evolved the capacity to develop culturally transmitted social norms that regulate social behaviour, including norms regarding appropriate marriage systems and the number of permissible partners. These norms in turn influence mating behaviour, and as I described earlier, such cultural memes—for instance monogamy or polygamy—can themselves evolve in Darwinian fashion as they are transmitted through societies with greater or less success.

Henrich's report then described the history of marriage systems in the West, covering some of the same ground as the affidavit of Stanford historian Scheidel, and Witte, the legal historian put forward by Canada. Henrich also described the prevalence of polygamy in the cross-cultural record, remarking as he did on the fact that "polygamy" and "polygyny" can, for scientific purposes, virtually be treated as synonymous, given the incredible rarity of polyandry across human cultures.

Then, having set the stage, Henrich turned his attention to setting out, exploring, and testing a theory of the expected consequences of the practice of polygamy on a nontrivial scale in a given society. After establishing that, for reasons of evolved psychology, polygamy overwhelmingly manifests as polygyny, Henrich discussed the consequences of the mathematics, first using a simplified example of polygamy's creation of a pool of unmarriageable men (at p 21 of his report):

> This illustration reveals the underlying arithmetic that can result in a pool of low-status unmarried men. Imagine a society of 40 adults, 20 males and 20 females ... Suppose those 20 males vary from the unemployed high-school dropouts to CEOs, or billionaires ... Let's assume that the twelve men with the highest status marry 12 of the 20 women in monogamous marriages. Then, the top five men (25% of the population) all take a second wife, and the top two (10%) take a third wife. Finally, the top guy takes a fourth wife. This means that of all marriages, 58% are monogamous. Only men in the top 10% of status or wealth married more than two women. The most wives anyone has is four.

> The degree of polygynous marriage is not extreme in cross-cultural perspective ... but it creates a pool of unmarried men equal to 40% of the male population who are incentivized to take substantial risks so they can eventually participate in the mating and marriage market. This pattern is consistent with what we would expect from an evolutionary approach to humans, and with what is known empirically about male strategies. The evidence outlined below shows that the creation of this pool will likely have a number of outcomes.

The first outcome of the "pool of unmarried men," according to Henrich, is an increase in crime. Men without reproductive prospects are "incentivized to take substantial risks so they [could] eventually participate in the mating and marriage market." If Henrich was correct, the model would predict increased criminality and antisocial behaviour where there are pools of "excess" young men.

Henrich tested this hypothesis in a number of ways. On a foundational level, he asked whether marriage does actually decrease criminality, such as murder, robbery, and rape. He found compelling support for the idea throughout the literature. One study suggested that marriage reduced a man's likelihood of committing a crime by 35 percent. This result was thought to be particularly robust because the study did not simply compare the relative criminality of married versus unmarried men, but rather tracked men throughout their lives, from a reform school at age seventeen to the age of seventy. In the study, crime rates decreased with marriage, as expected, but then increased if and when those men were widowed or divorced. The fact that this study used its subjects as their own "controls" made its results particularly compelling: marriage reduced male criminality, supporting the hypothesis that more unmarried men in the social "marketplace" would necessarily mean more crime.

To test this larger conclusion, Henrich employed three "prongs." First, he examined whether the degree of polygny correlates with crime across countries; second, he introduced a nonpolygamy-related proxy (the presence of unmarried men) to look for equivalent effects on criminality; and finally, examining the effects on differing sex ratios *within* countries (to avoid confounding comparisons of "apples and oranges").

In the first prong, the cross-country survey, Henrich found compelling data to indicate that an increase in the degree of polygyny in a country will correlate, in a statistically significant way, with higher rates of serious crimes, in particular murder and rape. This result remained robust even where wealth (as measured by per capita GDP) and other factors, such as location in Africa or proximity to the equator (where most poor, violent countries tend to be located) are controlled for.

The second prong produced similar results. When, instead of degree of polygyny, the researchers looked at the percentage of unmarried men aged fifteen and over in a country, they found similar, statistically significant results: the more unmarried men a country has, the higher the rates of murder, rape, and robbery it could expect to experience.

This led to Henrich's third prong by which he proposed to test his "pool of unmarried men" thesis. He looked at different types of situations where, for one reason or another, societies had created an imbalance between the numbers of males and females. Some of the studies were historical: for instance, Henrich demonstrated the relative violence of "frontier" societies, overwhelmingly male, in the early days of settlement in the North American West and Australia. But by far the most compelling studies were those that had recently been coming from India and China.

In China, the relative number of males to females had risen quite dramatically between 1988 and 2004 as a consequence of the gradual implementation of that country's notorious "one-child policy" coupled with Chinese parents' preference for male children. As Henrich had promised me while he was developing his data, the resulting increase in crime (it doubled) was extremely compelling, because the one-child policy had been implemented at different times in different Chinese provinces. Crime would go up in one province as its heavily male cohort reached adolescence, but it wouldn't go up in the neighbouring province, which didn't introduce the policy until a couple of years later. Then, a couple of years later, it went up in that province too. This permitted those analyzing the data to be very confident that it was the gender imbalance that was creating the increase, exactly as psychologists, anthropologists, and historians might predict.

It was not just the fact of the crime increase that was bracing, it was the extent. The China studies indicated that a very small increase in the sex ratio (0.01) led to a 3 percent increase in crime. If the ratio increased a little more, but still not even to the level where you'd be certain to notice it in a room of boys and girls (say an increase to 0.09), crime would increase by a full 27 percent. And the crimes being increasingly committed in China were not those associated with higher-status males (such as white-collar crimes like embezzlement and fraud), but rather those one would expect to see among the pool of low-status males who would be, in the evolutionary psychology model, genetically desperate as their reproductive prospects teetered between zero and nonzero; in other words, violent crimes such as murder and robbery (curiously, rape did not show the same increase, but the study's authors suspected this was the result of a massive increase in prostitution in the same period as Chinese society struggled to accommodate the unmarriageable cohort).

India's sex-ratio imbalances also seemed to have a similar violent effect, with, for instance, the murder rate in Uttar Pradesh (with a male to female ratio of 0.97) being one-half that of nearby Kerala (1.12). The India data was not quite as compelling as China's, because it was not the result of the introduction of a particular government policy on a certain date. Still, it was all highly corroborative of the central thesis: there is nothing more deadly in a society than an abundance of young, unmarriageable men.

Having convincingly demonstrating the first harm of polygamy's cruel arithmetic, Henrich turned his attention to the other aspect of the imbalance which polygyny creates. This was the subject that had so captivated me early in the development of the theory of our case: wouldn't the shortage of women in a polygynous society lead to the recruitment of girls at an increasingly young age?

Henrich confirmed that his theory would suggest that polygamy would tend to depress the age of marriage for girls, and increase the age disparity between husbands and wives. Importantly, he predicted, this effect would not be limited to polygamous marriages, because *all* men in such a society, polygamous and monogamous, would be competing for the shrinking pool of brides, and so all would be driven to expand their pool of prospective brides through the sexual targeting of younger and younger girls.

Henrich admitted that testing the "child bride" hypothesis was challenging because most of the studies came from the least developed nations in Africa, making it "difficult to tease apart the effects of polygyny vs. all the other variables that might influence Africa's situation". To address this concern, Henrich looked at studies that compared only African countries among themselves and as against developing nations located equatorially on other continents. This study revealed that the average age of first marriage for women in the highly polygynous countries was 19.9; in less polygynous countries it was 22.7; and in comparable monogamous countries it was 25.0. In Canada, incidentally, it is about 29. Similar effects were seen with respect to the age gap between husbands and wives: 2.7 years in the comparable monogamous countries, 3.9 years in the less polygynous countries, and 6.4 years in the highly polygynous countries.

Then, Henrich presented the results of what he called "micro-level case studies," which compared monogamous and polygamous marriages within four particular (otherwise culturally homogenous) groups: Bedouin Arabs living in Israel's Negev; rural villagers in southeastern Turkey; the Arsi Oromo, agro-pastoralists from southern Ethiopia; and Aboriginals from Arnhem Land, Australia.

These studies appeared to confirm the trends discernible from the African comparisons. All the societies studied indicated that polygyny drives down the age of first marriage for women and increases the age gap between husbands and wives. An interesting (and not entirely expected) finding of this survey was that the child bride phenomenon was not completely evenly spread across society (recall the theory predicts that both monogamists and polygamists will marry younger in a polygamous society). Rather, there appeared to be an *additional* depression of brides' ages in polygamous marriage. This was highly suggestive that one plausible explanation was that polygamy is a "harder sell" than monogamy, and so polygamists will tend to target girls who are more compliant and less socially developed.

In Henrich's presentation, it became apparent that, even aside from obvious and measurable effects of polygyny, such as increased rape and depressed age of girls' marriage, the "commodification" effect had serious consequences for women's equality, because men, who at the end of day held monopolies on physical violence as well as having their hands generally on the levers of religion, government, and other institutions of influence and control, would exploit this to their benefit.

So the third major effect that might be predicted from an increase in polygamy is an increased tendency for men to control women. Again using sex ratios as a proxy, Henrich demonstrated that scarcity of women reliably correlates with depressions of every accepted measurable indication of female equality (such as increased fertility rate and lower divorce rates), cross-culturally. Importantly, Henrich's analysis also held true in highly developed nations. Even in developed countries in Scandinavia and Europe, higher sex ratios predicted lower participation of women in the labour force, lower illegitimacy rates, and lower divorce rates (all indications of reduced women's rights). In fact, the results appeared to be even more striking the more developed a nation was.

As Henrich reached his last Powerpoint slide and concluded his prepared presentation, I asked him if he could summarize for the Court the degrees of confidence he could attach to conclusions regarding the causation of any particular harm associated with polygamy. Henrich was candid. He said that he was very confident about some of the conclusions—for instance with respect to sex ratios and crime. Other asserted harms had compelling support in the literature, but Henrich frankly conceded that more study was needed to have a high degree of confidence in the causal nature of the relationship.

As an example of one of the more tenuously established harms, Henrich referred to evidence of the consequences of reduced paternal investment in offspring. Henrich referred to nineteenth-century census data from Mormon polygynous communities and to contemporary studies of African societies that provided some support for this idea. The Mormon data showed, somewhat counterintuitively, that infant mortality was higher among the wealthiest 2 percent than in the lowest 16 percent, despite the fact that the richest were on average ten times wealthier than the poorest. The reason appeared to be the increased incidence of polygamy among the wealthy. The patterns observed in recent studies of polygamous African societies were similar. To give only one example, amongst the Dogon of Mali, children under age ten in polygynous households were seven to eleven times more likely to die than in monogamous households, even though the resources, per capita, were equivalent across the polygamy/monogamy spectrum. Henrich was able to tentatively conclude "that in polygynous systems poor, but married, men will have no choice but to invest in their offspring while rich, high-status men will invest in getting more wives", but frankly conceded that more study was needed before he could feel fully confident of the findings.[2]

I was pleased he was able to admit where the connections suggested by the data were weak, because it emphasized the weight that must be accorded where the connections were judged by Henrich to be, as he put it, robust.

Wu's testimony two days previously had given me another opportunity. The charts Wu had produced of 2006 census data showed an excess of single men compared to women at virtually every stage of adult life. The

166

*amicus* apparently believed that this supported his view that any increase in polygamy would be swallowed by the mass; I believed that it showed just the opposite. Taking Henrich to the figures, I asked him about their significance. Henrich pointed out that they showed that the male/female ratio already favoured single males. Had it gone the other way, and there was an excess of single women in the marriage market, then an argument could be made that the system could absorb some cohort of unmarried males produced by polygyny. But with the balance as it was, I quickly got Henrich to confirm that the figures were irrelevant to his harm analysis. The social problems created by, say, fifty thousand more males in that pool would be the same whether your starting point was zero or, as Wu's figures suggested, 557,000.

In cross-examination Macintosh was uncharacteristically at sea. He toyed with an attack on the process leading up to Henrich's opinion (implying really that Henrich was parroting my ideas, which was, if somewhat bit absurd, also flattering), before suggesting that Henrich's work wasn't the sort of thing he would stake his professional reputation on.

Q But I take it it's your theory. Are you putting your professional reputation in front of the court on your basic conclusions?

A Yes. I am intending to publish a version of this document. I'll probably start working on that sometime in January.

Q All right.

A Which is to say yes to that question.

Henrich's science seemed unassailable, and in the end the *amicus* was forced to virtually concede the field, extracting from Henrich only that he did not actually *know* how much polygamy there would be if the legal barriers were removed. Henrich readily agreed: no one could know the future, but as he had said in his report, a "nontrivial increase in the incidence of polygyny . . . is quite plausible if polygyny is legalized, given what we know about male and female mating preferences."

Henrich was as well placed as anyone to make these sort of assessments because his principal field of study was cognitive/cultural co-evolution; that is, how practices spread throughout societies. So when I confronted him directly with the *amicus*'s argument that "it couldn't happen here," he gave a very thoughtful and (at least to my mind) persuasive answer. I should say that I wasn't the only one impressed, because Bauman would eventually quote this entire passage from the transcript in his reasons for judgment:

Q [S]o what do you say to that, that it couldn't happen here?

A   Well, I mean that's really a tough question, right? Do we have, say—have gender norms, for example, gone far enough that it's just going to form a kind of shield or wall against the spreading of polygamy. And, I mean, so one general caution there is that, you know, society changes quickly, so, you know, if you had told someone in the 1950s that the United States would have a black president and that most new doctors would be women, they probably would be surprised. So social changes can occur quickly.

In this context we have good reason to believe that polygyny is a kind of ready response of our evolved psychology, that it's easy for this to happen for both males and females. So even though women may have acquired gender norms, they're still going to be inclined to marry up, so to speak.

The other thing here—I'm just checking my notes—is that even if we put aside whether Canadians who have acquired sort of the general cultural values that maybe they are immune, but there's still going to be migration issues in the sense that I would expect that if polygamy did become legal in Canada, that there would be—you see different numbers for this, between fifty and one hundred thousand polygamous living families in the United States, certainly they'd want . . . many of them would be inclined to move north because they could live without the threat of the law in the United States. So that would be one thing. There would also be . . . I would think that Canada would be a destination for polygynous families from Africa and the Middle East. Canada would be the Western destination for any immigrants who were polygynous because no other Western democracy has legalized it. And then there is also underground polygyny both in the US and France. Presumably they would want to move here as well.

The other thing to keep in mind is that if immigrant communities become stable and become like polygynous communities in other countries that have legalized polygyny, the fertility is always higher in polygynous communities. It's just robust. So these communities are going to grow faster and merely by population demographics there will be more polygynous . . . communities will expand faster than monogamous communities.

And also I still think it's possible that because of our evolved psychology, that the idea of polygynous marriage will just spread—it's possible that it will spread amongst the majoritarian population. Of course I'm only speculating here. But in some of my research in the past six months, I have learned that India has had to legislate against

Hindus because Hindu men have tried to convert to Islam so that they can be able to marry. In fact, there's a famous Hindu actor who converted to Islam so that he could marry additional women.

That's actually . . . so one of the things I study is how when high-status people do things it's likely to transmit and spread through the social fabric. So I can see this and I can imagine this starting by actors and people of very high social status adopting . . . taking a second wife or whatever, and then it would become legitimized and could potentially spread. And I learned recently that . . . on actually a story on NPR, so my source is a news site, that there is . . . that among African-American Muslims in Philadelphia, polygyny is spreading in south Philly as well. I'm from Philly, not south Philly. So it seems to me plausible that this stuff could spread.

One final point is that the idea of serial monogamy has come up a lot and I see serial monogamy amongst high-status males as showing us that the psychology of polygyny is really there, right? So these are high-status men who divorce the older wife in order to marry a younger wife, and in a polygynous society they would just add a younger wife. It's a lot more convenient; you can still live with your children. So you could see where this thing might begin to ebb into mainstream culture.

Finally, I will mention . . . so I teach evolutionary psychology and as a consequence, I teach . . . sort of a longer version of what you guys saw today, and there's always this question at the end of it. Well, given everything you just said, we should be a polygynous society; why aren't we? And one of the ways I introduce that issue is I use clickers, so students can respond in real time to questions. And I put women only, right, so that only the women are going to click on this one. And I give them a choice: You're in love with two men. One is a billionaire, he already has one wife and he wants you to be his second wife. You'll be a billionaire. You will have your own island. Make it look pretty good. And then compare him to just a regular guy, identical in every way, but you will just be his first wife. And then the question to the women is what is the probability—I give them five choices—that you would be willing to go with the billionaire, and I was surprised that 70 percent of my female UBC undergraduates said they either would go with the billionaire, with a 75 percent or a 100 percent chance they'd marry the billionaire. And I said you're in love with both guys and they look the same and all that kind of stuff. So that makes me think that it's not as crazy as some people think. I used to think.

The last to cross-examine Henrich was Monique Pongracic-Speier, counsel for the BC Civil Liberties Association. Pongracic-Speier focused on Henrich's predictions regarding the spread of polygamy and its effect on women's rights. She was, like Macintosh, blunted, gaining little but the same concession: we really can't know, but the spread of the practice in the mainstream was nevertheless "plausible." But Pongracic-Speier approached her cross with an undertone of indignation, suggesting simultaneously both that it was crucially important to the liberty of Canadians that they should be free to adopt polygamy if they so chose, but also that they would certainly not do so given its demonstrated effects on women's rights. A sample question:

> You're *speculating* so in your *speculation* you would *speculate* that Canadian women would, if polygamy were decriminalized, start to backtrack on the rights that they fought so hard to win through the twentieth century?

The point was, of course, that women and men might make individual decisions to live polygamously for any number of reasons, including love, need, or economic self-interest (assuming their decision-making was free and informed), unknowing, or perhaps uncaring, that their decision was contributing to the effects that Henrich had documented. It would not be the first time that people have done things despite the potential for harm to others.

But of course, as much as I might have wanted to intervene and argue with Pongracic-Speier myself, Henrich was doing fine. In a calm and friendly response, he could only point out that altering sex ratios did seem to affect women's rights, even in developed countries like Norway and Sweden. Frustrated, the normally restrained lawyer momentarily forgot that her role on cross-examination was to ask questions, not argue with the witness, and finished with:

> And I say to you Dr. Henrich, in Canada that is entirely *im*plausible. Thank you, those are my questions.

And with that, Henrich was excused from the witness stand, and I exhaled for what seemed like a full minute.

We had placed almost all of our evidentiary case on the question of polygamy's social harms from a scientific point of view in Henrich's lap and he had delivered in spades. If Henrich were right, polygamy needed to be curbed. And Henrich appeared to be right.

After court that day, I walked past the *Vancouver Sun*'s Bramham in the hallway, and said with a wink, "I won my case today. Do you think anybody noticed?"[3] Bramham had got the point without the necessity of my churlish prompting. Her article in the next issue of the *Sun* described the clash between the evidence of Campbell and Henrich as being like "Dorothy from *The Wizard of Oz* meets Indiana Jones."

## Lori Beaman

Lori Beaman was the *amicus*'s next expert, a professor of religious studies from Ottawa University with a doctoral degree in sociology. Realistically, Beaman's appearance was the last chance for the other side to claw back some ground lost in the battle of the experts. It wouldn't turn out that way.

Beaman's affidavits were curious. Her main point seemed to be that when the judge is looking at harms associated with polygamy, he should be careful to be guided by the facts and evidence, not by religious prejudice. She said, again and again, that we should not simply rely on the negative accounts of people who've left these religions, because their stories might be telling us nothing more than that bad things can happen in polygamous marriages. But of course, bad things can happen in monogamous marriages too.

The undertone of her message was that, in banning polygamy, we were really just engaging in (as she put it at one point) "sexual morality, racism, nation building, colonialism and the importation of Christianity."

Beaman's qualifications as an expert were not in serious doubt, although it appeared from her resumé that she, like Campbell, was enamoured with "qualitative research." She was also obviously proud of the substantial Social Sciences and Humanities Research Council (SSHRC, pronounced "shirk") grants that she had been awarded to support her work.

I really was of two minds with respect to her cross-examination. As I described earlier, my default position with experts is that cross-examination should not attempt to undermine them, which is usually very difficult, but rather to get positive information that might be helpful. This was the tactic that was used with good success with Wu and even, to an extent, with Campbell. So I prepared a very short list of questions designed to help bolster our own case rather than attack the *amicus*'s.

But the more I discussed the matter with my colleagues, the more I became convinced that we would have to take on Beaman directly. She simply made too many statements that would carry some weight as "expert" opinion that seemed just plain incorrect, or at least unsupportable.

More to the point, slipshod scholarship in Beaman's two affidavits made all of her factual assertions questionable. Earlier in the summer, Zaltz had noticed that Beaman stated that polygamy was practised among Yemenite Jews in Israel. Zaltz questioned whether this was really the case, and I asked her to track it down. What Zaltz found would make for some very interesting cross-examination, as would her further research regarding Beaman's assertions regarding First Nations historical practices of polygyny. At best, it appeared that Beaman was engaged in rather lazy scholarship. At worst, she was, even accidentally, misleading the Court on issues close to the core of the questions before it.

More troubling, but less susceptible to ordinary cross-examination were Beaman's broad suggestions: that evidence of polygamy's harm was "mixed," that the FLDS had historically been targeted out of "stereotypes" based on "atrocity stories" of a handful of disaffected former members.

After giving it a fair bit of thought, I decided to set aside my default position favouring a perfunctory cross-examination, and instead to "go long" against Beaman. I would structure my cross-examination to proceed in an increasingly less friendly way, leading her through her mistakes and mischaracterizations over a couple of hours. Unfortunately for me, this change in strategy required intense preparation in the few days leading up to Beaman's appearance on the stand. I had to read all the papers and articles her affidavits referred to, to satisfy myself that I was right on each of the mistakes that Zaltz and I had found. I prepared a binder with Beaman's affidavits alongside each document I intended to take her to.

The main problem with Beaman's evidence was that she considered herself a "qualitative researcher," a description also used by Campbell. Focusing on stories instead of hard numbers, qualitative researchers attempted to find deeper meaning than might be available through more conventional sources of data. Sometimes they succeeded, but it appeared that often qualitative research simply permitted the researcher to set aside any notion of academic rigour and produced little more than a perspective on an issue, selecting whatever from her experience supported any given point she wished to make. By the time Campbell's testimony had finished, I think many in the courtroom were a bit suspicious of anything derived from "qualitative research."

Nevertheless, qualitative research had caught on in academia. Beaman was a Canada Research Chair at the University of Ottawa (albeit a Tier 2 Chair) and had been awarded literally millions of dollars of SSHRC funding to pursue her various projects.

When Beaman was sworn in she was asked by Ludmila Herbst, the *amicus's* co-counsel, to describe the field of sociology. She said:

> Sociology is essentially the study of human society at it's—it can be both the individual, the group or the societal or institutional level . . . [S]ociology aims to bring a critical consciousness to the examination of the interplay between individuals, groups, social institutions. . . . [J]ust to give you a quick example, one of my professors when I was do-

ing my graduate work studied his bodily experience of earthquakes, so that would be a very phenomenal study.

This was really too rich to allow it to pass by unmolested. Really? Earthquakes? I had to find out more, so when it became time to begin the cross-examination I said:

Q  Before I get started with the questions I had prepared to ask, some-thing you said—well, I have to ask: "his bodily experience of earth-quakes"? That's a field of sociology that someone is writing about?

A  Yes. It's a diverse field.

I was a bit mischievous with the next question:

Q  Would you call that qualitative or quantitative research?

There was a scattering of laughter around the courtroom. She said:

A  That's definitely qualitative.

I said: "Dare I ask if it's SSHRC funded?"
More muted chuckles, indeed Beaman herself took it as the playful dig that it was, and smiled, being a good sport. "I don't believe it was," she said. With preliminary questions out of the way and with the lunch break approaching, I turned Beaman's attention to her first affidavit, where she'd written:

> 7.  Polygamy as a religious practice exists across a number of religious traditions. For some who practise it, polygamy is integrally linked to their religious beliefs. For example, among Fundamentalist Latter-day Saints, the practice of polygamy has implications for the afterlife, follows in the footsteps of Joseph Smith, their founding prophet, and provides opportunities for a demonstration of a godly life. For some Muslims, polygamy fits within the Qur'an and thus links them to God and their religious tradition. *Some Yemenite Jews in Israel practise po-lygamy as an expression of their religious beliefs.* Some First Nations people historically practise polygamy, which can be linked to their religions [emphasis added].

So here was our religious studies expert saying that Yemenite Jews still practise polygamy in Israel. I asked her if she knew anything about this curious phenomenon. Did they get married in synagogues? How many polygamist Yemenite Jews in fact lived in Israel? She didn't have a clue, but was pretty certain that they existed over there, and she confirmed that it was a current phenomenon. She cited only one source in her footnote.

So, affecting some surprise, I took Beaman to the article she cited, which Zaltz had retrieved from the library. It was called "Marriage and Divorce Customs in Yemen and Eretz Israel" and had been written in 2006.[4] I quickly summarized the article for context. It was about the two waves of migration of Yemeni Jews to Israel, one at the turn of the twentieth century and then another much larger exodus after Israel's establishment, around 1949–50. And in fact it's an incredible story: 49,000 refugees were secretly airlifted out of Yemen on British and American transport planes; they landed in Israel. Virtually every Jew in Yemen was evacuated in a matter of months. And when they lived in Yemen, some had practised polygamy, which wasn't unusual in Yemen; their Arab neighbours were sometimes polygamist too. It wasn't very common among the Jews; however, a handful of them arrived in Israel with more than one wife. But that was sixty years ago.

I took Beaman to the article's discussion of polygamy, which ended with this sentence: "The phenomenon of polygamy is no longer practised among Jews in Israel." Here is the exchange:

Q  And then it talks about the history in Yemen and that sort of thing and it gets to the end and says, this the very last sentence of that section on page 67, it says this: "The phenomenon of polygamy is no longer practised among Jews in Israel."

A  M'mm-hmm.

Q  Now, you'll forgive me for being a little astounded, having gone back to the source you cite for the proposition that it's still practised in Israel, to find that the author you rely on says that it isn't. Could you explain that?

A  No, I would have to read the article in its entirety again.

Q  I'm going to ask you to do that over lunch if you have the time?

A  Sure.

That was just the beginning of the good doctor's difficulties. Next I moved on to her statement that "[s]ome First Nations people historically practise polygamy, which can be linked to their religions." Again, this had surprised me, as by then I'd read quite a bit about polygamy in First Nations history and I have never seen it linked to their religions.[5]

For this contention, Beaman cited four sources: a book chapter and a book by respected historian Sarah Carter; an article from Irving Hallowell from *American Anthropologist*; and a 2006 article by Susan Walter, from

*Ethnology.* I went through a list of reasons from those articles for why First Nations men and women practised polygamy: social status, economic advantages, political strategy, power-brokering, and so on. Then I said:

> Okay. So here's the thing, Dr. Beaman: In this entire book and in Sarah Carter's book chapter and in the two articles—correct me if I'm wrong—there is not a page, not a paragraph, not a *sentence* and *not a single word* linking polygyny in First Nation to any religious practice? Would you agree with that? Or any religious belief?

Suddenly, Beaman seemed less insistent that we avoid generalizations and stereotypes when describing religious beliefs. By now defensive, she said:

A  Polygyny is linked to their lifestyle and being aboriginal. And part of the problem in looking at aboriginals in particular is that we don't see a discussion of religious practice partly because religious practice is not understood in First Nations communities in the same way you or I might understand it as an institutional practice. And so it's embedded in lifestyle and in life and culture so that's where I begin with the aboriginals. It, in fact, was a practice related to who they were as a people and so as aboriginals understand their lives, spirituality imbues the entirety of their lives as I understand it, and therefore as any family forum, any way of being is all linked to their spiritual practice.

Oh, boy. So she can cite authorities for polygamy as a religious practice, and then argue that they don't support that proposition because "we don't see a discussion of religious practice . . . because religious practice is not understood" the same way? I pressed her:

Q  Where do you get that from any of the articles or the book that you cite as authority for the proposition that First Nations people historically practised polygyny linked to their religious?

A  Where do I get it?

Q  Yes.

A  Simply look at the whole view—at aboriginal lifestyle as a holistic lifestyle. I would revisit these—do the authors say specifically this is a religious thing? I can't remember. But looking at aboriginal peoples and how they understand their lives, they did not distinguish between spiritual practices and anything—any other part of their lives.

Q  So you would as easily say then their diet was linked to their religion?

A  I might say that although I haven't thought about diet.

Q Perhaps let me ask this. If you wish as an academic to support the proposition that First Nations people practise polygyny linked to their religion, based on those four pieces of material, then perhaps I could ask you also at lunch to take the binder with you and see if you can find anything in these materials that would support that proposition?

A I can do that.

It was going well. On my way out of the courtroom, a member of the audience approached me in the hallway: "I feel like mincemeat for lunch, after that." Oh dear. Sometimes you have to be confrontational with witnesses, but never more than is absolutely necessary. Beaman was not dishonest or especially evasive, so I hoped I wasn't coming across as harsh.

When she came back from lunch, Beaman confirmed that the Yemenite Jews article said the opposite of what she represented. She dug the hole only deeper when she tried to clarify that perhaps her knowledge of the secret practice of Yemenite Jews had in fact come from a *newspaper* article from the Salt Lake City *Tribune* in which some Jews of some sort seemed to have been debating polygyny, although she hadn't seen the article herself.

Huh? This was the "religious studies" expert who had cautioned us not to make rash assumptions without employing established social science research methods? She'll swear to a fact in an affidavit based on the rumour of the existence of a newspaper article on a topic that *might* be related to her assertion?

On the question of First Nations "religious polygyny," she confirmed that she could find nothing in the sources she'd cited that supported her contention. I glanced at the Chief Justice—we clearly had his attention. I could have pursued Beaman on these points to the point of humiliation, but the Chief Justice had the message. He would realize that Beaman's careless and casual use of authorities meant that her affidavits could not be trusted, that they could be misleading. Now it was my project to show just how misleading they could be. "I'll move on," I said.

I went through a number of other propositions that she had made. She had said that the social science evidence on polygamy's harms was "mixed" (it wasn't, really—some studies had documented worse outcomes in polygamy, and some had been unable to document harms associated with polygamy relative to monogamy, but no quantitative studies had shown *better* outcomes in any variable for polygamy over monogamy). In cross-examination she conceded that "mixed" just seemed to mean that not every single study had found and measured a particular harm.

But I wasn't really concerned that the Chief Justice was going to pay too much attention to Beaman's summary of the international anthropological evidence when it had the evidence of others far better qualified in the relevant fields. Of more concern were her assertions regarding the origin of the *Criminal Code* prohibition from 1890. If the *amicus* could show that the law was enacted for a religious purpose, then he might well win the case regardless of the demonstrated harms.

Beaman had sworn in her affidavit that:

> Reasons for prohibiting polygamy were wide-ranging. A review of the literature suggests that sexual morality, racism, nation building, colonialism, and the importation of Christianity were most prevalent.

Again, though, Beaman's own cited sources betrayed her. Isn't it true, I asked, that "a central rationale" for the criminalization of polygamy in 1890 was in fact to protect women and young girls?

She waffled about whether she would accept that it was a "central rationale." So I took her to Sarah Carter, Beaman's own source for the history of the prohibitions. Carter had written:

> Antipolygamists claimed that polygamy meant unmitigated lives of slavery, bondage, and horror for the wives.

Beaman acknowledged that. And so I read her another passage from Carter:

> Other concerns were that the Mormons would proselytize, dragging young non-Mormon girls into lives of degradation.

And then, straight to the point—I took Beaman to where Carter had written:

> *A central rationale* for eradicating polygamy was that women were to be saved from lives of slavery . . .

I pointed out that Carter had noted polygamy as a cause among the proto-feminists of the nineteenth century, who had vowed to "fight to the death that system which so enslaves and degrades our sex, and which robs them of so much happiness."

All this had been ignored by Beaman, who had summarized Sarah Carter's work as follows:

> The criminalization of polygamy was linked to colonial ideals about citizenship and an imagined vision of the nation state which was largely white and Christian.

In Beaman's view, the "rationale" of protecting women and girls was just "rhetoric" that she didn't feel it necessary to mention. The most prevalent reasons, Beaman argued, were "sexual morality, racism, nation building, colonialism, and the importation of Christianity." This fit nicely with Beaman's worldview, I'm sure, and with the *amicus*'s argument, but it didn't jive all that well with even those sources she herself relied upon.

By mid-afternoon we had reached our discussion about the 2008 raid on the YFZ compound near Eldorado, Texas. Like Campbell and a number of other "progressive" scholars, Beaman had dismissed the entire episode as simply an overreaction of a government motivated by moral panic and prejudice. She had written in her affidavit:

The consequences of a failure to move beyond stereotypes can be dramatic, as is illustrated by two incidents involving the FLDS Church in the United States . . .

Her first example of a "failure to move beyond stereotypes" was, of course, the 1953 Short Creek raid, where state authorities had moved against the FLDS community, rounding up the men and shipping women and children off. By then, the court had already heard that articles appeared in *Life* magazine critical of the raid, and the embarrassed government caved in and reunited the families. The Court had heard the testimony of Rena Mackert, who as a young girl had been reunited with her pedophilic father for years more of abuse after she was returned to his tender care. "My father had *seventeen daughters*," Rena had said through her tears. It had been a moving moment, so I didn't think I needed to show Justice Bauman how wrongheaded or at least simplistic Beaman's assessment of the 1953 raid had been. So I turned to the much more recent incident at YFZ, which was, in Beaman's view, the second example of "a failure to move beyond stereotypes." She had sworn in her affidavit:

The second incident occurred in 2008 when state authorities raided the Yearning for Zion compound of the Fundamentalist Latter-day Saints, removing over 400 children and placing them into state custody. . . . [T]he allegations of abuse were largely unfounded. Atrocity narratives and stereotypes played a role in preventing state authorities from more carefully examining the allegations against those living in those communities.

Beaman conceded that allegations of child brides and forced marriage had dogged the FLDS for decades. Now, it was true that the YFZ raid was precipitated by what turned out to be a hoax call from a mentally disturbed woman claiming to be a teenager in distress. But was it really fair to say that the "allegations of abuse were largely unfounded"?

We quickly established that Beaman knew very little about YFZ, which wasn't surprising given how little she seemed to know about other "facts" she had sworn to under oath. For her YFZ research, her footnotes indicated she was relying on a draft book chapter written by a Utah historian that we couldn't review because it hadn't been published yet. She also said she'd followed the story through newspaper articles. But, I asked, before swearing to the court that the allegations were "largely unfounded," had she consulted the 22 December 2008 report on the raid made by the Texas Department of Family and Protective Services entitled "El Dorado Investigation"? She said, "I did not have this report available to me." I replied:

Q  You didn't have this available to you. I downloaded it from the Web a few nights ago. Google found it but you haven't looked for that sort of thing?

By this time I think Beaman might have been liking me less and less.

A  I wasn't able to find it, no.

So I took Beaman through the report in detail. In a community of perhaps only 300 adults, the authorities had found 124 "perpetrators of child abuse or neglect" in ninety-one families, over 60 percent of the families at YFZ. In a two-year window, twelve children between the ages of twelve and fifteen had been married off to men as old as fifty-four. The parents had at least stood by as it happened, if they didn't enthusiastically participate. It was nothing short of institutionalized child rape in which the entire community took part. A dozen sexual assault charges had been filed, with so far seven convictions and sentences as high as seventy-five years.

But this is what Beaman called "largely unfounded allegations of abuse"? What Campbell called "unfounded," without even the qualifier "largely"? How many children needed to be raped before allegations might be considered founded? I took her back to her sworn statement to the court summarizing the event as an overreaction based on "a failure to move beyond stereotypes." I asked:

Wouldn't you agree with me, Dr. Beaman, that in light of the facts as at least you now know them, having read this Internet document, that that is a *woefully inadequate* conclusion?

Still Beaman waffled, demanding to know why the remaining abusers hadn't been charged. I said "I will make you a deal, doctor. I will answer your question if you answer mine." Herbst sprang to her feet, and objected: "With respect, I think the question that Professor Beaman was posing was intending to elucidate what the question was that was posed to her."

The Chief Justice looked at the witness and said: "I think I found the question fairly clear."

Beaman still would not admit that her summary was even incomplete. I looked at the Chief Justice, who, if I wasn't imagining things, also let the hint of incredulity show on his usually inscrutable face. If Beaman would not admit that the allegations were *not* "largely unfounded," in the face of such overwhelming evidence to the contrary, it was at the expense of her own credibility. I was done with her.

To close off, I asked her whether she found it suggestive that every society that allowed polygyny also seemed to have a problem with adolescent, or even pre-adolescent, girls being married off. This included, I noted, the Yemenite Jews of the mid-twentieth century as described in Beaman's own source article. "Isn't that suggestive to you of anything?" I asked, perhaps that male competition was driving down the age of marriage in those places?

Beaman's reply was, in context, terribly ironic. "I think we need to be sceptical," she said.

I couldn't think of a better note to end on. "Indeed we do," I said, and indicated that I had no further questions.

That same day, we learned some bad news: Strachan, the senior federal lawyer, had gone on sick leave, effective immediately. She would have no further part in the trial. Even her colleagues at the Department of Justice were confused; no one knew what had happened.[6] I would miss Strachan; she had always been a steady hand on the tiller. Into her place stepped Keith Reimer. By this point, our two teams had worked together closely for so long that we felt quite integrated. So I was pleased that the powers at Justice had asked Reimer to take the first chair rather than bringing in another senior lawyer from outside the file.

### Todd Shackelford

Todd Shackelford, the *amicus*'s next expert witness, presented an entirely different set of challenges and opportunities than had Beaman. Shackelford's credentials were more than impeccable: he was the director of the evolutionary psychology lab at Oakland University in Chicago and a renowned authority in his field. He was particularly noted for his work in the field of domestic violence, but (as we'll see), this was far from the extent of his expertise.

Shackelford had been retained by the *amicus* to provide a very brief (about two-page) affidavit which simply confirmed that there are significant levels of violence and other forms of abuse in monogamous marriages. This rhetorically set up the *amicus* to argue that Henrich's "negative correlates"—that is, harms that he associated with polygamy—"could also be found in monogamous marriages."

The idea that bad things happened in monogamous marriages, however, was not the same as saying they were "correlated" with it, because the question is, compared to what? Assuming that people are going to enter relationships, then surely we should be comparing one type of relationship with another. For example, if we are considering banning drunk driving because it causes too many injuries and deaths, does it really matter that injuries and deaths also occur from sober driving? Surely the important question is whether there are *more* injuries and deaths if drivers drink?

Henrich had read Shackelford's report and made this precise point in reply. The question, Henrich said, wasn't whether monogamy was good or bad, the question was whether polygamy was *worse*. But Henrich went further. Shackelford's own research was, like Henrich's, premised on evolutionary psychology. It indicated that the largest risk factor in domestic violence seemed to be the presence of *genetically unrelated* pairs in the household (I have described the basic research regarding this "Cinderalla effect" earlier). Shackelford also found that an age-gap between husband and wife was a major predictor of violence and thus abuse. Henrich's response simply emphasized that both of these problems could be much worse in polygynous households, where far more family members are unrelated (co-wives) or less related (half-siblings).

Napoleon is said to have remarked that "God is on the side with the best artillery," which I had always taken to mean that very little that a general does on the battlefield can overcome a failure to have adequately prepared the basics. In preparation for Shackelford's cross, I had read everything I could find about him. I had skimmed probably forty of his articles and closely read at least a dozen. He was clearly a leading researcher and writer in the field of evolutionary psychology (the lens through which he examined male aggression and intrafamily violence). He had also written a considerable amount on human mating patterns, and had cited some works with which I was familiar, including those of Steven Pinker. He had collaborated on many studies and reports with David Buss, undoubtedly one of the leading figures of the emerging discipline.

So I resolved that I would use my cross-examination, not to dismiss Shackelford as I had Beaman, but to reinforce our own arguments where they were supported by ideas from evolutionary psychology. I was confident, based on everything I'd read, that Shackelford would endorse all the elements of our case that were premised on, or subject to analysis involving, that field. If I had been wrong it could have been a disaster, so it was something of a gamble. But again, it went back to the conversation I'd had with the former Chief Justice Brenner in the coffee shop: if they're honest, and I'm right, they'll say so. And frankly, if this expert in evolutionary psychology thought we had it fundamentally wrong, the court should know that, and we would deal with a weakening of our case in a straightforward way.

If you want to rely on the evidence you expect the expert to give you, you need to bolster, or at least accept, his credibility and authority. It would seem disingenuous to attack an expert's qualifications or abilities, and then, when you are unsuccessful, to try to turn him to your advantage. It is far better to indicate to the court, *in advance*, that you would accept what a witness like Shackelford said within his expertise, subject to matters of reasonable divergence of views.

It's the legal equivalent of giving your enemy's gunfighter a loaded pistol and trusting that he'd point it at his own boss. It's a strategy based on two kinds of trust. First, you have to trust the witness to be honest. Everything I had learned about Shackelford suggested to me that he would come to Vancouver looking to help the court, so I did trust him, inasmuch as I could trust any witness I'd never met. But second and more important, for this to work, for your confidence to be projected through advance endorsement of your adversary's expert, you have to trust in the correctness of your case. If I am wrong on an essential element, then the witness *should* point it out, and I *should* lose the point. This wasn't ordinary litigation where I was looking after the positional interests of a client. The Attorney General's position was that there were grounds to justify the polygamy law. If it turned out that there weren't, then the Attorney General's position should change, full stop.

So in for a penny, in for a pound . . .

Each expert witness, upon being sworn in, is led through his or her credentials and resumé by the lawyer for the proffering party, in this case Tim Dickson for the *amicus*. When Shackelford had taken the court through his CV, the Chief Justice asked whether I wished to speak to his qualification as an expert. Shackelford looked at me from the witness box and smiled expectantly.

I said: "My Lord, it's my position that Dr Shackelford is extremely well qualified. He is, in fact, an internationally recognized leader in the field of evolutionary psychology and it's an honour to have him here."

After that introduction, I was praying that Shackelford would agree with pretty much everything I had to say to him over the next two hours.

He did. My understanding of the psychology and sociology of polygyny was summarized neatly by Harvard professor Pinker in a few pages of his book *How the Mind Works*. I knew that Shackelford had cited Pinker's academic articles extensively in his own work. I asked Shackelford whether he respected Pinker's work. "Deeply," he replied. So I read paragraph after paragraph of what Pinker wrote, pausing from time to time to confirm that Shackelford agreed with the Harvard professor. Each time he confirmed that he did. So the *amicus*'s own expert adopted significant passages, such as these:

> Whenever polygyny is allowed, men seek additional wives and the means to attract them. . . .

> Polyandry, by comparison, is vanishingly rare. Men occasionally share a wife in environments so harsh that a man cannot survive without a woman, but the arrangement collapses when conditions improve. Eskimos have sporadically had polyandrous marriages, but the co-husbands are always jealous and one often murders the other. . . .

> The most florid polygynists are always despots, men who could kill without fear of retribution. (According to the *Guinness Book of World Records*, the man with the most recorded children in history—888—was an emperor of Morocco with the evocative name Moulay Ismail the Bloodthirsty.) The hyperpolygynist not only must fend off the hundreds of men he has deprived of wives, but must oppress his harem. Marriages always have at least a bit of reciprocity, and in most polygynous societies a man may forgo additional wives because of their emotional and financial demands. A despot can keep them imprisoned and terrified. . . .

> Under polygyny, men vie for extraordinary Darwinian stakes—many wives versus none—and the competition is literally cutthroat. Many homicides and most tribal wars are directly or indirectly about competition for women . . . egalitarianism and monogamy go together as naturally as despotism and polygyny.

It wasn't really a cross-examination in any conventional sense; I felt more like Shackelford's co-panelist than his interrogator, and perhaps because he determined that I was genuinely interested in learning his answers, rather than in tricking him, he became increasingly forthcoming and animated. One after one, he confirmed every essential element of our case, and he would alternate between an emphatic "yes" and an even more emphatic "indeed!" or "correct!" Shackelford agreed that men were inclined to polygyny as a biologically optimal mating strategy. He agreed that the practice might be expected to drive down the age of marriage of girls, and increase the age gap between husbands and brides. He agreed that it would be expected to create a surplus of unmarried males, and that this was bad news as young, unmarried men are the most dangerous creatures on the planet. He accepted that a scarcity of women might lead to increased efforts by men to exert control over their partners' reproductive capacity. His depth of knowledge in each of these areas was quite profound.

To my pleasant surprise he also seemed to endorse the idea of monogamy as being a platform for the development of women's rights. The exchange went like this:

Q [Monogamy] may have all started as a bargain between and among men that set this standard for that equality. And we've heard theorizing that subsequent to that was the beginning of equality among men in Western society and that that formed the platform much later for the development of the equality of man versus woman, that once you had monogamy established on the basis of the selfish interests of men, suddenly it became a platform from which women could assert their own equality. Do you have any thoughts on that?

A I'm aware of the argument and it seems plausible but I'm not intimately familiar with the data that had been collected on that front.

Q I understand. But it seems plausible?

A Yes.

I loved this guy.

I minimized his disagreement with Henrich over how Shackelford's work on genetic unrelatedness and age disparity risks might play out in the context of polygynous households. Shackelford allowed that it was possible that the effects could be worse under polygyny, but he cautioned that the work done in the monogamous context could not simply be expected to apply "holus bolus" to polygamous families. Fair enough.

Shackelford didn't give me absolutely *everything* I wanted. I resolved to ask him last whether he thought polygamy could spread in modern North America. I expected a main argument of the *amicus* and Civil Liberties Association to be that "it couldn't happen here." Henrich had said the idea of spread within the mainstream population was plausible, at least within a couple of generations. Shackelford appeared much more equivocal. On the one hand, he said he "generally agree[d]" with Pinker's statement that "whenever polygyny is allowed, men seek additional wives and the means to attract them." He noted, however, that there were presently no "high-status" polygynist role models that others might emulate, and the present practitioners of polygamy seemed in fact to have little social status. This he considered a factor militating against the spread, or at least against its rapid spread.

I decided not to explore with Shackelford whether in fact potential polygamists might be high status within their particular communities, even if they were looked down upon in the greater population. He wasn't an expert on Bountiful or immigrant populations, and to be honest, the point seemed rather self-evident given the evidence of the hierarchy of men in the FLDS. So I thought the last thing I would try to extract from Shackelford would be an admission that the evolved psychology was sufficiently powerful so as to lead to polygamy's spread throughout even the mainstream North American population.

To this end I had a bit of an ace in the hole. While I had been reading through Shackelford's articles in preparation for his testimony, I came across one of his earlier studies, which was focused not on domestic violence but on human mating strategies. I put the article to Shackelford so that he might confirm what it said.

The article reported the results of surveys taken of California college students. They were asked, among other things, to rate the attractiveness of a spectrum of mating strategies: on the one hand, a high number of casual partners; on the other, monogamous marriage for a lifetime. Not surprisingly, there was a sharp difference in the preferences between men and women on the two extremes. But what genuinely was a surprise was the fact that a statistically significant number of men reported that their *actual* preference would be simultaneous marriage to as many as ten or more women. The result was even more striking because polygamy was not by any means the focus of the study—this intriguing finding was almost accidentally discovered while the researchers were looking for something else.

I also raised with Shackelford Henrich's informal "clicker poll," which found that the majority of his female students would become the second wife of a billionaire over the soulmate of a less wealthy but otherwise equivalent man. While Shackelford did express surprise at the degree of support for the idea, he wasn't surprised that it should be significant.

Even so, when pressed on the question of polygamy's potential spread in the mainstream, Shackelford first said that the spread of polygyny in North America is "plausible . . . terribly, terribly unlikely, but plausible." Nevertheless, almost in the next breath, he admitted that, of men who could "afford the costs . . . some would" pursue polygyny.

This was an answer that I was prepared to live with. Obviously, the exercise was completely speculative; arguably it was legally irrelevant. But the *amicus*'s argument did hold some rhetorical appeal: how can you criminalize people living polygamously on the basis of a suite of harms that have been proven in some contexts, but wouldn't occur if the prohibition was removed?

I ran into the BCCLA's counsel, Pongracic-Speier, in the hallway after Shackelford's cross examination, and I wanted to tease her a bit after the rough ride she had given Henrich. "You see Monique?" I asked. "They're all *my* witnesses in the end." She responded by saying that—every once in a while—what I said was true. She was smiling, but she still didn't seem happy about it.

## Rose McDermott

The final expert to testify before the Christmas break was Rose Mc-Dermott, a political science professor at Brown University in Rhode Island. She had been working for a number of years on the WomanStats database, which collected, codified, and analyzed data on indicia of women's status and rights from 172 countries around the world.

McDermott used regression analysis to determine the relationship, cross-culturally, between the presence of polygyny and other social ills that were hypothesized as connected. It was essentially a fresh and more comprehensive approach to the work of Kanazawa, Tertilt, and other researchers cited earlier by Henrich. Those had tested one or a few variables cross-culturally; McDermott's study was able to simultaneously test the strength of association between polygyny and dozens of its purported harms.

The database was indeed formidable; over 283 national variables were logged for each nation, everything from a country's GDP to the incidence of female genital mutilation. Importantly for our purposes, the database also ranked each nation according to "degree of polygyny" on a 5-point scale with 0 being the lowest and 4 being the highest incidence. This permitted correlations to be explored between the presence of polygamy and each of the other variables.

In her report, McDermott showed that, as polygyny increased in society, the age of marriage for women decreased, as did a whole host of other harms: maternal and infant mortality, teen pregnancy, high birth rates, sex trafficking, domestic violence, and militarism all closely correlated with polygyny. All of these harms would, she said, be predicted by an application of principles established by evolutionary psychology. This was true even where the omnibus potential confounding factor, socioeconomic development (as represented by GDP per capita), was held constant as a control. She had summarized:

> Based on the best data available to date in the world, including the majority of countries across the globe, I find that in polygynous societies, women sustain more physical and sexual abuse. They have more chil-

dren, are more likely to die in childbirth, and live shorter lives than their counterparts in more monogamous societies. In polygynous societies, women are more subject to sex trafficking and female genital mutilation while receiving less equal treatment than men, and encountering more discrimination under the law. In addition, girls are less likely to be educated, restricting a key component allowing for upward mobility and economic independence. In societies with high rates of polygyny, up to half of the boys are ejected from their primary communities, with incalculable effects on them. Moreover, the average individual in a polygynous society has fewer liberties than the average individual in a state which prohibits polygyny. A polygynous state spends more on average on defence, leaving fewer resources available for building domestic infrastructure, including projects devoted to health and education. This is quite a diverse set of effects, confirming the wide-ranging consequences of polygyny in societies in which women live as enforced second-class citizens, and the states of which they are a part.

McDermott's expert report concluded with a discussion of some anecdotal evidence of benefits arising from polygamous unions:

> More generally, while some individuals certainly claim to benefit from being in a polygynous union, there has been no statistical demonstration that polygyny benefits most men or women, boys or girls or society considered as a whole. Nor are any such effects manifest in the vast majority of the peer-reviewed literature examining a smaller number of cases than would be permitted by statistical analysis. Perhaps such a defence of polygyny, unlikely though it may be, could be made and supported with data meeting the standards which we advocate—verifiable, comprehensive, valid, and reliable. But for now it is fair to state that while polygyny's negative effects are wide-ranging, statistically demonstrated, and independently verified using alternative analytical tools, its beneficial consequences are circumscribed and at odds with the welfare of most.

McDermott's contribution to the evidence was considerable, in that it added authority to a central tenet of the argument of the Attorneys General. Like Henrich, McDermott's work focused on the harm done by polygamous *societies* as opposed simply to the harm of any particular polygamous union, and was central to our argument because it vaulted past the civil libertarian objections. Not only were innocent, consenting, egalitarian polygamists contributing to harm (even if they were causing no direct harm), there was really nothing they could do to reduce or guard against that harm. There could be no "good polygamy."

Macintosh took a more aggressive approach to the cross-examination of McDermott than he had with Henrich. He sought to undermine McDermott's findings by questioning both the method (which he suggested presupposed the causal direction of the relationships) and the reliability of the data. But in the end he seemed to get little traction.

When I first read McDermott's report and every time I thought about it afterwards, I felt a bit nervous because of one particular vulnerability. Her model, as I've explained, developed its regression analyses by first ranking every country in the world according to its "degree of polygyny," in her case on a scale from 0 to 4. And this is where my difficulty came in, because there was considerable disparity in the degree of polygyny McDermott found *among Western countries*. For instance, the team had rated Canada, not as 0 on the scale of polygyny (extremely rare), but as 1 (not uncommon). The United States had been rated as 2, which suggested a higher prevalence still. Yet both of these countries, I suspected, scored very well on the scales of almost all the alleged harms: that is, they had good education, maternal and infant health, life expectancy, and so on. The same could be said for Western European countries, which were rated mostly at 0 but also had some as high as 2.

Macintosh did make the point, under cross-examination, that the correlations were not exact. That is, there were also some "highly polygamous" countries that had (for instance) better education than less polygamous ones. But given the large number of surveyed countries and the high number of data fields, such outliers would be expected and did nothing to diminish the overall correlations (in fact, their presence may actually demonstrate how strong the overall connections were).

No, I wasn't afraid that McDermott's overall conclusions with respect to polygamy and its harms were vulnerable. But if I were the *amicus*, I would have explored a different point altogether.

What if we had taken McDermott's data and isolated and held constant *location*. That is, if we ran two separate analyses of polygamy's effects, one with respect to Western democracies in Europe and North America, and the other for everywhere else. My strong suspicion would be that, were we to do so, we would find the correlations of harm being strengthened in the "rest of the world"; but in Western countries, I believed that the correlations she was describing would be reduced, and might possibly even disappear. It was even conceivable that, in developed democracies, McDermott's graphed "harm slope" might actually go the other way—in other words, that *Western* countries with relatively more polygamy (France and the United States, for instance) might be better places to live, controlling for GDP or not, than their neighbours with lower levels of the practice.

What would be the point of that exercise? Well it would allow Macintosh to argue that, even if polygamy was harmful in every country in the world, there must be something about Western societies that made them exceptional to the general rule linking polygyny to harm (perhaps the pre-existent context of greater women's equality), or might suggest that there are other factors in the developing world that were confounding the larger analysis. Either way, if the numbers came out as I suspected they might it would help Macintosh argue that "it couldn't happen here."

But the *amicus* had chosen to offer no expert in rebuttal to McDermott (though if he had hired an expert who had tried and failed to undermine the work, I wouldn't have any reason to know about it), so we may never know how such an analysis would play out.

My own belief was that a negative or inconclusive result for polygamy's harms in Western countries (if in fact my suspicions were borne out and this *had* been the result) would be because McDermott's data on the degree of polygamy in the West was at least inconsistent. While we certainly had polygamists in Canada, it seemed difficult to argue that the practice was "not uncommon" in this country, a characterization that justified Canada's ranking as 1 on McDermott's 0 to 4 scale. Nor did it seem to me that the United States was appreciably more polygynous than Canada so as to earn it a 2. You could even argue that both were countries where the practice would, comparatively speaking, be thought to be a 0, or "extremely rare." The difficulty with reducing degree of polygamy to a small gradation scale, moreover, is that minor differences might be compounded once regression is applied. For instance, if we are correlating "polygamy" on a 0 to 4 scale with "defence spending," which might be a more objectively quantifiable measure, you run the risk of distorted analysis if, for instance, a society rating polygamy as 2 is not really twice as polygamous as a neighbouring 1.

In the end I don't think that, even had Macintosh focused on this avenue, it would have significantly undermined the evidence as a whole, because McDermott's overall results were very consistent with virtually every other source of information before the Court. In particular, even if you could sustain the argument that Western societies do not *generally* suffer from the very limited degree of polygamy practised there, subsets of our society do. And that, if the negatives could not find correlational support when comparing one Western country to another, it was because polygamy was so rare that even significant differences (let's say if polygamy were twice as common in the United States as it is in Canada) could not measurably affect global measures such as girls' education. This, we would argue, spoke in favour of criminalization's continuance, rather than its irrelevance. But I must say I am curious to see how these numbers would in fact play out. I understand that McDermott's WomenStats data is freely available online, so the further analysis that I suggest could easily be undertaken by another expert on statistics.

After McDermott had finished, the Chief Justice thanked the lawyers for their efforts in keeping matters on track:

> We've made I think tremendous progress in developing an unparalleled evidentiary record on the issues that we're struggling with, and we are all engaged in an extraordinary exercise. It seems to me that's been made plain in the last few weeks. The progress to date is a credit to all counsel. The level of lawyering has been extremely high. I thank you. It has as well been demonstrated or marked by the high degree of civility between counsel and our progress to date reflects that as well. So thank you for that.

We finished 2010 in, I thought, very good shape. Our own evidence had gone in smoothly and was well received. The experts for the *amicus* had either been dismantled, like Beaman, or had proven themselves far more helpful to our case than theirs, as had Wu and Shackelford. Campbell, the *amicus*'s principal expert witness, had been neutralized on her own research but had nevertheless gone on to help us by endorsing some important elements of our case. It had been a very good month.

Over the three-week hiatus in the trial, I was frequently asked, by people who had heard how things were going, whether Macintosh, Wickett, and the other challengers' counsel were doing a good job on the other side. I had given a lot of thought myself to the question of what I would be doing in their position—a litigator, like a chess player, tries to think about his case from his opponent's perspective as much as from his own. The truth is, if I had been given Macintosh's job, I would have focused on the elements of the case where I had the strongest chance of winning. In my own opening submissions to the Court, I had identified three fields of battle in this case: purpose, harm, and interpretation. We had to win all three. All the evidence we had heard, indeed almost all the evidence that we would ever hear, had to do with harm, but this was not where the legislation was most vulnerable. I had concluded that Macintosh should be prepared to lose the field on the question of harm; however, he would nevertheless fight a rearguard action by refusing to concede the point, putting in some minimal evidence, and forcing us to expend energy defending our case on harm while he focused on his two potential magic bullets. If he could prove either that the legislation was enacted for a religious, rather than secular, purpose or that the legislation cast too broad a net, when properly interpreted, then he would win—at least until Parliament amended and re-enacted the provision.

Macintosh's strongest arguments were almost purely legal, so I felt limited overall confidence despite how well the evidentiary phase was proceeding. To put it bluntly, despite all the evidentiary ground I felt we had gained, I had no idea whether we would actually win the day. But our victories so far meant that the case would be decided on evidence that *could*, if the law went our way, support the prohibition of polygamy.

## Strategy and Tactics

### The Three-Front Fight

Litigation isn't warfare, thank goodness, but it's not chess either. There are some other similarities that make military analogies very tempting, and they're helpful if you don't take them too far.

Most large-scale litigation is pursued on a broad, grinding front. Lawyers don't tend to focus their energies and resources where it might most count; they simply attack every fact and every argument equally. I've never had the patience or endurance for that approach, nor do I often have the luxury of the unlimited resources that can make it a winning strategy. Despite the image of the government as a bottomless pit of money, the fact is that our lawyers are often out-resourced, outnumbered, and outgunned in any particular case.

I conceived the polygamy trial, as I've said, as a three-issue case: purpose, harm, and interpretation. Harm was the broad, central front. It was where we had to be meticulous, build up a comprehensive army of evidence and witnesses, and present our case methodically. Visualized on a battlefield, it would be where most of our forces would be, in the middle, advancing slowly but inexorably.

I knew enough about Macintosh to know that he understood mobile warfare; he knew that the battle wasn't set piece, that litigation was dynamic, and although deep preparation was necessary for success, it wasn't often sufficient. You had to be prepared to move; you had to be alert. So all the time, like Alexander the Great, Macintosh would keep his fastest cavalry behind the front, riding back and forth behind his main troops, waiting to find some opportunity, some slip, some break in the main front that he could dash in and exploit. If he were lucky, or if we were careless, he might parlay such an opening into a fatal thrust. We might give him an opportunity on the harm front to eviscerate our case.

I expected that Macintosh would not put force on force. He wouldn't concede harm, but he knew he couldn't resist along the whole front. His better arguments were purpose and interpretation: mainly legal, rather than factual questions, and areas of obvious vulnerability. These were our sensitive flanks, and this is where Macintosh would put strong resources. As we pushed forward on harm, he would give ground, but no more than he had to; he'd try to grind us a little as he retreated while he pushed ahead on the flanking movements. He hoped that as long as he could keep us focused on harm, we wouldn't be prepared for his attacks on the wings.

So it was a relief, at the half-time mark, that this had not occurred. Macintosh's cavalry had prodded and probed, but found no traction and no opening to exploit. Our main forces had advanced most of the length of the field, and had proven formidable. We had won the centre, though we still had some mopping up to do. We had also, wherever possible, re-inforced our flanks as we went along. And we had our own cavalry, mobile and effective. Every chance we got to hack away at their case on the sup-posedly religious purpose of section 293, such as Beaman's testimony, we exploited to good effect. But Macintosh was at least as much of a strategic thinker as I. He would have known that the main battle for the centre would go against him; he had seen the evidence, in affidavit form, months in advance, and no doubt he had consulted some experts before deciding that he couldn't put up a full-strength opposition.

So I expected Macintosh in the second phase to lose interest in harm. I expected him to look for opportunities to use his cavalry more on the flanks; we had a couple of experts left to appear, and they might provide some help to Macintosh in cross-examination. But my feeling was that Macintosh and his all-star juniors would most usefully spend January sharpening their swords for the legal argument to come, when all effort would shift to the wings.

## The FLDS Wild Card

Another frustrating aspect of the case, which became acute as we prepared to break for Christmas, was the constantly shape-shifting presence of the fundamentalist Mormons themselves. The FLDS and its bishop, James Oler, had been granted Interested Person status at the very beginning, and it was clear that Wickett, their lawyer, had been working with Macintosh, at least in a limited way, to coordinate the presentation of their evidence.

Prior to the hearing, Wickett had achieved an unprecedented victory when he had obtained an order permitting him to put before the Court anonymous affidavits of FLDS members. The order said that the affiants could give their evidence without identifying themselves, and if they testi-fied (behind a screen, at their option), they could not be asked any ques-tion that might tend to identify any other person who was in a relationship that might be criminally polygamous. This was a considerable advantage to Wickett, and a considerable difficulty for us, as it would sharply constrain our ability to test the evidence of Wickett's affiants.

But when the affidavits arrived in August, some of them were not anonymous. There was one from Merrill Palmer, the principal of Bountiful Elementary and Secondary School (BESS), which dealt mostly with a description of the education system in the community. And there was another from Oler himself.

Oler's affidavit described something of the structure and rules of the community, and contained a great deal of material on which we would look forward to cross-examining him. Oler downplayed the expulsion of boys from the FLDS, and asserted that any criminality at Bountiful would be promptly reported.

But Wickett was concerned that, in keeping with "the spirit" of the anonymity order, we should not be able to cross-examine Oler or Palmer about their "personal lives."

This I couldn't agree to. Both Oler and Palmer were polygamists, and it was said that both had married teenaged girls. Certainly, as central authority figures in the community, they would likely know the details of every child married in Bountiful and perhaps many in the United States too. We had lots of questions for them. I told Wickett that there could be no deal restricting cross-examination, and that if he wanted to shield his client's officials from difficult questions that were relevant to the issues before the Court, he should seek an order. Just before Christmas break, Wickett told me that he would be withdrawing Oler's affidavit. The fate of Principal Palmer remained to be seen.

# Round Two: January 2011

## W John Walsh

The first witness of the New Year was an expert put forward by the FLDS: John Walsh. Walsh was a self-described religious scholar who had testified as an expert witness on behalf of FLDS members at a number of hearings and trials in Texas. As I researched his background, I didn't know quite what to make of him.

His academic credentials were not what anyone would call "A" circuit: his PhD was from the University of Wales, but it, like his Master's in Jewish Studies (from Chicago's Spertus Institute), had been completed through distance education, generally viewed as a poorer alternative to residential study. His CV listed no scholarships, bursaries, or awards, and no academic publication record to speak of. In fact, he appeared to have done no professional work as a scholar at all, aside from the consulting work he performed for lawyers.

But when I spoke to his Master's supervisor at Spertus, a very well-regarded Jewish Studies scholar who had also been a reader of Walsh's PhD thesis, he raved about Walsh's erudition and integrity. And when I obtained a copy of Walsh's thesis and read it through, I had to admit it was an impressive piece of work. But the thesis had nothing to do with fundamentalist Mormon groups, and, whatever the quality of his education, Walsh claimed an expertise in the FLDS faith, arising from "eighteen years of study."

The affidavit itself had some odd assertions. Walsh argued that a Mormon (including FLDS) prophet is actually less of a dictatorial figure than the Pope, because the prophet is not infallible. Setting aside the fact that the Vatican no longer asserts papal infallibility, this statement seemed incredibly naïve, even if it were true from a theological point of view. The Pope cannot tell you who to marry, reassign your family, take away your house, or expel you from your community. Warren Jeffs could do those things, and did.

With respect to child brides, Walsh's view was that FLDS girls exercise a "real choice" in who to marry, by which he meant that some have said no to an arranged marriage and not been expelled from the church. He argued that there is no FLDS doctrine teaching minimum age for marriage, that this decision is made family-by-family. Walsh wrote that "most" FLDS women marry at the age of majority. His sources on these points seemed terribly tenuous.

When I searched online for anything attributed to Walsh on the Internet, what I found was just plain weird: a series of bloglike articles by a "W John Walsh" on various topics connected to Mormonism in general, and polygamy in particular.

And the Walsh who emerged on the Internet was an unabashed cheerleader for polygamy. A website collection of articles on Mormonism contained a bizarre pseudo-Socratic "script" supposedly authored by Walsh, designed for someone trying to persuade a sceptic of the righteousness of plural marriage (in fact, one script each for men and women). Here's a sample piece of the proposed dialogue:

> [Walsh to the sceptical man]: If marriage is a way we prepare for eternal life, would more family life help you prepare even better? I think so. Personality conflicts can be overcome through righteous living, repentance, forgiveness, and patience. Large families help you prioritize your time, money, and efforts. You can't waste time doing things of little worth. You must spend your time focusing on raising your family,

teaching them how to work and about the Gospel. The traits you develop in this family can only further your development as you strive to become more like the Father of us all.

[Man, grateful for Walsh's tutelage]: I never thought about it that way. I thought plural marriage was mostly about sex, but I can see it is actually designed to make us more like our heavenly parents.

Walsh closed the article with a quote from hyperpolygynist Brigham Young, which he introduced with these words:

If you are someone who objects to plural marriage, then I would challenge you to search within yourselves [*sic*]. There is no doubt in my mind that your attitude towards plural marriage will determine your place in eternity.

Whoever wrote this wasn't a disinterested expert: John Walsh was beginning to look like a true believer.

Wickett, the FLDS lawyer, had asked before the Christmas break if we really needed to bring Walsh to Court. He said he was concerned for costs, but I couldn't see how it would cost any more to bring Walsh than any other US-based FLDS witness. I suspected that Wickett had seen the way the *amicus*'s experts' testimony had gone (the collapse of Beaman and the thorough co-opting of Wu, Shackelford, and even Campbell), and was keen that his man (and his case) should avoid the same fate.

Greathead and I pondered the implications of letting Walsh off the hook. We decided that we couldn't give him a pass unless he removed some of the contentious stuff from his affidavit, particularly his bland reassurances regarding questions of consent and agency (he seemed to be suggesting that it was fundamentally impossible for a Mormon to coerce another because of the primacy of human agency in the faith). But should we call him anyway? He could be useful in that he did appear to have knowledge of FLDS teachings and doctrine. Perhaps he could confirm some of the information in the Warren Jeffs book *In Truth and Light*, which we had obtained through Greathead and Horsman's American contacts.

In the end we decided he should come, and we assigned his cross-examination to Ross, the very capable junior lawyer we had borrowed from Civil Litigation. In truth I really wanted to handle Walsh myself, but Ross had earned a turn in the limelight, having toiled for months putting our evidence together. She was, in any event, more familiar with the contents of *In Truth and Light* than any of us. Ross was also a "Jack Mormon," a former or lapsed member of the mainstream LDS, and so had the background to think on her feet if the cross-examination became a theological tug-of-war.

I did decide that I would do the first part of the cross-examination, dealing with the qualifications of Walsh to give his evidence. Compared to most of the other academics from whom the Court had already heard, Walsh, with his one questionable publication and rather underwhelming education, did not compare favourably. I wanted to point out the weakness of his credentials, in the expectation that the Court would not take too seriously his evidence on matters beyond his core expertise.

I also wanted to put to Walsh the bizarre article that was posted online in his name, and ask him to explain why he wrote such a peculiar piece, and so this was the first place I went. To my surprise, Walsh disclaimed any memory of having written the article. He allowed that he might have, over a decade ago, but dismissed the website where the article was found, suggesting that the site was simply a collection of reposts and other miscellany, God knows how heavily edited. It was hard for me to believe that a scholar of any description could not look at the article and immediately say either that he did or did not write it. But that's what he said: maybe he did, maybe he didn't.

Because Walsh had refused to positively identify the writing as his own, it couldn't be entered as an exhibit. But l felt confident that taking Walsh to the article would have the twin effects of making Walsh a more careful witness (because an expert will be more fastidious in testifying if they understand that you've done your homework and can nail them if they divert too much from their prior work) and planting in the consciousness of the Court that Walsh's testimony should not be accorded a large amount of weight.

Walsh's testimony was, at the end of the day, an anticlimax. He tempered some of the controversial statements in his affidavit, and did provide us with two unexpected but welcome pieces of evidence. He confirmed that *In Truth and Light* was a source of doctrine for the FLDS. And, incredibly, he testified (in his direct examination) that somewhere around half of mainstream Mormons would practise polygamy if the laws were changed to permit it:

A   The LDS did not renounce the principle of polygamy [in 1890]. What they did is they've made a practical realization that they would not be able to continue as a community under the pressure they were receiving from the American federal government. And therefore they decided that they would cease the practice of polygamy due to this pressure, but at that time they maintained that they still believed in the principle of polygamy.

Q   And has that . . . from a theological standpoint has that position changed or evolved over time within the LDS church?

A   It officially has never changed. Informally you would say that probably within the LDS church today there are two major groups. I couldn't put an exact number, whether it's 50/50 or 60/40, but they are both substantial groups. One group would like the return of polygamy, and believe that's a holy principle that should be eternally practised. Another large group, possibly larger than the first group, would like to see polygamy not returned. They believe it's an archaic practice and so they would like it not to return.

So officially the church has never altered its position on polygamy, but informally the millions of members of the LDS church are kind of divided into those two camps.

I wasn't going to place much stock in anything Walsh said about polygamy, because I felt fairly confident that, despite his vague memory, this W John Walsh was in fact the same W John Walsh who was so evidently pining for the return of the practice on earth (and I think that the same thought might have occurred to Bauman). Walsh seemed to me to be a guy who had began as a keen, even somewhat obsessive, amateur researcher of Mormonism but who had over time reinvented himself as a serious scholar and, in the course of so doing, had either rethought his views on polygamy or learned to keep them to himself. If the latter were the case, it would explain his wildly high estimate of support for polygamy in the LDS church (Walsh wouldn't be the first advocate to overestimate support for his views).[7] In any event, Walsh now was heavily invested in his own respectability, as he had become something of an "expert for hire" in US polygamy-related prosecutions, where he would make other questionable claims based on his understanding of LDS and FLDS doctrine.[8]

Nevertheless, if the *amicus* wished to rely on Walsh, he must swallow the whole meal, including Walsh's way-high estimate of the number of would-be polygamists among mainstream Mormons, and this could only undermine the *amicus*'s "it couldn't spread" argument.

## Rebecca Cook

Rebecca Cook was Canada's witness, an expert in international human rights law with a particular focus on women's rights. She is a professor of law at the University of Toronto and chair of international human rights law at that institution, where her teaching focuses on international women's rights, including a course on polygamy. Her academic credentials were phenomenal; she had a PhD from Columbia and Master's degrees from both Columbia and Harvard. She was a fellow of the Royal Society of Canada and had authored or co-authored seventeen books, 111 peer-reviewed articles, numerous legal briefs, and on and on, all focused on international human rights, especially women's rights and health.

Cook had been asked to address the harms of polygyny as viewed through the perspective of international human rights law, and to look at states' practices with respect to polygamy, and to opine on Canada's obligations.

In 2006 Cook had prepared a report for the government of Canada on polygamy, particularly as viewed through the perspective of international human rights law, and her affidavit to the Court was in significant part an updating of that project. She summarized her literature review of the harms of polygyny as follows:

> Based on my review of various international instruments, case law, relevant literature, and case studies, the weight of authority leads to the conclusion that polygyny has detrimental effects on women, and on society more generally. Polygyny structures the marital relationship unequally on the basis of sex. A core right—the right to take additional spouses—is extended to one spouse (the husband), but not the other (the wife). This asymmetry is premised on sex and sex role stereotypes that ascribe to men and women different attributes and characteristics that ostensibly warrant an unequal distribution of rights and obligations in marriage. In addition to these inherent wrongs of discrimination against women, polygyny is often associated with a number of material and health harms, though these harms vary within and across different social and legal contexts.

Cook testified at length about the nature and content of international law. Her basic position was that the asymmetrical structuring of a polygamous marriage is inherently wrong because it is offensive to women's dignity and equality. Like other experts before, she also identified harms to women's physical and mental health, material harms for both women and children, and also particular harms to the children of polygynous marriages.

Cook said that the trend internationally is to forbid polygyny through criminalization or family law rules.

As for Canada's obligations, her basic conclusion was that Canada had a duty under a number of international instruments, including the *Convention on the Elimination of All Forms of Discrimination Against Women (CEDAW)* to take all necessary measures to eliminate polygamy. Under very effective "friendly" cross-examination by counsel for West Coast LEAF, Cook confirmed that this obligation included a duty to protect against discrimination by both state and nonstate actors. Cook also confirmed that Canada had entered no "reservations" with respect to *CEDAW*.[9]

Herbst's cross-examination of Cook indicated which way the *amicus*'s argument would eventually go. She focused most usefully on the law of England, which since 1861 has had a criminal prohibition on bigamy, but has never added a provision to address polygamy *per se*. There is a controversy in England whether the bigamy law captures polygamy; if it does not, then there is a ready-made argument for the *amicus* that Canada, which has a bigamy provision like England's, does not require the extra prohibition on polygamy.

The argument repeats the one that occurred in Canada prior to the enactment of the 1890 law. England's bigamy law of 1861 was adopted into Canadian law upon Confederation, and would become part of the *Criminal Code*. But when Stenhouse converted to Mormonism in the late 1880s and joined the Mormon settlers in Southern Alberta, he argued that the bigamy provision did not apply to Mormon polygamy, or polygamy at all. It was this possible "loophole" that led to our polygamy law in the first place.

## John Witte

Dr John Witte, Jr, another expert witness for Canada, was a professor and director of the Center for the Study of Law and Religion at Emory University. Witte was qualified as an expert in legal history, marriage and historical family law, and religious freedom. His evidence canvassed and summarized the development of Western thought on polygamy and monogamy, beginning in ancient Greece and Rome.

A main point of introducing Witte's evidence was to emphasize that the prohibition on polygamy was not a Christian phenomenon. Witte described the function of monogamous marriage as described by classical philosophers, including Plato, Aristotle, Cicero, Musonius, Hierocles, and Plutarch, who referred to it as a source of private goods for men, women, and children, and of public goods for rulers, citizens, and society. He described how these philosophical views were legislated into formal institutions during the subsequent period of classical Roman law. The law restricted marriage to men and women who were of the age, fitness, and capacity to marry. No other sexual relationship had the status of marriage at Roman law, and no other institution could produce legitimate children, but there seemed no need to actually ban polygamy until 258 CE, when Roman emperors became explicit in prohibiting and punishing the practice. An Imperial Prescript from this period provided:

> It is in general obvious that no one who is under the authority of the Roman name can have two wives, since also in the Praetor's Edict men

of this sort were branded with legal infamy (*infamia*). The appropriate judge, when he learns of this matter, will not allow it to go unpunished.[10]

Witte went on to describe how, with the Christianization of the Roman Empire, the imperial proscriptions were melded with the teaching of the early Church, which had by then also adopted an officially monogamous position, to the point where, by the fifth century, Western theology and law were united in prescribing monogamy over all other forms of mating or marriage behaviour.

Until the Enlightenment, the enforcement of the polygamy prohibition was mainly for ecclesiastical authorities. But with the anti-establishment movement in England, Scotland, and America in the seventeenth and eighteenth centuries, arguments emerged against polygamy that were framed in rational terms. The advocates of monogamy said that children benefitted from more committed investments in the children of a nuclear family, and from the exclusivity and paternity certainty afforded by monogamy. Also, for the first time, the equality and dignity of men and women, and their mutual support, protection, and edification were offered as unqualified goods of the dyadic marriage relationship. This was important to our painting of the portrait of the polygamy prohibition as secular, rather than religious, law. Witte's Enlightenment philosophers clearly regarded polygamy as a dangerous institution that caused real harms to women, children, men, and society. Witte concluded:

> And what this underscores, at least to me, is that the prohibitions against polygamy are pre-Christian and post-Christian in their formulation in the West. Pre-Christian in that we have these formulations already in Greek philosophical texts and especially in pre-Christian Roman law, and post-Christian in that the architects of modern liberalism and the very formulation of what goes into a just liberal society are making clear that if we want to respect rights, if we want to respect dignity, if we want to respect the needs of all individuals in society and their inalienable and alienable rights, it is critical to maintain an institution of monogamy and prohibit and criminalize the institution of polygamy.

Witte's point was that Western legal tradition has declared polygamy to be an offence for 1,750 years. Over that time, the polygamy prohibition has been consistently justified on the basis of harm: (1) harm to women including exploitation; commodification; social isolation; co-wife conflict; discrimination; and impoverishment; (2) harm to children, resulting from discord, violation, and exploitation in the home, and the problems of diminished paternal investment; (3) harm to men created by the inequality of marriage opportunity and ostracization of younger men; and (4) harms to society resulting from social disorder and disharmony.

None of this, of course, was evidence that the harms actually existed or could be attributed to polygamy *per se*. That was not the point of Witte's recitation. Instead, his job was to speak to the motivations for the criminal prohibition, which legal academics like Baines, Beaman, Campbell, and Strassberg had generally assumed, in the absence of evidence, resulted from Victorian prudishness, colonialism, and prejudice. Witte's evidence clearly established that the prohibition was neither as recent nor as shallow as many had been led to believe.

Witte's evidence for Canada overlapped considerably the affidavit we had filed from Walter Scheidel, the chair of the Classics Department of Stanford University. In the end we were able to relieve Scheidel of his obligation to appear (he had by then taken a temporary posting at a university in the Middle East), and his evidence went in by affidavit alone.

The cross-examination of Witte focused on the fact that he had previously sworn an affidavit in the same-sex marriage cases. At that time, Witte's history had been used to support the deep roots of the prohibition on homosexual unions, and the clear suggestion was that Witte had been wrong about heterosexuality as a foundation of Western society then, and he was wrong about monogamy now. It was a fair point to make, and Witte, to his credit, confronted it directly, and gave quite a moving exposition of how his own thinking had evolved along with society's on the subject of gay marriage. Now, Witte explained, we had come to understand that we needed to extend all the goods of monogamous marriage to our gay and lesbian "brothers and sisters." This was different in kind from polygamy, because there is no corresponding extension of goods; there was only a bad institution. It was a persuasive distinction and eloquently made.

The exchange began when Tim Dickson, the *amicus*'s junior co-counsel, confronted Witte with an article he had written during the debate in the United States over same-sex marriage. In that article, Witte had urged caution in endorsing gay marriage, saying, "It's far too early in the debate to resort to constitutional brinkmanship to force change on a reluctant majority or to close doors to a resilient minority." On the witness stand, Witte explained:

> And I dare say in the ensuing ten years since I wrote that op-ed we have done exactly the kind of careful cultural—constitutional and cultural ventilation. We have done exactly the kind of prudent calculus that is necessary to think about issues of sodomy, issues of same sex relationships, recognizing that there are brothers and sisters in our own families, recognizing that there are members of our communities, rec-

ognizing that there are people in various professional communities of which we're a part who are same sex parties and who engage in same sex practices and who have children in same sex households.

And we have come to learn over time, as I say in my summary a few minutes ago, that the traditional attributes and goods that attach to other sex marriages, heterosexual marriage in the past, the classic goods of mutual love and support and companionship. The classic goods of mutual protection from sin and harm, and the classic goods of mutual procreation and nurture and education of children can be achieved in same sex households as much as they can be achieved in other sex households.

And it's just because of that recognition, that is, the dyadic structure that is duplicated in the same sex household with the goods attached to it, that has compelled a number of communities to come around on the question of same sex marriage and to recognize that same sex brothers and sisters deserve the same rights at law that other sex brothers and sisters deserve. And that the institution of marriage, when rendered plastic enough to include them within the definition, in point of fact helps substantiate and implement the goods that historically are ascribed to heterosexual marriage.

And children within same sex households are flourishing, partners within same sex households are flourishing, and communities that recognize same sex household are now flourishing. And notwithstanding the fact that we are still engaged in a culture war about this question, and we will over the next 50 years, we have done exactly what I'm calling on the community to do in this brief op-ed of 2000 or 2001. And we've come to the conclusion in a number of different churches and in a number of different states and in a number of different cultural communities, that same sex parties need to be treated the same way as other sex parties when it comes to union.

## Carolyn Jessop

Among the "survivor stories" of the modern literature of polygamy, the saga of Carolyn Jessop is by far the best known. Her autobiography, *Escape,* rose to number two on the *New York Times* best-seller list; her follow up, *Triumph,* had also done well.

Jessop is a former member of the FLDS, married as a teenager to Merril Jessop, a notorious figure who was now a bishop in that organization.

On the stand, Jessop told the terrifying tale of her life with Merril and her harrowing predawn run for freedom with her seven children. She recounted the life of subservience in the Hildale/Colorado City community, where she was not permitted to handle money (except to make minor purchases and return with the change). She described the conflict among the co-wives, and the constant surveillance by the Church's own volunteer "God Squad" and the local police, also controlled by the FLDS.

In person Jessop was almost preternaturally pleasant, with the hint of Texas in her accent. Jessop's recounting of her early-morning escape, bundling up her children into the van while the rest of the large family still slept, having arranged for non-FLDS relatives to meet her a few miles outside the community (she couldn't drive further because her vehicle, like most in the community was not licensed), had everyone in the courtroom on the edge of our seats. Nobody, she said, had ever been able to escape with their children—always they were brought back by relatives, "friends," the God Squad or the FLDS-controlled police. Jessop told of how, during the escape, her young daughter ran back into the house, and of her awful dilemma: should she leave with six, or go back for her daughter and risk losing all seven from the delay? The story was simply heartbreaking and horrifying.[11] And she spoke of her efforts to start a new life on the outside as a single mother of seven children.

On cross-examination, Wickett asked a number of questions about Jessop's income from her books and the auction of the movie rights to *Escape*. As it turned out, although the book had done well, it wasn't making her rich, earning her in the low six figures over five years. "It helped me get off welfare," she allowed. Jessop also said that she did a number of professional speaking engagements every year. Wickett asked if she was getting paid to testify in Canada. "No," she said.

The gist of Wickett's brief (and I should add respectful) cross-examination was that Jessop's experience was the result of two evil men: her husband, Merril, and Warren Jeffs, the head of the FLDS. It was surprising to us that the FLDS's own lawyer seemed eager to throw the current prophet of the church under a bus. The brief was obviously leaning towards the argument that it wasn't polygamy that was the problem, that bad experiences were just bad experiences and could happen in any context.

Entirely uncoached, Jessop deflected the suggestion that it was Warren Jeffs who was the problem, not polygamy itself. "I believe polygamy created Warren Jeffs," Jessop said simply.

Jessop's appearance at the trial was big news. Her recounting of life in the FLDS, with detailed accounts of beatings, oppression, and "water torture" (a method of obedience training where children—even babies—were spanked until they cried then held face up under a tap until they became exhausted) became the front-page headline of the following day's *Vancouver Sun*.

Jessop had been our first "live" witness with direct experience living within the FLDS. We had, by then, shown about a dozen videos of others, but Jessop's appearance took the "on the ground" evidence to a new level. It was at once sobering and inspiring to hear her courageous story.

## Matt Davies

Matt Davies was a psychologist put forward by the *amicus* as rebuttal witness to Beall. He was a counsellor with some limited experience dealing with members of polygamous communities. Davies's affidavit took exception to Beall's description of FLDS survivors' diagnoses based on post-traumatic stress disorder (PTSD). He suggested instead that persons who had left the church simply had "cognitive dissonance" and may be rationalizing their decisions to become "apostates" by emphasizing the negative in their experiences. Davies was also the *amicus*'s final expert witness. His academic credentials were thin; he was a practitioner, to be sure, and seemed to have some views on polygamy. But apart from his attack on Beall, his affidavit did not cause me much concern.

But Davies had another connection to the case. When Carolyn Jessop had discovered, some weeks before her scheduled testimony, that Davies would also be a witness, she revealed to us that Davies had treated her children, and that she had some things that she would like to say about him.

It was shaping up to be a very interesting two days; Jessop testified on January 12, and Davies was scheduled back to back, due to appear the following day.

On the stand, Jessop had described her experience with Davies. He had been hired, she said, by her estranged abusive husband after Carolyn fled. On her first meeting with Carolyn, according to her evidence, Davies sent her home with a book on polygamy and suggested that she should learn to accept the practice. Her memories of Davies had been uniformly negative. In the hallway at the break, we saw Davies, who had been flown up in anticipation of testifying the next day.

When Jessop had finished testifying there was a great deal of anticipation. What would Davies say about Jessop's allegations? Greathead had been preparing for weeks for Davies's cross-examination, enlisting other members of the team to assist her to become an expert on everything from the controversy surrounding PTSD diagnosis to the intricacies of American standards of practice in psychiatry. She had also prepared a series of questions based on Davies's treatment of Jessop's children, and was working late into the evening after Jessop's testimony had concluded. Craig Cameron with the federal Department of Justice was likewise fine-tuning his cross-examination questions at 10:35 that night when an astonishing e-mail was received from the office of the *amicus*: Davies, it said, would not be testifying. The *amicus* was withdrawing his affidavit.

What had caused the *amicus* to pull Davies at the eleventh hour, after flying him up to Vancouver to testify? It could have been any number of concerns, either of the *amicus* or of Davies himself. The *amicus* would only say in Court that he had determined that Davies's evidence "would not be helpful" to the Court. But they had not realized this until 10:35 the previous evening? We, of course, will never know. But it appeared to me that morning that the *amicus*'s case, at least to the extent that it relied on expert evidence, had now completely unravelled.

## Brenda Jensen

Our final two "direct experience" witnesses were former members of the leading families of the Bountiful community.

Brenda Jensen was a daughter of Harold Blackmore, who founded the fundamentalist Mormon community at Lister, British Columbia, on his eighty-acre farm. As I recounted earlier, Harold had established the small group there only to see himself pushed aside by his uncle, JR "Ray" Blackmore, in the early 1960s. Jensen had moved, with her father, to Short Creek in 1964, and then had followed him when he left the FLDS and moved to nearby Hurricane, Utah, a few years later.

Jensen spoke of the establishment of the Lister FLDS enclave, and life as a girl growing up in a fundamentalist Mormon community. She described, more than any other witness, the deterioration of the FLDS culture from a few committed families to an abusive and oppressive institution where girls were raised to be married and produce children as soon as possible. She eloquently discussed her father's developing disillusionment with the church leadership (which she, like Beall, described as part of a "caste system" of privileged families within the FLDS communities), who would meet over drinks and discuss the distribution amongst themselves of young girls who were approaching marriage age. She recounted her family's forced exile from Bountiful and the machinations that led to the signing over of the Bountiful property to the church's United Effort Plan trust.

More than anyone else, Jessop's testimony put the Bountiful part of the case into a solid historical perspective, and it also led me to think hard about the community in a different way: not as the Northern outpost of a bizarre church (which of course it had become), but rather as the outgrowth of a small group of well-meaning but catastrophically misdirected pioneer families whose "peculiar institution" had eventually either consumed them or spit them out.

## Truman Oler

The very first question put to Truman Oler asked him simply to confirm that the affidavit filed in the proceeding was his. This was done with all witnesses, each of whom would glance at the document, perhaps flip through the pages to their signature at the back, and answer affirmatively.

Not Oler. Handed a copy, he stared at the first page silently for perhaps ten seconds. Then he turned to the second page, another ten seconds, concentrating. The silence grew, spread over the courtroom. You could see people's backs straightening. What was wrong? Was there a problem with the affidavit? Oler turned to the third page, paused to read, then the fourth, and so on. Finally, he was done, and looked up: "Yes, that's right."

I will probably be unable to adequately describe Oler or his impact as a witness. I can describe him physically—a bit over six feet, very athletic build, a strong jaw, and close-cropped hair softened only slightly by wire-framed glasses. An impressive figure, but nothing too remarkable. It was when he spoke that you just had to listen.

To begin with, he would pause for perhaps ten or twenty seconds before answering a question, any question. Sometimes the pause would be much longer. At one point Horsman, who was leading him in direct examination, thought he didn't understand a question when he hadn't answered in perhaps half a minute, and began to clarify it. "I'm thinking," he said.

When Oler did answer, he spoke very slowly, in a stream of consciousness. He would start an answer only to seemingly think of a better way of putting his views across, switching midsentence to a different grammatical structure. He seemed to exist in a universe all alone with the question, and when he finished answering it, he would look up at Horsman almost as if coming out of a trance. It was very soon apparent that he was a remarkably intelligent man, and very wise for his twenty-nine years.

Oler had been a grade 9 dropout, and described working for Winston Blackmore's businesses as a labourer, earning two hundred dollars per month making fence posts and logging. Eventually his natural mechanical skills put him in the firm's repair shop. It was an unremarkable, even typical, career path for someone in the FLDS trying to prove themselves worthy of respect and, hopefully one day, the "assignment" of a wife.

Truman was a son of Dalmon and his third wife Memory Oler, which made him the full brother of Jim Oler, the current bishop of Bountiful,

Warren Jeffs' handpicked leader of the community. It also made Winston Blackmore, Memory's brother, his uncle.

Oler described, in his slow and sometimes halting way, the trials of growing up in the polygamous community—lack of parental attention, segregation of boys and girls (who were taught to regard each other as "poisonous snakes"), constant religious instruction, lack of any educational opportunity ("I didn't even know what college was"), and on and on. He described the raising of girls to be essentially baby factories, and the fates of the boys who could only live in hope of one day being permitted to marry, albeit marry a person not of their choosing.

Remarkably, Oler had no rancour for his former co-religionists, describing them as "some of the best people you'll ever meet." He thought Blackmore was a "good guy," and had obviously been badly shaken when Blackmore and Jim Oler effected the Split in 2002. Oler had left soon afterwards and described a community riven by petty backbiting and hypocrisy. He also detailed what it was like to become an "apostate" in the eyes of the community, ostracized even by members of his own family.

Most touching were his descriptions of the difference in parent-child relationships on the "inside" compared to his experience since becoming a father of two boys. Horsman asked:

Q  Has becoming a parent influenced your thinking about the way you were raised?

Oler paused, off in his world. He said softly, "Becoming a parent . . ." Horsman thought he might not understand the question.

Q  I mean in terms of your relationship with your children.

Oler looked up:

A  I'm just thinking here for a minute. Sorry.

Q  I have to stop interrupting you.

After another pause, Oler said, stumbling a bit over his words:

A  It has changed me so much... The way the men are raised. . . it is the women's responsibility to take care of the children every day and the men go out and work. They don't spend any time with their families even when they do have the time off. I can't see why personally. . . . I can't see why someone—why they would have so many children if they don't want to take care of them. Like I don't know, I don't know . . . I can't think of nothing more important than spending the time off I do have with my children. It's the most important thing in the world to me and I—and I see the needs that just the two of them have, and I can't even imagine trying to spread what little time I do have, and be able to give, and to be able to give my wife a little break from her day just to watch the kids for a little while. That's something they never would have had, the ladies, they never would have had a chance to get a job or work. They were basically having babies I guess as long as they physically can. But you . . . yeah, I just don't understand, like, why.

I know I have one brother who goes out and works. He has three wives. I don't know how many children and he goes out and works for months on end and never sees the kids and I know—and I witnessed with my own eyes, one of my older brothers who worked all the time come home to see one of his little babies. And he picked up the child and the child started to cry. He was afraid—he was afraid of him. He didn't even know who he was. That's—I don't know what I would do if I went home and I picked up my boy and he didn't know who I was. I couldn't handle that.

Oler was crying.

THE COURT:     Would you like a break, sir?

THE WITNESS:  It's okay. It's okay.

Oler was asked about the circumstances of his leaving, and facing the horrific decision that, everyone was convinced, would send him to eternal damnation. He described the cold reception he received now in every interaction with his mother, and how she had made it clear to him that, as far as she was concerned, it would have been better off if he had died. When he again broke down sobbing on the stand, I dare say half the courtroom was crying too.

A     The only contact I have with her is on my—if I make the initiative to call her, and even when I do, I find myself not wanting to call her again from the way that I am treated. When I do see or talk to her I just don't understand the way—well I do understand being involved in the religion the way they are and the way they do things but I just don't—I just wish there was something I could do so that . . . so that my mother could see that I am a good person. I don't hurt anyone. I don't break any laws. I don't—I don't hurt my family. I help my family. I help people I can. She looks at me as though I'm lost and she has said—she has said before that I am—she feels I am basically—that I would be just as well off as if I was dead. She said that before. And one time—I never told these ladies [Horsman and Greathead, who prepared Oler's affidavit] this story—but one time she told me a story of . . . she had one time had a stillborn child. I don't know—I don't think that's part of the fifteen [his mother's fifteen other biological children] but I hadn't heard of this until this story she told me, and this was after I left. She told me this story of the stillborn child and . . . in a way that made me feel she wished I was that child.

Oler was trying to get out the words:

That—I said did I . . . I just wish she didn't have to feel that way about me. How feeling like that can be God-like, I don't know. She hasn't—she does have no interest. I thought she would be very proud of me going back to school. And if I talk to her most of the time she treats me as if I am a stranger if I call her on the phone. There's no, "Hey how are you, how are the kids, what have you been up to?"

Q And that's because you've left the religion?

A That's because I left and she just cannot—she just thinks it's the end of the world.

On my way home in the car that night, I would listen to a CBC reporter refer to Oler's testimony as "unbelievably powerful." "It's a cliché," he said of the day's evidence, "but you literally could have heard a pin drop in that courtroom."

For me, the crescendo of the day, and in some ways of all the live witnesses' evidence, was the final answer given by Oler. Horsman had pointed out to him that, in his affidavit, Oler had said that he didn't like to talk about his past, about Bountiful or polygamy, that he was just tired of it. So Horsman asked him why, if that was the case, he had agreed to provide evidence in the reference:

Q I just want to ask you about one last portion of your affidavit, and it's the paragraph where you make the point, and you state it quite frankly, that you're tired of talking and thinking about your childhood and teenage years in Bountiful. That's at paragraph 25. Do you remember that portion of your evidence?

A I remember talking about it, yes. Here.

Q I expect there's many places in the world you would rather be right now than in that chair and I wondered if you could explain to the Court the reasons why you've agreed to be involved.

Oler paused, thought, and began another long halting speech that drove home the tragedy of life in the FLDS:

A   One of the main reasons . . . there are several . . . but when I hear and have the experience of trying to contact my family and the contact I do have with them and others, and I hear their experiences, it's just heartbreaking to me. And if there's any way, if there's any way, I don't know . . . I feel . . . and I know from the last, my last years there, the enclosed state which they have gotten in, the fact that they are not allowed access to television, computer access is very limited, Internet. I don't think—I don't know, maybe hopefully, hopefully the fact that I am here and what I have talked about can maybe get to some of the ones on the inside so they can see. And it would be so nice to one day be able to go down to the house I grew up in and see my family and have them treat me like a son, a brother, a friend.

I just—I just do not understand why they should have to go through their lives like that. They just . . . they're just . . . my mother shouldn't have to tell her child to go. Why they would be able to—why they would—I don't know. I—I don't think they even know what they're doing. I'm sure someone at the top of all this, there's a select few that are living a very good life off the benefits from what all—all the people involved are doing. They won't, they won't look at—I don't know, they don't look at it—they can't see the harm they're doing.

I feel for the most part most of the people involved I know most of them involved, especially my family, are very, very good-hearted people. They're—they're for the most part some of the best people you can meet on this earth, they're so kind hearted and everything. But they're just—they just don't know what they're doing and what they're being and the harm they're having, and all for no reason, and they do it all in the name of God and I just feel it is . . . just not necessary at all to take, to take a child, boys, young boys, young girls' ability and will to think away from them.

You really *could* have heard a pin drop as he paused again before shifting his attention to the legal question in the case:

And I've been thinking because I always hear—and I have heard well I guess Winston is the first one that always says it, the *Charter of Rights* or whatever. *Charter of Rights and Freedoms* to live to teach the religion, but I never really knew what that was.

Oler then made reference to section 2 of the *Charter*, which protects freedom of religion:

> I looked it up a little bit on the Internet and I read through that second—that second *Charter* and that one—the one thing they're trying to do is use that right to protect themselves . . . but . . . the teaching of that one religion is taking away all the rest of the rights on that *Charter*. And I just—it's just—I don't know if they—we never as children knew of charters and rights and freedoms, but I just don't understand. Well, I guess I kind of understand now but it's just—it just doesn't feel right to me why I know it's not for children to have to go through what I went through and all for no reason.

He looked up at Horsman, signalling that his answer was finished: "Well, they're personal reasons, but . . ."

The courtroom took a collective intake of breath. "*The teaching of that one religion is taking away all the rest of the rights on that Charter.*" That was our case, reduced to a single short sentence by a twenty-nine-year-old heavy-duty mechanic who could have been anything he'd wanted if he'd been raised somewhere else.

MS. HORSMAN: Thank you Mr. Oler. Those are my questions in direct, My Lord.

THE COURT: Thank you. Mr. Wickett?

Wickett had a pretty good sense for when to stay in his seat, a valuable trait not universally found among lawyers.

MR. WICKETT: No questions, My Lord.

THE COURT: Thank you.

Then, something unexpected from the *amicus*:

MR. MACINTOSH: My Lord, I have no questions, but I think my role as *amicus* permits me to thank you, Mr. Oler, for coming forward and testifying with the enormous stress and difficulty it's obviously presented for understandable reasons. And I wish to respectfully thank him for doing so and . . . thank you, sir.

The only hesitation in saying that, My Lord, is obviously I don't think it's right for the Court for me to start doing that routinely, and I won't, but I thank you sir.

THE COURT: Anybody else? And I share those remarks. . . . Thank you, Mr. Oler for coming to court. You're excused, sir.

Weeks earlier, when Horsman, Greathead, and I had been discussing which of our witnesses to call to appear, Horsman had insisted that we needed to hear Oler, that he would blow us all away. The way she spoke about him was almost reverential. I said, "Karen, I think you love Truman Oler."

Horsman smiled. "After you hear him testify, you will love Truman Oler too."

That night, Horsman and Greathead took Oler and Jensen out to dinner to thank them for their time, travel, and testimony. I declined an invitation to join them, and raced for the ferry home to Bowen Island.

The practice of law can take a lot of your time, and during my time with the government I spent half of most weeks in Victoria. Even when I'm at home I am often working. My wife might often feel like a single parent, and my son and daughter don't have me around much during the week. After Oler's testimony, I felt the overwhelming need to hug my kids before they got to bed. I think that night I might have squeezed them so hard it hurt.

## Stephen Kent

The final expert witness was Dr Steve Kent, a professor of sociology at the University of Alberta. We had decided not to ask Kent to be a witness for the Attorney General, despite the fact that he was one of the most prominent academics in Canada speaking and writing on polygamy. I felt that he was too much of an advocate, and that the debate that he had been participating in with the likes of Campbell and Beaman was superficial and the resulting work lacked the rigour and exactitude of the expert reports that we would be introducing at trial. Kent had really contributed two things to the debate over polygamy—he had compiled and summarized literature on polygamy's harms (which was superfluous now in light of other expert evidence) and he had offered his legal opinion on the polygamy law's constitutionality (which was irrelevant as that was the question now before the court). Canada seemed to share our reluctance, and agreed that we had all the points Kent could make covered through other witnesses.

But Kent had been keen to participate, and had contacted Stop Polygamy in Canada. Brian Samuels, though aware of the possible draw-
backs, thought the benefits outweighed the risks and retained him to
produce an affidavit/report.

Kent's report was basically a reiteration of the arguments he had made
in his previous publications. It had the air of advocacy. In fairness, Kent
had been such an advocate that to attempt at this point to produce a report that purported to be completely fair and balanced might have seemed
worse; this was part of the conundrum that had led us and our federal
counterparts, early in the process, to decide not to approach Kent to be an
expert for the Attorneys General.

I also decided I wouldn't be there in court for Kent's testimony. At
that stage, most of the day-to-day trial work was being done by Greathead and Horsman, as shepherds of the Bountiful/FLDS evidence, so my
attendance wasn't required and, when I had showed up in recent days, I
had sat in the gallery rather than at counsel table. I thought that if I did
not even do that, it would be a signal to the Court, if there was any doubt,
that Kent's evidence was not any necessary part of the Attorney General's
case. I was concerned that Kent would be the last chance for the *amicus* or
Wickett to get anything useful from an expert, and I was worried about
how he would fare in cross. I did suggest to Greathead that she conduct a
"friendly cross" just to establish the authoritative status of a couple of historical texts that I planned to rely on in my closing submissions, and she
would. With that, I hopped on a seaplane and flew to Victoria to spend
the balance of the week putting out some administrative brush fires and
working with my co-counsel Karrie Wolfe to write our factum for the
Supreme Court of Canada in the Safe Injection Site case.

At the end of the day I received the unofficial transcript. It was more
or less as we had expected. Kent's evidence in chief had gone in smoothly
enough, but he had been seriously challenged through an effective cross-
examination by Wickett. Wickett got Kent to agree that the authorities
he cited were selected because they supported Kent's conclusions that polygamy was wrong and should be prohibited. He also meticulously pointed out areas where Kent's conclusions on certain harms were tenuously
supported, and in fact where the best evidence indicated that they were
illusory.

In our own case, we had been careful to ensure that the harms we attributed to polygamy were supportable on the best evidence possible. For
instance, in the popular press it was often reported that polygamy was
associated with genetic disease, and in particular a form of retardation
sometimes called Polygamist Down's Syndrome, or Fumarase Deficiency.
We mentioned this as a risk of polygamy in our original Statement of

Position filed in March, months before the exchange of evidence, but the more I looked into the issue the more concerned I became that the association between polygamy and genetic disorder was no more robust than it would be in any small, insular community with a fairly limited genetic pool. Thus the problem was the insularity, rather than the polygamy; that was causing the problem. So by the time of our opening statement, I had dropped Polygamist Down's from the list of harms we would seek to prove.

Another persistent complaint made regarding polygamous communities, including Bountiful, was that they were riven with welfare fraud and other exploitations of social services. The theory was that the men would have a dozen wives and countless children, who would be a source of income from the state. Certainly in Canada, there was no evidence of this. In fact a call to the relevant government officials in British Columbia early in our investigation confirmed that *nobody* in Bountiful was on welfare. The evidence from the American communities, when the surface was scratched, seemed ambivalent at its very best. As a consequence, we had never alleged welfare fraud as a harm that could be associated with the practice of polygamy. We wanted to ensure that the harms we did identify were backed by bulletproof evidence, not conjecture or worse, myths arising from popular prejudice.

Insisting on a high degree of rigour from expert evidence is not just important from a strategic point of view, it also gives counsel any number of tactical advantages. Rigorous research gives better results, and scientists tend to admire efforts in this direction. In the Polygamy Reference, we were confident not only that our experts were good, but also that, if the other side's experts were legitimate, they would agree with our own.

Unfortunately, Kent had rather uncritically endorsed both the genetic disease and welfare fraud complaints as true, and on fairly tenuous evidence, mostly from the popular press. It was a simple matter for Wickett, on cross, to dig down a little and expose these harms as arguably chimeric, and in so doing cast doubt on the other harms that Kent attributed as well. He did a very good job, and I reckoned that, come closing arguments, not even Stop Polygamy in Canada would be relying too much on the evidence of Kent.

## Alina Darger and Mary Batchelor

The most succinct type of constitutional challenge to the polygamy prohibition was embodied by two "independent" fundamentalist Mormon women, Alina Darger and Mary Batchelor.

Darger was the daughter of a polygamist who had two wives and thirty-two children, living in two neighbouring houses in a Salt Lake

City suburb. She appeared to live an ordinary, middle-class existence; she graduated from high school and had a series of ordinary jobs. She now lived in a polygamous household with two other wives and twenty-four children. She fondly described the closeness of her polygamous family growing up, and her conscious decision to practise plural marriage in her own life (she married at twenty to a husband of the same age; her two plural wives, biological sisters, joined subsequently). Darger described her beliefs as follows:

> It was more of a process, because growing up, of course, I—you know, I lived in a plural family and I loved that experience and I thought it was really amazing, and I always felt like I had somebody close and to care for me.
>
> And then as I got older, I would talk about it with my siblings and say, what do you think? Will you—do you want to do it or do you not want to live this way? And I always felt I wanted to do that. And in talking with them, I did realize that there are a lot of sacrifices to make, and even watching my parents, and that it would be a harder road than if I had just chose a monogamous marriage, but I felt like, you know, growing up, what was so rewarding to me and what was so special to me, I wanted to have that in my family and continue on with that.

She described a fairly egalitarian existence, where important decisions were made among the adults by consensus. She allowed that paternal attention was a concern, but was proud of the fact that her husband made an effort to get to know each of his children.

Like Darger, Batchelor was an "independent" living in the Salt Lake suburbs. She too spoke sincerely and emphatically about the central role of polygamy in her faith.

> Plural marriage is a very vital and intricate part of my belief system, and I do not believe that I can achieve the fullness of my potential as a woman and as well as a daughter of God without it. It's a very meaningful part of my belief system.

Darger and Batchelor rejected underage marriage as well as "placement" by church leaders. Like Darger, Batchelor married as an adult; unlike Darger, though, Batchelor's plural marriage fell apart three years later when her sister wife left the marriage. Subsequently, Batchelor has considered herself an "involuntary monogamist." She has seven children, the eldest of which are in college. Under direct, we were introduced to the fact that Batchelor's former sister wife was not of enamoured of polygamy as was Batchelor herself.

Q And I realize describing three years in a sentence or two is obviously not easy, but in any event, describe as best you can, briefly, the three years of plural marriage.

A You know, we had some very good times, some really positive times. We had some very bonding moments. She and I had some strong bonding moments together. And we had some very challenging times. It was hard. It especially was hard when the marriage broke down and there was a loss of trust, and it was a heartbreak for me when she left.

Q M'mm-hmm. And she became a third wife in another plural marriage at that time?

A She did.

Q And she is—is now, or at least at some stage, she became a spokesman against polygamy?

A She became the founding director of Tapestry Against Polygamy.

These witnesses—Darger and Batchelor, presented a unique perspective and a robust challenge to the constitutionality of section 293. Their experiences bridged the gap between the mainstream practice of multi-partner conjugality and the closed fundamentalist communities. They were, in some ways, religiously motivated polyamorists, one might say the "good polygamists." They spoke generally of positive experiences with polygamy, and as such they embodied the "reasonable hypothetical" that we had known all along we would have to confront: a person whose religious practices of multiple marriage were barred by the polygamy law, and yet whose relationships could not be in any way linked with most of the harms that were well established in the closed communities of the FLDS and others.

We could make the point, and we did, that all might not have been as rosy in polygamy as the witnesses suggested. Batchelor's disgruntled sister wife, as noted above, had left the marriage and founded Tapestry Against Polygamy, one of the most vocal US-based antipolygamy organizations. Under cross-examination, Batchelor's description of her experiment with polygamy seemed somewhat less idyllic than her written accounts would suggest, particularly when put in context with the recollections of her one-time sister wife, Vicky Prunty, who had been the women's husband's first wife and had left after three years after her husband had also married Batchelor.

Horsman, who led the cross-examination, took Batchelor to Andrea Moore-Emmett's book *God's Brothel*, which has a chapter entitled "Vicky." In that book, "Vicky" paints a very different picture of polygamy than

Batchelor did, recalling it as a time of oppression and abuse, and describing "Greg" and "Marlene" (pseudonyms for Batchelor and the husband) as little short of fundamentalist religious fanatics. Batchelor responded mostly by denying that "Vicky's" account was factual, but Horsman's point was well made—Batchelor, a self-declared advocate for polygamy and against criminalization, had a retrospective view on polygamy that certainly wasn't the only way of interpreting the facts, even of her own marriage.

But things got really interesting when Robert Danay took over the cross-examination for the federal Attorney General. Danay wanted to explore Batchelor's knowledge of the "child bride" phenomenon, and pointed out that, in the survey presented by "Principle Voices" (Batchelor's pro-polygamy advocacy group), almost half the respondent polygamous wives indicated that they had married between the ages of fourteen and twenty. After scoring several other good points, Danay moved to Batchelor's thoughts on Tom Green, the notorious fundamentalist Mormon who had taken a succession of young girls as brides. Danay referred to the "Principle Voices" book:

Q  There's a discussion that starts at the bottom of page 42 and goes over onto page 43 about an individual by the name of Tom Green?

A  Yes.

Q  And this is the Tom Green who was convicted of bigamy and child rape as well?

A  Yes, he was.

Q  And I'm going to hand you a document. Now, the document I've just handed you is entitled "Polygamist Guilty of Child Rape" —

A  Okay.

Q  — with the subheading "One of Utah Mormon Tom Green's 5 Wives was 13 at Marriage"?

A  Yes.

Q  And I'm just going to quickly read a few lines from it and make sure we're talking about the same Tom Green from your book. And it says here:

> Polygamist Tom Green was convicted of child rape Monday for having sex with a 13-year-old girl who became his "spiritual wife," and had a child with him in 1986. Fourth District Judge Donald Eyre took just 30 minutes to find Green guilty for his relationship

with Linda Kunz, who is now his legal wife. The nonjury trial lasted about an hour.

The judge had already rejected defence arguments that the statute of limitations had run out and that the case should be thrown out because the alleged rape didn't take place in Utah.

And skipping down, it says:

Green, who has four other "wives" and 30 children in all, including seven with Kunz, already is serving a five-year sentence for bigamy and criminal nonsupport. He was convicted in May 2001.

And:

Kunz was called to the stand Monday but refused to testify. Spouses do not have to testify against each other. "We don't feel like this was a crime," she said after the verdict. Prosecutors submitted her testimony from previous hearings, as well as her 1973 birth certificate and the 1986 birth certificate of the couple's first child, Melvin.

"Basically, this comes down to math," Eyre said. "We know a normal human gestation takes nine months."

So I'll just stop there. And from what you understand, is this article discussing the same individual who is being discussed in your book on page 42?

A   Yes.

Q   And do you know Tom Green personally?

A   I have met him.

Q   In what context did you meet him?

A   Shortly after I got married, he came by my house to watch something, a video that we had, and so I met him at that time, I think.

Q   Why would he have come to your house to watch a video?

A   He heard from somebody that we had a video, and he wanted to see it, so he called and asked to come over.

Q   So your family must be on some friendly terms with him, I imagine?

A   We do know him now obviously. I haven't had contact with him. I saw him one time after he went to jail. But I met him. You asked me when I met him. I believe —

Q   When he came to your house?

A   He came to my house shortly after I was married.

Q  Okay. So is he friends with your husband?

A  I don't—we are associations.

Q  Association?

A  We know him.

Q  Okay. Now, if you go on to page 43 of your book where you continue to discuss the Green case, you see you discuss sort of your view or the authors' views of how fundamentalists reacted to the Tom Green case?

A  Right.

Q  And in the paragraph that begins with "while many fundamentalist Mormons disagree with Green on some issues, particularly his extreme openness about his plural marriages," if you skip down, you see that it says

> Besides four counts of bigamy, Green has been charged with "rape of a child." This charge is viewed with great irony since the "child" is his own wife who has remained a happy member of his family for 16 years. Fundamentalists perceive the extraordinary measures against Green as especially vindictive, despite claims of protecting children, since the intent and the outcome would be to break up his family.

A  Right.

Q  And those words are in your book?

A  They are.

Q  And you didn't object to them being included?

A  I didn't.

Q  Given your familiarity with Mr. Green, I wonder if you might answer a couple more questions about his arrangements. You're aware that he married 7 girls ranging from ages 13 to 16?

A  I actually am not that familiar. You would have to refresh my memory.

Q  So you may have at some point known that he married that number?

A  I knew Linda. I knew Hannah. I knew Shirley.

Q  So I'm told—and you can confirm—that when they were married, Green married Linda Kunz at the age of 13?

A  We learned that during the trial.

Q  And he married a woman named Shirley Beagley when she was 15?

A   I don't know.

Q   And LeeAnn Beagley when she was 14?

A   I have no knowledge of that other than what I read.

Q   How about Allison Ryan who was 16 when she married Mr. Green?

A   I never knew Allison.

Q   Cari Bjorkman who was 15?

A   I met—I met Cari.

Q   And Hannah Bjorkman who was 14?

A   I don't know when they were married.

Q   And —

A   So I'm relying on your information —

Q   Okay.

A   — is what I'm saying. I'm —

Q   And so you don't know if he married Tally Dawson McKinley [phonetic] when she was 14?

A   I don't know who she is.

Q   Okay. Are you aware that Mr. Green was married to two mother-daughter sets?

A   I am aware of that.

Q   And neither you nor your husband had any concerns with Mr. Green coming to your house to—for a movie night?

Danay's cross-examination of Batchelor was as effective as it was subtle, because it brought home that even those who sought to espouse and defend polygamy, the "good polygamists," recognized the child bride phenomenon even as they tended to de-emphasize its prevalence. But Batchelor's evidence under cross-examination revealed something that would become a recurring theme: a disturbing lack of *concern* with the fact that children were targeted, an elusive implication that, if plural marriage were truly God's will, then we needn't fuss with details like the age of the girls involved. This eerily calm acceptance of children being married off to middle-aged men would also emerge through the evidence of the FLDS's anonymous witnesses.

## The FLDS's Anonymous Witnesses

Throughout the trial, some important evidence for the other side seemed to disappear, not unlike that star you catch in your peripheral vision that winks out if you actually look at it. As I mentioned, Oler had filed an affidavit for the FLDS, and then apparently decided he didn't want to face cross-examination. The *amicus*'s psychologist Davies had withdrawn his affidavit after his former client, Jessop, had testified. And then, two weeks from the end of the trial, Wickett confirmed that Palmer, the principal of BESS, would not be testifying after all and would withdraw his own affidavit, which described how wonderful the FLDS-run school system was.

I wasn't surprised that Palmer had scarpered. Aside from his knowledge about Bountiful's somewhat perfunctory education system, Palmer had a lot of knowledge about child brides. He had reputedly married his own two wives as teenagers; I had been looking forward to questioning him about that. I also wanted to plumb the depths of his knowledge about all the girls in his school whom he watched being married off to older men in the community. Why, I wondered, didn't he feel it was his obligation to report these relationships to the authorities? It was regrettable that the Court would be deprived of his answers.

The highlight of the last week was the much-anticipated appearance of the FLDS's anonymous witnesses. In advance of the exchange of evidence during the summer, Wickett had applied for, and received, an order to protect his clients' witnesses from either self-incrimination or incriminating others as polygamists.[12]

Prior to the hearing of any lay witnesses, we came to an agreement with the other participants that each side would relinquish their absolute right to cross-examine every affiant, on the understanding that we could each decide which of our witnesses to call in direct, and those persons only would be cross-examined. The others would be permitted to put in their affidavits alone.

I had some misgivings about this. For instance, one FLDS witness had put in an affidavit that was, almost verbatim, identical to a second we received at the same time. Clearly one of these witnesses had simply accepted what was put in front of her and signed off on it, changing only a few sentences here and there (for instance, one witness said she was married, and one said she wasn't), but most of the affidavits' substance was, word for word, identical. Soon after delivering these affidavits, Wickett withdrew the second one. It would have been a lot of fun to cross-examine the remaining "clone" on her affidavit, and show her the identical one, and ask whose words these really were. At the very least, it would demonstrate that one or other of the affiants was simply a drone repeating what she was told to say. Perhaps they both were. But the remaining affiant was not one of those Wickett was proposing to call in direct. Did I really want to give up making my point in cross?

This agreement was the subject of a lot of wrangling and second-guessing, but at the end of the day all sides abided by it. The ongoing challenge was that Wickett kept changing his mind regarding which of the anonymous witnesses he intended to call.

For instance, it was apparent that anonymous Witness 1 was almost certainly Oler's mother. Witness 1 was one of the witnesses that Wickett had listed to call. After Oler's testimony, we looked forward to cross-examining her on the striking inconsistencies between the way she characterized her ongoing relationship with her unnamed errant son, and the way Oler had described it. We were confident that Oler's evidence had been so compelling that any disparity in the accounts would be resolved in his favour, and Memory Oler's evidence would be severely undermined as a result.

But after Oler's testimony, Wickett had a change of heart and told us that Witness 1 would not be called. We could, I suppose, have insisted that she appear, given that she was on the list, or that if she wasn't prepared to, her affidavit should be withdrawn. But we saw little utility in that. Sure, her affidavit, misleading as it may appear in light of Oler's testimony, would stay in the record. But if the court figured out that the terrible son she was referring to was Oler, I believed it could only weaken her evidence, not his. So, not without some reluctance, we relinquished our right of cross-examination.

However frustrating this might have been from our side, from Wickett's it must have looked especially bleak. The FLDS's two ranking witnesses, bishop James Oler and school principal Palmer, had withdrawn their affidavits rather than face cross-examination. Anonymous Witness 8 and her cloned affidavit had blipped briefly in and out of existence. Witness 1, who we believed to be Memory Oler, had been scheduled for direct evidence, and then withdrew after her own son took the stand and knocked it out of the park. Witness 11 was added to the list for direct examination, and then taken off. And Davies, the *amicus*'s psychologist who had been expected to defend the FLDS as mostly harmless, had been pulled after Jessop had savaged him from the witness box. On the other side of the ledger, we had not suffered any comparable ignominy, and all our evidence was still before the court.

Wickett's final selection was to have anonymous Witnesses 2, 3, and 4 appear to give live evidence. This was interesting, because Witness 4 was another who had not been on Wickett's original list.

Under our original trial plan, I wouldn't have been cross-examining any of the Bountiful witnesses. For this FLDS-focused part of the trial, Greathead was in charge. But it looked as though she would need to be in Victoria for part of the Tuesday that the witnesses were due to appear, and so we divided them among us. Greathead would do the cross of Witnesses 2 and 3, and I would prepare for Witness 4.

As it turned out, this proved to be lucky for me, because as I reread Witness 4's affidavit, I realized that I believed I knew who she was. And if I was right, I very badly wanted to talk to her.

Witness 4 identified herself in her affidavit as having four co-wives. We knew from the demographic breakdown of the FLDS's Bountiful community (which Wickett had provided us before the trial) that there were only two such five-wife families living there. And it was a notorious fact that James Oler, the FLDS's bishop of Bountiful, had five wives. So Witness 4 was possibly one of the teen brides of the bishop, and given her age it was almost certainly the young woman who had been the subject of the 2009 criminal charges against Oler, the quashing of which in 2009 had led to the reference. And after Oler had married that girl at age seventeen, he had taken a fifth wife who was only fifteen at the time of her marriage. She too had been married in the United States and brought up from Hildale. Oler, by then, was in his forties.

So, in my estimation, if Witness 4 had participated in the recruitment of a fifteen-year-old American into Oler's family, she could be both the victim *and a perpetrator* of child exploitation and trafficking. I was very much looking forward to asking her questions, not with a view to incriminating her, but more to learn how people could think this was normal.

The approach would be delicate. I wanted to avoid the possibility that Wickett would pull Witness 4 and her affidavit rather than having her testify, which he might do if he knew the questions we proposed to ask. In fairness, I had told Wickett that he should assume that we actually knew the identities of the witnesses we would cross examine. He had responded that this didn't bother him, provided that we avoided asking questions that would reveal their identity or those of other polygamists. I don't know whether Wickett knew all the details we did about Witness 4 and her family, but I had to assume that he understood her vulnerability. So I thought we needed to be very careful with our cross-examination of the first witness, Witness 2, so as not to "scare off" Witness 4 (Witness 3 was scheduled to follow the other two).

To prevent the anonymous witnesses from being visually identified, the court staff had arranged for the hearing to proceed by a video link. All counsel except the FLDS lawyer would be in Courtroom 55 as usual, along with any members of the public who wished to watch. However, the witness, Wickett, the Chief Justice, and a court clerk would be in another courtroom across the street. The video link would ensure that no one but these four could see the witness; the feed into Courtroom 55 showed only the Chief Justice and Wickett. We would listen to direct examination, and conduct our cross-examination, through the audio feed.

As I mentioned, the first anonymous witness would be Witness 2. She was a forty-something plural wife who had been born and raised in the Bountiful FLDS community. Wickett got the basic facts from her: her mother, one of five wives, had had fifteen children. Witness 2 was the junior of two wives in her household, and had nine children of her own. Interestingly, she described her own marriage as having been triggered from her desire to leave the community and attend college. The somewhat perfunctory nature of the arrangement was described as follows:

A    Okay. When I was 16 years of age I was very much interested in attending college, and so when I was talking about this to my parents they suggested that in order to help me and support me through the college that marriage would be a good idea. And so I thought about that for awhile and I decided that I did want to get married and so they went and spoke with our prophet at the time. My father came back and we had a discussion about it. He mentioned a name of one of the elders in you're church at the time although I did not know him well. I knew he was in good standing with the church. And he told me this man has no idea that his name has been placed here and you do not have to marry him if you do not want to. He will never know whether you said yes or no and I felt good about him and I married him.

On cross-examination by Greathead and Reimer (for the Attorney General of Canada), it emerged that Witness 2's sister wife was also her biological sister, and had also married her husband at age sixteen. The witness had borne her first child at seventeen and a second while still a teen. Her husband, at the time of her marriage at sixteen, had been twenty-nine.

Witness 2 described the belief system of the FLDS, something of the structure of the Church, and its rules regarding the segregation of boys from girls and the strict dress code for women, which required dresses from neck to wrist and ankle, which were worn even when swimming in the creek.

Most touching was her account of her own daughter's marriage at age fifteen. She clearly appeared quite conflicted about it. She didn't want her daughter to marry so young, and neither did her husband. Her husband went to the bishop, Winston Blackmore, to protest the idea.

Q And what was it that your husband spoke to the bishop about?

A He—he told me that he voiced to Winston that he didn't feel good about [redacted] my daughter getting married and—and there was a discussion there and it was ultimately left to her to decide—my daughter.

Q So notwithstanding the concerns of your husband that he expressed to the bishop your daughter ultimately got married at 15.

A Yes.

A little bit later, Witness 4 was given the opportunity to elaborate on the reason she had eventually agreed to her daughter's early marriage:

Q Now, for your—we've talked a bit about your 15 year old, your daughter who at 15 got married. Did you attend her wedding ceremony?

A Yes I did.

Q And so did you—you ultimately consented to your daughter's marriage?

A Yes, I did.

Q And your husband consented as well?

A Yes.

Q And why did you consent?

A Because her partner was 19 years of age. It was a monogamous relationship and I felt that I could be close by to her to help her in the event she had children which I was able to do and that's why.

Q So would you have not granted your consent if she was entering into a plural marriage situation at 15?

A I would have not allowed it.

Greathead returned later to the invidious choice faced by this mother:

Q Witness No. 2, you've told that you consented to your 15-year-old daughter marrying monogamously but you would not have consented to a plural marriage. So I'm wondering is it fair to say that in your mind a marriage to a man that was about the same age as your daughter and the man that she fancied was preferable to your daughter being placed in a plural marriage, married to a man much older and perhaps sent away to somewhere like Short Creek?

A Yes.

So an interesting window into FLDS marriages. Witness 2 put her name forward to marry a stranger at sixteen so she could be accorded the rare privilege of attending college outside the community. She consented to the marriage of her own daughter at fifteen to a nineteen-year-old man, at least in part because she did not want her girl to be placed with a much older man in a polygamous family. Yet the witness, at every opportunity, stressed how happy and content she was, and how much choice and agency she felt women had with respect to the FLDS rules.

The witness was also questioned about her explanation for the failure of postsecondary achievement at Bountiful: in her affidavit, she complained that the community was forced to spend its resources defending US-based church leaders facing criminal charges. She complained that church members lived at the "poverty level" as a result, and had no money to invest in higher education. On cross-examination, Witness 2 revealed that, in addition to their regular 10 percent tithing to the church, members had been asked for periodic contributions of hundreds of dollars each for the defence expenses of church leaders accused in the United States of participating in the sexual assault of children.

And what about the idea that they couldn't afford university? Greathead confirmed with the witness that she was aware that scholarships, bursaries, and student loans were available. And Greathead asked if the witness had ever known of an instance where a Bountiful student had applied to a university, been accepted, but had been unable to attend for lack of resources. The answer was no. Then Greathead suggested that it might be family priorities that were preventing the allocation of resources to education:

Q  So there's 19 children in your family?

A  Yes.

Q  So you mention that you live at the poverty line?

A  I believe we do.

Q  And is it possible—I'm going to put a proposition to you that you live at the poverty level because you've been trying to raise 19 children on the family income that you have?

A  I wouldn't say that is the only reason.

Q  It's one of the reasons though?

A  It could be, yes.

Bauman at times seemed to grow impatient with Greathead's methodical questioning of Witness 2, and I could understand why: one of the things she was trying to establish was a foundation for the introduction of our Vital Statistics evidence on teen births in Bountiful. The Vital Stats evidence, compiled by an analyst named Bruce Klette, compared teen births at Bountiful with those in the surrounding area and the province. It showed that a lot of girls were having babies in Bountiful. But because "Bountiful" isn't any recognized geographic area, and because the FLDS doesn't have public membership rolls, the government analyst had selected birth records for the Bountiful "cohort" on the basis of location and surname. Therefore we needed to establish that the communities he identified were in fact places of residence for FLDS members, and that the names he searched for (surnames such as Blackmore, Palmer, and Oler, given first names such as Moroni and Nephi) were in fact identifiable as recurring in the FLDS.

But the Chief Justice almost certainly had not yet read the Klette affidavits, so he would have had no idea why Greathead was taking the witness through lists of names "characteristic of the Bountiful community" or spending time with a map of Bountiful's surrounding settlements. So, I suspect, we tested his patience with Witness 2.

As the cross-examination progressed, I was also getting concerned about the length of time Witness 2 was taking, but for a very different reason. If Witness 2's evidence took all day, then Wickett would have overnight to ponder whether or not to call Witness 4. Wickett had examined his witness for only about half an hour that day, and had elicited very little that wasn't already in her affidavit. Greathead's cross-examination had by then gone on for three hours, and was constantly revealing information that seemed harmful to Wickett's case, or at least that was very helpful to ours. It seemed to me that Witness 4 would be even worse for the FLDS.

As a result, I had become fixated on the idea that Wickett would withdraw Witness 4's affidavit and shuffle her back into the shadows, because that's exactly what I would have done. So I pressed the other counsel who had signed on to cross-examine for an early conclusion to the evidence so that we could at least start Witness 4 that afternoon—once she had begun her testimony, even in chief, withdrawal wouldn't be in the cards. To my disappointment, Witness 2 ran out the afternoon, and I had a very sleepless night, worried that I would receive another late night e-mail, this time announcing that Wickett had pulled Witness 4.

The next morning we gathered again around the cameras and video screen. I could see Wickett at the podium on the TV, and silently prayed that he wasn't about to announce the withdrawal of his witness. To my immense relief, when court commenced he introduced Witness 4 and had her sworn. Game on.

I had prepared my questioning very delicately to get at the basic facts of Witness 4's marriage without identifying anybody. To my relief and somewhat to my surprise, Wickett asked her during his brief direct examination how old she had been when she was married. "Seventeen," she replied. This was information that had not been in Witness 4's anonymous affidavit. Wickett also elicited that she had been raised in an FLDS community in the United States, and assigned in marriage to her husband, whereupon she had moved to Bountiful. There was now no doubt in my mind that she was who I believed her to be, and I would question her on that assumption.

As I say, Wickett's direct examination was again very brief, perhaps twenty minutes. He walked her through her short affidavit, in which she described her education. She had attended BESS, and was now taking business administration at the College of the Rockies. She was articulate and self-assured; she sounded, for all the world, like a fairly normal, somewhat ambitious young woman, albeit one with some very peculiar religious beliefs and an obviously unusual way of life. This explained her selection as an affiant: superficially, her story was one of the few "success stories" they could produce. But under cross-examination I expected we would learn the details of what it means to be a girl in the FLDS.

The witness had been born in Hildale, but raised in another American community. When she was sixteen, she said, she had put herself forward for marriage. A few days after her seventeenth birthday, she was told that she was marrying a Canadian man whom she didn't know (though she said that she had dreamed of his face before). The wedding happened thirty minutes after she learned his identity. Two hours after that she was on the eighteen-hour drive to Bountiful, equipped with a letter from her parents to the border officials, claiming that she was going to Canada to "visit an aunt" and "stay with a friend." Her new sister wives were informed of the wedding by a phone call from the husband, after the fact. Since then she had remained in Canada on a series of student visas, which might help to explain her passion for the College of the Rockies' business programs. Her ambition, she said, was to become an accountant for the community.

Six months later, her husband did it again. Another American FLDS girl, but this one was fifteen. The sister wives were again informed by phone after the fact. Another long car ride. I was trying to be kind in cross-examination, but Witness 4 could not entirely escape, I thought, responsibility for what happened. A fifteen-year-old girl, a thousand miles from home, in a foreign country, "ordained by God" to have sex with a forty-year-old official of her own church. And it was all happening in this witness's home, with her obvious approval. When I asked her whether fifteen was just too young to be married to a middle-aged man, she replied that the new girl had seemed "very responsible" to her. Very *responsible*? So I asked the following questions:

Q Okay. Now, you're aware, Witness 4, that since 2008 the church has announced a policy of not marrying anybody below the age of legal marriage in any particular jurisdiction?

A Yes.

Q Do you agree with that policy?

A I do.

Q Why?

A I just think that's a good age to be married. For people nowadays.

Q What age is that?

A 18.

Q 18 is a good age to be married. Better than 15?

A 18 is a good age.

Q Better than 15?

A I guess.

Q Better than 17?

A Sure.

Q Do you as a sister wife feel that you are equal to your husband in the household?

A Equal in terms of other sister wives, or . . .?

Q No, I'm sorry, I mean equal *vis-à-vis* your husband?

A Equal as my husband . . .

Q Equal to your husband?

A I don't know if I understand what you mean.

Q I guess what I'm asking is if you consider yourself to be equals in the relationship or if you consider one to be more important than the other?

A Equal in the relationship.

Q It sounds to me like you're struggling with the concept?

I wasn't trying to be cute, but obviously I wasn't getting far with the idea of equality. I moved on, but I couldn't leave the question of age and agency just yet:

Q  Now I just want you to answer from your own experience and your own attitudes. You are a member of a household in which to your knowledge a 40-year-old, 40-something perhaps has married a 15-year-old girl and the man has a position of status within that girl's church. Would it ever occur to you to discuss that situation with any authority?

A  To discuss someone else's life with an authority? No that wouldn't occur to me.

Q  It wouldn't occur to you to report that to the police for instance?

A  If I felt like someone was doing something someone was in an abusive situation or was in harm being harmed of some sort I would feel to report that to authorities.

Q  And if it was happening in your own home that would give you a special responsibility, wouldn't it?

A  Yes.

Q  And it's probably needless to add but you never did that with respect to this 15-year-old girl's situation?

A  Was that just a comment or you wanted me to comment on that.

Q  I want you to confirm that was the case.

A  That I happened to see someone in a harmful or abusive situation and I didn't report?

Q  No ma'am. That you never reported to the police or any other authority the 15-year-old's situation?

A  No.

Q  And that to your knowledge no one else in the Bountiful community ever reported it?

A  I don't know that.

Q  You don't know of any reporting?

A  I don't have any idea what anybody else did or said.

Q  But you never received any inquiries that would suggest somebody had or did you?

A   No one ever came up to me and said I think there is something serious happening. You should report that to the police.

Q   Okay. And you considered it God's will that this 15-year-old should marry your 40-something-year-old husband; is that correct?

A   That it was a revelation from God, yes.

When I had finished cross-examining Witness 4 we had a real sense of the gulf between us. Here was a young woman, obviously bright, a college student, so mainstream in so many respects and probably regarded by those who knew her as a very nice person. Yet here was a person who could calmly describe the removal of a fifteen-year-old girl from her American family to be married to a forty-something church official in Canada, on no notice to anyone (least of all the girl) as if this were the most normal, even desirable, thing in the world. Not that she had struggled with this and concluded that it was right—the idea that it might be even remotely questionable did not, *could not*, have occurred to her. The enduring mental image I have of Witness 4 is her, at seventeen, and her fifteen-year-old sister wife, riding the yellow school bus to BESS. And her husband waving the bus off in the morning. And Palmer, and the other school officials, welcoming the girls' arrival, knowing full well what was going on with his newly arrived young charges. Everybody happy and smiling, the girls soon to be mothers. It was a scene wrapped in so much "middle America" imagery, yet just so . . . weird.

The last anonymous witness was Witness 3, a twenty-two-year-old woman who was studying during the summers in the United States to become qualified as a teacher. In the meantime, she was teaching at BESS on a "letter of permission," which is an authorization from the Ministry of Education to permit a person to teach without the usual education or qualifications.

Unlike most of the FLDS's other witnesses, Witness 3 had no direct experience as a polygamous wife; in fact she was unmarried. She was apparently being put forward, like Witnesses 2 and 4, to support the proposition that educational opportunities were not being denied young women in the FLDS generally or at Bountiful in particular. If you took these three women as representative you might think that college education was routine among the women of Bountiful. But to me, Witness 3's evidence revealed a different angle on the FLDS's approach to higher education.

Witness 3 had begun her studies in 2008 along with four other women from Bountiful, all of whom planned to get teaching qualifications and return to BESS. The FLDS provided the group with a house in Utah, and her family assisted with the costs of education. Clearly, the Church was supporting women's education, but only in those narrow fields that would serve its interests. It needed teachers and midwives because if it did not have its own people in these government-scrutinized and regulated professions, then "outsiders" would occupy them. It did not, it seemed, indicate that the children of Bountiful had, as the witnesses suggested in their affidavits and direct testimony, limitless opportunity to pursue any career or life that they wanted. The FLDS's efforts had already had some measure of success: all the teachers at BESS were members of the church.

Greathead asked Witness 3 the same questions we had posed to Witnesses 2 and 4: apart from midwifery, nursing, and education, do you know of a person from Bountiful who has a job that requires a university degree? She acknowledged that she didn't know of anyone.

This is quite extraordinary when you think about it. Bountiful is a small community, to be sure, about 1,000 people. But you would still expect that someone, anyone, in the sixty-year history of the community would have earned professional qualifications at university—a doctor, a lawyer, a veterinarian, whatever. But witness after witness indicated that it had never happened. In fact, no one knew of anyone at Bountiful even applying for a degree program at any of the province's dozen-plus universities. For whatever reason—probably mostly simply cultural norms against it—nobody from the Bountiful FLDS had ever exploited their supposedly limitless career choices.

Part of this was probably because the schools of Bountiful had not been certified to grant its grade 12 students the "Dogwood"—the standard BC Diploma confirming graduation according to provincial standards. Instead they were given diplomas from the school itself. Although Witness 3 could proudly say that no postsecondary institution had ever refused to accept her grade 12 credentials, she also conceded that she had never submitted her diploma anywhere but the College of the Rockies (a community college based in Cranbrook that does not require grade 12 graduation for many of its programs) and the Southern Utah University.

Having been both a student and teacher at BESS, Witness 3 was in a good position to discuss the curriculum at the FLDS-run school. She described an environment where there had been no sex education or life skills classes, but daily religious instruction.

I am often asked by lawyers what I think of the anonymous affidavit idea. In truth my feelings are mixed. It worked out very well in this case, in that a great many truths were put before the Court that might not otherwise have been there. However, this was due to two circumstances. First, the vast majority of the information was only gleaned because we knew who the anonymous witnesses were, or at least we believed we did. And second, the witnesses themselves, while at times somewhat reluctant and a bit evasive, never (at least as far as I could tell) answered a question dishonestly. Had they lied, and if we had not known who they were, it could have been a disaster. Even knowing who they were, how could we challenge a lie without revealing their identities? Fortunately the problem did not arise—whatever else these women might have been, they were honest witnesses.

That evening, I went out for dinner with Arvay. As usual we gossiped about who was doing what on the constitutional scene, and it was a very pleasant way to unwind after such an intense day in court. Arvay remained very interested in the case, and wanted to know my impressions of how the evidence was shaping up.

I encouraged Arvay to consider the idea of returning to the reference as Winston Blackmore's counsel, at least for the purposes of making closing submissions, if he could do what he needed to do in the time we had left. It's hard to imagine a constitutional argument that wouldn't be better with Arvay's participation; I thought it would improve everyone's game.

But I had real doubts that Blackmore himself would put in an affidavit and expose himself to cross-examination, even if he could be granted leave to do so at this late stage; from what I knew Blackmore had married too many girls, too young over the years. Moreover, the evidence of some of the witnesses suggested that his practice of employing boys and girls to work on his logging and other operations would be fertile ground for inquiry. Although no doubt charismatic and a powerful witness in direct, he would be incredibly vulnerable in cross. So, although I would have loved to have had my *Inherit the Wind* moment of a showdown with the erstwhile bishop, I didn't expect it to happen, and it never did.

## The Vital Stats Evidence

On Thursday the 27th of January we argued for the "late" admission of our Vital Stats affidavit, the one from Klette summarizing the government's knowledge of teen pregnancies at Bountiful.

I was satisfied that we didn't absolutely need this evidence. The individual witnesses' testimony, even that of the FLDS's witnesses themselves, proved beyond the shadow of a doubt that child brides and teen pregnancy were not only rampant at Bountiful, they were the norm, as was the importation of girls from the United States to feed the marriage market north of the border. But, if Klette's analysis was any indication, the empirical data bore this out, and so his affidavits would be useful corroboration and might give the Chief Justice some comfort that the pattern he was seeing in the individual evidence was not simply coincidence.

The Klette affidavit examined 833 births to 215 mothers in thirteen years. There were eighty-five teen births identified in the Bountiful "cohort." One in 10 babies in the Bountiful cohort had been born to a teenager. That's high—more than double the local average and almost four times the provincial average of 2.7 percent. But Klette explained that this wasn't the whole story. Because Bountiful mothers had so many children, the teen pregnancy was made to seem artificially low because all of the mothers' subsequent births swamped the data. If you were to ask the question a different way, that is, at what age do mothers in Bountiful have their *first* child, then it leaps out at you: eighty-five mothers—one-third—were eighteen or younger when they had their first child. Klette indicated that this was seven times the provincial rate. Unsurprisingly, two of the teens had three children each by the time they were eighteen; sixteen had two children each by that time.

The Klette analysis also revealed other helpful facts: the average age gap between Bountiful's mothers and fathers at the time of a child's birth is nearly double the regional and provincial averages. And fully 87 percent of the teen mothers in the database listed their own place of birth or residence as Hildale, Utah, which was powerful corroboration of the longstanding allegations of child-smuggling.

No question, this information was compelling. But we were seeking to admit it late, on the second-last day of trial. It had taken literally months to pull this data together and get the necessary approvals from the director of Vital Statistics to use this information in the reference proceedings. Elaborate confidentiality protocols had been designed to protect the women and girls whose stories were identified in the documents.

The *amicus* was understandably concerned by the late arrival of the evidence. Dickson, in a well-presented argument, argued that there was no evidence that the Bountiful cohort was actually representative of the community practices and many reasons to think it might not be.

But the most important thing we were trying to get before the Court wasn't Klette's summaries about what the birth records said; it was the records themselves. The *Vital Statistics Act* says that birth registration records are admissible in court as proof of the truth of what is recorded on them. And in my view, each of these records, filled out in their adolescent hand, told a story. Usually it was a young girl from the United States (generally Hildale/Colorado City) having a baby in Canada with an older, often considerably much older, man. After the testimony of Witness 4, recounting both her and her fifteen-year-old sister wife's arrival from the United States, these stories had an impact, a grounding in reality.

The next morning Bauman made his decision: all of our evidence would be admitted, subject to cross-examination and the right of the *ami-*

*cus* to present evidence in rebuttal to the Vital Stats numbers. This, and one or two other miscellaneous matters, would proceed in a little over a week, from the 7th to the 9th of February. But, for all intents and purposes, the trial proper was over.

After the conclusion of the brief court proceedings that Friday morning, January 27, I sent around an e-mail to all participants' counsel inviting them to join me for a drink at the lounge at the Hotel Vancouver. Wickett and Dickson were there; Cameron, Reimer, and Danay came from the federal team; Brent Olthuis, Robyn Trask, and Kasari Govender also attended, as did most of my provincial colleagues.

After a period of time, we were surprised by Chief Justice Bauman, who with his characteristic nonchalance stopped at our table and surveyed the collection of friendly colleagues who had days before been crossing swords. Like a jilted husband confronting his wife and her lover, Bauman said with perfect timing, "Well, *this* is awkward . . ." I assured him that we were on the verge of settlement, and we all had a laugh.

Lawyers are warriors for the working day, but they can be the best of friends when the ceasefire is called at the end of the shift. In fact they should be friends, because so much in the legal system is premised on lawyers' mutual trust and confidential, off the record conversations. Without these social times, the law would be unnecessarily confrontational, and cases, particularly big and complex ones, would become bogged down in pissy letters and secret strategies.

Unfortunately, the same collegiality cannot apply between lawyers and judges without jeopardizing the appearance of impartiality and fairness, and many who leave the profession for the bench find their isolation from their former colleagues to be suffocating. Others take to it with grace and good humour. Chief Justice Bauman wished us goodnight and moved to the other end of the bar.

The consensus in the media was that the case against polygamy was compelling. On the Monday following the last days of hearing, the *Globe and Mail* referred to the cross-examination evidence of the anonymous witnesses, and the evidence as a whole, and called for the polygamy provision to be upheld as a reasonable limit on the free exercise of religion. Bramham in the *Sun* went further, demanding a prosecution for sexual exploitation based on the facts revealed through the cross-examination of Witness 4.

## The Education Evidence

The main evidence phase ended on January 27, with a couple of minor matters left to resolve. First, CBC was back with an application to televise the closing submissions of the reference in March and April. And second, we had agreed to provide our witnesses on Education and Vital Stats to be cross-examined. To almost no one's surprise, CBC succeeded in their application. The Chief Justice invited them to submit a detailed plan within two weeks. It would be an interesting experiment.

But before the break we had a bit more evidence to introduce and test. We knew that, cross-culturally, polygyny is correlated with poor educational outcomes for women. We had requested information on the graduation rates from Bountiful's competing schools (Mormon Hills and BESS), to see whether expectations were borne out. The results were put in two affidavits by Ed Vanderboom, the province's chief inspector of independent schools, and Brent Munro, a data analyst with the ministry.

The education evidence from Bountiful was intriguing, if not conclusive. The data demonstrated unequivocally that Bountiful students have a very low completion rate, in that they almost never earn provincial accreditation for grade 12. This appears to be the case for both boys and girls. Of the students who were in grade 7 at BESS between 1994–1995 and 2003–2004, only 7 percent of female students and 6 percent of males were issued either a Dogwood or Adult Diploma. This compared to provincial averages of 78 percent of females and 72 percent of males. It is a tiny fraction of the completion rate for aboriginal students in the province (41 percent). As well, it cannot be explained by reference to the fact that BESS does not offer provincially accredited graduation, because it remains a small fraction of that of other isolated communities where this is also the case, such as Alert Bay in the Far North, and Bowen Island, where I live.

Nor can the rates be explained by reference to a theory of "poor start," as might be the case with, for instance, aboriginal populations or other small rural communities where a lack of resources, or endemic health or substance abuse issues took their toll. The day before the education witnesses appeared, the Fraser Institute issued its annual report card on British Columbia's elementary schools. This controversial report ranked British Columbia's schools according to how well their students did on a standardized grade 4 provincial examination. To the shock and horror of many, in 2010 BESS was rated as a perfect ten, the best elementary school in the province.

Some saw this as evidence that the numbers were being fudged, either through outright fraud or through extra attention in school to the tested subjects. How could students at such a maligned school actually be receiving a superior education? Didn't the report undermine all our evidence showing that the Bountiful education system was failing?

But I actually thought of the Fraser Institute report as *helping* our case. If it were true that, at least as of grade 4, BESS students are among the most accomplished in the province as measured by the provincially standard Foundation Skills Assessment (FSA) test, then clearly, something is happening to turn ordinary elementary students into high school dropouts in Bountiful. That something was, again, the arithmetic demands of polygamy: girls were being "streamed" towards a future as wives and mothers, and boys are, actively or passively, encouraged to manual labour jobs or eased out of the community altogether.

We had already confirmed that there did not appear to have been a single Bountiful student who had gone on to earn professional accreditation in anything but nursing, midwifery, and teaching. Truman Oler had said that he didn't even know what college was until he became an adult.

And nursing, midwifery, and teaching are, perhaps not coincidentally, the three professions where church control would be particularly advantageous in keeping the prying eyes of outsiders away from issues around the sexual exploitation of children. The birth registration records we had seen showed a volume of similar stories—those of teenage mothers, mostly brought up from the United States, and their mature adult husbands. That would probably also have become obvious to health-care practitioners at Bountiful who weren't involved in the church or community. And what of the school officials? Witness 4 described how, after she and her fifteen-year old sister wife were brought up from the United States to marry their husbands, they rode the school bus together to BESS. She also noted that school officials, like all other members of the community, to her knowledge expressed no concern at all that the two had become the plural wives of a man in his forties. It is difficult to imagine any other context where this could be considered anything but worthy of official concern in the school setting.

Of course, we had been hoping to ask these questions of the BESS principal, Palmer, but the FLDS had withdrawn his affidavit, as it had bishop James Oler's, and so the opportunity would not arise. In the end, the men of Bountiful left the women of Bountiful to take on what must have been an extremely stressful and unpleasant task. Then, just days after Vanderboom testified, we learned that Palmer had quit as the principal of BESS.

## The Girls of February

Once these last pieces of evidence had been entered into the record, it was time to turn our attention to the written submissions that would form the basis of our closing arguments. I had been working on them on and off since the reference began, and a good framework had been developed, but it was now time to comprehensively review and incorporate the evidence into the argument, and to sharpen our understanding and presentation of the applicable law.

But we had no sooner retooled away from the presentation of evidence when we were presented with perhaps the most breathtaking and dramatic evidence of the entire hearing: details of the fate of dozens of FLDS children, whom I came to call "the girls of February."

It began like this: on February 11, Greathead, who'd developed a very productive working relationship with the Texas Attorney General's prosecutor in the YFZ case, received a query from Eric Nichols, the Texas prosecutor of YFZ cases. He asked: "As we are getting ready for the trial of Warren Jeffs, I need to ask a favour. I would like to ask for your help in tracking down public birth records (if they exist) for two of our victims." He then named two girls, and said, "Both of these girls were born in the Bountiful community."

> Also, I imagine it is too late for you to use this information in your case, but let me know if you would have an interest. I know you asked me a long time ago about girls who were taken from Canada to Texas, and we have discovered these two.

Greathead replied:

> Hi Eric,
>
> Further to my last e-mail I do have a question about the named girls.
>
> Is the allegation that they have been married to Warren Jeffs and if so, when does Texas say they were married to him.
>
> Thanks
>
> Leah

Then, the bomb dropped. Nichols responded:

> We have found records indicating that each was placed in a "spiritual" or "celestial" "marriage" to Warren Jeffs on 12/16/2005, with the "marriages" occurring at the YFZ Ranch. They were both obviously twelve years old at the date of the "marriages." They were driven down from Canada to Short Creek earlier that month by their fathers . . . after Warren Jeffs notified these men that the girls would be "sealed" to him. [One girl's mother] also made the trip from Canada to Short Creek. The girls were then transported from Short Creek to Texas by FLDS operative John Wayman.

This blew our next weeks sideways—we'd been planning on a fairly leisurely preparation of our written argument, which was due March 4, and had divided tasks among the team. Now, we had to decide what to do about this new information. Should we try to get it before the Court, though evidence deadlines had long passed and only closing submissions remained?

Our first priority was to contact child protection authorities in Canada, since the two girls in question were still only seventeen, legally minors. That done, what next? The Texas authorities did not know whether the girls had remained in the United States or had returned to Canada (Jeffs had been in jail since 2007 on charges of child rape and was extradited to Texas in November 2009, just as the reference trial was starting). As far as anyone knew, their parents continued to live in Canada. But this was a matter for police and prosecutors, not for the civil litigators of the Constitutional & Administrative Law Group. Our involvement should be focused on ensuring that the right authorities had all the information we did.

But when we searched back through the government files for records of these girls, we rediscovered a 2008 letter from Texas child protection authorities to their counterparts in British Columbia's Ministry of Children and Family Development (MCFD). The letter had described records indicating the "celestial marriage" of a thirteen-year-old girl from Bountiful to Jeffs at James Allred's home near Short Creek in 2004.

Three girls, now. Twelve and thirteen years old. Greathead, Horsman, and I discussed it, but there really wasn't any question—this was relevant evidence and we needed to try, at least, to get it before the Court.

This wasn't as simple as putting it in an affidavit. Even if the Court would permit us to tender the evidence at this very late stage of the proceeding, it was by no means certain that Texas would be happy with our doing so. Our relationship with the Texas prosecutorial authorities was always delicate. Nichols, the Texas prosecutor, was now in private practice but was continuing to handle the YFZ prosecutions. He had always been as helpful as he could be to our lawyers, and vice versa, but we each had our limits. Texas, at that time, was involved in a number of secret grand jury investigations and more than a dozen prosecutions arising from the information gained through the execution of two search warrants at YFZ in April 2008. They were willing to share all kinds of information and documents, but only where they were already in the public record through introduction at Texas court hearings.

For my part, I had been concerned from the beginning that the reference should not become a form of an alternative criminal investigative process. And as the case evolved, as it became more focused on Bountiful, and as witness after witness (including the FLDS's own) took the stand and described what clearly appeared to be criminal behaviour, my caution in this respect grew. So we were grateful for all the assistance Nichols could offer in locating witnesses and facilitating introductions, and we took whatever public-domain records he could provide us, but I never had pressed the issue of access to confidential documents in Texas custody.

However, now we needed something from their archives if we were going to put the facts that had been revealed to the Court. After some discussion, we reached an agreement whereby we could use the records, subject to some qualifications. And so, on February 18, barely a week after first word of the girls was received, we filed an application to the Chief Justice to admit the records from Texas on the three girls, under seal and with undertakings of confidentiality. We would also file their birth registration records, also under seal, to prove their ages. The Chief Justice, who was travelling at the time, agreed to hear us by telephone the following Friday, February 25.

No sooner had out application been filed than the press latched back on to the story. Bramham at the *Sun*, not surprisingly, was first out of the gate, with an Internet article within hours of the filing reporting "a startling development in the polygamy story." The headline read "Shocking allegations point to child smuggling by Bountiful polygamists." Bramham had written stories about Canadian girls at YFZ since 2008 and was ready to write another story prodding British Columbia into action. As the story evolved, Bramham sprinkled the coverage with video footage, and even with photos of Jeffs with another of his child brides from the Texas proceedings. Her article ended with "Police and justice officials need to review the evidence, track down these fathers and mothers and charge them." Fair enough, I suppose. The children's information was now in the hands of the police and child protection authorities, with whom we had little contact.

Bramham wasn't the only one on the case within hours. Keith Fraser for *The Province* had a piece the same evening: "New evidence about alleged child brides from Bountiful prompts application to re-open polygamy trial." We had expected the interest, of course. The Attorney General, Barry Penner, was well briefed and handled the questions with a suitable mix of concern and distance. But as it turned out, we were just at the tip of a child-smuggling iceberg, and as we scrambled to work with the Texas authorities to put together an affidavit with the relevant church records in order to back up our application, fortune again intervened.

Among the documents Texas sent us were excerpts of a book called the *Dictations of the President Warren Jeffs*. This was the obsessively kept transcribed diary of the FLDS prophet over a period of years. It meticulously recorded almost everything Jeffs did in a day during the period when the YFZ ranch was being built and populated. In that period, Jeffs shuttled from one FLDS community to the next, running his little empire by cell phone, eventually in secret as he became a fugitive in the summer of 2005.

One of the things Jeffs was doing in that period was performing marriages, which he dutifully recorded in his *Dictations*. Here is the description of Jeffs's marriage to the thirteen-year-old Bountiful girl on 2 March 2004, mentioned earlier in this chapter. But this passage also refers to a second girl, who was fourteen. (I have reproduced these passages here with the redactions (XX) that we would use when we presented the passages in affidavit form, to protect the identity of child victims, or at least to make them less obvious.):

> Then we were past 1:00 o'clock p.m. I sat down with [Father of Child A] and his wife and his daughter, gave a training on the redemption of Zion in brief, in summary, and this girl was called on a mission; and they received it joyfully. And there [Child A], age thirteen, was sealed to Warren Steed Jeffs for time and all eternity, with James Allred and [Father of Child A] witnesses. I delegated LeRoy Steed Jeffs to be mouth.
>
> After they went to eat a little in Jim's kitchen, I had [Father of XX] bring his wife [Mother of XX] and daughter [XX] and gave them a training, which they received joyfully. [XX] was sealed to Warren Steed Jeffs for time and all eternity. She is age fourteen, age fifteen next Monday. LeRoy Steed Jeffs as mouth, delegated by me. [Father of XX] and Isaac Jeffs were witnesses on that marriage. I then had those young girls stay upstairs until I could leave—[XX] with her mother and little [Child A] with Naomie. You are smiling. I am smiling. I rejoice in the Lord's will. These young girls have been given to me to be taught and trained how to come into the presence of God and help redeem Zion from their youngest years before they go through teenage doubting and fears and boy troubles. I will just be their boy trouble and guide them right, the Lord helping me. I need to work with them more. Now I have a quorum of seven young girls living at R1.

And when we reviewed this entry dated 2 March 2004, we found a description of the marriage of three *other* girls on that date.

> I had arranged for [SH] and Dr. [LB] to meet me by 11:00 a.m., had them on call, but I did not have them brought to me until past 1:30 p.m. We then commenced the marriages and I will list those. I like to do them in order. I had Jim Oler bring [XX], and [XX] was sealed to Kendall Lucas Johnson Jr.; and [XX] was married to Jeremiah Johnson,

son of Kendall Johnson, the daughters are daughters of [XX]. The witnesses were LeRoy Jeffs, James Oler, and James Allred for those marriages. And then Brandon Seth Blackmore received [XX], daughter of [XX], son of [XX]. James Oler stayed for that wedding.

The two first-mentioned girls were from Bountiful; they were seventeen at the time of their marriage. Most significant, however, was the obviously central role played by Oler, the bishop of Bountiful and a participant in the reference. The passage documented that in March 2004, two children were delivered to Jeffs to be married to other men— delivered by Oler himself. The girls were Oler's own sisters.

The third child mentioned was an American girl, who was married to a man from Bountiful. This girl was sixteen, and we knew a little about her already because she was one of the "teen mothers" who had been recorded as giving birth in Bountiful some time thereafter. We were beginning to be able to take advantage of a real convergence of information from several jurisdictions.

So now, barely three days before we were due to be back before the Court, we had hard evidence of six trafficked girls—five going to the United States from Bountiful, and one coming the other way.

And it didn't show any signs of stopping there.

On the evening of February 22, I received an e-mail from Nancy Mereska of Stop Polygamy in Canada, passing on an anonymous tip she had received that, in April 2006, three more Bountiful girls had been married in Colorado. Within hours, another member of the public passed along information on the same three girls. By the next morning we had confirmed the girls' ages—two were seventeen, one was eighteen in 2006. So now we had *nine* teen and preteen girls, eight from Bountiful heading south, and one from Short Creek coming to Canada. Add that to the two we had before (Witness 4 and her sister wife from the United States, who'd been seventeen and fifteen at their respective marriages) and you had more than a pattern, you had a pathology. We scrambled to amend our notice of application and drafted a supplementary affidavit in Greathead's name. On Friday we would argue to admit evidence with respect to all nine girls.

Thursday night Bramham called to give me the heads up that the *Sun* would be running a front-page, above-the-fold headline in the morning on the child trafficking. The story was the result of Bramham's cross-referencing the information we had released through our affidavits (which didn't give any information that would identify the girls involved) with her own sources that now included copies of many of the *Dictations* of Jeffs, which Bramham had sourced elsewhere. The *Sun* story, Bramham warned me, would include the names of the two Bountiful fathers who had delivered their twelve-year-old daughters to be married to the prophet in 2005, Brandon Seth Blackmore and MacRae "Mack" Blackmore. So Friday morning the story of the trafficked girls was news again. "12-year-old girls delivered for marriage" read the headline in the *Sun*. The newspaper also revealed another detail that we had decided not to: that the two teenagers personally delivered to Jeffs by Oler in 2004 were in fact Oler's own sisters.

The hearing itself was a bit anticlimactic, and lasted a little over half an hour. The *Vancouver Sun* reported:

> On Friday, Craig Jones, B.C.'s lead lawyer in the constitutional case, asked Chief Justice Robert Bauman to admit the diaries and other church documents, even though the evidentiary phase ended last month.
>
> Jones noted that it is the first evidence of the extremity of the early sexualization of girls in Bountiful. Former residents testified that the youngest girls they knew of were in their mid-teens. Jones argued that it shows the "commodification and trafficking in girls," which was predicted by ethnographer Joseph Henrich, economist Shoshana Grossbard, and others.
>
> He described the new information as essential to refute McGill law professor Angela Campbell and University of Ottawa classics professor Lori Beaman, who testified that child brides are historical anomalies and that allegations of abuse within the Bountiful community are unfounded.
>
> But more than that, Jones said information such as what is in Jeffs' diary entry quoted above refutes the notion promoted by the B.C. Civil Liberties Association and law professor Martha Bailey that it's okay to decriminalize polygamy because other laws deal with harms such as child brides and human trafficking.
>
> Chief Justice Bauman gave a tentative "yes," agreeing that B.C. can tender the information. He also agreed that FLDS lawyer Robert Wickett will have seven days after receiving it to challenge its admissibility.

Then, of course, Bramham asked the obvious question:

> But now that at least some of the information is out, the more pressing question is: When will B.C. file criminal charges?

Now, putting together our evidence on the trafficked girls was in the hands of Greathead and Bevan, who were working with the Texas Rangers and the prosecutor to track down all the relevant documents and put them in final form. We would hand over anything we could to the RCMP and MCFD officials investigating the most recent revelations, but the flow was a one-way street. We expected to know no more than members of the public about the status of the investigations. We would have to put that aspect of the case out of our minds.

But the courtroom goings-on continued to be well publicized, even if they weren't dramatic. The combination of the hearing, the filed materials, and the *Sun* headlines gave the issue a high public profile. CBC's *As it Happens* ran a segment on Bountiful (interviewing Bramham), and through the weekend the *Globe* and *Province* newspapers picked up the story of the renewed probe into the Bountiful allegations.

The heat was on the government as it hadn't been since 2008, at least. The media was demanding answers: What was the government doing? Why had it taken so long? In a followup story Friday night, the Attorney General was weighing in too. The *Vancouver Sun* reported:

> On Friday, Attorney-General Barry Penner said the polygamy case was one of his top priorities.
>
> "Bountiful and polygamy are quite disturbing to me and I strongly support the legislation [the criminal code offence of polygamy.]"
>
> Penner noted that he asked RCMP last Friday to investigate the new information and to look particularly at any evidence that might support criminal charges of child sexual exploitation or parents procuring their children for sex.
>
> He went on to say, "I'm offended by any suggestion of what has been alleged to have taken place [12-year-olds becoming brides] is akin to marriage. . . . What this is is a lot of middle-aged men wanting to have sex with children."

But others were determined to hold the government's feet to the fire. The *Sun* quoted British Columbia's formidable child advocate, Mary-Ellen Turpel-Lafond:

> "The ministry cannot hide behind privacy at this point when there is a constitutional reference on the issue," she said. "The public needs to know that when there is an allegation that comes forward that a child may be subject to some form of sexual exploitation that that is promptly and thoroughly investigated."
>
> She said she was "deeply troubled" that over the last four years, despite an RCMP investigation and court challenge, the public still remains

in the dark about what might be happening with adolescent girls at Bountiful.

"We have a very important set of public values to address here and it may engage the criminal law, it may engage child welfare, and it may require us to rethink a few things," she said. "I hope [The RCMP] has a team that will look at the issue completely because I think at this rate there are some very significant concerns about the well-being of some children from British Columbia," said Turpel-Lafond.

This was all very good news for those of us on the polygamy team who had never understood the inertia of the BC government, and of the prosecutorial authorities, over three decades of allegations and investigations.

Perhaps most amusing was that Winston Blackmore, James Oler's bitter rival and the previous bishop of the FLDS at Bountiful, came out of obscurity to decry the latest revelations. In a series of interviews, he was saying basically that none of that teen bride smuggling stuff would have happened on his watch. I heard an interview on CBC Radio, when the reporter listened to Blackmore's indignant condemnation of Oler, then asked, mischievously, what was the youngest girl Blackmore had ever married. Of course Blackmore, who had twenty-five wives, had married many of them as teenagers, including several fifteen year olds. He stammered through an evasive answer, saying that "I said what I said and did what I did in the past" but that he was now "looking forward" and besides, "this interview was supposed to be about the other guy." He didn't know about the twelve year olds, he said, and if he'd been in charge he'd never have allowed it.

But the story of the trafficking of child brides at Bountiful wasn't over yet.

No sooner had we got the Chief Justice's order permitting us to tender evidence of the nine girls than Bramham found another. She told me that she'd heard that Oler's own daughter was married off in the United States in June 2004. She knew the location and the dates, and before long she had the girl's age, apparently from independent sources. Could we confirm it?

Of course, we couldn't give her the information that we had before it was put before the Court, and Bramham knew that, but she had to ask. Anyway, it was beginning to look like her sources were as good as ours.

So I followed up on her query about Oler and his young daughter. I looked at the (by then publicly available) *Record of the Prophet Warren Jeffs* for June 2004 and sure enough, there it was in the dictation of the prophet from 24 June 2004, the following passage:

I called Jim Oler last night and told him to bring his daughter [XX] for her to get married, that Jim Oler would receive a wife, and that Brandon Blackmore and his son Zane should come and receive the training and that Brandon's daughter [XX] should come and be married that they should wait in Cedar City, Friday morning, until I called.

The next day, the three weddings had been dutifully recorded. So here's Oler, having taken his two seventeen-year-old sisters down to be married in March 2004, now called upon to give away his fifteen-year-old daughter and to receive a fifteen-year-old wife, all on the same day. The church records show that Oler's daughter was married at 1:23 pm, and Oler wed his new bride (his fifth) exactly eleven minutes later. The third Bountiful marriage that day (Jeffs performed eighteen marriages in seven hours on that occasion) was another of Brandon Blackmore's daughters, apparently heading off to another American household.

So what had begun with evidence of two trafficked twelve year olds had become nine a week later, then twelve by the following Monday morning. And it continued to mushroom. By the Monday afternoon we had firm information on twenty-seven child brides smuggled to and from Bountiful. Every day Greathead was on the phone with her Texas Rangers, pleading with them to search through the archives for more evidence on a new girl, and Bevan was asking Vital Stats for yet another birth registration record. And we were turning over all the information we could, as soon as we could get it, to the RCMP and child protection investigators, who had launched a major investigation based on the new material.

For my part, while I tried to help Greathead and Bevan where I could, I was being pulled three ways from Tuesday by constant requests for more information, for briefings, for summaries and reports. And in the midst of it, I was trying to review two and a half months of trial transcripts and affidavits for references to put into our closing submissions. I hadn't slept so little since I was a young associate at Bull, Housser & Tupper. I was hardly ever home, and when I was, I was working. My wife was straining to keep the family functioning without me, and my plans of running the LA Marathon in March were fading with every missed training run. I began to pass off work to other lawyers, and relied on friends to take over speaking engagements to which I had rashly committed months before. But I knew the pace couldn't be sustained for very long. The famous American litigator David Boies supposedly used to ask his associates from the Cravath's litigation team, "Do you want to sleep, or do you want to win?" Once, a few days before the submissions were due, I actually fell asleep while typing at my desk. And I knew my colleagues were being pressed just as hard. Government lawyers exist in a world without overtime pay or bonuses for extra hours worked. Some respond to this by making it a nine-to-five job, but this doesn't really work in litigation. The people who worked with me on the polygamy file did whatever it took to get the job done, and that meant a lot of weekends and evenings, unpaid.

But it was getting ridiculous as February became March. We knew, with twenty-seven potential child victims, we had to draw the line at some point—if we waited until all the girls were chased down and their information compiled, we would never get the affidavit material before the Court, and god knows how many more would be discovered as Greathead continued to review the Texas material. So we made a decision to put together all of what we had on the first thirteen; Greathead prepared the affidavit of Texas Ranger Nick Hanna, and it was finalized on the last day of February.

Wickett had been granted seven days to ponder whether he wanted to raise an objection to the admissibility of the Hanna affidavit, but we didn't have any time to sit around and wonder what he would do. We now had only three days to complete our closing submissions, a document that would eventually be 168 pages long.

## Polygamy's Hidden Crimes

The way I saw it, the evidence of the "girls of February" was further rebuttal to what was, on the face of it, one of the *amicus*'s most attractive arguments: If the problem is the youth of brides, or exploitation, or trafficking, or erosion of women and children's rights, then why not rely on laws against those activities instead of the polygamy prohibition? Or why not modify and extend them?

Our response was that implementing stricter child-exploitation or trafficking laws, or effecting the more vigorous enforcement of those in place, is only an answer to the extent that such crimes are reported, investigated, and prosecuted. This is obviously not the case, and in fact the crimes upon which the FLDS and *amicus* apparently were advancing as alternatives (sexual exploitation of a minor, sexual assault, trafficking in persons, and so forth) are both underreported and difficult to investigate and prosecute, and this is particularly true with respect to insular populations of vulnerable immigrant groups or closed religious communities where polygamy is mostly likely to prosper.

At trial, every expert witness who was asked the question confirmed that, even *outside* closed and insular religious communities, crimes within the family are severely unreported, especially crimes against children. Thus, permitting an activity (polygamy) that will increase harm (including criminal harm) against children or women cannot be supported on the basis that the harm can be adequately addressed through enforcement of other laws. It simply cannot.

You might recall, as I often did in those days, that the bishop of the FLDS, Oler, had declared in his affidavit that in all "instances where members of the community have been suspected of criminal offences . . . reports have been made to the police." Yet Oler himself, the Texas records had revealed, had taken a fifteen-year-old "bride" and given away his own teenaged daughter in a wedding performed by Jeffs; he had conveyed at least two other teenagers to the United States to be married by Jeffs. If these things were not criminal, what on earth was?

The *Criminal Code* section 153 says:

Sexual exploitation

**153.** (1) Every person commits an offence who is in a position of trust or authority towards a young person, who is a person with whom the young person is in a relationship of dependency or who is in a relationship with a young person that is exploitative of the young person, and who

(*a*) for a sexual purpose, touches, directly or indirectly, with a part of the body or with an object, any part of the body of the young person; or

(*b*) for a sexual purpose, invites, counsels or incites a young person to touch, directly or indirectly, with a part of the body or with an object, the body of any person, including the body of the person who so invites, counsels or incites and the body of the young person.

. . .

(1.2) A judge may infer that a person is in a relationship with a young person that is exploitative of the young person from the nature and circumstances of the relationship, including

(a) the age of the young person;

(b) the age difference between the person and the young person;

(c) the evolution of the relationship; and

(d) the degree of control or influence by the person over the young person.

Section 150.1 sets out that there is no defence of consent for a charge of sexual exploitation. The point of the law, in other words, was to capture behaviours whereby consent was obtained, but shouldn't have been.

The law recognizes that certain relationships are so potentially exploitative that they must be absolutely barred in the teenage years. For the purpose of the sexual exploitation laws, a "young person" was defined in 2003/4 to be between the ages of fourteen and eighteen; below fourteen, there could be no consent to sex. More recently, the age of consent to sex has gone up to sixteen, so exploitation laws now apply between sixteen and eighteen.

There are at least two other provisions setting out crimes relevant to the "girls of September." Section 170 of the *Code* makes it an offence for a parent or guardian to procure their child "for the purpose of engaging in any sexual activity prohibited by this Act." And section 171 makes a householder liable if he or she "knowingly permits a person under the age of eighteen years to resort to or to be in or on the premises for the purpose of engaging in any sexual activity prohibited by this Act." In other words, parents who give up a child to be exploited can be held criminally responsible, and so might the other adult members of the household that receives the child as a "celestial bride."

But in the case of these "marriages," like those of Witness 4 and her younger sister wife, nobody called the police. Nobody complained to child welfare authorities. Nobody—not the schools, not the church, not, apparently, any member of the community—thought that the marriage of a fifteen- or seventeen-year-old girl to a church official in his forties was wrong. The full details of the crimes would never have come to light but for the evidence of Witness 4 under cross-examination. So, in my argument, we couldn't simply rely on laws against sexual exploitation to solve the problems created by polygamy.

Then consider the revelations at the YFZ compound. That raid found twelve marriages of children between twelve and fifteen years old (not including the two twelve year olds we'd just learned about)—twelve prosecutions for child sexual assault and for other crimes. Scores of perpetrators of related abuses. And again, no member of the community ever reported these facts to the authorities, and the closed and insular nature of the compound ensured that they weren't known outside. It was only a hoax call from a woman *pretending* to be a member of the community that triggered the authorities to act.

Needless to say, nobody in the Bountiful community said a peep to anybody outside when three young girls, aged twelve and thirteen, were taken south to marry the prophet.

It is a nice idea that the harms that go hand in hand with the practice of polygamy could be addressed if only the practice would be brought into the sunlight through decriminalization. But there is no reason to believe that this would happen. Polygamy builds insularity precisely to hide the abuses that it requires to sustain itself through generations. It requires it to

shield the methods of control and indoctrination that will guarantee the
next generation of willing child brides.

## The Beginning of the End: March 2011

On the day we filed the Attorney General's written submissions, March 4,
it was announced that the new premier-elect, Christy Clark, had decided
to replace Seckel as deputy minister to the premier and head of the public
service. This was a great blow. Since leaving his post as deputy Attorney
General, Seckel had retained a keen lawyer's interest in the ongoing work
of the group, including the polygamy case. Now he was gone from government altogether.

There were other transitions that month: we got a new premier and
cabinet when Clark won the leadership of the BC Liberal Party. Clark decided to retain Barry Penner as Attorney General. Although I had hoped
for the return of de Jong, if for no other reason than we had a comfortable
working relationship and he had been very involved in the polygamy file,
I was warming to Penner despite his very earnest style. He would make a
point of stopping by my office when he was in the building, and showed
an interest in the rotating collection of rifles and shotguns that I displayed
(for some reason even I only imperfectly understand) on my office wall.
He was obviously very smart, and had been doing yeoman's work reading his way into the files, including polygamy, which he would frequently
discuss whenever we weren't talking about Second World War infantry
weaponry.

We all suffered the loss that month of Brenner, the former Chief Justice and my frequent morning interlocutor at the Glass City Café. Brenner
had been only sixty-four and in our interactions he seemed to be at the top
of his game; it was said that he died suddenly while chopping wood. It was
very sad event, compounded for me by the fact that the special sitting of
the Court in his honour was scheduled for the next month on a day where
I was due to be in Ottawa and could not attend.

After our written submissions were filed, we had two weeks to wait for
the *amicus* and his allies to file their own. Months before the final schedule had been set, my wife and I had planned a short trip to California, and
as it turned out, the trip, only six days, would have me in the United States
when we received the other side's arguments.

The submissions arrived, on schedule, on March 17, while I was exploring Disneyland with my family. The *amicus*'s document alone was over
300 pages, and there were also substantial submissions from the BCCLA
and the CPAA. Assured by Bevan, who read them first, that they didn't

contain any major surprises, I resolved not to read anything myself until after the trip was done. This was especially so because Bevan suggested that I would be irked by how the *amicus* had characterized the evidence, which she said made her feel as if we did not all hear the same witnesses. And there was also a *tone* to the submissions, she suggested, that might ruin my enjoyment of the vacation. Should we reply? I asked her. If so, only briefly, was her thought. If the challengers' manner of argument was irksome to us, perhaps it was better left intact to irk the judge also.

So my family moved on from Anaheim to Santa Monica, where I ran the marathon in a record downpour, and I returned a few days later to prepare in earnest for the closing submissions, where we would try to present, in a complete and cohesive way, the case for section 293, the case against polygamy.

# PART 6
# The Case Against Polygamy

## The Convergence

Sometime at the end of the evidentiary phase of the hearing, the *amicus*'s co-counsel Dickson and I were discussing the schedule of the exchange or our written submissions. It had occurred to me that, given all that we knew about the positions being advanced by the other, it didn't make much sense to have too much back-and-forth, with the *amicus* putting in his argument on breach, the Attorneys General responding to that and adding our argument on section 1 justification, and the *amicus* then responding to that (and heavens knew where all the intervenors would fit in). Dickson was reluctant to proceed that way. "We need something to shoot at," he was saying with respect to our section 1 argument, "we need to know what your argument's going to be."

I had to laugh—Dickson was giving me too much credit for cleverness. I responded that our argument was going to be very simple: "It's *harmful.*"

Now, Dickson had a point about the sequence, and before long we agreed with the *amicus*'s proposed schedule for exchange of arguments, even though it put us up against a tight timeframe. But I wasn't exaggerating much when I summarized our expected submissions. Once you were past the *amicus*'s "silver bullet" argument (that is, his assertion that the very purpose of the law was discriminatory), every aspect of the case would come down to what the Court found with respect to the harms of polygamy.

The main theme of our closing submissions was the "convergence" in the evidence of harm. It was a term I had borrowed from Henrich, who had used it to describe how the results of the various studies he reviewed "converged" to support the theories of polygamy's harms. In our case as a whole, the convergence was in how, with respect to each of the negative correlates of polygamy, the stories of individuals and the anecdotal observations of academics also fit in with the expectations of the experts. This convergence was nowhere more striking than in the evidence of the sexual targeting of girls.

The impact of polygamy on girls had been the centrepiece of our evidentiary efforts. It was a harm that was, along with the lost boys phenomenon, most directly tied with the cruel arithmetic, and the victims were so clearly innocent that no one could argue for the idea that their rights should be sacrificed on the altar of their elders' religious freedom or personal liberty. So our closing submissions, which began with the phrase "a polygamous society consumes its young," focused heavily on the evidence of the early sexualization of girls.

We began our submissions on this most obvious point by observing that Mormon polygamy has, from the beginning, been noted for the youth of its brides. Joseph Smith was said to have married several teenagers. The historian Van Wagoner had written of nineteenth-century Mormon polygamists:

> Although defenders of Mormon polygamy stress that the principle was intended for religious rather than sexual purposes, plural wives tended to be much younger than their husbands. A 1987 study completed by the Charles Redd Center for Western Studies at Brigham Young University found that 60 percent of the 224 plural wives in their sample were under the age of twenty. The man was usually in his early twenties when he married his first wife, who was in her late teens. When he took a second wife he was generally in his thirties and his new wife between seventeen and nineteen years of age. Men who married a third wife were commonly in their late thirties. The average age of third wives was nineteen as were fourth wives whose husbands by then were between thirty-six and forty-five.[1]

When the FLDS community at Short Creek was raided in 1953, the action was justified in part on the basis its residents were engaged in a "conspiracy to commit statutory rape." The governor of Arizona described Short Creek as:

> dedicated to the wicked theory that every maturing girl child should be forced into the bondage of a multiple wifehood with men of all ages for the sole purpose of producing more children to be reared to become more chattels of this lawless enterprise.[2]

Now, of course, a politician saying something doesn't make it true. In the reference, though, the evidence of child brides at Bountiful and throughout the FLDS communities in North America was simply overwhelming. Recall how one of Campbell's interview subjects reported that at least twenty-three of her twenty-five sisters were married before reaching the age of eighteen. Anonymous Witness 2 married at sixteen, as did her sister wife (also her biological sister). Her own daughter married (monogamously) at fifteen. Witness 4, as I discussed at some length earlier, married at seventeen and her sister wife married at fifteen. And of course, there were the girls of February, as I have called them, whose stories had been revealed by cross-referencing the YFZ raid with birth records. And by the time of our closing submissions, there had already been a number of prosecutions in Texas that involved evidence of numerous young brides.[3]

Beall had estimated that 30 percent of his female patients from polygamous marriages (from inside and outside the FLDS) were married at sixteen or less.

Greathead and Horsman compiled for the closing submissions a parade of underage marriages from their video affidavits: Ruth Lane, former wife of Winston Blackmore, reported him as having married two fifteen year olds among his other, slightly older, teen brides over the years: "They can stretch it however they want," she had said. "They were fifteen." Susie Barlow had been assigned into marriage with her fifty-one-year-old cousin when she was sixteen; Lorna Blackmore had a daughter assigned to bishop Oler when she was sixteen and a daughter assigned to Oler's half-brother when she was seventeen. Jessop was married at eighteen to a man who was thirty-two years older than she was. Jessop also testified that her sister wife Tammy was eighteen when she married the eighty-eight-year-old "Uncle Roy," who would go on to marry a seventeen year old when he was "around ninety-six." Winston Blackmore was said to have required Teressa Wall to marry at seventeen. Teressa described her thirteen-year-old sister being forced to marry their cousin, and another sister at eighteen marrying Rulon Jeffs when he was well into his eighties. Rena Mackert was married at seventeen. Mary Mackert spoke of the former prophet Leroy Johnson taking a twelve-year-old wife. Truman Oler described the typical age of marriage for girls in Bountiful as sixteen. Again and again, the testimony was the same.[4]

Some empirical corroboration of this overwhelming anecdotal evidence was also found in the birth registration records from Bountiful, which indicate that about a third of mothers identified by the BC Vital Statistics Agency official Klette as coming from Bountiful first gave birth as teens, a rate that is some seven times the provincial average.

Teen pregnancy, of course, is only one indicator of the real problem: the sexual targeting of girls by much older men in a polygynous society. The usefulness of teen birth statistics at Bountiful was that, as even the *amicus*'s expert Campbell confirmed, they are a virtually conclusive identifier of teen *marriages* (because out-of-wedlock pregnancies in Bountiful were, she said, unknown). In his own closing submissions, the *amicus* had argued that teen pregnancy is also a problem in other cultures or particular communities, and this is so. But it is not the pregnancy that is at the heart of the problem with polygamy. The problem with polygamy is that girls will be raised to become adolescent—or even pre-adolescent— sexual targets of much older men. The evidence of that phenomenon from Bountiful and the FLDS was overwhelming, while there was no evidence of this harm in other communities that the *amicus* identified as having high teen-pregnancy rates. Presumably, teen pregnancy in those places was the more familiar kind, where young people engage in risky behaviour with one another with serious consequences. It does not indicate or confirm a pattern of methodical predation on girls by persons in positions of authority.

Campbell in her affidavit (as in her academic writing) had glancingly characterized child brides at Bountiful as a "historical" phenomenon, and a practice "no longer followed." We noted, however, that she simultaneously reported that some of the Bountiful women to whom she spoke described themselves as dedicated to eliminating the practice, something which should hardly be necessary were it not an ongoing concern. Moreover, we pointed out, one mother interviewed by Campbell, who had married at sixteen, bemoaned the fact that her own daughter had become a teenaged bride despite the mother's misgivings. Anonymous Witness 2, a woman in her forties who had married at sixteen, told a very similar story of seeing her daughter marry at fifteen. The marriages described by anonymous Witness 4 (her own and that of her sister wife, at ages seventeen and fifteen respectively) were not "historical" as I defined the word, because they occurred in 2003 and 2004. The dozen child brides identified in the report of the Texas Child Protective Services at YFZ were married between 2004 and 2006 as young as twelve years old. The Attorney General had presented evidence of thirteen Bountiful girls married in the United States between 2004 and 2006, aged twelve to eighteen.[5] These facts, we said, indicated that Campbell's characterization of teen marriage as historical suffered from the same frailties of so much of her "qualitative research"—her tendency to uncritically adopt the stories told to her, even where there is readily available data and information directly contradicting her conclusions. This appeared to be particularly so where the data is inconvenient to her revisionist characterization of Bountiful and the FLDS as an unfairly maligned community of odd but generally harmless religious adherents.

Of course the challengers would argue that these were artefacts, not of polygamy, but of the peculiar culture of the FLDS and other fundamentalist Mormon communities. We responded that there was nothing in the Mormon, let alone fundamentalist Mormon, faith that dictates or encourages brides below the age of legal marriage.[6] If members of the FLDS were marrying younger than mainstream Mormons and others outside their community, it wasn't because their religion drove them to do so. Something else was afoot.

And of course, we said there was no mystery, given the simple arithmetic of polygamy. A polygamous society *ipso facto* creates a demand for more women than men. Absent importation of sufficient numbers of marriageable women, the principal source for a larger available pool of prospective partners will be younger and younger girls.

This was borne out by careful cross-cultural studies, such as those described by Henrich, which show that a society's degree of polygyny correlates with the youth of girls at first marriage and with the age disparity between the brides and their much older husbands. The correlation between polygyny and youth of brides also featured in the evidence of Professors Grossbard and McDermott. No evidence, we observed, was led to counter this observation, nor was the correlation questioned in cross-examination.[7]

As I have written earlier, you could not review the literature of polygamy without being struck by the simultaneous accounts of underage marriage. The propensity to marry adolescent girls had been noted as a peculiar feature of the Yemenite Jewish community, where polygamy was practised until the mid-twentieth century. Youth of brides and age disparity between men and women at marriage was also noted among the polygamous cultures of rural Turkey, southern Ethiopia, the Middle East, and Australia, according to Henrich. Among polygamous African immigrants in France, it was observed by the French National Consultative Commission of the Human Rights that:

> [Translation] Most of the time, these wives are young girls. . . . Married most often by force or in any case without having had a choice, they find themselves isolated, under the total domination of the husband.[8]

Again according to Henrich, on the American frontier, where there was a marked sex-ratio imbalance, marriages of girls as young as twelve or thirteen were reported. North of the border, the archival evidence assembled by Nelson, our articled student, showed that when Indian agents assigned to the Blackfoot First Nation complained to Ottawa about the polygyny there at the turn of the last century, they simultaneously reported the phenomenon of young girls being offered into marriage, with one Indian agent writing in 1903:

> There are instances here of parents selling, bartering, or giving their girls—under ten years of age—to be the wife of men of various ages. Furthermore, within the last year, several Indians have contravened the law regarding polygamy. I would like to know whether these Indians are to be allowed to retain these girls as wives, and whether the Indians who have plural wives are to go unpunished, providing they refuse to discard wife #2.

The concern was reiterated by the assistant Indian commissioner following a visit in the field, who noted that "I was assured that children as young as five years of age were so disposed of . . ." Sarah Carter also mentions this phenomenon among the polygynous Plains Indians in the same period. She wrote that contemporary reports of girls commonly marrying between the ages of sixteen and eighteen, but being "pledged or betrothed at a young[er] age," in one documented case at age seven.[9]

And there was more convergence with Henrich's evidence regarding the consequences of the rising male-female sex ratio in China. There, the practice of "minor marriage"—where an infant girl is promised in marriage to a wealthy family, was observed to have been "spreading rapidly" as the more numerous male offspring of the "one-child policy" reached adulthood.

We argued that the *amicus*'s counterevidence on the question of the youth of brides was indirect and unpersuasive. On the one hand, he could show that there are many factors contributing to teen pregnancy, and he could demonstrate that, at least with respect to older teens (younger than age twenty) the rates vary considerably across the province. But he introduced no evidence of any other community where "marrying" girls at fifteen, sixteen, or seventeen was widespread (never mind the practice of marriage to much older men, common in polygamy), and in fact he introduced no evidence of a single such "marriage" outside the fundamentalist Mormon faith. The *amicus did* introduce an essay through the Brandeis Brief that indicated that somewhat more mainstream Mormons marry as teenagers than do average Canadians, but not by much.[10] And again, there was no evidence at all that any member of the mainstream Mormon population has married as young (twelve to sixteen years) as members of the FLDS in Bountiful and the United States.[11] The FLDS expert Walsh confirmed in his testimony that there is no *religious* reason for church members to marry young.

We allowed that it was possible that Campbell was in one respect correct, in that since 2002 the incidence of child brides within the Winston

Blackmore side of the Bountiful Split had been reduced. But we also said that it is also possible that in this same period the incidence of plural marriage itself has been reduced, perhaps as a result of increased scrutiny, the threat of prosecution, or from a genuine liberalization of the community (in fact, Campbell, who said she has stayed in touch with many of her sources, reported that she had no knowledge of any plural marriage occurring on the Blackmore side of the Split since 2002). We noted also that in June 2008 the FLDS in the United States and Canada announced a policy whereby there would be no "sealings" of girls under the legal age of marriage. Perhaps predictably, it also appeared that there had been no sealings at all since that policy has been in place. The gist of all this was that while it may be possible that there were no "new" child brides in Bountiful, that was because there was no more "new" polygamy there, either.

The other most obvious result of polygamy's simple mathematics is that it will result in an increased number of unmarried boys and men, and in fact ensure that a significant number of men will never be able to marry. We argued the lost boys phenomenon from two main angles. First, of course, being turned out of a closed religious community is a cause of serious concern in itself; that is, the impact on the boys, and the society that must absorb them, is considerable. But there is another dimension to the problem as well and that is the impact on lack of marriage opportunities on societies that permit polygyny to spread.

The experts in the reference agreed that the more narrowly distributed are opportunities to reproduce, the more risk-taking and violent behaviour will be seen among men. This had been a main theme of the evidence of Henrich and had been extensively noted in the literature, especially the popular writings of Harvard's Pinker, who had memorably summarized the criminality of men "whose prospects teeter between zero and nonzero" and quoted Bob Dylan's line, "When you got nothing you got nothing to lose."[12] We were able to remind the Court that the *amicus*'s own expert evolutionary psychologist Dr Shackelford quite enthusiastically agreed with Pinker's description of polygamy that included the following passage:

> Under polygyny, men vie for extraordinary Darwinian stakes—many wives versus none—and the competition is literally cutthroat. Many homicides and most tribal wars are directly or indirectly about competition for women . . .[13]

There had been substantial cross-cultural evidence placed before the Court demonstrating how even a modest degree of polygyny may have an enormous impact on levels of crime and antisocial behaviour. Each of the various methodologies used by Henrich to test the causal hypothesis produced the same prediction: as the degree of polygyny increases and even a relatively very small pool of lower-status, unmarried men is created, crime rates (particularly violent crimes like murder and robbery) will increase, and strikingly so. Henrich noted that these predictions appear consistent with historical accounts of areas where marriage opportunities were scarce and with the anthropological record.

Historian Benjamin Bistline wrote of the arithmetic of polygamy in the closed communities of the FLDS:

> The birth ratio of boys to girls among the Polygamists is the same as it is anywhere in the world, pretty much one boy to one girl. If one man has even two wives, then some boy in the society must not get married. The doctrine of the Polygamists is that a man must have at least three wives to reach the highest degree of heaven. The perceived importance of a man goes up by the number of wives he has, thus the ratio of wives to a man is important; those in leadership positions have wives numbering into the tens. This causes a dilemma for the Polygamist Leaders, what to do with the surplus of boys.[14]

William Jankowiak, who spent fifteen years studying the FLDS communities at Short Creek and Centennial Park, put it as follows:

> There is a shortage of eligible women to marry in every polygynous society, and this is a primary factor responsible for intergenerational conflict in Colorado City/Centennial Park. Senior males are always on the marriage market and thus compete with younger men for mates in a limited pool of eligible women. . . . The competition for mates is acute. . . . Young men know . . . that if they do not find a girlfriend before they graduate from high school, they probably will never have one. Without a girlfriend, they will leave the community to find a wife.

The personal evidence from the FLDS and Bountiful had put a human face on the lost boys problem in much the same way it did for child brides. In those communities, we pointed out, the criminal harm itself might not be apparent, because the "excess" boys and men can simply be expelled, or will leave on their own when their prospects appear so bleak that they overcome family loyalties and religious affinity. The boys, the evidence showed, were turned out for real or imagined behavioural problems or "rebelliousness," a phenomenon touched on by many witnesses but most eloquently captured by Beall.[15] Jessop testified that as far back as she could remember, young boys had to be excommunicated or otherwise sent away from the community, a practice also described by Rena and Mary Mackert. Don Fischer testified that he was expelled from his church and community when he was fifteen years old. He and his brother were given $100 and a garbage bag with clothes. Others were simply made to see the writing on the wall, like Richard Ream, who was told point blank that he would not be eligible for marriage in the FLDS Church. Ream saw himself as having recovered from the experience, and in hindsight said: "Honestly, Warren Jeffs telling me to remove myself from that society is probably the only good thing the man's ever done for me." Others had been sent to work for church-controlled industries for little or no compensation, in what appeared to have been a common practice.[16]

Beall, the clinical psychologist, had testified about a number of young men he had treated whom he described as having been "expelled" from the American communities, and about the problems they encountered in the greater society. Carolyn Jessop told the story of "Sam," a friend of her son Arthur, who, unable to cope outside of the community, took his own life. Jessop explained that Sam's situation was far from unique:

> My concern is that Sam is just one of hundreds of these kids that are just fighting to make sense of something that you can't make sense of, and the people in his life that he cared the most about, being his parents, didn't want to see him. And it's hard to make sense of being—your parents taking you out and throwing you out with the garbage. And a lot of these boys are finding their way through it and maybe not in the most positive of ways, but I think Sam is just more of an awareness that they're not going to all make it. They're not all going to find their way through it.

The *amicus* and the FLDS had done their best to deny, or at least minimize, the lost boys phenomenon. For the *amicus*, Campbell said that none of her interviewees mentioned it as an issue (nor, as we had determined during her cross-examination, had she asked). In the face of the evidence going the other way, we countered that her evidence was unpersuasive. Indeed, under cross-examination Campbell had acknowledged that lost boys are frequently mentioned in the literature as a harm associated with polygamous practice, but agreed that she had deliberately avoided interviewing any males in the community on that or any other topic.

Sometimes attempts to evade the obvious problem of polygamy's cruel arithmetic led to testimony that was almost absurd. According to one of the FLDS's anonymous witnesses, for instance, the mathematical problem doesn't arise because boys in the community engage in high-risk activities or jobs and are simply killed off. If this were true, it would be a macabre manifestation indeed of evolutionary psychology's prediction of increased risk-taking among boys in a scarce marriage market such as that created by polygyny. Far more likely, the witness was exaggerating. Overall, we said, the evidence of lost boys driven from the community implicitly or explicitly because they have no future there was both predictable and compelling.

But by whatever means, it did appear that the Bountiful FLDS community had somehow dealt with the numbers problem. As the trial was getting underway, we had asked Wickett to provide us with a demographic summary of the FLDS community at Bountiful. The data that the FLDS had provided indicated a significant number of missing boys and men, compared to women. So, we said, either through the recruitment of new women (from American communities), the marriage of children, or through the effective expulsion of excess men (and, given all the convergent evidence, apparently through some combination of all three), it was clear that the demands of polygamy for a gender imbalance in the Bountiful FLDS community had been satisfied.

The comparative scarcity of marriageable women in the FLDS and similar groups provided a very useful tool of social control. The religion held that the achievement of the highest level of exaltation required the practice of polygamy in this life, and that one's eternal status is affected by marriage and procreation. This meant that a substantial proportion of the male population would be prevented from fulfilling their own religious ambitions in even a limited, monogamous way by the dominance of polygamy practised by a few older men. A number of the personal witnesses described the lengths they would go to in order to curry favour with the church authorities and secure a first wife. Indeed the promise of an opportunity to marry *at all* seemed to be an institutional control mechanism within the FLDS. Women increasingly became commodities by which powerful men sought to control others, and the religion and the structure of the society grew up around that idea.

But if women were to be commodified for the benefit of some men and the detriment of most, the impact on women and girls, we argued, was uniformly negative, both in polygamy and in the broader society where polygamy is practised at nontrivial levels. And in this area, polygamy's impact on women's equality, the convergent evidence was also very strong.

Again, our argument began with the predictions of the high-level experts, most particularly Henrich, who set out in his affidavit the basic principle that "[a]s women become scarce they tend to be viewed as commodities." This manifests through overt exertions of male control and dominance, including rape and sexual exploitation. Henrich said:

> In cross-national analyses, greater polygyny is robustly associated with higher incidence of rape, even when controlling for economic differences and including continental control variable. This same relationship

is found when the percentage of unmarried men is used instead of polygyny: more unmarried men, more rape.

Rape and other crimes are easier to quantify than other impacts on women's place in a given society, and we were aware that some academics proposed that women's scarcity in a polygamous society increased their value, an idea made popular by the journalist Wright and social scientist Betzig (remember her rhetorical question of whether one would rather be the third wife of JFK or the only wife of Bozo the Clown?).

But if this were so, one was compelled to ask, why did polygamy correlate so closely with the oppression and abuse of women and girls? The answer had been most eloquently addressed by Grossbard, the expert economist from the University of San Diego put forward by the Christian Legal Fellowship. Grossbard had studied the economic consequences of polygamy for almost three decades, and she had described in her affidavit the progression of her thinking from one of "polygamy is good for women" (based on "Chicago School" libertarian economic theory) to "polygamy is bad" (based on subsequent study of the real effects of the practice). She had explained that while in theory polygamy increases the value of women in the marriage marketplace, this added value is not captured by the women themselves. In fact, she said:

> As pointed out in Guttentag and Secord (1983) and Grossbard-Shechtman (1993), the high value of women in marriage markets in polygamous societies is expected to increase men's incentives to control women by way of political and religious institutions, such as arranged marriages and marriages of minors.

Here was the great irony of it. Polygamy made women more valuable, but that wealth would be distributed by those with the power—religious, economic, political, and in the end physical—to assert control over them. Grossbard, like the other experts who had conducted literature reviews, had observed that polygyny corresponded in the literature with both the youth of brides and arranged marriages, among a host of other negative impacts on women's free and equal participation in society. The number of correlations in accord with the expectations of control mechanisms had led Grossbard to conclude that the relationships are causal, not simply coincidental. Grossbard, after thirty years' study of polygamy, had summarized her conclusions in direct examination as follows:

> That, in the cultures and societies worldwide that have embraced it, polygamy is associated with undesirable economic, societal, physical, psychological and emotional factors related especially to women's well-being.

As I wrote earlier, I was impressed by another measure of polygamy's impact on women's interest that hadn't previously occurred to me. As a political economist, Grossbard considered it significant that, from the early suffragette movement in the United States to the present, it was *women's* groups who were at the forefront of antipolygamy activism. The report "Polygamy and the Rights of Women" from the Quebec *Conseil du statut de la femme* had made the same point in the international context, pointing to Egypt, Iran, and Morocco as places where women's groups are agitating for reform. Indeed the *Conseil* report is itself an indication of the concern of women's groups in this country. The gendered character of the opposition, in other words, was powerful evidence of the gendered nature of the problem.

We were able to show with convincing evidence that, worldwide, the degree of polygyny in a society correlated directly with a depression in virtually every accepted measure of female equality. Henrich had approached the problem using the same multipronged approach he employed when analyzing the youth of brides. The effect of polygyny on a host of women's rights was also the central focus of the massive project undertaken by McDermott and her team, and presented by the Attorney General of Canada.

The results, we said, were unmistakable: Henrich found that polygamy can be expected to increase age gaps between husbands and wives, decrease the age of brides, increase rape and sexual exploitation of women and girls, and encourage social institutions that commodify and control women. McDermott's analysis of her database of 171 countries, each rated for degree of polygyny, revealed the same thing. Using a regression analysis controlling for GDP, McDermott found that polygyny negatively correlated with virtually every possible indicator of female wellbeing, including age at marriage, maternal mortality, life expectancy, legal equality, and domestic violence.

The *amicus*'s experts Campbell and Beaman had opined that the evidence of polygamy's harms was "mixed" or inconclusive. What they appeared to mean by this is that some studies had found harm linked to polygamy, and some have not. They did not acknowledge that the overwhelming weight of the international cross-cultural literature indicated a positive correlation. They did not cross-reference their brief review of these studies with econometric modelling and case studies (as did Henrich) or conduct a comprehensive *de novo* data analysis (as did McDermott), and we suggested that their evidence should be discounted accordingly. In the end, I suggested, Beaman's and Campbell's equivocation on the question of polygamy's established harms bore some resemblance to Big Tobacco's fifty-year insistence that "correlations" between smoking and lung cancer were inconclusive, and emphasizing the causal "controversy" over what appeared to be a strong scientific consensus.

And again, the convergence in the evidence from the high-level predictions of the experts to the evidence on the ground was complete. For instance, one expected pressure in a polygamous society is with respect to reproductive control: in a male-controlled reproductive marketplace, you would expect to see women having more children as they have less power to control their reproductive health. As I described earlier in this chapter, this correlation was among those borne out in the international studies. It was also a feature that leapt out of the personal evidence that emerged from the FLDS communities in North America. It is accepted that as women become better educated and are presented with opportunities to meaningfully participate in the economy and institutions of a given society, their birth rate will tend to go down dramatically. This is why the number of children a woman can be expected to have in her lifetime is considered to be an important and useful marker of gender equality by the United Nations and other groups who track women's rights internationally.

So it was significant, we said, that in the FLDS as in other fundamentalist Mormon communities, extraordinary fecundity is the norm, with women having, in some cases, fifteen children (Truman Oler's mother) or even more.[17] Again, the religious beliefs developed to support the idea, through assertions that one's place in heaven would be influenced by the number of one's offspring. Jorjina Broadbent testified that her polygamist husband would say, "It's not quality we're looking for, it's quantity, how many children we have before this life is up" (Jorjina herself had twelve). There was no way of avoiding the phenomenon of fecundity at Bountiful, and the *amicus*'s expert Campbell acknowledged that large families are the norm there. Importantly, it was also Campbell's evidence that women could practice birth control only surreptitiously. Ever willing to put a positive gloss on the culture, though, Campbell seemed to present women's machinations to secretly control their reproductive capacity as a promising example of women's empowerment. Other witnesses emphasized repeatedly that birth control was not allowed, and some said that women had to have a medical excuse for not having children. Jessop, despite numerous progressively difficult pregnancies, testified that she had no choice whether to become pregnant, and sought desperately the "permission" of her husband to stop having children:

> But my concern after that pregnancy and especially with the other four where I got so sick with each pregnancy and I was terrified during that pregnancy I wasn't going to live through it and so I went to Merril,

because in the FLDS a woman doesn't have a right to choose whether she can have children. That is up to a man and he is inspired by God if there's a spirit that is supposed to be born to that woman. And if he sees you as worthy to be a mother in Zion and you refuse, it is considered a sin unto death. So it wasn't my place to choose to not have more children because I was having difficult pregnancies. That was—that was a choice that my husband would have to make and he held within his power.

It was clear from the testimony of Truman Oler, the brother of the Bountiful bishop James Oler, that women in the FLDS had been taught that they should want to have children as long as they were biologically capable. Another witness reported that girls in the Church are taught that their life's purpose is to get married and have as many babies as possible for the kingdom of heaven. He said: "They're not really treated as anything but cattle." All the women Beall counselled reported having been sexually and/or physically abused. "Unwanted sex was a common feature in these relationships."

Maximizing the female reproductive window was given as another reason for the depression of the age of marriage of girls. As Jensen explained, girls in her generation were turned over to the prophet to be assigned in marriage at sixteen because at that age the men "felt like a girl was mature enough to start raising a family, that she would have the length and time of her birthing span so she could produce more children, and all of this is for the glory of God. And it was very important that she start as soon as possible."[18] Teressa Wall described how, at her school "there was a class called child development and they would have all the girls go there and talk about their duties as a wife, their duties as a mother. Their greatest mission here on this earth is to multiply and replenish the earth. Their priesthood head [the male figure, either a father or a husband, who is considered to be in charge of a girl's or woman's life] is God to them. You obey your priesthood head no matter what."[19] Orders dictating a woman's reproductive behaviour came also from the FLDS prophet. Rena Mackert testified:

I remember distinctly being called into Roy Johnson's [the former prophet's] office and he demanded to know what I was doing to keep from becoming pregnant. He lectured me on the many kinds of birth control and how it was killing babies, and that if I was doing these things I was murdering the spirits that were supposed to come down through me.

But fecundity, we argued, was only half of the equation of reproductive control. In addition to forcing women to have babies in "approved
unions," a society where men dominate women's reproductive choice will
also feature strict prohibitions on sex *outside* of those unions. Thus, in the
FLDS, we saw a high degree of separation of children by gender, with
girls and boys taught to regard each other as "poisonous snakes," according to a number of witnesses. The segregation policy can be extreme in its
enforcement: Brent Jeffs had testified that he was shipped from his US
home to a "reform camp" in Canada after he was caught talking to a girl.
Likewise, Richard Ream testified that he was sent from Utah to work for
Winston Blackmore, to get him away from girls.

If church elders were unable to control boys' contact with girls, they
could not control female reproductive choice, because as Henrich had
pointed out, girls tend to choose boyfriends who are their age or only
slightly older. Teen boys and young men, therefore, were a special threat
to the power of the churchmen to obtain girls and women for themselves.
Because the FLDS religion held that God might reveal his matchmaking
intent through divine revelation, it developed that desperate teenaged
boys and young men were asserting "revelations" at an accelerating and
unsustainable rate. FLDS historian Bistline, in his work on the history of
Short Creek that we had introduced through his affidavit, had described
this phenomenon, observing in his book:

> By the mid-1950s this policy [permitting boys to approach girls with
> "revelations" that they were to be married] had become a major con-
> cern to the Priesthood Council. It created two problems. Any girl after
> reaching about 13 years-old would have a great number of suitors com-
> ing to her, all having claimed to have a revelation that she was to marry
> him, greatly confusing her young and tender mind. The other (and no
> doubt greater problem) was that the girls would invariably choose the
> younger man, making it almost impossible for the older Brethren to get
> new wives.

The solution, according to Bistline, was to tweak the religion to suit
the problem:

> The people were taught that only a member of the Priesthood Council
> could get a revelation of who a girl "belonged to" (should marry).[20]

This was a nice example of what we characterized as polygamy's "in-
vention" of the religious and social practices that sustained it. Religious
instruction provided the necessary preparation of girls to accept, even welcome, marriage to much older men, a process Beall described as "sexual
grooming" whereby young girls are "conditioned to marry at a young age,

267

to whomever the prophet directs." He said that this raised a "core issue" of "whether young women are capable of giving true consent to sexual contact."

The fact that polygamy depressed the age at which girls would be targeted had positive side effects for the privileged men in FLDS communities, because it eased their efforts to control them. This was a theme that had also arisen repeatedly in the personal evidence, particularly that of Wall and Jessop. Wall had said:

> [G]rowing up in Salt Lake when Rulon Jeffs was the leader, he was more—he really supported girls waiting until they were older, but in Canada girls for the most part were married 15, 16, and then as the years went by even younger and younger. And I know Winston was a big believer in he felt like well, let's get them married off while they're young and they don't have a mind of their own, you know. He really liked to get them married off young.

In polygynous societies, one expects that women will marry younger, and as noted, they do. But, we pointed out, this is not simply an absolute depression of age; women and girls also marry men who are considerably older. The effect is statistically significant with respect to first marriages, and becomes more and more so with subsequent marriages (polygynous marriages tend not to happen all at once, but rather, wives are added a number of years apart) to the point where, for instance, Witness 4, her husband's fourth wife, married him when she had just turned seventeen and he was in his late thirties or early forties. These differences in age, we submitted, made it difficult to imagine that such a relationship could be anything close to "equal," and indeed we pointed out that anonymous FLDS Witness 4, under cross-examination, appeared to have difficulty even understanding the term "equality" as it applied to husbands and wives.

Warren Jeffs explained marriage of girls in the FLDS in part because the young women were so malleable. Remember how in the diaries that had been seized in the 2008 YFZ raid, Jeffs described his marriage to yet another young teen, then wrote:

> These young girls have been given to me to be taught and trained how to come into the presence of God and help redeem Zion from their youngest years before they go through teenage doubting and fears and boy troubles. I will just be their boy trouble and guide them right, the Lord helping me. I need to work with them more. Now I have a quorum of seven young girls living at R1.[21]

We suggested that the mechanisms of control over almost every aspect of life in the FLDS had at times a wholly sinister aspect, particularly in the United States, with neighbours, and even the sister wives themselves, becoming part of an oppressive culture of surveillance and norm-enforcement. Beall had testified about the sister wives' constant presence as one of several bars to the "escape" of mothers who wish to leave. He had eloquently presented the constant stress, what he termed the "climate of danger" in fundamentalist Mormonism that was eerily reminiscent of accounts from totalitarian regimes throughout history. And Jessop's inspiring but terrifying account of her own predawn escape from both the FLDS-controlled police and the Church's own roving "God Squad" breathed life into the stories of the FLDS culture of mutual surveillance.

In the fundamentalist Mormon faith, the dominance of women by men is both doctrinal and institutional. The prophet is a man, as are all his lieutenants. The bishops are men. Each woman is assigned a "priesthood head"; initially, that person is her father, until she is assigned in marriage, at which point the husband takes over. Women may only enter the afterlife through their husbands, and may only enter the highest levels of the eternal kingdom by becoming plural wives. Needless to say, there are no "plural husbands." Beall referred to male domination that is the rule in FLDS communities as "an institutionalized power imbalance between males and females."

The clear result of all this was the sort of commodification that the experts would predict must arise in a society that permits polygamy. "Within the polygamous community," said Beall, "a woman is by and large an object." Again and again, we showed, the personal witnesses had made this harm too real for the Court.

Beall said the girls he counselled reported feeling like a "bargaining chip"—for instance, when given to older men in order to promote their father's standing in the community. After marriage, it appeared that a girl would simply become her husband's property. Jessop explained more than once how she was made to feel like chattel. She recounted that the day after she married Merril Jessop, as she sat amongst her new "family," he remarked that a dog is better than a new wife "because a dog is more loyal."

Jensen recalled her father Harold Blackmore's crushing disillusionment when he returned from meetings of FLDS elders where girls were bartered over and "distributed" among them. The arranged marriage of women, and especially of very young girls, was, on the evidence, the very essence of FLDS marriage practices, and the women's own aspirations be damned.

Henrich had quoted the anthropologist William Jankowiak's description of FLDS practices as follows:

In this setting, fathers often exchanged daughters in order to marry them . . . men wanted to marry off their daughters before they could decide to select from within their age cohort. By the 1990s Second Ward fathers began to negotiate marital exchanges not for themselves but for a favourite son, or in some cases a grandson.

Henrich also reported Jankowiak's findings that within Short Creek's First Ward, families also gave/give daughters as a kind of patronage to the prophet:

The prophet's age does not restrict families from offering their daughters to him. The reasons why fathers give their daughters to the prophet (often with a wife's encouragement) are to gain prestige and to obtain material and spiritual benefits.

Commodification is institutionalized in a religious setting through centrally arranged marriages. In the FLDS this was facilitated through the prophet's "revelations." There was some evidence at the trial of what was called "courtship marriages," at least among the more liberal families in fundamentalist Mormon communities, but by far the more common practice, it appeared, was that of "assignments" made on short notice. The FLDS's anonymous Witness 4, for instance, described her own marriage a week after her seventeenth birthday to a man she had never met. She had been married half an hour after learning his identity, and two hours after that she was being driven to Canada to begin her new life with her husband. In a similar episode years before, Jessop had been told she would be married when she was awakened from bed at two in the morning. Jessop was then kept within her parents' sight until the wedding could take place a few days later. These arranged marriages were featured in the testimony of virtually every personal witness, and the emphasis on lack of notice was similarly commonly reported in the FLDS.

Nor did the Church's control end when it "turned over" a girl to her new husband; there was extensive evidence that women and their children could be, and were, "reassigned" to other men at the whim of the prophet. Existing wives generally had little or no choice in the new marriage, and at times were not even informed of the wedding until after it has occurred.

Our expert evidence had led us to expect that the necessity to strictly control women's options in a polygynous society would lead to the development of a general culture of subservience and obedience of both children and adults, male and female. So it was significant that many witnesses described in detail the pliability of FLDS members. Beall said that "polygamous conditioning discourages independent thinking and feeling" and offered his opinion that this indoctrination impairs development and function of the brain in adolescence. Brent Jeffs described the main teachings of the FLDS as enforcing perfect obedience as the hallmark of perfect faith: "basically doing everything that they ask no matter what without question, without opinion, nothing."[22] Many other witnesses from the FLDS also emphasized the culture of indoctrination and the resulting impairment of independent and critical thinking. It was difficult to reflect on the testimony of Witness 4, who had so blithely described the circumstances of her removal and that of her teenaged sister wife from their American families to their new Canadian home, without wondering what had so bent her development as to make that seem normal or acceptable.

Training of children for obedience appears to have been extreme in fundamentalist Mormon communities and was a common theme of the personal and some expert evidence. Two personal witnesses independently described the use of suffocation of crying infants to instil obedience. Jensen testified as to the frequent use of physical violence to reinforce a rigid fealty, not only to parents, but to the dictates of the Church.

Perhaps the most extreme manifestation of the commodification effect is in the phenomenon of trafficking in girls and young women. At the high level, McDermott's regression analysis confirmed the association of polygamy with female trafficking cross-culturally, a phenomenon that Henrich had also predicted. The evidence from Bountiful was, again, striking in the degree of its corroboration. A number of the personal witnesses described the movement of teenagers from communities in the United States to be brides in Bountiful, and some also described movement the other way. Beall described the trafficking between the American communities and Bountiful as follows:

> I learned from my patients that most of them had travelled back and forth between what they call Short Creek, which means the Hildale/ Colorado City area, and Bountiful. There was a lot of travel back and forth especially as young girls, potential marriage partners, that kind of thing.

The BC Vital Statistics Agency's birth registration records showed that, of the sixty-five teen mothers documented in Klette's Bountiful cohort, over half (57 percent) had been born outside British Columbia (thirty-two in Utah, one in Arizona, and four in Alberta).[23] Witness 4 spoke of exactly this phenomenon: born and raised into the FLDS in the United States, she received an "assignment" by the prophet to marry a foreign stranger on a half-hour's notice. She was bundled into a car for the eighteen-hour drive north and taken across the border with a false note from the girl's parents (listing the purpose of the entry as to "visit an aunt"). Then the whole process was repeated with Witness 4's fifteen-year-old junior wife, half a year later.

But we argued, the most eloquent documentary evidence concerned James Oler, the bishop of the Bountiful FLDS community and a participant in this reference. In March 2004 FLDS records indicate that Oler delivered two teenaged sisters to the United States to be married by Jeffs. A few months later, he delivered his own fifteen-year-old daughter. Only minutes after witnessing her marriage, he himself married a fifteen-year-old American girl, bundled her into a car, and returned to Canada with her.

Ruth Lane, Winston Blackmore's former wife, testified that Blackmore married her a week after he married two American sisters, all in the United States; Blackmore drove back to Canada with his three new wives. Truman Oler testified that girls from the United States were always being placed with men in Canada, and vice versa, and that it was common for girls to be sent across the border for marriage.

We also, by then, knew something of the scale of movement of girls *from* Bountiful. In 2004 and 2005 at least three girls, aged twelve and thirteen, were taken to the United States by their parents to be "celestially married" to Jeffs. The church records referenced in the affidavit we had introduced by Texas Ranger Hanna indicated more than a dozen girls trafficked between Bountiful and the FLDS communities in the United States, with an ongoing investigation of many more.

In other contexts, the importation of brides into a polygynous community might offset the age-depressing effects of polygyny. The ancient Greeks, for instance, used their economic and military resources to secure a supply of sex slaves to satisfy wealthy men's desire for multiple partners that persisted notwithstanding their society's official adoption of the monogamous standard. The same pressure-valve effect did not pertain at Bountiful or elsewhere in the FLDS because the entire pool of fundamentalist Mormons is affected by the practice of polygyny on both sides of the border. So while there may be more girls and women available through trafficking, this does not ease the negative effects of the cruel arithmetic. Trafficking in the FLDS, we argued, was simply a reflection of the intensity of the market in young girls created by polygamy.

Another significant point of convergence, we submitted, was in the evidence that polygamy leads to poor educational outcomes, particularly but not exclusively for girls and women. It became apparent during the reference that Bountiful students had historically experienced a very low high-school completion rate, in that they almost never earn provincial accreditation for grade 12 completion. Of the students who were in grade 7 at BESS between 1994–1995 and 2003–2004, only 7 percent of female students and 6 percent of males were issued either a Dogwood or Adult Diploma signifying completion.

As I mentioned earlier, the FLDS had introduced evidence through its cross-examination of Vanderboom (from the BC Ministry of Education) that, at least as of grade 4, BESS students are among the most accomplished in the province as measured by the provincially standard FSA test. Clearly, we argued, something was happening in Bountiful to turn ordinary, even exemplary, elementary students into high-school dropouts. In the Attorney General's submission, the natural inference to be drawn was that girls were being streamed towards a future as wives and mothers, while boys, if they stayed, are expected to serve the local industries as menial labourers.

When we dove beneath the expert reports and the statistics figures and reviewed the evidence of the personal witnesses, the picture came into sharp focus. Many of the witnesses testified that education was not valued in the FLDS, and many children did not finish high school. The FLDS Records seized by the Texas authorities included the following note:

Dear Uncle Warren, In regard to sending children to school, we have Kendra who is now seven years old and she desires to go to first grade. . . . She knows she has to be obedient and sweet at home before she can go to school. LeAnn [the writer's wife] has finished 8th grade and is wondering what I would like her to do. Unless you direct otherwise, I would like her to be home where there is much to do in taking care of the children, house and yard.

Some witnesses spoke of the emphasis on acquiring "practical skills" such as mechanics, midwifery, etc. Some of these skills, coincidentally, served the interests of the Church's hierarchy, who owned the businesses that benefited from a ready supply of cheap labour (Blackmore and Oler were both successful businessmen in an environment where, in theory, all enterprise was supposed to be in service of the Church). Others, we argued, were useful means of keeping the prying eyes of outsiders away from the systematic predation of girls (teaching and midwifery, for instance, needed to be done by "insiders").

This devaluing of education beyond the elementary years was a frequent theme of the personal witnesses—girls left school to start families, boys to work. Oler recalled that the boys at Bountiful joked that all they needed to do was learn to count to 175 because that is how many fence posts were in a bundle. Truman left school after grade 9 to go to work, and testified, "I don't even recall knowing what a college was through my younger days." Wall said that her husband Roy, who grew up in Bountiful, "got snatched out of school and sent to work" in seventh or eighth grade.

Teressa explained that "Winston felt like that boys were getting a better education working than in books and so I don't know very many boys at all that actually finished high school. There was some so bad they didn't even know how to read and they were sent to work." While he was a member of the FLDS, Jessop's son, Arthur, was only allowed to attend school until the end of grade 7. After that, from the age of twelve until fifteen (at which point he left the FLDS with his mother), he worked construction with his brothers, something for which he was well prepared because he had worked around heavy equipment since he was six years old. There was a bright side to this story, though: after leaving the FLDS, Arthur had completed his high school and became the first of Jessop's twenty-six sons to go to college. Other boys, such as Truman Oler, had also at least partially recovered from their early education deprivation, but only after they left the Church.

And to say the least, things were not better for the girls. Jessop had testified that she had believed that there was a real need for doctors in the Short Creek community, and that her own desire had been to be a pediatrician. Yet she was pulled out of school at grade 8, and had to beg to complete high school through a home program. She testified that she had pleaded with her father to ask the prophet (Leroy Johnson at the time) for the opportunity to attend college so that she could become a doctor. Her father was hesitant about even asking the prophet. Jessop described Johnson's response:

> Uncle Roy said I could not be a doctor, but he would give me permission to be a teacher. However, if I wanted to pursue a college education I belonged to Merril Jessop and I would have to marry him before I left. The other understanding is that Merril would be my priesthood head. He would own me. I would be his. If he decided that he didn't want his wife to have a college education, there was that conflict, but Uncle Roy had given permission, so there was also the opportunity that I might be able to.

FLDS historian Bistline wrote in a passage of his book, referenced in his affidavit, that:

> The Polygamists teach that love is not necessary before marriage. Women are inferior to men and must learn to school their feelings, yielding to the desires of their husband. The girls of Colorado City Polygamists are considered as chattel, to be used by the leaders to reward faithful men of the Group for their support of the Priesthood Work.
>
> Very few of them ever achieve any more than bearing as many children as possible, usually between the number of 15-20. Most are expected

to work, turning what money they earn over to their husband to use as he sees fit. A few become school teachers to work in the public schools, while others become nurses to work in the hospitals of nearby communities. None are ever allowed to become professors, doctors, lawyers, or achieve other professional goals. Mostly they work at whatever unskilled jobs are available in the area.

It is commonly accepted, even acknowledged by each of the FLDS anonymous witnesses, that not a single Bountiful student has gone on to earn professional accreditation in anything but nursing, midwifery, or teaching. These are, I have argued, the three professions where church control would be particularly advantageous in keeping prying eyes of outsiders away from issues around the sexual exploitation of children. Witness 4 described how, after she and her fifteen-year-old sister wife were brought up from the United States to marry their husband, they rode the school bus together to BESS. She also noted that school officials, like all other members of the community, expressed to her knowledge no concern at all that the two had become the plural wives of a man in his forties. It is difficult to imagine any other context where this could be considered anything but worthy of official concern in the school setting. No female fundamentalist Mormon from Bountiful, apparently, has ever gone on to earn a university degree.

Against all this evidence of poor educational outcomes, the *amicus* and FLDS really had precious little to offer. The anonymous witnesses that they put forward, such as 1 and 4, appeared to have been selected in part because they had at least taken some steps towards postsecondary education. But these were outliers, selected to be (in the first case) a teacher because the FLDS had apparently realized early that they could not permit outside educators to see what was going on in the schools and community. Witness 4 was studying business and accounting at the local college, but the weight of her testimony seemed to indicate that a central motivation for staying in school was to avoid deportation on the expiry of her student visa, which had been repeatedly extended since her arrival in Bountiful as a teen.

As a result, the challengers could not rebut or deny that educational opportunities appeared to be sharply constrained, and instead fell back on assertions that, in demanding better, the governments we represented were attempting to impose middle-class values on a different culture. This is a fair point as far as it goes, but, we said, it didn't go that far. Certainly, people ought to have a choice about whether to "buy in" to the mainstream view of the good life. But surely also the fact that *nobody* took that option in Bountiful was indicative of the reality that the choice was really not there after all. The sad fact was that, while opportunities for women in higher education blossomed throughout the rest of the country in the postwar period, a girl growing up in Bountiful and remaining with the FLDS appeared to have less of a chance of earning a university degree than a girl in Afghanistan, Somalia, or Sudan.

In addition to these harms that we believed had been amply demonstrated on a balance of probabilities (and then some), we also argued that there were harms that, while not the subject of conclusive proof, nevertheless were sufficient to give rise to a "reasonable apprehension of harm." The work of Scheidel of Stanford University, like that of Henrich and Witte, demonstrated that the social imposition of universal normative monogamy was concurrent with the growth and success of the Western democratic way of life and the development of a rights-based culture. We noted that a number of respected theorists suggested that one would not be possible without the other. Again, Harvard's Pinker put it concisely and memorably when he observed that in recent centuries "egalitarianism and monogamy go together as naturally as despotism and polygyny."[24]

We of course had to concede that, despite the experts' universal observation that rights-based democracies appeared to be incompatible with polygamy, the precise causation could not be determined (that is, does monogamy contribute to democracy, or does democracy lead to monogamy, or is there another development that leads to both?).

Our own expert, Scheidel, after extensive review of the available literature, noted that "the causes for the 'rise of the West' continue to be hotly debated in the academic literature and no consensus appears to be in reach." In other words, the hypothesis is plausible, but unprovable.

More speculative, perhaps, but no less thought-provoking was the fact that, to so many Canadians, polygamy seemed almost instinctively "immoral." Obviously, one always has to be very careful about these judgments: they could have evolved in societies because they provided a cultural-evolution advantage, or they might be the result of innate human tendencies to prejudice that we should properly guard against. So we were careful not to place too much emphasis on the undermining of "morality" as a harm. Nevertheless, we recognized that the Supreme Court *had* said that morality was a proper subject for the criminal law, and that it is open to Parliament to legislate "on the basis of some fundamental conception of morality for the purposes of safeguarding the values which are integral to a free and democratic society."[25] The Court in *R v Malmo-Levine* had said, though, that this does not justify codification of "mere 'conventional standards of propriety' but must be understood as referring to 'societal values beyond the simply prurient or prudish.'"[26]

In our closing, we accepted that, if harm to conventional standards of propriety were all that supporters of section 293 could invoke, justification for the polygamy ban would be tenuous indeed. The challengers' arguments seemed largely premised on the belief that the prohibition against polygamy was, as a societal value, "simply prurient and prudish." We said, obviously, that the evidence demonstrated otherwise. But even so, we said that the fact that socially imposed monogamy is so deeply imbedded in the moral fabric of our society cannot be dismissed lightly. The courts' deference to Parliament on matters of morality, while anything but absolute, reflects an understanding that strong moral codes may evolve for an important reason, even if that reason is imperfectly understood at any given time.

Finally, we argued that polygamy was inherently degrading of Canadian values, in particular the values of equality and the protection of vulnerable groups. We said that, regardless of whether you accepted the explanations of evolutionary psychology, it was plain that polygamy, when permitted, reveals itself overwhelmingly as polygyny. In every significant religious or cultural manifestation, this means that the women in the relationship are limited to one partner of the other sex while the men are not. This inequality reinforces the simple apparent mathematics of a polygynous household: the suggestion that a man is "worth" several women.

Bevan and I collaborated on much of the language we used to express the harm to the value of equality, including our concluding paragraphs on the topic. Because the language is mostly hers, and the case so eloquently put, I am excerpting them here in their entirety:

> 263. Equality is one of the fundamental values of Canadian society—it is enshrined in sections 15 and 28 of the *Charter*, and its protection is beyond "simply prurient or prudish" concern. The more important the institution, the more important it is that we honour the right to equality within that institution. Marriage is an institution sufficiently fundamental to Canadian life that it was the subject of careful constitutional assignment in 1867. It is certainly true that our ideas of what marriage is and should be has changed over time, but the centrality of the human pair bond remains a defining characteristic of Canadian culture, to the point where its recent extension to gays and lesbians is seen as a watershed moment in those groups' quest for equal dignity and status.

> 264. Section 293 protects women and children from commodification and exploitation. A criminal law may be justified without proving direct harm if it protects vulnerable groups, such as racial minorities, women, or children. This law protects women, children, and in particular vul-

nerable female members of immigrant populations and discrete and insular religious sects.

265. More broadly, to the extent that polygyny is inherently unequal and conceptually degrading to women and girls, the prohibition serves to advance their equality throughout society. Equality within the family unit is especially worthy of legal reinforcement. Children experience societal norms first and most importantly within those units, and that is especially true within closed or insular minority groups where other cultural influences are *ipso facto* limited. And while it is true that gender inequality can exist within monogamous marriages, it is not a defining feature of such marriages, as it is of polygynous ones.

266. This last point is worthy of some weight, because an important role of the criminal law is public denunciation; it is an expression of society's deepest values, including, in this case, the value it attributes to women's equality.

## The Legal Arguments

The most obvious challenge to section 293 was based on its impact on freedom of religion. It was clear that marriage in most polygamous traditions was entwined with religious beliefs (you have noticed I have avoided saying polygamy is "based on" or "derived from" religion because I actually believe it is the other way around, but that's beside the point).

We could not live in a society where the religiosity of a practice renders it automatically immune from prosecution. There are very few crimes, from petty fraud to genocide, that have not, at one time or another, been excused on religious bases. Some clearly criminal activities, such as female genital mutilation, "honour killings," ritual animal sacrifice, and cannibalism may be closely connected with deep religious or cultural beliefs. So the religious origin or nature of a prohibited activity, we told the Court, is not the end of the analysis, but the beginning.

Joseph Smith's embryonic Mormonism was born in the United States when the American Revolution and the *Bill of Rights* were still young. To help put things in historical perspective, we can recall that Thomas Jefferson was president when Smith was born in 1805, and would still be living when Smith reported his discovery of the Golden Plates to his followers in the early 1820s. As polygamy in Mormonism grew, the revolution was still very much a work in progress, and the 1789 Constitution was within the living memory of most grandparents.

More than anyone else, Jefferson was the author of the constitutional separation of church and state, and it is useful to remind ourselves just how revolutionary the idea of a secular citizenry was at the time. There were two elements to Jefferson's concept of the relationship between the state and religion: anti-establishmentarianism, which provided that there must be no official state religion, and a "free exercise" guarantee that the state will not interfere with the religious practices of its citizens. Both were embodied into the First Amendment to the Constitution, which began:

> Congress shall make no law respecting an establishment of religion, or prohibiting the free exercise thereof . . .

Although this was, as I say, the first national *constitutional* expression of freedom of religion (one that could not simply be repealed), the prototypical religious freedom law actually predated the US Constitution by more than a century. It was a statute of the British colony of Maryland, and provided that "No person or persons . . . shall from henceforth be any waies troubled, molested or discountenanced for or in respect of his or her religion nor in the free exercise thereof." The title of this law was the *Maryland Toleration Act,* and its choice of language suggests the difficulty that is implied in all the documents and jurisprudence on religious freedom since: precisely what need the citizenry tolerate in the name of the free exercise of a citizen's faith?

Over time it has been recognized that even a secular state could frustrate the free exercise of religion by passing laws that are neutral on their face but disproportionately impact a certain religion. An easy modern example would be the prohibition of burkas or face veils, which, although it may apply to everyone, it would only have a religious impact on Muslims and a handful of others. The fear is that through such ostensibly neutral laws, both elements of the First Amendment protection would be offended: not only is free exercise undermined, but the state is, through restricting practices of religious minorities, able to indirectly impose a state-sanctioned model of religious propriety.

On the other hand, if something truly is worthy of prohibition, does it matter whether it is done for a religious purpose? The US Supreme Court, and subsequently the Canadian Supreme Court, recognized that there were valid reasons to pass laws despite a disproportionate impact on particular religions; laws against murder or assault might infringe on the exercise of religions that favour human sacrifice or vampirism. But these are broad prohibitions against activities (killing and attacking others) that are more usually nonreligious in nature. Far more problematic is the face veil ban I moot above, because it is a prohibition of an activity that *usu-*

*ally* has a religious foundation. This might also be said for the prohibition against polygamy because it is a type of family arrangement that is often interwoven with religious belief.[27] In such cases, it is generally thought that there must be some real indication of the activity's harm in order to justify the state's intervention. Otherwise, ostensibly neutral laws could be arranged so as to simply crowd out one religion or another.

In the analysis that has developed in Canadian law, there are two stages to determining whether a law breaches the *Charter*'s protections of religious freedom, which the Supreme Court had articulated in a case dealing with a challenge to a bylaw that prevented orthodox Jews from maintaining a religious structure known as a *sukkah*:

> [A]t the first stage of a religious freedom analysis, an individual advancing an issue premised upon a freedom of religion claim must show the court that (1) he or she has a practice or belief, having a nexus with religion, which calls for a particular line of conduct, either by being objectively or subjectively obligatory or customary, or by, in general, subjectively engendering a personal connection with the divine or with the subject or object of an individual's spiritual faith, irrespective of whether a particular practice or belief is required by official religious dogma or is in conformity with the position of religious officials; and (2) he or she is sincere in his or her belief. Only then will freedom of religion be triggered.[28]

Granted, the evidence indicated that it is possible for individuals to observe any religion in which polygamy is accepted or encouraged without actually practising polygamy; although some, including some fundamentalist Mormons, definitely appeared to believe that there were advantages in the afterlife to those who practised as opposed to simply espoused "the Principle." We therefore accepted that some people practise polygamy in accord with deeply held religious views within the meaning of the cases.[29] Nor could we dispute that the infringement on that practice by the imposition of criminal sanction was trivial or insubstantial.

The *Amselem* case was significant in other important respects: first, it reiterated the rejection, dating from *R v Big M Drug Mart Ltd*,[30] of a distinction between religious views and practices, holding both to be equally protected. And second, it rejected the notion that the protected views must be part of an established faith, or even shared with others: it was enough that they were sincerely held by the individual asserting the right. So we could not argue, for instance, as many scholars and commentators did, that the FLDS wasn't "true" Mormonism.

Our main point was that, since the early *Charter* case of *R v Big M*, the Court had confirmed that "religious freedoms were nonetheless subject to limitations when they disproportionately collided with other significant public rights and interests," and that "the invocation of freedom of religion does not, by itself, grant immunity from the need to weigh the assertion against competing values or harm."[31] Justice Iacobucci had written in *Amselem*:

> [O]ur jurisprudence does not allow individuals to do absolutely anything in the name of that freedom. Even if individuals demonstrate that they sincerely believe in the religious essence of an action, for example, that a particular practice will subjectively engender a genuine connection with the divine or with the subject or object of their faith, and even if they successfully demonstrate non-trivial or non-insubstantial interference with that practice, they will still have to consider how the exercise of their right impacts upon the rights of others in the context of the competing rights of private individuals. *Conduct which would potentially cause harm to or interference with the rights of others would not automatically be protected.* The ultimate protection of any particular *Charter* right must be measured in relation to other rights and with a view to the underlying context in which the apparent conflict arises [emphasis added].[32]

Our case was built around harm, and we said the outcome must be the same whether these harms were seen as negating the very right of religious freedom under section 2(a), or whether they should be more properly considered at the section 1 stage as "justification" for the *prima facie* infringement.

However, we pressed for an interpretation of the *Charter* that would deny harmful religious practices even *prima facie* protection. We argued that, where the "competing values" at issue were themselves protected *Charter* rights, it is appropriate to weigh them in the balance at the section 2(a), rather than the section 1 stage.[33] Even where polygamy could be said to rise to the level of a fundamental tenet for *Charter* purposes, we said, we could not concede a breach of section 2(a) because the practice is inherently harmful and infringes on the fundamental rights of others. Unfortunately, in this we were up against the weight of the jurisprudence and academic commentary, which suggested that the Supreme Court of Canada had moved away from internal limits to section 2(a), holding that weighing the rights and interests of others should occur at the section 1 stage. Peter Hogg, Canada's leading constitutional authority, wrote:

> The idea that freedom of religion authorizes religious practices only so far as they do not injure others has been abandoned by the Supreme Court of Canada in favour of an unqualified right to do anything that is dictated by a religious belief.[34]

No doubt, Professor Hogg was correctly summarizing the evolved position of the Court, but the whole idea nevertheless seemed absurd in its application. If the Court, as its views were summarized by Hogg, was correct, then any crime at all—from writing a bad cheque to mass murder—would be a protected exercise of religion if a single individual sincerely believes that there was a religious imperative, or even a religious permission, to commit it. In every case, under this analysis, it would be up to the government to justify the infringement. This protection, which would go well beyond even that afforded to expression (where expressive actions have been held to be unprotected in many contexts), seemed (and still seems to me) morally and philosophically unsustainable.

At the end of the day, at what stage the harm was weighed made little difference in the polygamy case, because the analyses of breach of section 2(a) merged with the question of arbitrariness under section 7, and with justification under section 1, as it had in the recent decision of *AC v Manitoba (Director of Child and Family Services)*. In that case, Chief Justice McLachlin (concurring) had written:

> In this case, the s. 7 and s. 2(*a*) claims merge, upon close analysis. Either the *Charter* requires that an ostensibly "mature" child under 16 have an unfettered right to make all medical treatment decisions, or it does not, regardless of the individual child's motivation for refusing treatment. The fact that A.C.'s aversion to receiving a blood transfusion springs from religious conviction does not change the essential nature of the claim as one for absolute personal autonomy in medical decision making.[35]

Here, the essence of the fundamentalist Mormon claim, like that of a polygamous Muslim, is the same: one for "absolute personal autonomy in [marriage structure] decision making." As such, we said, the asserted right must be weighed against the social interest in placing restrictions upon it. This could be analyzed under section 2, section 1, or section 7, but the answer must be the same: personal autonomy and religious freedom must yield to the more substantial interests at stake.

There two final unique aspects relevant to the religious freedom claim that we emphasized at a couple of stages in our closing. The first was that, because polygamy is most harmful when it is twinned with an external, binding authority that purports to sanction it, the religiosity of the practice itself exacerbates the harm. We pointed out that the evidence that had emerged from expert and lay witnesses alike indicated that the greater the religious fervour with which polygamy was interwoven, the more harmful it can be expected to be. This would not be so with respect to almost any other imaginable case asserting a religious right to do something prohibited. In fact, you could argue, the opposite was more generally true: carrying a concealed knife might be reasonably feared to lead to more serious assaults, but perhaps fewer when the knife was a *kirpan*, the ceremonial dagger worn by observant Sikhs.

Aside from freedom of religion and the section 7 "liberty" violations (to which I will return later), there were some other breaches alleged by certain of the challengers with which we had to grapple. The CPAA made an argument under section 2(b)'s protection of free expression. The group suggested that "conjugal polyamory" is a protected expressive activity.

Justice Pitfield in the same-sex marriage case *EGALE Canada Inc v Canada (Attorney General)* had held that "the words 'freedom of expression' are not apt to describe the formalization of the legal relationship that is marriage."[36] Though polygamous marriages are not *legal* relationships, the analogy is apt.

Of course, our argument was that the bulk of what was considered "polyamory" did not fall within section 293's prohibition. But to any extent that it did, it was difficult to comprehend the commission of a crime as an independent protected form of expression *per se*. Any nonsecret breach in the face of a law is, on some level, an expressive act—it is, at least, an expression of defiance of the law. This does not elevate every flagrant crime to the level of protected speech. Parking a car, the Supreme Court had confirmed, can be an expressive activity. If section 293 is otherwise valid law, we said, freedom of expression could not be used to permit its breach.

Perhaps less of a stretch were the arguments of the *amicus* and some other challengers based on the *Charter*'s section 2(d), which protects freedom of association. Here, the *amicus* said that, because section 293 permits multipartner sexual activity, but not "polygamous groupings," it violated the freedom of association. The associational arguments of other challengers appeared to be similar.

The scope of freedom of association had been most recently considered by the Supreme Court of Canada in *Health Services and Support—Facilities Subsector Bargaining Assn v British Columbia*.[37] In that case, the Court had decided that the protections of 2(d) should be extended to include collective bargaining. It had done so after finding first that an interpretation of section 2(d) that precludes collective bargaining from its ambit would be inconsistent with Canada's historic recognition of the importance of collective bargaining to freedom of association; second, that collective bargaining is an integral component of freedom of association in international law, which may inform the interpretation of *Charter* guarantees; and finally that interpreting section 2(d) as including a right to collective bargaining was consistent with, and indeed, promoted, other *Charter* rights, freedoms, and values.

In the Polygamy Reference, we pointed out that the challengers did not suggest that there is any authority in the caselaw for inclusion of polygamous marriage as protected under section 2(d). Indeed, we noted, the argument that freedom of choice in intimate partners is a protected form of association was rejected by the British Columbia Court of Appeal in an "adult consensual incest" case, *R v MS*, above. In that case, the court had relied on the Ontario Court of Appeal's decision in *Catholic Children's Aid Society of Metropolitan Toronto v S(T)*, for the proposition that the protection in section 2(d) was clearly designed to protect association with persons beyond the primary family unit. Tarnopolsky JA wrote of his reasons in *Catholic Children's Aid Society*:

> The freedoms of assembly and association are necessarily collective and so mostly public. Our constitutional concerns have not been with assemblies within families or associations between family members. Rather, the protections we have been concerned with are for those assemblies and associations that take us outside the intimate circle of our families.[38]

It was also significant, we argued alongside Canada, that freedom of association was raised by claimants in both the British Columbia and Ontario challenges to the exclusion of same-sex couples from the traditional definition of marriage, but no court in any province accepted that section 2(d) could be engaged by the inability to marry.[39]

There was very little in the evidence that could support an argument based on the *Health Services* case. The Court had heard nothing regarding the history of associational guarantees in the family setting, such as would be required to establish a historical case for inclusion. The challengers had produced no evidence supporting the idea of polygamous marriage as a component of association at international law (and in fact, we pointed out, if there was a consensus in international law it was that polygamy should be banned). Finally, they had articulated no argument that a right to polygamous marriage was consistent with or promoted other *Charter* rights, freedoms, and values. In fact, we said, given the evidence of the nature of polygamy's harms, it clearly did the opposite.

No, aside from religious freedom, it was clear that the constitutional impact was around the "liberty" interest protected by the *Charter*'s section 7. We had to concede that section 293 engaged section 7 of the *Charter*, because it permitted imprisonment. Any criminal law with penal consequences triggered scrutiny under that section. But some of the challengers were asserting broader protections, asserting the infringement of the "liberty to marry a person of one's choice." The BC Civil Liberties Association (BCCLA) also suggested that section 7's "security of the person" protection was engaged through the consequences of criminalization in the form of "psychological stress," which might be also linked to the insularity of Bountiful and other polygamous communities and which could tend to make residents of those communities reluctant to access health and other services.

We acknowledged that liberty may be engaged under section 7 without the threat of imprisonment. In *Malmo-Levine*, the Supreme Court of Canada summarized the law as follows:

> 85 In *Morgentaler, supra*, Wilson J. suggested that liberty "grants the individual a degree of autonomy in making decisions of fundamental personal importance", "without interference from the state" (p. 166). Liberty accordingly means more than freedom from physical restraint. It includes "the right to an irreducible sphere of personal autonomy wherein individuals may make inherently private choices free from state interference": *Godbout v. Longueuil (City)*, [1997] 3 S.C.R. 844, at para. 66; *B. (R.) v. Children's Aid Society of Metropolitan Toronto*, [1995] 1 S.C.R. 315, at para. 80. This is true only to the extent that such matters "can properly be characterized as fundamentally or inherently personal such that, by their very nature, they implicate basic choices going to the core of what it means to enjoy individual dignity and independence": *Godbout, supra*, at para. 66. See also *Blencoe v. British Columbia (Human Rights Commission)*, [2000] 2 S.C.R. 307, 2000 SCC 44, at para. 54; *Buhlers v. British Columbia (Superintendent of Motor Vehicles)* (1999), 170 D.L.R. (4th) 344 (B.C.C.A.), at para. 109; *Horsefield v. Ontario (Registrar of Motor Vehicles)* (1999), 44 O.R. (3d) 73 (C.A.).

In *Godbout v Longueuil (City)*, LaForest J, writing for three members of the Court, found that the choice of residence was a "liberty interest" within the meaning of section 7 (the remainder of the Court did not consider section 7). He quoted approvingly from the respondent's factum:

> [Translation] Residence determines the human and social environment in which an individual and his or her family evolve: the type of neighbourhood, the school the children attend, the living environment, services, etc. In this sense, therefore, residence affects the individual's entire life and development.[40]

On analogous reasoning, we were driven to accept that fundamental choices of family arrangements engage the liberty interest in section 7, and although the cases were not determinative of the issue, we were prepared to argue on the basis that section 7's liberty interest is engaged with or without the threat of incarceration. The consequences of this concession were limited given that liberty was in any event engaged by the penal sanctions of section 293. However, it did require that Court must weigh this infringement of liberty as well in the "fundamental justice" analysis, particularly with respect to whether the statute was unconstitutionally disproportional in its effects. Again, this would come down to a weighing of harm: the harm to the accused by being imprisoned or prevented from freely participating in banned forms of conjugality, against the harms that we said were caused by the practice of polygamy itself.

As for the BCCLA's argument that "security of the person" was at issue, we acknowledged that, in *R v Morgentaler*, Dickson CJ accepted that "serious *state-imposed* psychological stress"[41] could trigger section 7 protection. In *Malmo-Levine*, it was agreed, at least in *obiter*, that preventing a person from gaining access to medical help may engage section 7.

The BCCLA appeared to be arguing that the fear of prosecution is "serious state-imposed psychological stress," and moreover that the insularity to which this leads was depriving individuals of the opportunity to access needed medical and other services. There was also some suggestion that the insularity of the communities like Bountiful (which they argued was induced or exacerbated by the criminalization of polygamy) made the commission of crimes against those persons more difficult to defend against.

Fear of criminal prosecution no doubt has contributed to making the residents of Bountiful, and American FLDS communities, secretive and insular. But, we asked, was this really a fear of prosecution under section 293 (which had not been prosecuted for a century until 2009, and was declared in 1992 by a representative of the Crown prosecutor's office to be unconstitutional and unenforceable), or was it fear of prosecution for the other crimes that polygamy causes?

In any event, we said, there is in this case no evidence of serious psychological harm resulting from any state action. Witness 2 had said in her affidavit that her seven-year-old child had terrible fears about authorities "coming to get us," but then she confirmed under cross-examination that this could only be as a result of what the boy had been taught by members of the community, not as a result of any state action *per se*.[42]

The FLDS, as I have said, had a morbid obsession with myths of government persecution that were inculcated in children virtually from the cradle. These served well to foster a sense of suspicion of the "outside" and facilitate more rigid community discipline. We argued that if the Chief Justice accepted the evidence that criminality at Bountiful—the trafficking in and sexual exploitation of girls, for instance, or harsh physical abuse in order to instil discipline and obedience—is ancillary to the creation of the supply of child brides that polygamy demands, then decriminalizing polygamy is unlikely to make Bountiful less insular. It seemed fantastic, we said, to suggest that these crimes are hidden because polygamy had been driven underground. These crimes were hidden because they were crimes, they flowed from polygamy, and they needed to be kept secret in order for their perpetrators to be able to continue committing them.

And further undermining the suggestion of a *causal* relationship between criminalization and insularity there was, we said, conflicting evidence even of *correlation*. The *amicus*'s expert Campbell readily admitted that Bountiful, once a community so insular that it had the reputation for entirely shunning contact with the outside world, had in recent years become less insular and more open (at least the "Blackmore faction," which was the subject of her study). She acknowledged that this renewed engagement with the outside world came at a time when Bountiful residents (some of whom had been, according to her, unaware that polygamy was even illegal) came under increased legal scrutiny and the criminal prohibition increasingly weighed on their minds.

Q  Right. So it's safe to say I think then in the timeframe in which criminalization has been weighing more heavily on residents' minds that that has also been a period in which the community has been less insular and isolated; is that true?

A  I think that's a fair parallel.

Only one witness from Bountiful had spoken to the expected effects of decriminalization on the insularity of Bountiful. Witness 4 testified that she expected that the community would remain insular and isolated after decriminalization. That is, she said, the way she liked it:

Q  So your expectation is that if polygamy were decriminalized then—and combined with your hope that your community would remain isolated and insulated you would—you would expect that if it was decriminalized you would be able to continue that isolated and insulated existence; is that right?

A  Yes.

Overall, we said, the evidence on the harm of insularity was weak. No challenger could point to any incident where a person had suffered any injury as a result of a reluctance to approach authorities for fear of being "outed" as a polygamist. While it was not inconceivable that such a thing could happen, it was far from the sort of harm, we said, that could outweigh the demonstrated perils of removing the criminal sanction.

Like the protection of religion in section 2(a), protections for infringements of "life, liberty and security of the person" are not absolute. They could be infringed if doing so accorded with "the principles of fundamental justice." In a section 7 challenge, it was up to the person alleging the breach to identify just what these supposedly offended principles were, and we would argue how "harm" permeated every aspect of this analysis too.

The challengers identified three principles of fundamental justice in their section 7 argument that they said were violated: arbitrariness, overbreadth, and disproportionality.

However, there is also another principle that was never clearly articulated as such: one of the challengers' section 7 arguments appeared to be that, even if it were permissible to ban polygamy involving children or coercion, it is a violation of the principles of fundamental justice to criminalize consensual, adult polygamy where there is no harm in the relationship itself. The argument integrated notions of liberty to make life choices (discussed earlier in this chapter) with a simultaneous assertion of harmlessness, folding consent and privacy into arguments based on harm. We said that these two things—the question of consent (going to liberty) and the question of harm (going to fundamental justice) should be kept conceptually distinct at the section 7 phase, but we were prepared to deal with both.

With respect to liberty and harm, we noted that the appellate courts had upheld incest laws in the face of section 7 attack in the context of consensual, adult incest without proof even of a power imbalance. In the incest cases, the Courts found that the harm of incest *generally* justified its prohibition in every case, even where there was no actual harm to the participants.

Perhaps more powerfully, we were able to point out that the Supreme Court of Canada, in *Malmo-Levine*, rejected the idea that fundamental justice necessarily requires an element of harm to be present, either in an individual case or in society generally. Moreover, it was equally clear that *no* claim for breach of fundamental justice could succeed where harm from the prohibited activity *is* demonstrated beyond *de minimis*. Gonthier and Binnie JJ wrote for the majority in *Malmo-Levine* (at para 133):

> We do not agree with Prowse J.A. that harm must be shown to the court's satisfaction to be "serious" and "substantial" before Parliament can impose a prohibition. *Once it is demonstrated, as it has been here, that the harm is not de minimis, or in the words of Braidwood J.A., the harm is "not [in]significant or trivial," the precise weighing and calculation of the nature and extent of the harm is Parliament's job. . . . The relevant constitutional control is not micromanagement but the general principle that the par-*

*liamentary response must not be grossly disproportionate to the state interest sought to be protected* [emphasis added].

Nor, *Malmo-Levine* confirmed, did it offend principles of fundamental justice to impose laws that reduce risk of self-harm to individuals, as well as to society itself. This, we said, succinctly defeated the idea that "consent" might be a constitutionally mandated defence, as it were, to criminalization of a given activity:

124 [W]e do not accept the proposition that there is a general prohibition against the criminalization of harm to self. Canada continues to have paternalistic laws. Requirements that people wear seatbelts and motorcycle helmets are designed to "save people from themselves." There is no consensus that this sort of legislation offends our societal notions of justice. Whether a jail sentence is an appropriate penalty for such an offence is another question. However, the objection in that aspect goes to the validity of an assigned punishment—it does not go to the validity of prohibiting the underlying conduct.

125 A recent discussion policy paper from the Law Commission of Canada entitled *What is a Crime? Challenges and Alternatives* (2003) highlights the difficulties in distinguishing between harm to others and harm to self. It notes that "in a society that recognizes the interdependency of its citizens, such as universally contributing to healthcare or educational needs, harm to oneself is often borne collectively" (p 17).

There was, we said, after *Malmo-Levine*, no argument that it is a principle of fundamental justice that social harm, or indeed any harm beyond *de minimus*, must be demonstrated before Parliament can act. And more particularly, it was emphatically *not* an independent principle of fundamental justice (that is, apart from arbitrariness, overbreadth, and disproportionality) that the harms of an activity must outweigh the deleterious effects of the prohibition. In any event, we said, in this case such a call wouldn't even be close, given the harms caused by the prohibited activity.

It *is* a principle of fundamental justice that laws should not be arbitrary. In the recent decision of *Chaoulli*, McLachlin CJ and Major J (with Bastarache J concurring) had defined the concept (at paras 130–31):

A law is arbitrary where "it bears no relation to, or is inconsistent with, the objective that lies behind [it]." To determine whether this is the case, it is necessary to consider the state interest and societal concerns that the provision is meant to reflect: *Rodriguez*, at pp. 594–95.

In order not to be arbitrary, the limit on life, liberty and security requires not only a theoretical connection between the limit and the legislative goal, but a real connection on the facts. The onus of showing lack of connection in this sense rests with the claimant. The question in every case is whether the measure is arbitrary in the sense of bearing no real relation to the goal and hence being manifestly unfair. The more serious the impingement on the person's liberty and security, the more clear must be the connection. Where the individual's very life may be at stake, the reasonable person would expect a clear connection, in theory and in fact, between the measure that puts life at risk and the legislative goals.

The Supreme Court of Canada had also said that the utility of its chosen methods is an area in which Parliament is entitled to deference. In *Malmo-Levine* at p 657, the majority had written:

> Questions about which types of measures and associated sanctions are best able to deter conduct that Parliament considers undesirable is a matter of legitimate ongoing debate. The so-called "ineffectiveness" is simply another way of characterizing the refusal of people in the appellants' position to comply with the law. It is difficult to see how that refusal can be elevated to a constitutional argument against validity based on the invocation of fundamental principles of justice. Indeed, it would be inconsistent with the rule of law to allow compliance with a criminal prohibition to be determined by each individual's personal discretion and taste [emphasis added].

In order to be found arbitrary, a law must bear *no* relation to, or be inconsistent with, the state's legitimate objective. Here, the objective was to reduce polygamy and its attendant social harms. Section 293 clearly bore a relation to that objective, and was not inconsistent with it.

We suggested that all of the arguments advanced with respect to arbitrariness were re-articulations of two basic assertions: first, that polygamy causes no harm, or second, that if it does cause harm, the criminal prohibition in section 293 is ineffective at reducing polygamy.

We responded that the harms attributable to polygamy could no longer be doubted in light of the evidence presented at trial. The only real question under the rubric of arbitrariness was whether the law was effective at deterring or reducing polygamy, and we said that this really wasn't a question for section 7 at all, but rather ought to be considered under section 1's inquiry into whether there is a "rational connection" between the law's objective and the means used to achieve it.

The Supreme Court had recognized that it is another principle of fundamental justice that criminal legislation must not be overbroad. In *R v Heywood*, Cory J wrote for the majority:

> Overbreadth analysis looks at the means chosen by the state in relation to its purpose. In considering whether a legislative provision is

overbroad, a court must ask the question: are those means necessary to achieve the State objective? If the State, in pursuing a legitimate objective, uses means which are broader than is necessary to accomplish that objective, the principles of fundamental justice will be violated because the individual's rights will have been limited for no reason. The effect of overbreadth is that in some applications the law is arbitrary or disproportionate.

Reviewing legislation for overbreadth as a principle of fundamental justice is simply an example of the balancing of the State interest against that of the individual.

. . .

In analyzing a statutory provision to determine if it is overbroad, a measure of deference must be paid to the means selected by the legislature. While the courts have a constitutional duty to ensure that legislation conforms with the *Charter*, legislatures must have the power to make policy choices. A court should not interfere with legislation merely because a judge might have chosen a different means of accomplishing the objective if he or she had been the legislator.

. . .

[B]efore it can be found that an enactment is so broad that it infringes s. 7 of the *Charter*, it must be clear that the legislation infringes life, liberty or security of the person in a manner that is unnecessarily broad, going beyond what is needed to accomplish the governmental objective.[43]

As I have emphasized throughout, it was fundamental to our argument that, as with incest and obscenity, many of the harms associated with polygyny exist whether or not any particular polygynous relationship is directly harmful to the participants, and irrespective of the degree of consent in any particular relationship. As such, we said, the Court should find that the harms at large, without aggravating circumstances in a particular case, are sufficient to support a blanket ban on polygyny.

All polygynous relationships, we said, contributed to the "marketplace" harms described by the experts Henrich, Grossbard, and McDermott. In addition, each carried with it, if not realized harm, at least an increased *risk* of harm to the participants and children inherent in the family form.

Much effort was spent by the challengers to show the impact of the law on polyamory, in light of the evidence of the relative innocuousness of that behaviour. They sought to "fold in" as much polyamory into section 293 as possible; we suggested that this was something of a mug's game.

We rejected the idea that it was possible, let alone necessary, to "hive off" or exclude something called polyamory from the *Criminal Code*'s prohibition of polygamy. The application of criminal law could not be reduced to an exercise in subjective self-definition, such as the proposal by the CPAA that persons who declared a belief in "equality" should be exempt. We noted that there had been many defining distinctions suggested for polyamory: the degree of consent, the "loving nature" of polyamorous relationships, the "honesty" of the participants, or their assertedly "egalitarian" design or absence of patriarchal trappings. None, we said, had any legal coherence.

In truth, it would appear that most relationships that the CPAA described as polyamorous would not meet the criminal definition of polygamy under section 293. If they did meet the definition, that is, at the point where they become "marriages" or "marriage-like" through the influence of a binding authority or otherwise, then they were, we said, criminally polygamous and ought to be banned.

If section 293 is justified, at least in part, on the basis that its objective is to protect women, could it still sanction prosecution of both husbands and wives? Several of the challengers pointed to the law's application to all participants in a polygamous relationship as proof of clumsy overreach. The *amicus* had written in his reply opening (at para 40):

> Obviously, it would be absurd to criminalize the alleged victims. But that is precisely what s. 293 does. The polygamy ban does not simply target those who might exploit others for their own interests; rather, it criminalizes all participants, alleged victims and alleged wrongdoers alike. It is hard to conceive of a law more flagrantly overbroad in its effects.

Here, the challengers' objection was based on the false premise that the sole legitimate objective of section 293 is the protection of the polygamous wives. Now, certainly, the women in any given polygamous relationship may or may not have been easily characterized as "victims." But our fundamental point was that the risks and harms created by polygamy, to the participants, to children, and to society at large, occurred regardless of the individual circumstances of the participants. While in many, perhaps most, cases, the wives themselves will suffer harm, this harm was not the sole source of, or justification for, the prohibition.

Again, our reasoning is paralleled in the application of the incest laws. These laws were clearly intended to protect children against, *inter alia*, exploitation by parents, and yet they (at least on their face) criminalized both parties to an incestuous union. Similarly, women and even children may be subject to prosecution under the *Criminal Code* for creating obscenity or child pornography. Here, we said, society was entitled to rely on the common sense of judges and prosecutors to ensure that the *prima facie* blanket prohibition was not unreasonably applied, and on the Constitution to ensure that, in any particular case, the punishment is not grossly disproportionate to the crime, as we would discuss.

The challengers rejected our reliance on discretion in prosecution, but doing so suggested that it could *never* be appropriate to prosecute a wife in a polygamous marriage. But is that so? In a case like that of Witness 4, where a husband and three fully adult sister wives participate in a polygamous marriage with seventeen- and fifteen-year-old girls, should they be held completely immune from account? And if it were true that polygamy caused social harm even where practised only by fully consenting adults, then the wives' status *as such* should make them liable, or at least to some extent morally blameworthy, for entering into an enterprise that is socially harmful.

Now, much of the anticipated argument against section 293, however it was characterized in terms of legal analysis, could be reduced to this: jailing harmless polygamists is a disproportionate response to any problems associated with some polygamy, and would cause more harm than good. So a distinction must be drawn between the justification of *criminalization* and the justification of *imprisonment*. This reference, we said, was only about the former. Because there was no minimum sentence for polygamy under section 293, any question of unconstitutional disproportionality must be addressed through *Charter*-compliant sentencing in a particular case. In *Malmo-Levine*, the Supreme Court rejected the idea that marijuana laws were unconstitutional because a maximum of seven years' imprisonment was an impossibly harsh response to harmless possession and use of marijuana. The majority stated (at paras 164–65):

> The requirement of proportionality in sentencing undermines rather than advances the appellants' argument. There is no need to turn to the *Charter* for relief against an unfit sentence. If imprisonment is not a fit sentence in a particular case it will not be imposed, and if imposed, it will be reversed on appeal.
>
> *There is no plausible threat, express or implied, to imprison accused persons—including vulnerable ones—for whom imprisonment is not a fit sentence* [emphasis added].

In polygamy, we argued by direct analogy, if a sentence of incarceration was grossly disproportionate to the crime on its facts, then it would be a sentence that could not, constitutionally, be imposed. This did not call into question the constitutionality of section 293, as long as, in at least some instances, incarceration *would* be a fit sentence. The Court had of course heard numerous stories of predation on countless young girls by polygamist officials of the FLDS church. It may well be that such behaviour would warrant a custodial sentence. In other cases, incarceration would clearly *not* be proportional to the crime. This was not a question that went to the constitutionality of the provision.

Apart from the consequences of *disobedience*, the challengers asserted that there were harms associated with *obedience* to the law. That is, that obeying the law requires that Canadians subvert their desires to explore multipartner personal arrangements at the point where those arrangements become marriages, or marriage-like, and thus criminal.

We accepted that the restriction on a "freedom to be polygamous" had deleterious effects on some persons. But, we pointed out, any criminal law restricts one's ability to do as one pleases, and all deprive the aspiring criminal of the profits (financial, emotional, or otherwise) that one might gain through the commission of an offence. The point of the criminal law is that it holds all to the same standard of behaviour.

In a Rawlsian sense, we said, criminal laws represent an *ex ante* bargain whereby citizens agree to restrain their self-serving behaviour in pursuit of the greater common good. The polygamy prohibition was just such a bargain. Men agreed not to take more than one wife, and women agreed not to share a husband with other wives, in order to have the benefits of a more equal, stable, and responsible society. As with any criminal law, there would be those who see the advantages of being outside this bargain as weighing more heavily than the broader social benefits; they would find themselves in the *ex post* position of opportunity and power. The sacrifice would be, for them, greater. This did not undermine the legitimacy of the criminal law; in fact, we argued quite the opposite: it confirmed it.

The *amicus*'s religious equality argument was found in two paragraphs of his opening statement: the first alleged a discriminatory *effect* of section 293; the second also described a discriminatory effect, but appeared to go further and reiterate a discriminatory *purpose*:

> 54. Section 293 breaches section 15(1) for many of the same reasons as it breaches section 2(a). The provision draws a distinction between religious practices which the state deems to be acceptable (monogamous marriage) and those that are subject to criminal sanction (polygamous marriage). Even if not prosecuted, religious practitioners of polygamy are stigmatized by the law and treated as less worth of respect and concern.

I was fortunate in that Greathead had litigated many important section 15 cases and was well familiar with the jurisprudence. She drafted a comprehensive explanation of section 15 and its evolution and interpretation. At bottom, though, our argument on section 15 was that arguments advanced under it were simply misconceived.

Any religious-based differential treatment that results from section 293, we said, originated with the behaviour of the religious adherents. The prohibition simply recognizes the very real differences between those who practise polygamy and those who practise monogamy. In *Alberta v Hutterian Brethren of Wilson Colony*, McLachlin CJ held (for the majority):

> Assuming the respondents could show that the regulation creates a distinction on the enumerated ground of religion, it arises not from any demeaning stereotype but from a neutral and rationally defensible policy choice.[44]

At bottom, the *amicus*'s "equality" argument was that, because the state had criminalized a practice that, for some, was religious, and because it did not criminalize a practice (monogamous marriage) that was, for some others, also religious, it was engaging in religious discrimination. This was similar to the *Hutterian Brethren* case, where the Court found that the section 15 argument added nothing to the section 2(a) "freedom of religion" argument, and the question of infringements upon religious belief would be more appropriately analyzed through that section.[45] The Chief Justice of Canada wrote in *Hutterian Brethren*:

> There is no discrimination within the meaning of *Andrews v. Law Society of British Columbia*, [1989] 1 S.C.R. 143, as explained in *Kapp*. The Colony members' claim is to the unfettered practice of their religion, not to be free from religious discrimination. The substance of the respondents' s. 15(1) claim has already been dealt with under s. 2(*a*). There is no breach of s. 15(1).

Aside from religion, the other ground upon which the challengers relied in their section 15 discrimination argument was that of marital status. We accepted that the Supreme Court of Canada had identified marital status as an analogous ground for the purposes of section 15. However, there was no indication in the jurisprudence that that analogously protected group should be understood to include persons who are engaged in marital arrangements that are (otherwise legitimately) prohibited by the *Criminal Code*.

The test for establishing an analogous ground had been established in *Corbiere v Canada (Minister of Indian and Northern Affairs)*, where the majority wrote:

It seems to us that what these grounds have in common is the fact that they often serve as the basis for stereotypical decisions made *not on the basis of merit* but on the basis of a personal characteristic that is immutable or changeable only at unacceptable cost to personal identity. This suggests that the thrust of identification of analogous grounds at the second stage of the *Law* analysis is to reveal *grounds based on characteristics that we cannot change or that the government has no legitimate interest in expecting us to change to receive equal treatment under the law* [emphasis added].[46]

In other words, if the Court accepted that there was a reason to distinguish polygamous marriage from monogamous marriage (for instance, on the basis of harm), then "practitioner of polygamy" could not be an analogous ground for section 15 purposes, either under marital status or otherwise.[47] If it were, then being a criminal of any sort would be a grounds for protection from discrimination (and the more heinous the crime, the higher level of discrimination of course).

No we said, the bulk of the challenger's arguments regarding *Charter* breaches should be set aside. The real question in the reference was whether the infringements on religious freedom and liberty could be justified. Section 1 of the *Charter* provides that the rights and freedoms it describes are subject "to such reasonable limits prescribed by law as can be demonstrably justified in a free and democratic society." This requires the application of what's called the *Oakes* test.

The first two aspects of the *Oakes* test ask whether the government has a "pressing and substantial concern" and, if so, whether the measures adopted are "rationally connected" to that concern. Both of these are, we argued, infused with the weighing of harm. That is to say, if there *was* harm from polygamy, or the reasoned apprehension of harm, then there was a pressing and substantial concern under the first branch. Because the measure in question was a *criminal prohibition*, it followed virtually automatically that, once the harm of polygamy was demonstrated, measures to prevent the harm would be found to be rationally connected for *Charter* purposes.

Harm has a particularly important role in the context of the criminal law. To justify criminalization, the Attorney General had to show the "reasonable apprehension" of a harm that is "not insignificant or trivial." Once that is done, according to the Supreme Court, "the precise weighing and calculation of the nature and extent of the harm is Parliament's job."[48] In the case of polygamy, we argued that the requirement to show harm had been met and far exceeded.

The second part of the *Oakes* analysis required that the measures taken be rationally connected to the objective of the law, in this case the reduction of the harms attributable to polygamy. The rational connection requirement is satisfied where there is "a link or nexus based on and in accordance with reason, between the measures enacted and the legislative objective."[49] Here, we could rely on the obscenity case of *R v Butler*, where the majority had written:

> Accordingly, the rational link between s. 163 and the objective of Parliament relates to the actual causal relationship between obscenity and the risk of harm to society at large. On this point, it is clear that the literature of the social sciences remains subject to controversy.
>
> . . .
>
> While a direct link between obscenity and harm to society may be difficult, if not impossible, to establish, it is reasonable to presume that exposure to images bears a causal relationship to changes in attitudes and beliefs.[50]

The test of rational connection "is not particularly onerous."[51] The threshold was low, as had been reiterated by the Court in *Hutterian Brethren* (at para 48): "The government must show that it is reasonable to suppose that the limit may further the goal, not that it will do so." And as Justice Lamer had pointed out in the prostitution reference, if the object of a criminal law is to reduce the harm from the crime, then it is virtually *ipso facto* rationally connected for *Charter* purposes:

> Regulating or prohibiting the cause is at least one method of controlling its effects. A piece of legislation that proceeds upon such a premise does, in my view, exhibit a rational connection between the measures and the objective.[52]

In *RJR-MacDonald Inc v Canada (Attorney General)*,[53] the Court had been satisfied that the targeted activity (tobacco consumption) caused massive social harm. What was far from certain, however, was that the criminal restrictions on advertising would reduce that consumption. In that case, the majority in *RJR* inferred causation (and thereby mitigation) through "reason and logic" rather than strict proof. In our case, we said, we had no need to rely on supposition, presumption, or "reason and logic." We had proof of the harm, and proof that the prohibition of polygamy was protecting against that harm, notwithstanding the handful of prosecutions.

The challengers' "ineffectiveness" argument was premised on the idea that historically, section 293 had been neither prosecuted nor was it acting as a deterrent, and yet polygamy still did not flourish. We responded that Parliament is not required to demonstrate that a criminal activity would have been more prevalent if it had not been criminalized. But even if that were necessary, we said, the evidence before the Court was that the law had functioned historically as a prophylactic and deterrent; and that, if upheld, it would continue to do so.

In 1887, the year Card arrived with his settlers, there were forty-one Mormons in Southern Alberta. By 1891 there were 359 Mormons in Cardston and vicinity, but the colony was growing rapidly, almost doubling in size by 1894[54] and reaching nearly 10,000 by 1911 (10.8 percent of the population of Southern Alberta).[55] There was no comparable Mormon presence anywhere else in Canada at the time.

After the enactment of the *Criminal Code*'s antipolygamy provisions, Card's settlers in Southern Alberta continued to reassure the Canadian government that they had no intention of living polygamously there. And, as I noted earlier when describing the history in more detail, almost without exception, the Mormons were true to their leaders' word, at least to the extent that they did not actually *live* polygamously in Canada.

Soon after the criminal law was amended, the LDS Church in Salt Lake City issued the 1890 Manifesto declaring that the Church would endorse no marriages that were "contrary to the laws of the land."[56] According to Palmer, "the Manifesto effectively ended the fears about a large-scale migration of Mormons coming to escape anti-polygamy laws." Most of the press commentary regarding Mormons in the next few years was positive, and in 1893 Lethbridge's Mayor Bentley is reported to have told the press on a visit to Central Canada that "polygamy was 'unknown' in the Mormon settlements in southern Alberta," adding that the Mormon settlers were "all conspicuously honest."[57]

In our submissions we pointed out the contrast between the experience of LDS polygamy in prerevolutionary Mexico and Canada. Mexico had, at the time, an antibigamy provision, but never extended it to polygamy and tacitly agreed that the settlers in that country could practice plural marriage "quietly."[58] There were no bars on polygamist men bringing in additional wives, and they did so. The Mormon historian Embry wrote of LDS polygamy after 1890:

> According to one contemporary nineteenth-century account, the practice of polygamy in the colonies was "almost universal" and "close to 100 percent of the people then living at Juarez Stake [Mexico] were so attached to this order that it was the very woof and warp of their domestic life and also the theme and central idea of community worship."

Embry confirmed the rarity of the practice of polygamy in Canada after the enactment of the revised provisions and the issuance of the 1890 Manifesto:

> In contrast [to Mexico], Latter-day Saints in Canada lived a *de facto* monogamy. Husbands usually lived with one wife in Canada, leaving their other wife or wives in the United States. . . . To date, only three men can be proved to have brought more than one wife to Canada: John Lye Gibb, Franklin Dewey Leavitt and Thomas Rowell Leavitt. Their wives lived in different communities. . . . As William L. Woolf, who grew up in Alberta, explained, "The Canadian government['s] . . . agreement was generally adhered to." Interviewed in 1972, he remembered "four to six" men who lived with more than one wife in Alberta.[59]

Another leading historian of the period, Hardy, agreed that the different legal response to LDS polygamy in Canada and Mexico was the reason for the absence of the practice in this country:

> With the amendment of Canadian law in 1890, identifying the private ceremonies employed in Mormon multiple marriages as prohibited, the intent of the earlier Canadian statutes was made explicit. Unlike in Mexico, where legal intent also existed but was never reified, the Canadians moved to meet Mormon plural marriage in the same way as it had been done in the United States with the *Edmunds Act* of 1882. The result was that, although plural family life existed in Canada after 1890, as it did in the United States, it was both less frequent and less openly acknowledged than in Mexico.[60]

The polygamy Manifesto drove the practice further underground among Latter-day Saints in the United States, and it did not become public until 1904 that there had been authorized plural marriages in the LDS after 1890. In that year, LDS president Joseph F Smith issued the Second Manifesto, and the Church began to discipline and excommunicate its recalcitrant polygamists.[61]

As noted earlier, there are some historical accounts of a very few Mormon men (three documented cases) cohabiting with two wives in Alberta in the subsequent decades, and also some reports of plural marriages solemnized by Amreican-based LDS officials, but the practice by the mid-twentieth century seems to have entirely disappeared, and indeed John Horne Blackmore, who represented the region in the House of Commons, was excommunicated from the LDS when word reached Salt Lake City that he had even spoken in favour of polygamy (Blackmore himself married only once).[62] Palmer summarized:

Charges that Mormons were practicing polygamy in secret were misleading and wildly exaggerated. A rearguard attempt was made by a few Mormon leaders to keep polygamy alive in southern Alberta, but it was limited to a handful of people, and plural wives did not live in Canada.[63]

There is, therefore, no record of any contemporarily known or officially confirmed case of polygamy among fundamentalist Mormons in Canada between 1890 and 1953. Nor is there any record of any complaint being made to any police force that any particular Mormon person was violating the laws against polygamy. Virtually every Mormon man, including those who had been polygamous in the United States, refrained from living polygamously in Canada. The few who carried on the practice, to the extent that it continued, did so in secret, with their wives living apart in different communities, and polygamy appears to have become virtually nonexistent among the Latter-day Saints in Canada by World War II. McCue wrote of the period that "interest in Mormons subsided as polygamy became less of an issue, and the newspapers seldom mention them after 1890."[64]

In the Utah Territory, where the law against polygamy had been imposed *after* the Mormons settled, the experience had been diametrically different. Polygamy had flourished prior to the passage of the federal antibigamy legislation in the United States. After its passage, a wave of prosecutions followed. Between 1885 and 1889, somewhere between 970 and 1,300 Mormon men had been convicted of bigamy or unlawful cohabitation, or an average of almost one a day for four straight years.[65]

So, far from being a "dead letter," we argued, the 1890 Canadian polygamy and bigamy amendments, backed by the threats of rigorous enforcement by the federal government, had precisely the effect that Steele of the NWMP had wished in his report of 1899: they prevented the practice of polygamy from gaining a "foothold" on the Canadian frontier as it had in the Utah Territory and prerevolutionary Mexico, where the lack of explicit laws or government acquiescence had the opposite effect. In fact, the Canadian foothold would not be established until a handful of Canadian Mormons who had taken an interest in polygamy founded Bountiful in the late 1940s.

The obverse of the challengers' ineffectiveness argument was their assertion that the law was unnecessary: they suggested that, if polygamy were decriminalized, the small numbers of practitioners would be insufficient to create any of the social harms demonstrated by Henrich. The *amicus* went so far as to say, in his opening submissions:

> If 293 is struck down, as I say it must be, as a matter of law, then what happens, *and all that happens*, is that being a polygamist no longer turns someone into a criminal.

In the case of the polygamy prohibition, we responded, we were entitled to rely on "reason and logic" for the idea that at least *some* persons would take up the practice of polygamy if it were not criminally barred. But there was also, we pointed out, considerable evidence on the point.

We noted that evolutionary psychology supported the idea that polygyny is, for men who can afford it, an advantageous mating strategy, as it permits a wealthy male to have both multiple partners and still adequate investment in the offspring.[66] If the principal tenets of evolutionary psychology are correct, then humans will have a tendency to adopt the practice when the environment permits it. As described earlier, both experts in evolutionary psychology, Henrich (for the Attorney) and Shackelford (for the *amicus*), considered the phenomena of "serial monogamy" (particularly divorce and remarriage to sequentially younger women) and patterns of infidelity and overlapping relationships among North American men to be suggestive that males were adopting essentially polygynous mating strategies to the extent that they are legally and socially able. Shackelford agreed that laws had been enacted to control the practice of serial monogamy by imposing costs upon it.[67]

Both Shackelford and Henrich spoke of indications that surprising numbers of university students appeared willing to entertain the idea of polygamy. In Shackelford's study, more than 5 percent of male respondents indicated that their "ideal" mating behaviour would involve simultaneous marriage to between two and ten women (a percentage that Shackelford considered, if anything, low). In Henrich's impromptu "clicker" quiz of his female third-year university students, 70 percent said that, given the choice between becoming the second wife of a billionaire or the only wife of an otherwise identical middle-class man, they would either very likely or certainly choose the billionaire, a rate that Henrich (and Shackelford) thought surprisingly high. Shackelford had said under cross-examination that he thought 17 percent would be a more expected figure:

Q But nevertheless it doesn't surprise you that a significant portion of even well educated presumably successful, unlimited-option university women would select that option given those choices?

A No, it doesn't surprise me, yes.

The experts had been quite properly reluctant to speculate on the rate at which polygyny might spread in the mainstream if permitted. Henrich agreed that it was unlikely to turn Canada into a significantly polygynous society immediately, but considered that, in fifty years, its nontrivial adoption (and a loss of ground on women's equality and other factors) was "very plausible." He had held this position in the face of vigorous cross-examination by the *amicus* and the BCCLA.

Shackelford, the *amicus*'s expert, was ambivalent. On the one hand, he said he "generally agree[d]" with Pinker's statement that "whenever polygyny is allowed men seek additional wives and the means to attract them." He noted, however, that there were presently no high-status polygynist role models that others might emulate, and the present practitioners of polygamy seemed in fact to have little social status. This he considered a factor militating against the spread, or at least against its rapid spread.

When pressed on the question, Shackelford first said that the spread of polygyny in North America is "plausible . . . terribly, terribly unlikely, but plausible." Nevertheless, almost in the next breath, he agreed that, of those men who could "afford the costs . . . some would" pursue polygyny.

Oddly, we noted, it had been the FLDS's rather unnerving expert on Mormonism, Walsh, who appeared most enthusiastic about the possibility of polygamy's proliferation. As I described earlier, he estimated that as many as half of the millions of "mainstream" Mormons would embrace the practice if it were permitted.

Of course we knew that high degrees of polygyny were possible among otherwise recognizably Western communities in North America (it might have been going too far to describe them as mainstream). The wealthiest and most powerful FLDS leaders had accumulated many wives. Winston Blackmore was generally thought to have around twenty-five. Rulon Jeffs had eighty at the time of his death. Warren Jeffs was thought to have had more than sixty by the time of his arrest. Paul Kingston (current leader of the Kingston group) had fifteen wives when Rowena Erickson was still with the group, and now probably has thirty.

As Henrich had pointed out, the preconditions for what the literature called hyperpolygyny are present in North America with its excessive disparity in wealth and status. This, coupled with an already established group of polygamists including hyperpolygynists, suggested that polygamy's practitioners would have an even greater impact than they do in cultures where wives are generally few. Henrich concluded in his first report:

> If this combination of theory and evidence is correct, legalizing all forms of polygamy will principally result in an increase in polygynous marriages by wealthy, prestigious men.

Wu, the University of Victoria demographer brought in as an expert by the *amicus*, confirmed that he had no knowledge of polygamy or its potential for expansion. The expert political economist Grossbard rejected the *amicus*'s suggestion that because monogamy and industrialization are closely correlated, polygamy simply could not catch on in a complex society such as Canada. Grossbard emphasized the experience of France, where a thirteen year "window" of decriminalization had led to a community of two hundred thousand members of polygamous families in that country, a point made also in the Quebec *Conseil du statut de la femme* report.

We argued that the human drive to polygamous practice was sufficiently strong that it could even lead some to convert to unfamiliar religions. Recently, the Supreme Court of India had attempted to close the door on what had become a widespread practice of Hindu men converting to Islam in order to take a second wife under an Indian law that permits polygamy for Muslims but not for Hindus: *Thomas vs Union of India*.[68] Nevertheless, since that time a number of very high-profile Hindus, including Bollywood stars and high government officials, had married second wives after a "conversion" to Islam.[69] This problem of the spread of polygamy among the educated urban elite had apparently become sufficiently worrisome that the Law Commission of India has recommended changing the laws of marriage to stop it.[70]

If the challengers had succeeded, of course, resort to such artifice would not have been necessary. Polygamous marriage would be available to any regardless of belief or religious practice. But the fact that persons were willing to change religions (or in some cases perhaps create religious dictates) to facilitate polygamy indicated, we said, that the domestic adoption of the practice should not be discounted.

Of course, we allowed, it was also possible that the evolutionary psychology model was incorrect, and the apparent robustness in the practice of polygyny is related to cultural factors, especially the structural inequality of men and women. In such a case, the argument went, we need not worry about polygamy happening here.

This argument had been put in economic terms by economists Gould et al:

> In developed countries, bans on polygyny seem to be effective, but this is most likely due to the low demand for polygyny in equilibrium. In this sense, we follow the line of reasoning in Becker (1992) and Jon Elster (1989) by arguing that laws and norms may effect behavior, but they rarely evolve if personal incentives are weak to uphold them. Our model should be considered an attempt to explain how personal incentives to become polygynous decline naturally with development and, therefore, align themselves with laws and norms to reinforce a monogamous outcome.[71]

We responded that such an argument was hardly reassuring, for several reasons. First, even if polygyny were attenuated with development and the equality of women, parity between the sexes—economic, social, political—was in 2011 hardly a completed project in Canada.

Second, we noted that it was uncontroversial that the factors that are proposed as attenuating polygyny's negative effects, from women's equality to economic development, are not equally distributed throughout the country. There are many communities where women's rights are not culturally recognized, even if they legally exist. And it was within these communities—immigrant enclaves and even Bountiful itself—that polygamy could be expected to spread first.

Third, we argued, it was clear that polygamy can spread rapidly even where women and children are accorded the fullest possible legal rights. If any proof is needed, it was provided by our "petri dish" at Bountiful. Polygamy among Mormons in Canada swelled from a single family of a husband and two wives (Harold Blackmore's) in 1947 to a community of over a thousand by the turn of the century, where men had as many as twenty-five wives. This happened despite the fact that women's *legal* rights were as advanced in Lister as they were elsewhere in Canada. As the rights of women and children advanced in general, so they withered in Bountiful. In light of this experience, it was simply not possible to say that "it couldn't happen here."

Then there was the "elephant in the room": immigration. At present, we said, the illegality of polygamy acted as a bar to immigrants who wished to bring their polygamous families to Canada, and it restricted persons who have moved here from polygamous societies to adopt the practice in Canada after relocating. It was uncontroversial that Canada is a preferred immigration destination from the developed world, including from countries where polygamy is practiced.[72] If Canada were to become the only nation to decriminalize polygamy, we said, it would be "the only game in town"—the only possible immigration destination for polygamist families.

The lesson of France was plainly before the Court. That country had introduced a family reunification policy permitting immigration by members of polygamous families in order to spur immigration in response to postwar labour shortages. A review of the literature reveals the catastrophic consequences as the numbers of polygamists in France swelled to hundreds of thousands. The research indicated that the situation for polygamist immigrants in France was dire indeed: often worse, in fact, than in their home countries. The French government had reversed direction in 1993, but the damage was already done and the harms persist almost two decades later. Indeed, the "re-criminalization" of polygamy seems to have added yet another layer of oppression on the victims of polygamy, indicating that decriminalization is not something that can be approached as any kind of whimsy, because it was not simply a harmless social experiment.[73]

Aside from the developing world, of course, there would be immigration from polygamists presently in the United States, including fundamentalist Mormons and the others who Walsh described as inclined to the practice, and other Western countries who would view Canada as a preferred destination.

In short, we summarized, "reason," "logic," and all the evidence in this case indicates that if polygamy were decriminalized, its practice could be expected to increase in a nontrivial way.

The next, and probably the trickiest, stage in the *Oakes* analysis is "minimal impairment." In our submission, the evidence of harm in this case was more than sufficient to demonstrate that *some* government action was justified. The question was therefore: was section 293 the *right* prohibition, or at least one that fell within the range of reasonable alternative measures?

The challengers presented two main arguments with respect to minimal impairment. The first was that the law was unnecessary because the harms of polygamy could be addressed through alternative means; the second is that, if a polygamy law is justified, it could capture less than the present law does. This latter was, therefore, another iteration of the overbreadth argument already addressed in these submissions in the context of section 7 of the *Charter*, so I need not repeat our arguments made in that respect.

But what of alternative means? The challengers of section 293 would say (and many commentators in the popular press would repeat it): "[I]f the problem is the youth of brides, or exploitation, or trafficking, or erosion of women and children's rights, then why not rely on laws against those activities instead of the polygamy prohibition? Or why not modify and extend those laws first?"

This assertion implied that Parliament was restricted from imposing complementary measures to address social harms, and we argued that this was not so. In *R v Sharpe*,[74] the accused argued that, if the problem animating the prohibition of child pornography is that it leads to further exploitation of children (even assuming that there was no abuse involved in the making of it), then the solution would be the enforcement of laws against that activity; the "market reduction" targeted by the law against simple possession was, according to this argument, unnecessary. Chief Justice McLachlin rejected the idea, writing:

[A]n effective measure should not be discounted simply because Parliament already has other measures in place. It may provide additional protection or reinforce existing protections. Parliament may combat an evil by enacting a number of different and complementary measures directed to different aspects of the targeted problem: see, e.g., *R. v. Whyte*, [1988] 2 S.C.R. 3. Here the evidence amply establishes that criminalizing the possession of child pornography not only provides additional protection against child exploitation—exploitation associated with the production of child pornography for the market generated by possession and the availability of material for arousal, attitudinal change and grooming—but also reinforces the laws criminalizing the production and distribution of child pornography.[75]

But more important was the point that implementing stricter child-exploitation or trafficking laws, or effecting the more vigorous enforcement of those in place, was only an answer to the extent that such crimes are reported, investigated, and prosecuted. This was obviously not the case, and in fact the crimes upon which the FLDS and *amicus* would rely as alternatives (sexual exploitation of a minor, sexual assault, trafficking in persons, and so forth) were both underreported and difficult to investigate and prosecute, and this was particularly true with respect to insular populations of vulnerable immigrant groups or closed religious communities where polygamy is mostly likely to prosper. The Utah Supreme Court in *State v Green*[76] quoted Richard A Vazquez:

> Given the highly private nature of sexual abuse and the self-imposed isolation of polygamous communities, prosecution may well prove impossible. This wall of silence may present a compelling justification for criminalizing the act of polygamy, prosecuting offenders, and effectively breaking down the wall that provides a favorable environment in which crimes of physical and sexual abuse can thrive [emphasis added].[77]

Every expert witness asked the question had confirmed that, even outside closed and insular religious communities, crimes within the family are severely unreported, especially crimes against children. Thus, permitting an activity (polygamy) that would increase harm (including criminal harm) against children or women could not, we said, be supported on the basis that the harm can be adequately addressed through enforcement of other laws. It simply could not.

This was perhaps the greatest point of philosophical departure between my own position and that of my erstwhile BCCLA colleagues. I simply could not endure the thought that they would be prepared to sacrifice the interests of innocent children through what I saw as a philosophical blindness towards, or perhaps I should say an unreasonable denial of, indirect victims.

The association had taken a similar position in *Butler*; the Court had said they were wrong. They were wrong again in *Sharpe*, and in the second *Little Sisters* case. I appreciated their caution regarding "indirect harm" arguments based on mere speculation or supposition, and I, like them, remained suspicious of the quality of proof in, for instance, *Butler*. But when indirect harms were proven in Court, and when the harms were as serious as child rape and exploitation, how could they be held irrelevant when weighing the liberty interests of adults, even "consenting" ones?

The bishop of the FLDS, Oler, had declared in his affidavit that in all "instances where members of the community have been suspected of criminal offences . . . reports have been made to the police." As I described earlier, Oler purported to withdraw his affidavit rather than face cross-examination upon it. I very much would have enjoyed asking him some pointed questions, because, as we now knew, it was Oler himself who was recorded as delivering his two teenaged sisters to be married to Jeffs in 2004 and later witnessing the marriage of his fifteen-year-old daughter in Mesquite, Nevada, minutes before collecting his own fifteen-year-old bride. Polygamy laws made that activity illegal, and a prosecution had been commenced against Oler for violating section 293 (with respect to allegations of his "marriage" to another teen bride). That prosecution, of course, had been quashed by the decision of Justice Stromberg-Stein, along with that of Winston Blackmore. But even in light of all that we know about him, Oler has never faced charges for trafficking, exploitation, or other offences.

We argued that the pattern of apparent criminality within the FLDS demonstrated eloquently why the harms caused by polygamy could not be addressed through the enforcement of child exploitation, sexual assault, procurement, or other laws. Were it not for a very particular confluence of events—the prank call to Texas authorities, the keeping by the FLDS of meticulous records of its own abuses, and the testimony of the FLDS's anonymous witnesses in this reference—the details of this behaviour would never have come to light. Indeed, even with such compelling documentary evidence, there still remained a question of whether the crimes detailed could ever be prosecuted; without the cooperation of the victim, it is very difficult to prove sexual contact as an element of exploitation or assault, unless the girl becomes pregnant while still a teen. And surely, we said, public policy could not require the government to wait until that point before addressing such a serious social harm.

We allowed that it was a nice idea that the harms that go hand in hand with the practice of polygamy could be addressed if only the practice would be brought into the sunlight through decriminalization. But there was no reason to believe that this would happen. Polygamy needs insularity to hide the abuses that it requires to sustain itself through generations. It required insularity to shield the methods of control and indoctrination that would guarantee the next generation of willing child brides.

From a legal standpoint, in any event, the Supreme Court had made it plain that Parliament should be given great latitude for dealing with social harms once they have been identified. The Court in *R v Butler* wrote:

> Finally, I wish to address the arguments of the interveners, the Canadian Civil Liberties Association and Manitoba Association for Rights and Liberties, that the objectives of this kind of legislation may be met by alternative, less intrusive measures. First, it is submitted that reasonable time, manner and place restrictions would be preferable to outright prohibition. I am of the view that this argument should be rejected. Once it has been established that the objective is the avoidance of harm caused by the degradation which many women feel as "victims" of the message of obscenity, and of the negative impact exposure to such material has on perceptions and attitudes towards women, it is untenable to argue that these harms could be avoided by placing restrictions on access to such material. Making the materials more difficult to obtain by increasing their cost and reducing their availability does not achieve the same objective. Once Parliament has reasonably concluded that certain acts are harmful to certain groups in society and to society in general, it would be inconsistent, if not hypocritical, to argue that such acts could be committed in more restrictive conditions. The harm sought to be avoided would remain the same in either case.

> It is also submitted that there are more effective techniques to promote the objectives of Parliament. For example, if pornography is seen as encouraging violence against women, there are certain activities which discourage it—counselling rape victims to charge their assailants, provision of shelter and assistance for battered women, campaigns for laws against discrimination on the grounds of sex, education to increase the sensitivity of law enforcement agencies and other governmental authorities. In addition, it is submitted that education is an underused response.

> It is noteworthy that many of the above suggested alternatives are in the form of *responses* to the harm engendered by negative attitudes against women. The role of the impugned provision is to control the dissemination of the very images that contribute to such attitudes. Moreover, it is true that there are additional measures which could alleviate the problem of violence against women. However, given the gravity of the harm,

and the threat to the values at stake, I do not believe that the measure chosen by Parliament is equalled by the alternatives which have been suggested. Education, too, may offer a means of combating negative attitudes to women, just as it is currently used as a means of addressing other problems dealt with in the *Code*. However, there is no reason to rely on education alone. It should be emphasized that this is in no way intended to deny the value of other educational and counselling measures to deal with the roots and effects of negative attitudes. Rather, it is only to stress the arbitrariness and unacceptability of the claim that such measures represent the sole legitimate means of addressing the phenomenon. Serious social problems such as violence against women require multi-pronged approaches by government. Education and legislation are not alternatives but complements in addressing such problems. There is nothing in the *Charter* which requires Parliament to choose between such complementary measures.[78]

The analogy with polygamy was, we argued, apt on a number of levels. If the Court accepted that the harms we described were caused by polygamy, then, as the Court in *Butler* pointed out, there can be no obligation upon Parliament to deal only with the symptoms.

The second assertion made by the challengers under the rubric of "minimal impairment" was that, if a polygamy law were justified, then *this* polygamy law captured too much. Could, in other words, a less minimally impairing ban achieve the same goals? As we had also argued under section 7, it was difficult to see how it could.

The main areas of overinclusiveness argued by the challengers were three. They suggested (at various times and in different ways) that the law could be more carefully tailored if it: (1) did not include polyandry or same-sex partnerships; (2) did not include any nonexploitative, consensual adult multiparty relationships; and (3) applied to only the men in polygynous households. No actual language had so far been proposed that *might* make the provision constitutional.

We had already dealt with these concerns in the course of our assertions made under the headings of "interpretation" and "overbreadth" under section 7. We said that, properly interpreted, the law did not apply to polyandry or same-sex multiparty relationships. However, the main point to be made was that redrafting the law to capture only exploitative or underage marriages, or to apply only to polygynist men and not women, would not help for the simple reason that the harms of polygamy are felt throughout a society, regardless of whether they are felt in any particular relationship.

The difficulty in requiring, as West Coast LEAF and the BCCLA would have, elements of exploitation or inequality in order to commence a prosecution for polygamy was the same. If polygamy is harmful, it was not necessary or desirable to parse it into good and bad polygamy by reference to its consequences in any given situation. And needless to say, given that on all the evidence religious polygamy is, if anything, worse than any secular variant, there could be no "reasonable accommodation" for religion as there might be with, for instance, helmet or kirpan exceptions for religious Sikhs.

The final argument from the challengers with respect to minimal impairment was an assertion that the prohibition in section 293 is unnecessary, argued by way of international comparison and legal history. The argument went like this: Until 1890, Canada and Great Britain shared virtually identical criminal prohibitions on bigamy. In 1890, Canada bolstered its law with the specific provisions regarding polygamy; Great Britain did not. Now, more than 100 years later, Great Britain and Canada are *both* experiencing low levels of polygyny, according to comparative sources such as McDermott (whose team rated both countries as 1 on the 1 to 4 scale of degree of polygyny).

This argument was appealing on the surface but had many difficulties. First of all, as described at length elsewhere, the uncertainty about the application of the bigamy prohibition to polygamy that existed in Canada in 1889 endured in England. It was not possible to know whether English bigamy laws, like the almost identical American versions in *Reynolds* and *Holm*, would be applied to bar polygamy or whether they would not. And as for assessing the impact of the English legal framework on the spread of polygamy in that country, we really had very little evidence on either subject—that is, the state of the law (including immigration practices, enforcement policies, and so forth) *or* the presence of polygamy.

But the argument from international comparison foundered most badly on the shoals of the hard experience of other nations: the example of prerevolutionary Mexico, which became a haven for polygamist Mormons at precisely the time when Canada did not, arguably because it had no polygamy law *per se* and did not enforce the polygamy law against the immigrants; and the sobering example of France, which relaxed its own laws for a period of thirteen years and experienced a massive wave of polygamous immigrant families. And there was the United States itself, which followed up the relatively ineffective bigamy provisions of 1862 with the far more comprehensive legislation of the 1880s before polygamy was brought to heel there.

The final element of the *Oakes* test requires the government to demonstrate that the beneficial or "salutary" effects of the law outweigh the

*The Case Against Polygamy*

detrimental impacts. We said that the evidence indicated that reduction in polygamy has the following beneficial effects, all of which had been described in the evidence of harm:

- increased per-child parental investment, with expected increase in the mental and physical wellbeing of children overall;
- reduced social strife, conflict, and crime that is expected as a result of more uneven distribution of the opportunity to marry;
- reduced average age gaps between husbands and wives, increasing equality in marriages;
- reduction in the sexual predation on young girls;
- reduction in incentives for male control over women and their reproductive capacity; and
- consistency with Canada's international treaty and legal obligations.

In addition we pointed out that eliminating the right of citizens to marry polygamously increases the opportunity of others to marry at all. In *Miron v Trudel*,[79] the minority opinion in the 4:4:1 split (dissenting in the result but not on this point), made some important observations about marriage as not only a fundamental institution,[80] but also a fundamental human right that was formally recognized under the United States Constitution[81] and international law.[82] The Court did not, we said, have to recognize any legal aspect to the right to marry; it need only recognize its more widespread distribution as a social good.

The *amicus* in his opening statement had taken sharp exception to this argument, suggesting it disparaged women by treating them as a resource to be distributed to placate men. These arguments were repeated in the *amicus*'s closing submissions, where Herbst argued that polygamy "criminalized women for failing to distribute themselves more equally among men," a rhetorical flourish that I had thought to be unadulterated sophistry (but somehow quite brilliant nonetheless). We pointed out that there was something of an irony in this position, given that it seemed to be, on the evidence, the polygamists who appeared to be "trading" in women and girls; we for our part were not suggesting that there is some duty on the state to ensure that marriage opportunity is equally spread throughout the population, or that someone might be subject to criminal sanction just because their life choice (for instance, a decision not to marry) would impact someone else's right to marry at all.[83] But to the extent that the *Charter* is involved in the balancing of rights throughout society, it was not, we said, irrelevant that in denying one class of persons the right to marry plurally, the law is distributing the right to marry overall more equitably through society.

And of course, there was also the evidence that prohibiting polygamy might lead to increases in levels of democracy, human rights, and economic development. How these effects had played out in Canada, and how they might be affected by decriminalization, could only be the subject of reasoned speculation, but given their fundamental importance to Canadian society, we argued that we should not put them lightly in peril.

The deleterious effects identified by the *amicus* and FLDS and their allies fell into two broad categories. The first category contained a number of asserted harms:

- the stigma and discrimination against practitioners of polygamy;
- the insularity caused by fear of prosecution; and
- the harms of the criminal process itself (possible arrest, prosecution, incarceration).

We made one general observation about all of these deleterious effects: they were, we pointed out, visited on persons who *violate* the law, not on persons who *obey* it. This may seem self-evident and thus unimportant but it was not. The weight or harshness of the criminal process is properly considered under the question of "gross disproportionality" under sections 7 and 12. Where a law has met this test, the harms visited upon the *criminal* should not be resurrected at the section 1 stage.

And under section 1, it was not the role of the courts to weigh, in a global sense, *all* the negative effects of criminalization against the benefits gained. Rather, the benefits of prohibition should be weighed only against the harms to the exercise of the *Charter* rights breached.[84] So in the case of polygamy, it would not be relevant to consider, at the section 1 stage, any deleterious effect except that affecting the free exercise of religious, expressive, or associational rights. This meant that only if section 15 were found to have been breached would it be appropriate to consider factors such as stigma.

The second broad category of asserted deleterious effects, and the one that *was* properly considered at the section 1 stage, involved the consequences of *obeying* the law. These, we conceded, were legitimately considered at the section 1 stage. They include essentially two ideas. First and most obviously, there was a deprivation of religious freedom. For those very few persons in Canada who believe that polygamy is *ordained*, rather than simply permitted, by their religions, this deprivation could be significant.

Second, we also conceded that there may be an equivalent loss of secular liberty—the loss of the freedom to choose to have more than one wife or to share a husband with another wife. But, we said, in order for this to rise to the level of deleterious effect under section 1, it must be a deprivation of liberty that was not in accordance with the principles of fundamental justice. The Supreme Court had long held that any law that does not survive a section 7 challenge will be impossible to justify under section 1, except in cases of dire emergency, and so it must be taken as a given that, if the analysis had proceeded to this stage, section 7 has not been violated. As a result, we said, the deleterious effects that may be legitimately viewed at the proportionality stages were reduced to one: the loss of religious freedom.

We pointed out that fundamentalist Mormonism appeared to be the only religion that *mandates* polygamy. Islam's only religious dictate with respect to polygamy is to place restrictions upon its practice; there is no suggestion that the practice itself has a religious origin. Mainstream Mormons may or may not believe that plural marriage in the afterlife is an advantage, but they accept that, in the present, God's laws can legitimately yield to governments'.

It was arguable, of course, that the FLDS church and faith arose from a desire to practise polygamy, rather than the reverse. I myself am inclined to this view. But this was really, given the scope of the harms attached to polygamy, of little consequence. A religion may hold as a central tenet human or animal sacrifice, punishment of religious transgression by stoning or immolation, genocidal war, or infanticide. The only time a criminal law has been struck down because of conflict with religious practice was in the early case of *Big M* itself, and there it was the religious *purpose* of the law that offended.

The only way a polygamy prohibition could *not* offend religious practice would be if it were to hive off a religious exception or accommodation, as did the Sunday-observance law upheld subsequently in *R v Edwards Books and Art Ltd*.[85] But such an exemption, we argued, would defeat the very purpose of the polygamy prohibition, if for no other reason than, as we had earlier submitted, the polygamy law was legitimately focused on the "core" and most harmful forms of multiparty marriage, those invoking a binding authority, it is naturally and almost uniquely at odds with religious teaching such as the FLDS's. That is to say, unlike virtually any other act that might be defended on the basis of religious freedom—the wearing of a turban or kirpan, the erection of a *sukkah*, and so on—religiously mandated plural marriage was harmful (and thus the legitimate target of the criminal law) in part *because* of its religiosity, and the more profound and controlling the religious belief, the more harmful it can be. It was the *religious* nature of plural marriage that permitted the cradle-to-grave indoctrination of adherents into the acceptance of the practice; it was the *religious* nature that has permitted it to expand so rapidly in Bountiful from a single family in 1947 to about a thousand souls today.

Most types of polygamy may be, on balance, bad, but religiously mandated polygamy was, we said, many times worse.

We urged the Court to consider the question of religious impairment in the context of the true objects of the protection. The evidence of those who have left the FLDS indicated the extent to which that religion is used, not as a vehicle for self-fulfilment, but as an impairment of it—as a mechanism of control, not liberation. Adherents were taught that if they disobeyed the direction of the church leaders, they were going against God; and if they persisted, they were expelled from the only community they had known. Once expelled, the member was an "apostate" and could be shunned even by family members. Surely, we said, this was not the purpose of section 2(a)'s protections.

Bevan made another important contribution to this aspect of the argument by emphasizing that, as I described earlier in my discussion of section 2(a), the religious practice being defended was, in itself, discriminatory against women as it embraced only polygyny. As such, Bevan wrote, *Charter* values of equality and dignity were *promoted*, not offended, to the extent that the practice could be curtailed. If the nature of the exercise of an infringed right was itself distant from the values the *Charter* was designed to protect, the weight accorded its infringement as a deleterious effect at the balancing stage should be minimal, at best.

At the end of the day, we said, if the harms attributable to authoritarian patriarchal polygyny generally, and fundamentalist Mormon polygyny in particular, were accepted by the Court, and given the inherent inequality of *all* known traditions of religious polygamy, then restricting this manifestation of religiosity must be seen as, on balance, a salutary, rather than a deleterious, effect.

## Interlude

When all participants had finished our submissions and the Chief Justice had thanked the counsel and, by name, the court staff who had assisted throughout the process, we had only to go away and wait. I was asked on a number of occasions how long the wait would be; my belief was that it would be between three and nine months away (as it turned out my guess wasn't bad; it was seven).

But time didn't stand still, and neither did anybody's practice, so our little polygamy team had a last drink together and scattered to the winds. We all had other files to attend to—I needed to prepare for the Supreme Court of Canada argument in the *Insite* case and had a number of other appearances already dotting my calendar, and of course there was much to catch up with on the management end of the group as well. I was also being increasingly drawn into a number of controversies surrounding Oppal's latest project, the Missing Women Commission of Inquiry, which was threatening to spin out of control as Oppal publicly confronted the government over the issue of funding for participants' counsel.

But nobody who had worked on the Polygamy Reference could let it go entirely. We had begun the exercise as a great legal challenge, but it had in the end become personal for each of us, as the dry arguments were replaced, stone upon stone, with the stories of Rena Mackert, Truman Oler, and the little girls whose impossibly young faces stared back at us from photos in the YFZ documents.

So it was something of a vicarious victory when, on 9 August 2011, the last of Jeffs's luck ran out in San Angelo, Texas.

In 2006 Jeffs had been living as a fugitive, shuttled around among safe houses and seedy motels by a close group of acolytes, planning his church's new settlement at YFZ and pausing here and there to marry and be "married" to a succession of supplicant and compliant girls and young women. The FLDS's "Prophet, Seer and Revelator" had found himself on the FBI's "Ten Most Wanted" list as a result of Utah allegations that he had arranged "marriages" between very young girls and much older men in the Church.

On the evening of 28 August 2006, a Nevada State Trooper pulled over Jeffs's Cadillac Escalade SUV not far from Las Vegas. The truck had drawn the trooper's attention only because its temporary licence plates weren't visible. Jeffs was travelling with Naomi Jeffs, perhaps his favourite wife, and his trusted brother Isaac, whom he frequently assigned the task of performing Jeffs's own marriage ceremonies. Jeffs was recognized and arrested; also found in the car were $55,000 in cash, sixteen cell phones, several laptop computers, and a number of disguises including three wigs.

While Jeffs was awaiting trial in Utah, Arizona got in line by filing eight counts against him for crimes alleged in that state. On 25 September 2007 Jeffs was convicted of two counts of being an accomplice to rape, and sentenced to five years to life for each count. He was then moved to Arizona, where in February 2008 he pleaded not guilty to charges there. After some troubles with that case, the Arizona charges were dismissed on 9 June 2008 and Jeffs was returned to Utah where his lawyers were pursuing an appeal on the basis that the judge's jury instructions had been flawed.

Eventually Jeffs's appeal would be successful, and the Utah Supreme Court would order a new trial in July 2010. But by then the die had been cast. The Texas authorities had raided the YFZ ranch in April 2008. After the initial controversy surrounding the immediate fates of the children seized by child protection authorities, police and prosecutors began to pore through a room full of church records and other documents seized in the raid, often from hidden locations. What they found was damning—almost incredibly so. And for the first time, there was an extraordinary amount of evidence pointing squarely at Jeffs as not just an accessory to the rape of FLDS children, but also as a principal perpetrator. Texas filed its charges, and requested Jeffs's extradition.

While he waited for Jeffs, Texas lead prosecutor Nichols began knocking off other senior FLDS members one by one, relying on the evidence from the YFZ raid.

Jeffs's extradition process began in July 2010, at about the same moment that his Utah appeal was finally successful. He was held in custody and despite a spirited fight by his attorneys was moved to Texas in December of that year. After that things moved quickly, and following a two-week trial in July and early August, Jeffs was convicted for having sex with two of his followers, twelve and fifteen years old.

Since his 2006 arrest and the Utah prosecution, Jeffs had become increasingly erratic in jail, and more and more the figure he struck was pathetic rather than fearsome. He would renounce, and then reclaim, leadership of his church; he would fire a succession of lawyers; and he would issue manifestos from prison and excommunicate FLDS members for a host of wrongs, real and imagined. There were reports of attempted suicide (both by hanging and by banging his head on his cell walls) and hunger strikes, which on one occasion had resulted in a court-ordered tube being inserted into his stomach.

By the time of his Texas trial, Jeffs was representing himself, and badly. His opening statement became a tirade against what he insisted was religious persecution. Every witness was an opportunity for a religious lecture. And when his turn came to make closing submissions, Jeffs fell silent: he actually did not speak for over twenty minutes before uttering "I am at peace" and sitting down.

Not that there was much he could have said in his defence. The evidence at his short trial was deeply disturbing and utterly damning. The Texas prosecutors had the benefit of an intense amount of documentation—FLDS records could be cross-referenced with the diary entries of Jeffs and matched to birth records including those from British Columbia, where at least five of Jeffs's two dozen underage brides originated. In one case DNA evidence proved that he had impregnated a girl when she was fourteen. But Texas also had graphic audio recordings that Jeffs himself had made—recordings of his rape of a twelve-year-old girl in front of several others, after which both are heard to say "Amen." He was also heard instructing his "quorum of twelve" young girls in obedience to his sexual "comfort," including that they shave their pubic hair to please him, and God. Nichols put the evidence in methodically, like nails in Dracula's coffin, ignoring Jeffs's impotent rants from the prisoner's dock.

On 9 August 2011 Jeffs was sentenced to life in prison for the aggravated sexual assault of a twelve year old, and an additional twenty years for sexually assaulting the fourteen year old. Under Texas law, he won't be able to apply for parole until he is 100 years old.

The members of the erstwhile polygamy team weren't the only ones in British Columbia to track these developments. Jeffs remained the spiritual leader of at least half the Bountiful community, and the cooperation between the Texas authorities and our reference team had contributed important evidence in the cases on both sides of the border.

The Jeffs conviction allowed Bramham to renew her calls for a task force. How, she asked (in a column entitled "Texas convicts polygamist pedophile while British Columbia dithers"), could it be that Jeffs is convicted for a pattern of raping and abusing teen and preteen girls, several of whom had been shipped from Bountiful for that purpose, and yet every member of the community in British Columbia that had supplied Jeffs's teen "brides" had never even been charged?

It wasn't a bad question.

Attorney General Penner continued to take a personal interest in the Bountiful case, and things began to move along as he read his way into the file. I learned that Penner's attention could be a mixed blessing; in sharp contrast to Oppal and de Jong, Penner felt no compunction about communicating directly with "line" counsel, and because I was dealing with several hot topics of the day he sometimes seemed to regard me as his personal lawyer. With respect to polygamy, at least, I thought this was a good thing; perhaps, I thought, I could use this privileged access to persuade him to appoint a new special prosecutor, or otherwise kickstart the investigation and prosecution of wrongdoing at Bountiful.

But it wasn't to be. Penner, who had recently become a father for the first time, soon concluded that his time in public service had reached its end, and to my great surprise (and, as near as I can tell to the surprise of everyone else except, perhaps, his family), on August 18, nine days after Jeffs' conviction, announced his resignation as Attorney General. Soon he would also resign his seat in the legislature and return to the private practice of law. Into the role of Attorney General came Shirley Bond, the formidable Solicitor General, who despite her undoubted skill and intensity of work habits, was not familiar with the file.

Eventually, Bond would become, if anything, even more determined than Penner to act on Bountiful, but for the moment at least, it seemed that momentum generated by the Texas developments had been lost.

# PART 7
# Decision and Aftermath

## Judgment Day

On 8 August 2011, the day of Jeffs's sentencing in Texas, I received a brief note from Christine Judd, the Chief Justice's law officer. Could we provide her, she asked, with the names of our counsel as they might appear on the first page of the Court's Reasons for Judgment?

Could this mean that the judgment was imminent? It seemed so, but it had only been four months since the trial had ended. This would be quick in a routine case; for something with the complexity of the Polygamy Reference, it seemed impossible. I resisted the temptation to pry some improper information from the ever-proper Ms Judd, and submitted the six names of our lawyers who had appeared: myself, Greathead, Horsman, Bevan, Ross, and Zaltz.

The next day I received a phone call from Ms Judd: "I realize that my e-mail yesterday might have led you to believe the judgment was imminent," she said. "I don't want anybody to expect that it will be released this week or next week . . ."

So we exhaled. And waited as summer turned into fall. A second false start came on October 14, when Global TV ran a story on its *16:9* program on Bountiful. The reporter, Carolyn Jarvis, had apparently become the latest "outsider" to be wooed by Winston Blackmore with promises of exclusive access to "his" community, and Global had produced a documentary which said very little new. However, everybody's attention was gripped by Jarvis's repeated statements to the effect that the decision in the reference was expected "within days." In a teaser for the documentary on Global's morning show, Jarvis told the hosts that Global had been informed by the Chief Justice's office that the judgment would be down that week or the next. We inhaled again. Then . . . nothing. Not that week, not the next. Not the week after that.

Finally, on 8 November 2011, we received notice that the Court would release its reasons on 23 November 2011, precisely a year and a day since the trial had begun.

Two months earlier, Sarah Galashan, the CTV reporter, had asked me whether the Court would do a "media lockup," where the court reveals the judgment to sequestered reporters in advance of its public release, so that the press could more effectively comment once it is made public. As far as I knew, the BC Courts had never done one, but it was an occasional practice of the Supreme Court of Canada in particularly high-profile cases. I passed the idea along to the Court through Ms Judd, and apparently it had been embraced by the Chief Justice. As a consequence, the Court had arranged "lockups" for both media and counsel.

The lockup was not the only unusual aspect of the decision's release: the two-week lead time was also much longer than the ordinary two or three days' notice provided by the Courts to counsel. This was a mixed blessing; it helped to plan our month, for sure, but it also meant that those in government charged with preparing to deal with the various outcomes—communications people, law enforcement, and executives up to the Attorney General herself, would be asking a lot of questions and demanding briefings and messaging on all possible outcomes, of which there were an almost infinite number.

Some counsel had placed friendly bets on the date of release, and others preferred to guess at the length of the written reasons. Deputy Attorney General Loukidelis guessed that the judgment would be 400 pages. I thought it would be shorter, at around 150. Loukidelis's estimate turned out to be far closer than mine, but in any event it was clear to us that it would be a very lengthy decision, and had no doubt consumed a great deal of Chief Justice Bauman's attention given that it had been produced in seven months, still a relatively short period of time.

Later in the same day that the notice had been distributed, November 8, I attended the annual Bench and Bar Dinner, a popular banquet held in a ballroom of a downtown hotel. Not surprisingly, I saw the Chief Justice as we were being seated. As I mentioned earlier when I described Bauman's good-humoured intervention in our post-trial drink at the Hotel Vancouver, lawyers and judges working on the same case tend to be careful when they ran into each other at social events. The collegiality of bench and bar embraces social contact, but discussion of the substance of any case before the judge, even one in which the lawyer is *not* involved, should be avoided. Government lawyers, in particular, should be concerned not to be seen as too friendly with the independent judiciary, so there is often something of an awkwardness in anything longer than a perfunctory greeting. Even so, I couldn't resist a quip to Bauman about the inordinate lead time his announcement had provided. "Now you can sleep and I can't," I said.

"I've been sleeping fine all along," he replied with a smile, and I had to admit that he had all the appearances of someone who had.

In my job things never go quite as planned. As judgment day approached, I had tried to shuffle some important but not-yet-critical matters off my plate to deal exclusively with polygamy in the days leading up. This hadn't been easy—I had taken on the defence of a petition that had been filed against the government by John Doyle, the Auditor General, seeking access to documents detailing the province's various programs of legal indemnities. The co-respondents in the matter were David Basi and Bob Virk, whose case had made the word "indemnity" synonymous with allegations of government waste, corruption, and sleaze. It was the latest episode in a notorious saga, and was the subject of intense attention both inside and outside government. The issue in the case was how to facilitate the Auditor General's access to documents that were subject to legal privileges, and the case was messy as it concerned decades of confidential files from dozens of cases, with hundreds of potentially affected parties.

Nor was this the only thing on the go. On the Monday, just two days before the scheduled release, I had to appear briefly in court to put in an appearance on a constitutional case where a defendant was challenging a municipal bylaw that prohibited the smoking of hookahs in Vancouver cafés. Soon after noon I was on the float plane to Victoria, where I had been asked to brief the Attorney General and others on the polygamy decision so that she was fully prepared to respond on Wednesday morning. With the hookah case appearance behind me, I had been looking forward to a clear day and a half to restart the polygamy machinery in anticipation of the decision.

But that Monday afternoon when I settled into my Victoria office and fired up my laptop, I saw a flurry of urgent e-mails. The Occupy Vancouver protesters, whose "tent city" had been finally evicted from the lawn of the Vancouver Art Gallery by an injunction granted the previous Friday, had packed up and re-established their camp outside the doors of the Vancouver Law Courts Complex. Media reports suggested that this move had been taken in retaliation for the court's decision moving them along. The judiciary, needless to say, was not impressed, and the Attorney General was determined to act quickly and decisively to ensure unfettered access to the courthouse building. I was told to get myself on a helicopter and back to Vancouver, and be prepared to be in court by first thing the next morning to seek an injunction. This I did—the injunction application the following day was successful; an order was granted that permitted assembly and protest, but banned the erection or maintenance of the obstructing structures or otherwise interfering in the operation of the courts.

While I was otherwise "occupied" (sorry), Horsman had taken over the briefing responsibilities on the polygamy file, and the Attorney General would be prepared.

The Chief Justice's staff had arranged for a number of "lockup" rooms in the basement of the courthouse to be available for the various participants, and the Attorney General of BC lawyers were given one of our own, down the hall from the *amicus* and the federal Attorney, who also each had a dedicated space. The remaining Interested Persons had a larger room, and representatives of the press were all together in an unused courtroom. Loukidelis, Doug Eastwood, the Attorney's strategic counsel, and Chris Tupper, her ministerial assistant, would be gathered in her office at the Victoria legislature awaiting our release from the lockup, at which point we could call and let them know the result. It would be me and Horsman who waited in our lockup room, and we had a last few minutes of wild speculation about what the judgment would say.

At 8:30 am on November 23, Ms Judd went from room to room with a stack of copies of the printed reasons. As soon as we saw the size of the documents in her arms, we realized that a thorough reading in the one-and-a-half hours wouldn't be possible—each copy was obviously hundreds of pages long (357 pages, as it turned out). I don't know about Horsman, but there was a nervous unsteadiness in my hands that wasn't entirely attributable to my morning Starbucks. Out of litigators' habit, Horsman and I flipped to the last page and started reading backwards. That proved confusing, so we started again at the front, where the Chief Justice had summarized his decision in the first fifteen paragraphs.

It seemed that we had won, and as we flipped through the pages it became apparent that we had won quite convincingly.

Given the length of the decision, even in the hour and a half allotted to us we could not read every detail. Nevertheless, it was obvious that the Court broadly endorsed our theory of polygamy and its harms, and had meticulously set out the evidence we and the federal lawyers had presented, calling it "overwhelming." Henrich's and McDermott's evidence was central, but the Court noted that the key was, indeed, the "convergence" between the expert predictions and the evidence on the ground. Polygamy was harmful, the Court said, again and again. Henrich was right. Campbell and Beaman, the *amicus*'s experts who had so casually glossed over reports of child abuse in the FLDS, were "somewhat naïve."

Ten o'clock came quickly, and Ms Judd again stopped by to release us from the lockup. Horsman went back to the office to send a summary e-mail of the decision. I stayed in our room and called Eastwood's cell phone. "Doug, it's a clean win," I said, and I listened as he repeated the news to the room.

I could hear cheering in the background, then some confusion, and silence. Doug explained to me that I would have to wait to say more, because the Attorney General had jumped up at the news, and had run down the hallway with her deputy to break the news to her cabinet colleagues.

On speakerphone, I explained some nuances of the decision. The Court agreed with us that there was no infringement on freedom of expression, association, or equality rights. As expected, the Court did find that the expression violated freedom of religion under section 2(a), and that it affected liberty interests under section 7. But these infringements were justified under section 1 of the *Charter* because of proof of polygamy's harm. Apart from one small tweak (the Chief Justice said that the law could not criminalize minors who engaged in plural marriage), the law was valid and enforceable.

The Attorney General was effusive and articulate. She had taken over from the departing Penner only months before, and like him had become personally very interested in the polygamy file. As a woman, in particular, she said she was incensed by the abuses of girls reported at Bountiful. She told me that day that we had "done a great thing for Canada, and you and your team should take a moment to reflect on this right now. It's a great victory, and we're all grateful."

Health Minister de Jong, who as Attorney General had given his blessing to the trial court reference idea and had been personally involved in the early planning and the approval of the reference questions, called my cell phone that afternoon from a plane on the way to a federal/provincial territorial ministers' conference in Halifax. De Jong was, I think, the only one of the four Attorneys General for whom I've worked who had never phoned me directly, so I was quite touched that he had made the effort to track down my number. Also impressive was the gesture of Deputy Attorney General Loukidelis, who would take the time to handwrite personal messages of thanks to each of the lawyers, paralegals, and secretaries who had worked on the file.

## Chief Justice Bauman's Reasons

Justice Bauman began his reasons by noting that there were really two competing "essential issues" before the Court. He wrote:

[2] Here, the Attorney General for British Columbia has said in opening that the case against polygamy is all about harm. Absent harm, that party accepted that s. 293 would not survive scrutiny under the *Charter.*

[3] The challengers, led by the *Amicus Curiae,* counter (primarily) that this case is about a wholly unacceptable intrusion by the State into the most basic of rights guaranteed by the *Charter*—the freedom to practice one's religion, and to associate in family units with those whom one chooses.

. . .

[5] I have concluded that this case is essentially about harm; more specifically, Parliament's reasoned apprehension of harm arising out of the practice of polygamy. This includes harm to women, to children, to society and to the institution of monogamous marriage.

Having accepted our framework, and the requirement that we imposed on ourselves to show harm, the Chief Justice offered this summary of the evidence before him:

[6] Based on the most comprehensive judicial record on the subject ever produced, I have concluded that the Attorneys General and their allied Interested Persons have demonstrated a very strong basis for a reasoned apprehension of harm to many in our society inherent in the practice of polygamy as I have defined it in these reasons.

The Chief Justice neatly summarized the harms of polygamy in the paragraphs following, which it is useful to reproduce here at length:

[8] Women in polygamous relationships are at an elevated risk of physical and psychological harm. They face higher rates of domestic violence and abuse, including sexual abuse. Competition for material and emotional access to a shared husband can lead to fractious co-wife relationships. These factors contribute to the higher rates of depressive disorders and other mental health issues that women in polygamous relationships face. They have more children, are more likely to die in childbirth and live shorter lives than their monogamous counterparts. They tend to have less autonomy, and report higher rates of marital dissatisfaction and lower levels of self-esteem. They also fare worse economically, as resources may be inequitably divided or simply insufficient.

[9] Children in polygamous families face higher infant mortality, even controlling for economic status and other relevant variables. They tend to suffer more emotional, behavioural and physical problems, as well as lower educational achievement than children in monogamous families.

These outcomes are likely the result of higher levels of conflict, emotional stress and tension in polygamous families. In particular, rivalry and jealousy among co-wives can cause significant emotional problems for their children. The inability of fathers to give sufficient affection and disciplinary attention to all of their children can further reduce children's emotional security. Children are also at enhanced risk of psychological and physical abuse and neglect.

[10] Early marriage for girls is common, frequently to significantly older men. The resultant early sexual activity, pregnancies and childbirth have negative health implications for girls, and also significantly limit their socio-economic development. Shortened inter-birth intervals pose a heightened risk of various problems for both mother and child.

[11] The sex ratio imbalance inherent in polygamy means that young men are forced out of polygamous communities to sustain the ability of senior men to accumulate more wives. These young men and boys often receive limited education as a result and must navigate their way outside their communities with few life skills and social support.

[12] Another significant harm to children is their exposure to, and potential internalization of, harmful gender stereotypes.

[13] Polygamy has negative impacts on society flowing from the high fertility rates, large family size and poverty associated with the practice. It generates a class of largely poor, unmarried men who are statistically predisposed to violence and other anti-social behaviour. Polygamy also institutionalizes gender inequality. Patriarchal hierarchy and authoritarian control are common features of polygamous communities. Individuals in polygynous societies tend to have fewer civil liberties than their counterparts in societies which prohibit the practice.

[14] Polygamy's harm to society includes the critical fact that a great many of its individual harms are not specific to any particular religious, cultural or regional context. They can be generalized and expected to occur wherever polygamy exists.

As we had reviewed the evidence during the trial, we had repeatedly emphasized what we called (borrowing a term from Henrich) the "convergence" in the evidence—the way in which the expert predictions from psychology, anthropology, economics, and so forth played themselves out again and again "on the ground" in polygamous societies, and most obviously in Bountiful and the other FLDS communities. This struck a chord with the Chief Justice, who allowed (at para 492):

[492] The AGBC referred on a number of occasions to the remarkable convergence of the evidence on the question of harm, from high level predictions based on human evolutionary psychology, to the recurring harms identified in intra-cultural and cross-cultural studies, to the "on the ground" evidence of polygyny in contemporary North America. As I proceed through the evidence, this convergence becomes increasingly striking.

Perhaps the most gratifying sentence was this:

[1044] On the whole of the evidence here, I conclude that the Attorneys General have certainly demonstrated a reasoned apprehension of harm associated with polygyny. Indeed, they have cleared the higher bar: they have demonstrated "concrete evidence" of harm.

I was very interested to see how the Chief Justice would deal with the most controversial aspect of our case's theory, the ideas taken from the field of evolutionary psychology. We had used Henrich's (and indeed Shackelford's) expertise in this field because we had to explain why polygamy was not a gender-neutral pursuit, and never could be. That is, the harms we demonstrated arose from polygyny, and were in part a consequence of the gender imbalances it created (leading to the sexual targeting of girls and the ejection of "excess" boys, etc). We needed to prove that, if polygamy were permitted, it would manifest overwhelmingly as polygyny, and our evidence was that this tendency arose from evolved behaviours.

A couple of days before the decision I ran into West Coast LEAF's Govender on the street. While the reference was underway, Govender had been tapped to replace Alison Brewin as executive director of WCL, but had retained many of the duties of her previous position, litigation director, and was of course still a lawyer on the file. So with the release of the judgment looming we allowed ourselves a few minutes of the speculative banter familiar to lawyers everywhere, challenging one another to foretell the outcome. My prediction was vague—I was confident that we'd made our case for *some* polygamy prohibition, so I expected the Chief Justice to either uphold the law with a fairly restrictive definition of the offence, or strike it down while allowing that Parliament could re-enact a more carefully delineated prohibition. Govender's prediction, if anything, was more optimistic than mine. She thought that the Chief Justice was going to accept everything we said, factually, *except the evolutionary psychology*: "He's not going to go there. Sorry." This was an ongoing bone of friendly contention between us; I was convinced that the evolutionary theory was correct, or at least the best scientific hypothesis of the phenomenon of polygyny yet. Govender, though, was aghast—I don't think that's too strong a term—that a Court would rely on inherent and distinct male and female behaviours in support of legislation. Her views, I should say, were shared with many of our friends and colleagues whom I might describe as being on the progressive Left.

Immediately after we were released from the lockup I ran into Govender again, in the crowd of reporters, lawyers, and others gathering for *ad hoc* scrums on the courthouse steps. She wasn't too happy that the Chief Justice said (at para 538): "It is Dr. Henrich's acknowledged expertise in evolutionary psychology which he has applied to the question of polygamy that gives me comfort with his conclusions."

I had believed all along that our case would live or die on the strength of Henrich's evidence, and I have related earlier that it was at the close of his testimony that I had impetuously declared victory (not that I could have predicted the precise outcome, but at that moment I believed that we had proven the harm, and that the rest would be a fight over the interpretation of the provision and its breadth). So you can imagine my relief that the Chief Justice appeared just as impressed with Henrich's evidence as I had hoped he would be. In fact, Bauman's review of Henrich's evidence alone consumed at least fifteen pages of the decision, and the Chief Justice accepted all the harms posited by Henrich as real or reasonably apprehended.

The reasons reflect an equal appreciation for the global study undertaken by McDermott and presented by the government of Canada. McDermott, as you will recall, used sophisticated regression analysis to determine that the degree of polygyny in a society was significantly correlated with an impressive number of measurable harms—everything from education levels of girls to spending on armaments. Macintosh had pulled out all the dismissive rhetoric he could muster for McDermott, calling the report "abracadabra" and a "departure from anything reasonable," suggesting that McDermott's conclusion was that "evils around the planet were attributed by her to one man marrying more than one wife." Macintosh urged a "common sense" approach that, in his view, required that the Court ignore McDermott's statistics out of hand.

I had pointed out in my closing that, when you thought about it, McDermott's findings with respect to defence spending were not actually unexpected. Henrich had shown that a more polygamous society was a more dangerous society, because it needed to "deal with" the pool of low-status, unmarried men created. Perhaps they could be accommodated by employing them in wars, external or internal; if not, their increased anti-social and criminal behaviour could be expected to require heavy policing. Any of these eventualities would increase spending on weaponry and so a correlation would not be unexpected. That the challengers considered such a proposition as self-evidently absurd is indicative of the extent to which they did not fully appreciate the true nature of the case we were presenting.

The Chief Justice appeared to be of the same mind, in that he was prepared to accept what the evidence demonstrated, even if it was not immediately intuitive. With respect to McDermott's defence spending link, he wrote:

> [630] Certainly, Dr. McDermott's conclusion that there is a statistically significant relationship between the level of polygyny in a country and that country's per capita defence spending initially seems surprising. However, the fact that it was arrived at by the same methods as she used for her other seventeen dependent variables does not, as the *Amicus* put it at para. 416, reveal "the frailty of her entire report." Rather, the consistency of her methodology bolsters her results with regard to national defence spending.

> [631] The challenge to the national defence spending variable is an example of the manner in which the *Amicus* tends to overstate Dr. McDermott's conclusions . . .

Most gratifying for me was the extent to which we had persuaded the Chief Justice that there was something to the "marketplace" harms of polygamy encapsulated by my appropriation of Bramham's term "cruel arithmetic":

> [1333] I reject the *Amicus'* concentration on, and rather dismissive critique of, the harms associated with the so-called "cruel arithmetic" of polygamy. The existence of these harms has been demonstrated by the defenders.

If there is one thing about which I feel a sense of personal accomplishment about the polygamy case it was this aspect of our theory and the evidence we developed around it. Lawyers like to fool ourselves into thinking that we win or lose based on our talent and skill, but the bracing reality is that we are at the mercy of the facts. But we do have a choice about which facts to introduce and emphasize, and how. The development of the cruel arithmetic argument from a nice turn of phrase by Bramham into the comprehensive expert report of Henrich and the theory that underpinned our entire case for harm was something that might not have happened without my involvement. So when Macintosh and his allies attacked the concept so vigorously as self-evidently bad, I admit that I took it more personally than I should have, and perhaps I responded with some indignation of my own. Had I understood that the Chief Justice was "with us" on the point I might have toned down my emphasis somewhat.

Having accepted all of our evidence on the generalized harms of polygamy from the anthropological and sociopolitical evidence, Bauman turned to the specific.

Remember when Beaman, a professor of religious studies, had sworn evidence regarding the polygamist practice of Yemeni Jews and First Nations communities, before admitting on the stand that even the sources she cited provided no support for her assertions? I had felt particularly pleased at exposing Beaman's glib conclusion that the allegations of child abuse at the YFZ compound in Texas had been "largely unfounded." I had walked Beaman through the report of the Texas Child Protection Authorities, which she had never bothered to locate, that found 262 victims of child abuse or neglect (out of perhaps 400 children in the entire community) and substantial evidence of crimes even more sinister still. The Chief Justice wrote of this exchange:

> [756] In the face of this report, Dr. Beaman's conclusion that allegations of abuse were "largely unfounded" simply cannot be given credit, and the entire exchange between her and counsel on cross-examination leads one to be wary of those who would downplay the apparent dangers to children in FLDS communities.

Campbell, the "qualitative researcher" who had parlayed a few days in Bountiful interviewing a number of Winston Blackmore's wives and a few of their friends into SSHRC grants and a default position as Canada's leading academic expert on Bountiful, did not fare any better. The Chief Justice wrote:

> [758] Professor Campbell accepted, again at face value, that teen marriages in Bountiful have long been discouraged. Late in the evidentiary phase of this hearing we learned, from a more complete review of documents seized during the raid of the YFZ Ranch in Texas, that this may well not be the case. . . . I recognize that Professor Campbell's interviewees were predominantly from the Blackmore side of the community and that it may be that teen marriages are a thing of the past within that group. Nevertheless, the YFZ documents suggest that this is not the case with respect to the Bountiful community as a whole.

Overall, the Chief Justice was kind but categorically sceptical in his view of the evidence of Campbell and Beaman:

> [752] I found the evidence of these two witnesses sincere, but frankly somewhat naive in the context of the great weight of the evidence.

The final point of "convergence" in the evidence was with the evidence of the personal witnesses, which Bauman wrote had been "highly personal and very moving." As we had done in our closing submissions, Bauman methodically went through the testimony and matched the witnesses' stories to the categories of harm predicted by the experts from the literature reviews, cross-cultural studies, and behavioural predictions based on evolutionary psychology, and you could almost hear the tumblers of a lock clicking into place as he did so. The personal witnesses, who mostly put in their evidence through the video affidavits prepared by Greathead, Horsman, and Ross, hammered hundreds of nails into the coffin of the idea of a mostly polygamous society as one in which harms were no more prevalent than a mostly monogamous one.

The biggest surprise of Bauman's decision was how easily he dealt with what I considered to be the greatest problem facing the polygamy law: the idea that it criminalized behaviour that could not easily be associated with the harms of institutionalized polygyny that were easily demonstrated, because it captured secular and non-authoritarian polyamory, and its gender-neutral language implied that it equally applied to polyandry and same-sex multipartner marriage in addition to polygyny.

On the first point, we and Canada had suggested that secular polyamory—the act of living conjugally with more than one partner—wasn't "polygamy" as captured by the law. The Attorney General of BC said that polygamy required the invocation of some sort of authority, and the Attorney General of Canada said that it required an actual ceremony. The Chief Justice accepted a position halfway between us, finding that some sort of initiating ceremonial event was required for polyamory to cross the line to polygamy, but that actual proof of the ceremony was not something that needed to be proven as an element of the offence. His interpretation focused the use in the statute of the term "conjugal union," as opposed to a "conjugal relationship." I'm not sure how the Chief Justice's interpretation would play out, practically speaking, but the Chief Justice did appear to accept the underlying premise that, whether or not multipartner unions could be risky or actually harmful without the aegis of a sanctifying or enforcing authority, they definitely were when they crossed that threshold.

It is on the second point where Bauman most surprised me, and actually went beyond where we had urged. Unlike me, Bauman was completely untroubled by the extension of the polygamy prohibition to polyamory and same-sex relationships. In his view, such marriages served to undermine the positive obverse of negative polygamy: the institution of monogamous marriage. He wrote:

[882] I would expand upon an important point with respect to the purpose of s. 293. In my view, it is directed in part at protecting the institution of monogamous marriage. At first blush, this characterization of its object seems to undercut the thesis that s. 293 is directed at addressing harm—the harm viewed as arising from the institution of polygamy.

[883] I say this in response: the harms said to be associated with polygamy directly threaten the benefits felt to be associated with the institution of monogamous marriage – felt to be so associated since the advent of socially imposed universal monogamy in Greco-Roman society.

. . .

[885] The negative and the positive aspects of the polygamy prohibition are two sides of the same coin. The prohibition abates the harms to individuals and society associated with polygamy, and it protects and preserves monogamous marriage, the institution believed to advance the values threatened by polygamy.

This was ground on which I had been afraid to tread, because I did not believe that simply undermining the "traditional" model of the nuclear (heterosexual) family could be grounds for criminalization. If it were, then weren't we only a step away from recriminalizing homosexuality, or any number of other modern forms of relationship that were adopted as alternatives to the mainstream view of "family"?

But on reflection I think the Chief Justice's point was both subtler and stronger than any that had occurred to me. It was not enough that polyandrous marriage, for instance, meant fewer heterosexual dyads, as might have been also said of gay marriage. It was because the behaviour prohibited was of a type that caused the very harms decidedly attributable to polygyny; it simply did these things less directly than polygyny did. To look at it another way, holding polyandrists to the same rules as polygynists promoted the same private and public goods for everyone. This had been the point made very eloquently by Witte on the stand, but which hadn't sunk in with me at the time.

The Chief Justice deflected my imagined *in terrorem* slippery slope argument as follows:

[1037] The offence [of polygamy] is not directed at multi-party, unmarried relationships or common law cohabitation, but is directed at both polygyny and polyandry. It is also directed at multi-party same-sex marriages.

. . .

[1041] When all is said, I suggest that the prohibition in s. 293 is directed in part at protecting the institution of monogamous marriage. And let me here recognize that we have come, in this century and in this country, to accept same-sex marriage as part of that institution. That is so, in part, because committed same-sex relationships celebrate all of the values we seek to preserve and advance in monogamous marriage.

[1042] The alarmist view expressed by some that the recognition of the legitimacy of same-sex marriage will lead to the legitimization of polygamy misses the whole point. As Maura Strassberg, Professor of Law at Duke University Law School, points out in "Distinctions of Form or Substance: Monogamy, Polygamy and Same-Sex Marriage" (1997) North Carolina LR 1501 at 1594, the doctrinal underpinnings of monogamous same-sex marriage are indistinguishable from those of heterosexual marriage as revised to conform to modern norms of gender equality. This counters, as well, the argument advanced by many, that "in this day and age" when we have adopted expansive views of acceptable marriage units and common law living arrangements, the acceptance of polygamy, or at least the abandonment of its criminal prohibition, is the next logical step. This is said in the context of the sentiment often expressed that the "State has no business in the bed-rooms of the Nation." Here, I say it does when in defence of what it views is a critical institution—monogamous marriage—from attack by an institution—polygamy—which is said to be inevitably associated with serious harms.

The Chief Justice had one caveat in his overall finding that the law was constitutional: he held that it could not be used to prosecute a child bride (not that anyone had ever proposed such a thing), but that prosecution would be permitted if the polygamous marriage endured into adulthood.

I am determined not to be too fawning in accounting for my admiration of the Chief Justice's reasons. Obviously, because they largely conformed with our argument and accepted our evidence, I saw them as vindication (there is an old litigator's saw to the effect that "I never lost a case that wasn't wrongly decided"). I have written many submissions that were simply adopted by the Courts in their reasons, sometimes blatantly through cut and paste, sometimes more subtly through paraphrase or quotation. The Chief Justice's reasons in the reference, though, were entirely his own, not simply cobbled together from the parties' written arguments. He developed a theory of the case that was, while more or less aligned with ours, distinct and, I had to admit, where it diverged from ours, actually stronger and more cohesive. He referred to much of the evidence that we emphasized, but he also demonstrated a virtuosic command of the case and the evidence before him such that could, and did, pull out pieces from the record to make a particular point better than the parties had been able to. Overall, the decision was a *tour de force*, expressed in a voice that was matter of fact and, well, *wise*.

## Appeal Denied

In British Columbia there is a thirty-day deadline for an appeal from a judgment of the Supreme Court. Since Macintosh's appointment as *amicus*, he had been identified as one of the three "parties" in the case, which gave him, and perhaps only him, the right to appeal the Chief Justice's decision. Arrangements were made to continue his brief, and as the month after the judgment wore on, all were expecting that the *amicus* would soon be announcing an appeal.

So I was very surprised when, on December 20, Macintosh wrote a note as a courtesy, informing me and the federal Justice lawyers that he had decided not to appeal. The following day he issued a press release to the same effect:

> George Macintosh, as the court-appointed *amicus* in the polygamy constitutional reference case, has advised that he will not be appealing the findings of Chief Justice Bauman of the British Columbia Supreme Court. The Attorney General of Canada retains the power to have this matter considered further by the Supreme Court of Canada, and the Attorney General of British Columbia retains the power to have this matter considered further by the Court of Appeal for British Columbia. Accordingly, Mr. Macintosh at this time will not be elaborating on his decision not to appeal.

In neither communication did Macintosh give any reasons for this decision, because, as he said, the matter might still be considered by a higher court. Nor did Macintosh or his juniors elaborate on this with me privately. Like everyone else, I could only assume that the *amicus*'s team, having carefully reviewed the decision, had concluded that the findings of fact were simply too strong, too categorical in establishing harm, to permit a successful appeal of the judge's application of the law.

The Attorney General quickly issued a statement acknowledging Macintosh's announcement:

> We respect Mr. Macintosh's decision, as *amicus*, not to appeal. I would like to thank him and his co-counsel, Tim Dickson and Ludmila Herbst. They handled their responsibilities with dedication and skill, as we

expected they would when we chose Mr. Macintosh for this important role.

Macintosh was correct that his decision wasn't necessarily the end of the matter; the Attorneys General could still take the question to the higher courts through another reference. But as the *amicus*'s withdrawal sunk in, and the various options were considered and played out, it seemed better to leave the Chief Justice's comprehensive and categorical judgment as, at least for now, the last word on Canada's polygamy law.

That Wednesday night I went out for dinner in Victoria with Jamie Cassels, an old friend and collaborator (we had worked on the tobacco litigation, then co-written a couple of articles and a book, *The Law of Large Scale Claims*). Cassels, the former dean of law at the University of Victoria, had finished a two-term stint as the university's vice-president academic and provost, and was halfway through a two-year sabbatical. It was a celebratory dinner for reasons other than polygamy: I had received a call from the Attorney General the previous Thursday, telling me that I'd been appointed Queen's Counsel. Cassels had been one of my nominators for the honour, and the wine was flowing. Like everyone, he had been surprised by the news of the *amicus*'s decision. "What will happen now?" Cassels wanted to know.

I said we could refer the question to the Court of Appeal, or Canada could take it direct to the Supreme Court. Cassels thought about that, and shook his head. "Why would you, though? You have a great decision; it's not going to get any better." Cassels thought that the decision would remain persuasive despite being "merely" a decision of the trial court, in the same way that the findings of a public inquiry were generally accorded great deference. Cassels's view was certainly one I'd heard a lot lately: we should learn to take yes for an answer. A bit later that evening Cassels and I were joined by David Loukidelis, the Deputy Attorney General. Loukidelis and Cassels hadn't seen each other for a while, so the conversation quickly turned from work to just catching up with all the various goings-on in our family lives, but it did seem that there was little enthusiasm to take the polygamy case to a higher court.

Macintosh's official announcement was made only two days before the expiry of the appeal period. I kept one eye on the clock as the time ran out, wondering whether Wickett and the FLDS, or perhaps the BC-CLA, would scramble to appeal following Macintosh's demurral. I wasn't sure that either of them had a legal basis to pursue an appeal, as they were Interested Persons instead of "parties" (I didn't want to devote resources to tracking down an answer, because it would only matter if one of them did want to appeal and if we wished to oppose them). It appeared that neither considered an appeal wise, or perhaps both considered it impossible. In any event, no appeal was filed. Arvay was still out there as Winston Blackmore's counsel, and he too might have considered applying for standing to appeal. But Blackmore, indeed like Oler and any other potential criminal defendant, also may have perceived an interest in keeping the adverse precedent at the lowest court. If they were subsequently prosecuted, they could argue that the judge hearing their case was not bound by Bauman's decision.

This was technically true, but it would be technically true even if the matter were decided by the Supreme Court of Canada. A reference decision is, at least in theory, advisory only, no matter what the level of court, and in any event a criminal defendant might always argue that his own facts and circumstances, or his own legal arguments, demanded that a prior precedent be distinguished. In my view, a court of any level would give a healthy deference to the decision of the Chief Justice made after such a thorough and comprehensive review of the evidence on polygamy.

There was one undeniable effect of the Chief Justice's decision. Since the decades of opinions given by or to the Attorney General that section 293 was unconstitutional, any prosecution based on that section might be attacked because charging a person with violating a law while believing it to be unconstitutional was an act of, at least, bad faith. This concern—that charging a polygamist might be thought to be an abuse of process, or even constitute the tort of malicious prosecution—was now a thing of the past.

# Renewal

Despite the Attorney General's exhortation to reflect on our victory, we didn't have much time before we were overtaken by realities. Attention again focused on Bountiful; it had been nine months since the revelations of the trafficked girls—where were the criminal charges?

I suppose I was a little more sensitive than usual to the views of the press that week because, for the first time since joining the ministry five years previous, I was asked to speak to reporters—first, on Tuesday, after the Occupy injunction, and then again the next day, after the polygamy judgment. Both events took place on the steps of the courthouse and, with respect to polygamy, everyone wanted to know, "What next?"

By this point, no charges had been forwarded to the Crown, and the RCMP trip to Texas had been put off several times and was now scheduled for mid-December. No one knew what the Ministry of Children and Family Development was doing with their inquiries, but Mary Ellen Turpel-Lafond, the child advocate, was again calling for action, as were members of the media. Our own team, who admittedly had little knowledge of the mysteries of the criminal justice process, were completely perplexed by the glacial pace. Perhaps perplexed is understating it: Bevan, for one, was practically pulling her hair out.

I had always been at pains to keep the Polygamy Reference separate from police investigations of wrongdoing at Bountiful, but these worlds had collided as the reference drew to a close and we became inundated with evidence of the sexual trafficking in young girls. At first, our involvement had been funnelling all the information we could to the investigating authorities. Later, Greathead met with various officials in an attempt to coordinate a working group among various government agencies in Canada and the United States. But absent from the equation have been the prosecutors.

British Columbia's criminal justice system works differently from almost every other province. In Ontario, or in Alberta, or in just about any other province or territory, charges are "laid" by the police, who swear an information before a justice of the peace, and the prosecution is underway. In those places, the Crown takes over the prosecution, and may carry it forward to trial or decide to enter a stay. In British Columbia, in contrast, the police investigate, and then send a Report to Crown counsel. A prosecutor reviews the file, and then, if he or she considers that charges should go forward, "approves" them for prosecution.

In theory there is little difference between the models: in either case, the acquiescence of both police and prosecutors is required for charges to proceed. Practically speaking though, it was perceived that the "police charge" model established a default that, particularly in cases with some public profile, made abandonment more difficult and was thus more "law and order" focused.

But British Columbia's "Crown approval" model, in which the prosecutors are driven by reports from the police, coupled with the unusually independent culture of British Columbia's Crown counsel, had another apparent effect: Crown lawyers appeared reluctant to get involved at the investigative stage of the cases, compared to their counterparts in other Canadian provinces. At Bountiful, we had what appeared to be a criminal conspiracy involving dozens of victims, and possibly hundreds of perpetrators, of sexual exploitation and related offences. In my mind, the matter needed to be treated as a full organized crime investigation. Moreover, prosecution for sexual exploitation itself, which required that the government prove that the accused was in a position of trust or authority over the victim, would rely on a very sophisticated understanding of the religious, economic, and social context of Bountiful. All the cases were interrelated.

But Bond could not simply direct the CJB to help investigate or to prosecute. Justice Stromberg-Stein, in her *Blackmore* decision, had held that the Attorney General could not name the special—that was the ADAG/CJB's job. And indeed, after the decision in that case, it was arguable that *no* new special could be appointed because the original prosecutor, Peck, retained exclusive conduct of matters that fell within his 2006 mandate.

When Peck was re-approached in December 2011, he indicated that he had no desire to renew his conduct of the Bountiful prosecution, leaving the coast clear for a fresh appointment. Preparations were made for a "gazetted" instruction to CJB.

So on January 9, the Attorney General wrote a letter to CJB ADAG Gillen, instructing him to retain a new special prosecutor of the Bountiful cases to consider any charges *except* polygamy (that would be left, to be added after a final decision had been made on the prospect of re-referring the question to a higher court). Curiously, the matter was reported in the press, not as a threshold moment in the pursuit of child abusers in Bountiful, but rather as the moment of resignation of Rick Peck. But Peck had not worked on the Bountiful file for four and a half years, and had not really considered himself involved since his report in 2007 had been submitted. The point, as the *Globe and Mail* and *Vancouver Sun* seemed to grasp but many others did not, was that there was, once again, some momentum behind efforts to investigate and prosecute the historical sexual exploitation of girls at Bountiful.

A few days later, CJB announced the appointment of Terry Wilson, a well-regarded senior criminal lawyer to lead the prosecution. Notwithstanding his formidable reputation, Wilson wouldn't have been my first choice to lead the Bountiful prosecution. Everything I knew about the history of the case strongly suggested that, this time, it should be a woman in charge of the file—it just didn't seem to me that the succession of senior males that had looked at, and rejected, charges of sexual exploitation in Bountiful really *got* it, somehow. Two months after the announcement of his appointment, on 26 March 2012, the Attorney General announced that Wilson's mandate had expanded to include charges under section 293 itself. The press release that day said:

> After reviewing Chief Justice Bauman's comprehensive and compelling decision on the constitutionality of the polygamy section of the *Criminal Code*, government has decided against a referral to a higher court.
>
> . . .
>
> Legal counsel have advised me they are satisfied his decision will enable police and prosecutors to act with authority in investigating and

prosecuting criminally polygamous relationships. While the opinion of a higher court may be more persuasive in case law, the government does not believe a referral decision is necessary.

Still, as I write this, despite all the evidence uncovered in Texas and through the Polygamy Reference, despite even the testimony under oath of witnesses in the case, no person is facing criminal charges for what happened at Bountiful. I am beginning to wonder if anybody ever will.

# AFTERWORD
# The March of the Zombies

There are many definitions of the word "liberal." To the extent that the word is derived from the same root as *library*, it speaks to a certain mode or degree of learning—as in the "liberal arts" or a "liberal education." To some it means licentious or permissive, from the Latin *liber* for free or unrestricted. This is the characterization of liberal thought that has allowed the term to become something of a pejorative in the political lexicon of the American Right. But I have always preferred the definition of "liberalism" of Bertrand Russell, who considered it to be a state free of preconception and dogma, one willing to *learn* (I think it is charming and profound that the same Latin word, *liber*, means both "book" and "free," don't you?). A liberal, according to Russell, must always be prepared to let go of his dearest truths if the evidence pointed persuasively in the other direction. This was most famously expressed in a phrase attributed to John Maynard Keynes, who is reported to have said, "When my information changes, I alter my conclusions. What do you do, sir?"[1] Russell put it somewhat more comprehensively when he wrote (and we know he really did write it):

> The essence of the Liberal outlook lies not in what opinions are held, but in how they are held: instead of being held dogmatically, they are held tentatively, and with a consciousness that new evidence may at any moment lead to their abandonment.

This view of liberalism, however, is not the modern mainstream, and liberalism has taken on canonical beliefs of its own. One of these beliefs that had become dogma among many liberals (and here I include liberals on the libertarian end of the spectrum, many of whom who would consider themselves conservatives, politically) was the idea that alternative mating or marriage structures were not axiomatically harmful and therefore should be a matter of personal choice in which the state could not legitimately intervene. Taking this to be true in the case of, for instance,

339

same-sex marriage, liberal thinkers simply extended it, without much further thought, to polygamy. I would like to think that if Russell or Keynes had held this position, in light of the evidence presented in the course of the reference, they would have been prepared to change their conclusions.

But the "liberal" defenders of polygamy seemed relatively untroubled that all of their underlying assumptions about the practice—that it was not inherently harmful, and that in any event any harms could be effectively addressed by other laws—had been rather conclusively disproven, and even after the decision the skeptics persisted. I cannot blame them for holding their initial position (I held it too, once); my complaint is that they cling to it today. And they do: the same arguments that had been vigorously made, diligently and methodically weighed in light of evidence, and then thoroughly demolished by Chief Justice Bauman in his reasons are simply thrown up again as if the trial had not happened.

The *National Post*'s Jesse Klein, wading shallowly even by the standard of the kiddie-pool that is modern libertarian political thought, wrote a representatively vacuous opinion piece the day after Bauman's judgment was released. The article seemed generated by someone who had either not read the decision in the rush to meet a deadline or who had not understood the Chief Justice's fairly straightforward English. Granted, Klein did seem to have read the first and last few pages, but apparently he skipped the middle (I know, I know . . . "it was so *long*"). How else to explain his determination to refight lost battles, almost as if from the grave. Here's one example:

> Arguments that polygamy causes societal harm by taking too many women off the market become a moot point, because there is nothing to suggest that there would be widespread adoption of the practice. (Not to mention that if it were adopted by secular society, there would be no reason not to see relationships involving one woman and multiple men.)

No reason to believe that polygamy would manifest as polygyny over polyandry? Nothing to suggest that it would spread? Sigh. Klein simply ignored all the findings of fact that directly contradicted his assertions, and then concluded:

> The law . . . should not be so broad as to criminalize behaviour that hurts no one and is engaged in by consenting adults.

It really was as if Klein didn't know that the points he considers self-evident were vigorously argued by the participants and ultimately resoundingly rejected by the trial judge, not because their premises were logically flawed, but because all of the evidence went the other way.

This was a disappointment to me. But what could they say? I call the "common sense" civil libertarian arguments like Klein's "zombies." They simply can't be entirely killed, and they will be summoned into the streets by polygamy's apologists long after I have passed into dust. But what will also endure, I hope, is the Chief Justice's decision, and the masses of evidence it summarizes. For a year, we focused the legal fact-finding process on the phenomenon of polygamy with the principal purpose of assessing whether it was inherently harmful, and that process came to an unequivocal conclusion: yes. For a long time to come, glib assertions like Klein's can simply be met with reference to over 300 pages of exhaustive analysis.

The BC Civil Liberties Association, in contrast to Klein, seemed stunned into silence in the aftermath of the decision, a bit like that parrot from Monty Python ("He's pining for the fjords . . . lovely plumage, the Norwegian Blue . . ."). The association's press release on November 22 publicizing the imminent release of Bauman's judgment appears to have been the last written word of the association on the topic. I would have hoped that the BCCLA would admit that it had been wrong: that the available facts had changed, and like Keynes (or whoever) they were prepared to revisit their previous conclusions. Perhaps this hope was really just seeking some vindication for my very conscious departure from their camp on this issue. I guess I was really hoping to have persuaded my former colleagues that I had been right to move beyond the standard libertarian view of multiparty marriages.

I doubt that some could ever be convinced, and they will always find some support among academics who see their role as presenting perspectives rather than attempting to analyze available facts. Remember the evidence of the challengers' principal expert witnesses, Campbell and Beaman, whom the Chief Justice had charitably described as "sincere, but frankly somewhat naïve"?

My own view is that the work of these two academics, and others who seemed to argue from a predetermined set of conclusions (polygamy is harmless, prohibition is bigotry) was not simply naïve, it was dangerous. Their approach was based on a view that, if we perceived problems with Bountiful, then the problem must be *ours*, the result of moral panic and the "othering" of a religious minority. Campbell's research was scarcely worthy of the name: she was co-opted by Winston Blackmore and his proxies with what in the end was a simple bargain, even if she didn't recognize it as such—she and her assistant were granted privileged "access" sufficient to secure the raw material for her studies (and the prestige and grant money that might follow), and Blackmore would get an academic topspin added to his public relations volleys. This devil's bargain was eerily similar to Blackmore's extortionate proposal to Chief Justice Bauman himself at the beginning of the reference: unless you pay me a million or so for legal counsel, I will refuse you "access" to members of my community. If the Chief Justice didn't knuckle under, Blackmore had said, Bauman would be deprived of the direct evidence that would make his findings credible. The Chief Justice, to his credit, had refused.

What Campbell gave Blackmore in exchange for access was not money, it was the academic "beard" of "qualitative research." Campbell credulously parroted her interviewees' "voices" as they skirted around, diminished, or denied the harms, such as child brides and lost boys, associated with polygamy at Bountiful. Blackmore is himself an admitted and unrepentant serial predator of young girls (on Larry King Live he admitted some of his wives had been "under sixteen," though he accused one of the children of lying about her age: "but that's not unusual for women, is it?" he asked King, who chuckled along), and he had presided over an institution, the FLDS, which had been for decades little more than a puppy mill catering to the whims of its male priesthood overclass. Campbell unwittingly helped him present a picture of simple, misunderstood folk who just wanted to be left alone. The responses given by her interviewees (and I am here referring to the accounts in the public domain[2]) read like what they were—shallow platitudes elicited by a fawning and tentative inquisitor. It was clear that Campbell would rather have eaten her teacup than ask difficult questions about the age of Blackmore's wives or the fate of the community's excess boys. Ironically, the fact that the conversations were almost entirely pointedly meaningless was implicitly held as proof that that there was nothing all that sinister going on.

I would like to be able to dismiss the evidence of Campbell and Beaman as some sort of fraudulent outlier of academic endeavour. I would like to be able to say that it fell abysmally short of the standards that we expect of serious intellectuals. But the sad fact is that this kind of work is *de rigueur* among a powerful cohort in the "broad" field of sociology, which seems to view anything empirical as inherently suspicious. Legal academia, when it turns its attention away from the study of what law *is* and further into the field of what it *should be* is generally no better in its determined aversion to empiricism.

Campbell's "sociolegal anthropology" (my term) and Beaman's sociology had been, outside of the case, widely considered to be factual, to the extent that their work (particularly Campbell's) seemed to form the basis for much of the academic discussion around Bountiful. I know I am being harsh, but surely this speaks to the vapid state of the modern social sciences, where no one is there to discover *facts*, but rather to present *perspectives*. I do take great comfort, however, that the deception was so readily and completely made transparent through evidence and cross-examination at trial, perhaps the last intellectual forum where facts indisputably matter, indeed where objective truths are acknowledged to exist at all. It was not simply a "perspective" but a *fact* that children were being abused at the very moment when Campbell and Beaman, without any evidence at all, were assuring us that such reports were exaggerated and the result of moral panic or religious prejudice.

So maybe we should be sceptical of demands that we tolerate the "other," simply because they are the "other." And this leads me to other somewhat "illiberal" thoughts that have rattled around my head since my work on the polygamy case began: Those who defended the polygamists most strenuously did so from the unassailable position of liberal tolerance. Twenty years ago, that position overwhelmed all. Today, perhaps, it does not. Is it possible that one development of the last decade or two is that our notion of what we in Western democracies need to tolerate in the name of religious freedom has undergone a change, and perhaps a very significant one?

By the last part of the twentieth century, our improving understanding and recognition of the historical plight of many minorities had led to a protectiveness of those groups in the public discourse. By the time I entered law school in 1995, I don't think it's much of an exaggeration to say that a lot of the academy was deeply in the thrall of the belief that liberal tolerance required suspending criticism of any action that could be characterized as a feature of a different (that is to say, nonmainstream) culture or religion.

Some exceptions were allowed in the obvious cases, for instance, human sacrifice or female genital mutilation; but by and large the theory was that, contrary to the Whig version of history, Western rules and norms were not *better* than those of other countries, just *different*. For too long, the argument went, the imperial and colonial projects of the West had been underwritten by beliefs in our inherent superiority. It followed that every attempt to suggest that the fundamental beliefs of the "other" or the actions inspired by those beliefs were worthy of contempt could be met with an eruption of intellectual outrage and deft redirection. If Rwandan Hutus took to hacking their Tutsi neighbours to death with machetes by the hundreds of thousands, one could predict the reaction: vast oceans of ink would be dedicated to our own criticism of the imperial West, whose policies somehow, surely made them do it. In any event, we were told, we are in no position to judge *them*.

This peculiar Western blending of aggressive self-hatred and pacifistic tolerance reached a zenith, or perhaps it is better to say nadir, with the Salman Rushdie affair, an embarrassment which began in 1989. Rushdie, I'm sure you recall, was a British citizen who had written a novel, *The*

*Satanic Verses*, to which some Muslims, and particularly the fascistic (and, not irrelevantly, opportunistic) clerics of Iran, objected. The religious leader of that nation, the Ayatollah Khomeini, issued a religious edict, a *fatwah*, and offered a reward for Rushdie's head.

The proper response from a self-respecting liberal democracy ought to have been to call the Iranian ambassador on the carpet and send him packing (is there any doubt it would have been a "him"?) back to Tehran with a simple message: should Mr. Rushdie meet his end at the hands of someone hired or inspired by the Ayatollah, the bearded one and his senior minions would be notified of the event by the noisy arrival in each of their bedchambers of a submarine-launched cruise missile. I am not suggesting that this would have had any deterrence effect, general or specific. But it would have been a morally appropriate response, and at any rate far better than the incontinent, mewling apologies from many "thought-leaders" in the West (a not-insignificant number of whom hinted that Rushdie, through "insensitivity," had brought the death sentence on himself). At the least, a firmer response might have tempered the spread of Rushdie-cidal mania in the Muslim world, which eventually included serious threats (occasionally carried out) against his publishers and translators in many countries, and even as late as 2012 was the cause of unofficial and official censorship.[3]

And then all this was threatened to be repeated in 2005, when twelve editorial cartoons were published in the Danish newspaper the *Jyllands-Posten*. The cartoons depicted the Islamic prophet Muhammad in a number of controversial contexts, assertedly (and as it turned out, certainly ironically) in furtherance of a public debate regarding Islam's capacity for enduring criticism. What began as a few protests against the cartoons exploded into "spontaneous" violent outrage in the "Muslim streets," leading to as many as one hundred deaths. The Danish embassy in Pakistan was bombed; others in Syria, Lebanon, and Iran were torched.

But this was more than fifteen years after Rushdie's initial death sentence, and it seemed that the West had learned some lessons in the interregnum. This time, those voices advocating toleration of this intolerance would be muted, and the dominant reaction of the West was appropriately hostile and protective of the freedom of our citizens to participate in the public discourse. Some organized "buy Danish" campaigns; numerous publications reprinted the controversial cartoons in defiant solidarity with the embattled Danes. Foreign governments were called out for their clumsily obvious support of "spontaneous" anti-Western demonstrations. The matter, after a time, blew over. There were still some quisling voices to be heard, suggesting that the cartoonists and their publishers ought not to have provoked the psychotic Mullahs so. But by and large, the West stood up to the bullies, and by and large the bullies backed down.

What had happened in the meantime, of course, were the September 11 attacks and some degree of philosophical reflection in their wake. I am not one of those who believed that that day "changed everything"—I think in most peoples' daily lives it actually changed very little. But the year 2001 marked, I think, the beginning of an evolution in the way public intellectuals have permitted themselves to regard the collision between Western values and those of other societies, mainly those in the Muslim world. Only after the attacks was the discourse unshackled from the prevalent views of cultural relativism, and from the rather unthinking tendency of well-meaning writers to regard with hostility any suggestion that Western values of constitutionalism, human rights, and the rule of law were objectively superior to the systems of other societies. It was, in other words, okay again to use words like "civilization" as a way of distinguishing a better, more advanced, form of society.

If you believe in a liberal rights-based democracy, then you must accept that tolerance, past a point, is not only unnecessary but *undesirable*. Patrick Henry probably did not actually say "Give me liberty or give me death," and the classic declaration attributed to Voltaire, "I disapprove of everything you say but will defend to the death your right to say it," was written by Evelyn Beatrice Hall in tribute to him. The authorship is beside the point. What is important about these enduring phrases (aside from their very endurance, which I suggest is testament to their resonance) is that they are not passive promises of suicide, but rather calls to arms. Tyranny may be opposed by force, and liberals should be prepared to endure almost anything *except* the intolerance of others. If this seems self-evident or tautological to you then I am gratified, because for decades I would suggest that it was anything but, and it was the rediscovery of a sense of cultural judgmentalism—the idea that some cultural practices, and perhaps entire cultures were not only different but *worse*, and perhaps even that there was something that might be regarded as objective social *progress*—that helped to turn the tide against tolerance of polygamy in the new century.

This may seem like an easy point to make, and overall one that has little to do with polygamy, but I think it is salient for two reasons. First, as I've suggested, I believe that much of the official reluctance of the authorities to act against Mormon fundamentalist polygamists since the time of the Second World War has been informed by a sense that our intolerance of the practice should be better regarded as a manifestation of our own prejudices and cultural imperialism, rather than from a legitimate concern of direct or indirect social harm. And second, because it is not simply coincidental that the practice of polygamy is, globally speaking, most closely associated with those who set themselves as committed to a war on rights and freedoms generally, but more particularly on those of women and girls.

In other words, by the turn of the last century it was dawning on many that polygamy is one those religious and cultural practices where we might have been too unthinkingly devoted to diversity for its own sake. Think about it: in the sixty-five years since the last great global bloodbath ended and the "rights revolution" began in earnest, and in the middle of Canada which, in many ways, was at the cutting edge of that legal and philosophical upheaval, we watched as one of our communities went headlong in the other direction. The Bountiful FLDS grew from a tiny group of polygamists, religious fundamentalists on the point of plural marriage, but not, by most accounts, otherwise measurably illiberal, into a community where women's rights and the treatment of girls would cause approving wrinkles around the eye of any right-thinking Taliban patriarch. Where young daughters were—at times literally—exchanged for equally young "brides," where sexual psychopaths were given not only succour and sanctuary but indeed almost absolute power. Where the statistical chances of a girl going on to a university education was—without exaggeration—worse than in sub-Saharan Africa, Cambodia, or Afghanistan. In part by virtue of our own liberal ideal of tolerance and *respect* for rights, we became complicit in the brainwashing, commodification, and trafficking of an entire generation of girls in the heart of British Columbia and in Utah and Arizona.

My point is that our society's default position on tolerance has hardened over recent years, and that this probably affected the determination, throughout society, to do something about polygamy after years of inactivity. Perhaps the so-called war on terror, however ineptly led, clumsily executed, and avariciously inspired it may have been in any of its various theatres, is at least in some of its aspects a war between societies who are determined to be tolerant and those who aspire only for the opposite. And perhaps it was a fundamental seed of legitimacy in that struggle that freed us to think once again of some societies as simply more desirable, *per se*, than others. Certainly, people raised in all manner of environments may believe that their situation is both right and best. But what of those who had bases for real comparison? After September 11, maybe it was again all right to think that the hundreds of millions of people who aspired to leave less advanced societies (I'll take the risk of calling them that) in favour of more advanced civilizations (an even riskier characterization) were not simply the craven self-interested few of their kinsmen. After all, where was the pattern of immigrants going the other way—those who, tiring of the capitalist excess and anomie about which many in the West justly complain, decided to chuck it all in for the rustic easy life under a tribal warlord or one of the few remaining military dictatorships? Such inspired contrarians may exist, but I have yet to meet one. In the same vein, it is difficult to imagine parents anywhere else in Canada who would wish to raise a daughter or son in Bountiful. That might not mean everything, but it does, I would argue, mean *something*.

So what should happen with the polygamists of Bountiful? As a lawyer on the "civil side" of the Attorney General's ministry, I have no say in charge-approval, either as policy or in individual cases. However, given the history and where we find ourselves today, it seemed to me that it makes little sense to prosecute the majority of polygamously married adults. So if anybody asked me to set out a policy, it would be pretty simple.

We can and should say that, going forward, all polygamous marriages that come to the attention of the authorities will be subject to prosecution. With respect to subsisting or historical polygamous marriage, prosecution would only occur if it appeared that there were elements of exploitation, abuse, or a gross imbalance of power. This would permit the majority of existing polygamous marriages, and the families they supported, to continue, and run their course without government interference. I see little to be gained in tearing apart existing and functioning households, most of which include children of the wives involved, except where they were founded on exploitation or abuse. In this way, I think, polygamy in Bountiful would simply expire, as indeed it has already begun to do. And without polygamy, the abuses of the FLDS would fall away because they are not, we have seen, independent variables.

If the authorities were willing to take a comprehensive approach, I think it should begin with wresting control of the Bountiful properties away from the church's United Effort Plan trust. Control over the land and houses has been a significant source of the organization's hold over its members, and along with control over the distribution of wives (and, through "reassignment," even children), is the foundation of the despotism that still lingers there. Similarly, the church's grip on education in the community should be prised open. Real teachers should be brought in from outside Bountiful, and the influence of the church should be completely purged from any state-supported schooling in the area (can anyone believe that we should pay for a school with an incarcerated child rapist as its revered figurehead?). This will cost us money, but I would like to believe the children might be thought of as worth it.

Whatever remains of the FLDS power base at Bountiful should be disassembled, brick by brick if necessary, through a coordinated effort by all authorities involved. Some members of the community will protest at the demise of their way of life. Tough. For decades the community stood by as young girls were indoctrinated into blind obedience and then traded as collectibles among the community's powerful men. Parents, adult siblings and half-siblings, grandparents, teachers—every one of them was complicit in this, and in my mind they have relinquished any claim to the privilege of absolute control over their community's future. We gave them that right once, gave them the benefit of our blind eye, and they blew it. And I can't believe that they simply didn't know any better, or couldn't do anything about it. If the courageous men, women, and children who fled the community and others like it, and who risked their families and even their lives to alert the world, if they could find their moral centre, so could have the ones who stayed behind.

What I learned in the course of the Polygamy Reference regarding human nature and the evolution of societies has changed my beliefs about the future of human rights in Canada and elsewhere. I have come to believe that there *is* something like a destiny to human progress, that there *is* something that can legitimately be lauded as civilization. Yes, the polygamy case highlighted resurgent movements, be they among fundamentalist Mormons or Muslims, who would see the rights revolution reversed in favour of patriarchal despotism. But these are, in the great scheme of things, reactionary outliers; that they are fighting should not be taken to mean that they are winning. Of what consequence are Blackmore and Oler to the progressive development of rights in Canada? They can exploit and abuse individuals, but, as the reference decision showed, society will not tolerate them forever, and they will eventually be swept aside. And yes, there are men in the darkest backwoods of the Muslim world who would throw acid in the faces of schoolgirls, but these are also eventually impotent: their rage is not really against an imperial West so much as against the aspirations of the Arab Spring, and the relentless ambition for justice and equality that surrounds them on all sides. Such men and their beliefs are already, if uncomprehendingly, dead; their paroxysms of cruelty are not resurgent energy so much as the last twitches of a corpse. They are zombies also.

The Canadian Constitution is sometimes regarded as a "living tree," a metaphor which suggests not only vitality, growth, and development, but also that the rights it sets out will expand according to some pattern that is directional, if not entirely predetermined. I believe this is true. The will to freedom, dignity, and justice, and the capacity to compromise and cooperate in the pursuit of mutual liberty are, no less than polygamy, coded in our genes. But unlike polygamy, these better impulses of human nature promote, rather than undermine, the complex, rights-based, civilized society which has proven to be the most competitive and successful social structure.

None of this is to suggest that the project of a more just society is complete. There is more to do, every day. My confidence in the idea of progress does not lead me to conclude that we can be complacent; rather, it leads me to conclude that we *won't* be. That makes me, I suppose, an optimist.

# Notes

## Part 1: Beginnings

1   I hope I will be forgiven if I do not slavishly adhere to the customs of Anglo-Canadian legal nomenclature, which would require that I refer to "the Chief Justice," "Bauman CJSC," or "His Lordship." As with my frequent omission of other formal titles and subnominals, such as "Dr," "Professor," or "QC," I've made this choice to improve readability and avoid distraction.

2   These are recent law graduates who spend a year in the court assisting judges, mostly with research and writing. It is an excellent apprenticeship, particularly for aspiring litigators. From a lawyer's point of view, the number of clerks present in the audience indicates one of two things: either the judge has flagged the case as particularly demanding so as to require their assistance, or the clerks themselves have identified the proceedings as particularly interesting, because of the issues, parties, or counsel involved, and therefore worth a look. I suspect in the polygamy case both factors were at play.

3   *Big Love*, for those unfamiliar, is the story of a polygamous Mormon man trying to make it as an "independent" in Salt Lake City after leaving "the Compound" at "Juniper Creek" run by the "United Effort Brotherhood," all fairly obvious references to the real FLDS community at Short Creek and the United Effort Plan, the trust under which it operated. The fictional UEB in *Big Love* was based in Southern Utah with an outpost in Canada; it had child brides, lost boys, and a scary aspiring prophet with repressed homosexual tendencies who usurped his father's power after the elder man suffered a stroke. The show ran for five seasons, concluding in the same year the Polygamy Reference was decided.

4   I refer throughout to the "trial." Technically speaking, it was not the trial of an action, but rather a hearing of a reference proceeding. I prefer to ignore this formality because the Polygamy Reference had the basic structure of a trial, including live witnesses, gowned counsel, and so forth, and to call it such allows me to distinguish the main hearing from preliminary proceedings "in chambers."

5    Senior lawyers in British Columbia, as in England and other Common-
     wealth jurisdictions, are sometimes granted the title "Queen's Counsel."
     In British Columbia, the designation is an honorary title bestowed on a
     couple of dozen of the province's ten thousand lawyers per year. A number
     of the lawyers referred to in this book have been awarded their QC, but (as
     I mentioned in above note 1) to avoid some awkwardness and overformality
     of writing I have chosen to omit this and other subnominal designations
     from the text from here forward.

6    I had learned that *West Coast* LEAF should not be confused for a subsidi-
     ary of LEAF, the national organization based in Toronto. Indeed there
     seemed to be some sensitivity around the subject. Similarly, the BC Civil
     Liberties Association is unaffiliated with the Canadian Civil Liberties
     Association, and many of the members of the former (which was estab-
     lished first and has a genuinely national profile) consider the latter to be
     something of an Eastern usurper, and some might occasionally be caught
     derisively referring to the *Toronto* Civil Liberties Association.

7    *Reference re: the Constitutionality of s. 293 of the Criminal Code of Canada*
     [Polygamy Reference]. The judgment of the Supreme Court of British
     Columbia can be found at 2011 BCSC 1588.

8    This wasn't solely metaphor—Erickson's low-slung design was adopted
     only after the original proposal—for a Manhattan-scale skyscraper that
     would have been Vancouver's tallest even today—was abandoned as too
     dominant and imposing. Erickson's vision was of law courts as public space,
     rather than Dracula's tower.

9    It is a frequent surprise, particularly to American visitors, to learn that
     the "Supreme Court of British Columbia" is not actually the highest court
     in the province. It is called "supreme" to distinguish it from the "inferior"
     provincial courts, but is in itself below the appellate courts, which are the
     BC Court of Appeal and the Supreme Court of Canada, which is actually
     (as if it weren't confusing enough) the supreme court of Canada.

10   The ground level is called the second floor, and the public elevators reach
     only to the "fourth" (actually the third) after which you must walk some
     distance and take another elevator to the remaining levels. This was said to
     be a security measure, to hinder escape attempts by criminal defendants. In
     my observation it has trapped far more tourists.

11   A barrister in the English parlance is a trial lawyer, as distinct from a
     solicitor who advises clients but does not generally attend court. In Canada,
     a lawyer upon being admitted to his provincial law society is qualified to
     practise as either, or both.

12   The "purse" theory of the sash, I concede, has been persuasively attacked
     by historians of court dress who claim that it was never a receptacle for
     money but instead represents a vestigial hood that was part of the original
     "mourning gown." Although this explanation is at least as credible as mine,
     I find it far less charming and romantic and so choose to disbelieve it. And
     regardless of its actual origins, the lack of an equivalent feature on the
     gowns of judges, court clerks, and Queen's Counsel is proof that life can
     imitate legend to beneficial effect.

13 Some have written that the practice originated with the death of Queen Anne in 1714.

14 Two other fun but well-worn anecdotes surround these requirements. One particularly fussy judge is said to have criticized a female barrister for wearing a skirt to court. She is said (and I have heard this reliably verified) to have removed her skirt, then and there (having had the foresight to put on something underneath). In another story, a lawyer appeared in court wearing brown shoes. The judge, again a rather notorious pedant (should I prefer "stickler"?) said, "I can't hear you, counsel." The brown-shod lawyer resumed, to the same interruption again. The legend goes that the lawyer, not comprehending the nature of the judge's objection, assumed the problem was with His Lordship's faculties (some versions of the story employ a female judge), and simply kept speaking louder and louder.

15 *Supreme Court Further Amendment Act, 1905* SBC 1905 c 16, s 2. Not everyone was pleased with this decision, and there was a threatened rebellion when an admiralty judge refused to doff his wig, of which he must have been very proud, on the grounds that the admiralty court was in exclusively federal jurisdiction and therefore immune from the provincial law, which on its face applied "in any Court in this Province." I read about the dispute in a Washington State newspaper of the day, which reported the constitutional crisis north of the border with some wry amusement. I have since learned that the judge, Archer Martin, insisted on wearing his wig when he sat on admiralty cases until his retirement in 1940, and also required that counsel appearing before him do likewise.

16 Law Reform Commission of Canada, *Working Paper 42: Bigamy* (Ottawa: Law Reform Commission of Canada, 1985) at 29.

17 Law Commission of Canada, *Beyond Conjugality: Recognizing and Supporting Close Personal Adult Relationships* (Ottawa: Minister of Public Works and Government Services, 2001).

18 BC Civil Liberties Association, *Annual General Meeting Newsletter, 2001*, online: www.bccla.org/newsletter/01annual.pdf at 7.

19 Martha Bailey & Amy J Kaufman, *Polygamy in the Monogamous World: Multicultural Challenges for Western Law and Policy* (Santa Barbara, CA: Praeger, 2010) at 156.

20 *Ibid* at 133–42.

21 Bailey & Kaufman, *ibid*, cite an "A Currie" who, writing also for the Law Reform Commission of Canada, said: "Traditionally, polygamous marriages appear to be almost universally associated with inequality between the sexes."

22 2004 UT 76 at para 40.

23 2006 UT 31 at para 175.

24 Kathleen Tracy, *The Secret Story of Polygamy* (Naperville, IL: Sourcebooks, 2002) n 3 at 188–89.

25 Janet Bennion, *Women of Principle: Female Networking in Contemporary Mormon Polygyny* (Oxford: Oxford University Press, 1998).

26  Maura Strassberg, "The Crime of Polygamy" (2003) 12 Temp Pol & Civ Rts L Rev 353 at 357.

27  *Ibid* at 358.

28  Another example is the crime of assisting another to commit suicide. It is difficult to argue with the proposition that, in particular cases involving the terminally ill and terribly disabled for instance, to do so is an act of mercy and causes no harm. The legitimate basis for criminalization, if there is one, must lie in the weight of indirect harms that could accrue if the practice gained legitimacy. By coincidence of timing, a challenge to this very law was launched in British Columbia while the polygamy case was ongoing. Joe Arvay was counsel for the plaintiffs.

29  Shayna Sigman, "Everything Lawyers Know About Polygamy is Wrong" [2006] 16 Cornell J Law & Pub Policy 101 at 164.

30  Susan Drummond, "Polygamy's Inscrutable Secular Mischief" (2009) 47 Osgoode Hall LJ 317 at 358.

31  Strassberg, "The Crime of Polygamy," above note 25 at 364.

32  Beverley Baines, "Polygamy's Challenge: Women, Religion and the Post-Liberal State" in Kim Brooks & Carissima Mathen, *Women, Law, and Equality: A Discussion Guide* (Toronto: Irwin Law, 2010) [orig. (2007) 2 (no.1) *Les Ateliers de l'éthique* at 27].

33  Angela Campbell et al, *Polygamy in Canada: Legal and Social Implications for Women and Children* (Ottawa: Status of Women Canada, 2005).

34  Steven Pinker, *How the Mind Works* (New York: Norton, 1997) at 477.

35  Michelle Chan, "Beyond Bountiful: Toward an Intersectional and Postcolonial Feminist Intervention in the British Columbia Polygamy Reference" (2011) 16 *Appeal* 15 at 17.

36  Lori G Beaman, "Who Decides? Harm, Polygamy and Limits on Freedom" (2006) 10(1) Nova Religio 43.

37  Bailey & Kaufman, above note 19 at 3.

38  There is a lively debate about when Smith became a polygamist. He appears to have privately advocated the idea almost from the founding of the faith, but it did not become official church doctrine until 1852, eight years after his death.

39  98 (US) 145 (1878).

40  *Morrill Anti-Bigamy Act* (37th United States Congress, Sess 2, c 126, 12 Stat 501).

41  The 1604 law (*An Acte to restrayne all persons from Marriage until their former Wyves and former Husbandes be deade*) was worded as follows:

If any person or persons within his Majesties Domynions of England and Wales, beinge married, or which herafter shall marie, doe at any tyme after the ende of the Session of this present Parliament, marrye any person or person, the former husband or wife beinge alive, that then everie such offence shalbe Felonie . . . (1 JAC. 1. C. 11).

42  *Reynolds*, above note 39.

43  *Ibid.* at 164-65.

44  As an important aside, the American campaign against the Mormon church (there is no other way to characterize it) created a context quite distinct from that in which the Canadian criminalization of polygamy occurred. The LDS church in the United States had, by the time of founding prophet Joseph Smith's death in 1844, established itself in direct (and occasionally violent) confrontation with the government and rival groups. By the time of the legislation that threatened to disenfranchise Mormons and fragment the LDS church in 1887, the church was a monolithic political, cultural, and military presence in the already tumultuous West. The LDS church dominated the life of the territory of Utah and effectively formed the government there, and many of its members and leaders sought to establish an independent state.

45  *Reynolds*, above note 39 at 165–66.

46  Quoted in Tracy, above note 24 at 145.

47  The jury charge that was the subject of objection, interestingly, focused on the harms of polygamy to women and children:

> "I think it not improper, in the discharge of your duties in this case, that you should consider what are to be the consequences to the innocent victims of this delusion. As this contest goes on, they multiply, And there are pure-minded women and there are innocent children—innocent in a sense even beyond the degree of the innocence of childhood itself. These are to be the sufferers; and as jurors fail to do their duty, and as these cases come up in the Territory of Utah, just so do these victims multiply and spread themselves over the land."

48  *Holm*, above note 23 at para 58.

49  Jessie L Embry, "Exiles for the Principle: LDS Polygamy in Canada" (Fall 1985) 18 *Dialogue* 108 at 109.

50  *House of Commons Debates* (10 April 1890) at 3180.

51  McCue, below note 55 at 119.

52  *Ibid* at 120.

53  Legal definitions of "bigamy" and "polygamy" often overlap, but the former usually involves an attempt to go through a second *legal* marriage without dissolving the first. Some commentators, including, as we will see, Stenhouse, assert that the essence of bigamy is deception—the bigamist is either fooling his first wife, his second wife or (more usually) both, while he is also attempting to deceive the state. The polygamist generally makes no secret of his affiliations, at least to his partners.

54  Stenhouse's arguments, interestingly, anticipate those being advanced today by Chapman, who similarly argues that the English bigamy law (which is unchanged from 1861) does not address polygamy.

55  Robert J McCue, "Anthony Maitland Stenhouse, Bachelor 'Polygamist'" (Spring 1990) 23:1 *Dialogue* at 120.

56  Howard Palmer, "Polygamy and Progress: The Reaction to Mormons in Canada, 1887–1923" in Brigham Young Card, ed, *The Mormon Presence in Canada* (Edmonton: University of Alberta Press, 1990) at 114.

57  "Unlawful cohabitation" was not a crime on the Canadian books; this may have been a reference to the language of the 1882 *Edmunds Act* in the United States, which had attempted to flesh out the bigamy prohibition to prevent "unofficial" polygamous marriage.

58  McCue, above note 55 at 119–20.

59  *Ibid* at 121.

60  Mr Blake, *Debates of the House of Commons* (10 April 1890) at 3174.

61  *Ibid.*

62  Hon Mr Abbott, *Debates of the Senate* (25 April 1890) at 583.

63  *Ibid* at 585.

64  Hon Mr Dickey & Hon Mr MacDonald (BC), *Debates of the Senate* (25 February 1890) at 142.

65  I will refer to the fundamentalist Mormon settlement at Lister as Bountiful, even though it was not widely referred to as that until decades after its founding.

66  From the "Biography" on the inside covers of Harold Blackmore, *All About Polygamy: Why and How to Live it!* (Hurricane, UT: Patriarchal Society, 1978).

67  *Ibid* at 2.

68  *Ibid* at 3.

69  *Ibid* at 37.


# Part 2: On Human Nature

1  Even though it appears that almost all non-African peoples have a significant amount of *nonhuman* DNA by virtue of our interbreeding with (mostly) Neanderthals and Denovians, it does not appear to have made a measurable impact on behaviour—at least I am not aware of any literature suggesting such a thing. A good overview of the present state of knowledge is found in Kevin N Laland, John Odling-Spee, & Sean Myles, "How Culture Shaped the Human Genome: Bringing Genetics and the Human Sciences Together" (February 2010) 11 Nature Reviews Genetics 137–48. For an argument that recent evolution has led to measurable genetic dif-

ferences among peoples, see Gregory Cochran & Henry Harpending, *The 10,000 Year Explosion: How Civilization Accelerated Human Evolution* (New York: Basic Books, 2009).

2   K. G. Anderson, H. Kaplan, & Jane Lancaster, "Paternal Care by Genetic Fathers and Stepfathers" (1999) 20 Evolution and Human Behavior 405–31.

3   The seminal work on genetic relatedness and homicide is Martin Daly & Margo Wilson, *Homicide* (Hawthorne, NY: Aldine de Gruyter, 1988).

4   Greg A Tooley, Mari Karakis, Mark Stokes, & Joan Ozanne-Smith, "Generalising the Cinderella Effect to Unintentional Childhood Fatalities" (2006) 27 Evolution and Human Behavior at 224.

5   Only one study, of child homicides in Sweden, seemed to cast doubt on the phenomenon in that it found no statistically significant increased risk from stepparent murders. However, when closely analyzed, the Swedish study was revealed to suffer from a "denominator problem" because it failed to properly count the number of stepparent families in the population. When those adjustments were made, the Cinderella effect reappeared in Sweden too.

6   Daniel Gavron, *The Kibbutz: Awakening from Utopia* (Lanham, MD: Rowman & Littlefield, 2000).

7   Laura Betzig, "Sex, Succession, and Stratification in the First Six Civilizations" in Lee Ellis, ed, *Social Stratification and Socioeconomic Inequality* (Westport, CT: Praeger, 1993) at 37–74.

8   Jacob A Moorad et al, "Mating System Change Reduces the Strength of Sexual Selection in an American Frontier Population of the 19th Century" (2011) 32 Evolution and Human Behavior 147–55.

9   Some traits that are subject to intense selective pressure can, of course, develop very quickly. For instance, the prevalence of a rare gene permitting its bearer to operate at higher altitudes is now known to have spread among certain Himalayan people within a very few generations, but this is to be expected. Because only those with the gene could live in the high mountains, they were the only ones who could settle there; if their children didn't carry the gene they would die or be forced to move lower down. Some recent discussion of the speed of some evolutionary adaptations is found in J. Hawks, E. T. Wang, G. Cochran, H. C. Harpending, & R. K. Moyzis. "Recent Acceleration of Human Adaptive Evolution" (2007) *Proceedings of the National Academy of Sciences USA* 104:20753-8. A favourite story of Carl Sagan was the Heike crab (*Heikea japonica*). Japanese fishermen, it was said, would throw back crabs if patterns on their shells resembled human faces, out of the belief that these might be reincarnated Samurai warriors. Within a very few generations, virtually every Heike crab came to have the protective "faces" on their backs. Whether or not the Heike story is true or modern scientific folklore, every dog owner appreciates how quickly certain traits can be manipulated by selective breeding.

10   Steven Pinker, *The Language Instinct* (New York: Morrow, 1994) at 15.

11   Steven Pinker, *How the Mind Works* (New York: Norton, 1997) at 497–98.

12 Robert Wright, *The Moral Animal* (New York: Vintage Books, 1994) at 100.

13 Bruce Hoffman, "All You Need Is Love: How the Terrorists Stopped Terrorism" (December 2001) 288 *Atlantic Monthly* 5.

14 Pinker, *How the Mind Works*, above note 11 at 478.

15 Alan S Miller & Satoshi Kanazawa "Ten Politically Incorrect Truths About Human Nature" (July 1, 2007) *Psychology Today*, online: Psychology Today http://www.psychologytoday.com/articles/200706/ten-politically-incorrect-truths-about-human-nature.

16 *Ibid.*

17 Napoleon Chagnon, "Life Histories, Blood Revenge, and Warfare in a Tribal Population" (1988) 239 Science 985–92; C. T. Palmer & C. F. Tilley. "Sexual Access to Females as a Motivation for Joining Gangs: An Evolutionary Approach" (1995) 32 *Journal of Sex Research* 213–17.

18 Numbers 31:1–18.

19 As in, for instance, Deuteronomy 20:10–17:

> When thou comest nigh unto a city to fight against it . . . And when the LORD thy God hath delivered it into thine hands, thou shalt smite every male thereof with the edge of the sword: But the women . . . shalt thou take unto thyself; and thou shalt eat the spoil of thine enemies, which the LORD thy God hath given thee.

20 Richard Dawkins, *The Selfish Gene* (London: Oxford University Press, 1976). As I write this, not long after a number of lives were lost when the cruise ship *Costa Concordia* sank off Italy, there is much handwringing over the resilience of the "women and children first" injunction in maritime disasters. Critics think it is a vestige of altruistic chivalry, but that makes little sense. Perhaps its origin is much deeper: a society that privileged women and children (boys and girls) when faced with a catastrophic culling of numbers stands a much better chance of rebuilding its numbers (and thus maximizing its genetic bequest) than one that assigned places on the lifeboat randomly without regard to gender or age.

21 Wright, above note 12 at 100–1.

22 *Ibid* at 101.

23 There is perhaps one other interesting aside about Speaker Gingrich's mating and marriage strategies. Gingrich is a Christian, having been raised as a Lutheran, spent some time as a Southern Baptist, and ending up as a Catholic. Needless to say, none of these religions could have been said to have caused or inspired his polygamous behaviour. Conversely, his main opponent is the (apparently) fastidiously monogamous Mitt Romney (married for over forty years), who is a Mormon.

24 This emperor of Morocco was identified by Pinker as having the most recorded children in history—888; *see* Pinker, *How the Mind Works*, above note 11 at 477.

# Part 3: All Roads Lead to Bountiful

1   After the *Charter* was passed, governments scrambled to ensure that their laws were in compliance, and this did lead, occasionally, to an Attorney General taking the position that a law was unconstitutional. Ian Scott, Attorney General of Ontario, gives an example of an episode where he had concluded that the exclusion of girls from equal participation on hockey teams was unsustainable in the *Charter* era. Ian Scott, "Law, Policy and the Role of the Attorney General: Constancy and Change in the 1980s" (1989) 39 UTLJ 109 at 120. However, the public attack on the polygamy law is the only instance of which I am aware where a provincial Attorney General has publicly refused to enforce a federal criminal law on the grounds that it violated the *Charter*.

2   Grant Huscroft, "The Attorney General and *Charter* Challenges to Legislation: Advocate or Adjudicator?" (1995) 5 NJCL 125 at 149.

3   *Ibid* at 150.

4   The entire report has not been made public. The excerpts and description here are from the executive summary of the report, which was publicly released.

5   That year, the king had asked whether "when the whole kingdom is in danger" he may "command all the subjects of this kingdom, at their charge, to provide and furnish such number of Ships, with men, victuals and munition" and whether "the king [was to be] sole judge, both of the danger, and when and how the same is to be prevented and avoided." Most of the judges said yes to both questions, and Charles, pleased, published their opinion and set about seizing ships, men, food, and munitions. Outraged, Parliament passed legislation nullifying the king's expropriations and impeached some of the judges. Parliament was clearly not impressed with the innovation of the legal reference question, and the king himself was beheaded.

6   It was later reported by a newspaper columnist that the idea of a reference to the Supreme Court was an epiphany that came to "a senior government lawyer" in the middle of the night. It was widely assumed that I was that lawyer, and, worse, that I was the source of the information in the story. So I take this opportunity to set the record straight.

7   "Adjudicative facts" are the traditional stuff of trial court evidence—witnesses, documents, and so forth used to determine who did what, when, where. "Legislative facts" invite evidence to assist in the interpretation or adjudication of statutes: they might be government reports, *Hansard* debates, or social science evidence in the form of "Brandeis Briefs." Usually only evidence of legislative facts are permitted in the appellate courts. However, there have been extremely rare instances, like the notorious *Truscott* case before the Supreme Court of Canada in 1967, where the appellate court did hear evidence of adjudicative facts on a reference. This has happened perhaps three times in Canadian history.

8    Charles Lewis, "B.C. May Charge Men of Sect: A-G; 'Canadians Abhor' Behavior in Bountiful" *The National Post* (10 April 2008) at A1.

9    *Arkinstall v Surrey (City)*, 2008 BCSC 1214.

10   *Arkinstall v Surrey (City)*, 2010 BCCA 250.

11   A *Rowbotham* application was named after the case of *R v Rowbotham*, a 1988 decision of the Ontario Court of Appeal. In that case, the court had decided under the *Charter* that, where failure to provide funded counsel meant that an accused could not receive a fair trial, the proceedings should be stayed as an abuse of process. As so often happens, what the court had anticipated would be an issue in "exceptional" circumstances had twenty years later become routine, and *Rowbotham* orders had become little more than a second-tier of legal aid funding. With a virtual cottage industry of *Rowbotham* applications blossoming, they came to be assigned to lawyers in the Con Admin group, so that details of defence counsel funding would remain isolated from the prosecutors. Usually *Rowbotham* applications resulted in small cash outlays. But in major cases such as the *Surrey Six* murder trials and the *Bountiful* case, *Rowbotham* funding could easily result in millions of dollars in public money going to lawyers' fees.

# Part 4: A Case for the Trial Court

1    I have always had a great deal of respect for Stromberg-Stein, an extremely smart and dedicated jurist. But now, a couple of years later and after all the dreadful revelations of the systemic exploitation of children at Bountiful by Blackmore, Oler, and many others, I do wonder if her decision would have been the same had she known then what we know now about the fates that awaited many of the girls born at Bountiful and delivered into the hands of polygamist patriarchs like them. But I guess this question has to be added to the host of other "might have beens" or "should have dones" that dog litigators for years after cases gone awry. The fact is, but for her decision sinking the Blackmore/Oler prosecution, there would have been no reference case, and it is quite possible that the revelations of the scale of abuse at Bountiful would never have become known.

2    In the *Basi/Virk* case, for instance, the government had been forced to outlay millions of dollars in indemnities to government officials who had been prosecuted for corruption, and some commentators blamed the lawyers' comfort at the public trough for the length and complexity of the proceeding. Certainly, without strict controls, there was little incentive to leave even the most speculative stone unturned. Coincidentally, a subsequent decision on publicly funded counsel which put strict and realistic limits on *Rowbotham* and similar funding was penned by the same Justice Stromberg-Stein of Blackmore fame, who ruled that lawyers need to be offered the rates determined by the Legal Services Society, and not a penny more.

3    One of the ideas offered in support of a trial court reference would be that it was cost efficient. British Columbia had recent and painful experience

where government had agreed to fund adversarial counsel, only to see the proceedings spin catastrophically out of control with the lawyers profiting handsomely. The reference was thought to be a forum that would provide better and fuller evidence than one would expect in a single trial of a criminal accused, but be tighter and more efficient than a public inquiry, which were notoriously open-ended and expensive (the British government's Inquiry into the Bloody Sunday Massacre, to give an extreme example, is said to have cost several hundred million *pounds*). In the end, the costs to the Attorney General, which included government-funded counsel on both sides (but exclusive of court costs), was around $1.7 million from inception to the conclusion of the trial. Factoring in the fact that many of the expenses (salaries of government lawyers, for instance) would have been incurred in any event and the costs were closer to $1 million, about half of that used to pay expert witnesses for their time preparing their reports.

4   Arvay and Wickett apparently didn't know when they made this argument that it had, in fact, been the Chief Justice who had directed through the Trial Division Registry that the matter should be brought as it had been.

5   2009 BCSC 1668.

6   2010 BCSC 517.

7   All the opinions to which I here refer have been either publicly released or described in public documents.

8   It was, of course, in anticipation of this possibility that the second reference question was designed. If the law was not constitutional in all its applications, the reasoning went, then it should still apply in a case that "involved a minor, or occurred in a context of dependence, exploitation, abuse of authority, a gross imbalance of power, or undue influence." This narrower reading, it was hoped, might still capture the "bad" polygamy while leaving the "good," or at least harmless, polygamy alone.

9   Maura Strassberg, "The Challenge of Post-Modern Polygamy: Considering Polyamory" (2003) 31 Capital UL Rev 439 at 478.

10  *Ibid* at 477.

11  William G Blum, CSG, *Forms of Marriage: Monogamy Reconsidered* (Eldoret, Kenya: AMECEA Gaba Publications, 1989), cited by Strassberg, "The Challenge of Post-Modern Polygamy" at 478.

12  Strassberg's mathematics could only make sense if population growth outstripped demand for multiple brides by older men. But even then, pressures on adolescent and pre-adolescent girls would still result because, presumably, younger men would not always be content to wait until they were much older to find sexual partners.

13  Shayna Sigman, "Everything Lawyers Know About Polygamy Is Wrong" (2006) 16 Cornell JL & Pub Pol'y 101 at 178.

14  *Ibid.*

15  *Ibid* at 181.

16  *Ibid* at 178.

17  *See*, for instance, *Law Society of Upper Canada v Skapinker*, [1984] 1 SCR 357 at 384; and *R v Oakes*, [1986] 1 SCR 103 at 138. In *MacKay v Manitoba*, [1989] 2 SCR 357, Justice Cory wrote (at 361–62):

> *Charter* cases will frequently be concerned with concepts and principles that are of fundamental importance to Canadian society. For example, issues pertaining to freedom of religion, freedom of expression and the right to life, liberty and the security of the individual will have to be considered by the courts. Decisions on these issues must be carefully considered as they will profoundly affect the lives of Canadians and all residents of Canada. In light of the importance and the impact that these decisions may have in the future, the courts have every right to expect and indeed to insist upon the careful preparation and presentation of a factual basis in most *Charter* cases. The relevant facts put forward may cover a wide spectrum dealing with scientific, social, economic, and political aspects. Often expert opinion as to the future impact of the impugned legislation and the result of the possible decisions pertaining to it may be of great assistance to the courts.

> Charter *decisions should not and must not be made in a factual vacuum. To attempt to do so would trivialize the* Charter *and inevitably result in ill-considered opinions. The presentation of facts is not, as stated by the respondent, a mere technicality; rather, it is essential to a proper consideration of* Charter *issues.* A respondent cannot, by simply consenting to dispense with the factual background, require or expect a court to deal with an issue such as this in a factual void. *Charter* decisions cannot be based upon the unsupported hypotheses of enthusiastic counsel [emphasis added].

18  Constitutional reference cases are most often concerned with "division of powers" issues—an appellate court is asked to decide which level of government has authority over a certain topic. Evidence is minimal, and indeed often such cases are adjudicated based on either agreed or assumed facts.

19  Andrea Moore-Emmett, *God's Brothel: The Extortion of Sex for Salvation in Contemporary Mormon and Christian Fundamentalist Polygamy and the Stories of 18 Women Who Escaped* (San Francisco: Pince-Nez Press, 2004).

20  Polygamy is practised under customary law in Africa, most intensively in the band of nations that extends across the continent from Senegal in the west to Tanzania in the east. Within this "polygyny belt" it is estimated that 20 to 30 percent of married men are in polygynous unions, in incidence so high that it suggests a shortage of marriage-age males. See HG Jacoby, "The Economics of Polygamy in Sub-Saharan Africa: Female Productivity and the Demand for Wives in Cote d'Ivoire" (1995) 103 JPE 938 at 939.

21  Some have suggested that because this Koranic permission was issued after the battle of Uhad, which had literally decimated the male popula-

tion leaving many widows and orphans, it was intended for far narrower circumstances.

22  The research formed the basis of an article entitled "Polygamy and Wife Abuse: A Qualitative Study of Muslim Women in America" (2001) 22 Health Care for Women International 735.

23  All three of the Shafias were convicted of first-degree murder by a jury on 29 January 2012.

24  Meg Barker & Darren Langdridge, eds, *Understanding Non-Monogamies* (New York: Routledge, 2010); Deborah Anapol, *Polyamory in the Twenty-First Century: Love and Intimacy with Multiple Partners* (Lanham, MD: Rowman & Littlefield, 2010); Dossie Easton & Janet W Hardy, *The Ethical Slut: A Practical Guide to Polyamory, Open Relationships and Other Adventures*, 2d ed (Berkeley, CA: Celestial Arts, 2009); Tristan Taormino, *Opening Up: A Guide to Creating and Sustaining Open Relationships* (San Francisco: Cleis Press, 2008).

25  Strassberg, "The Challenge of Post-Modern Polygamy," above note 9 at 439.

26  Jessica Bennett, "Only You. And You. And You." *Newsweek* (29 July 2009).

27  *Muller v Oregon* (1908), 208 US 412.

28  The Chief Justice directed that, for the duration of the reference, a small room outside Courtroom 55 be set aside as a library. All the evidence (not under seal) would be duplicated and maintained in that room, which could be accessed by the participants, the public, and the press.

# Part 5: Trial Diary

1  The question about Brent Jeffs's error was never fully resolved. After Beall had testified, we contacted Jeffs to determine the source of his belief that he had been hypnotized by Beall. I was concerned that we had submitted misleading information to the court, and we should correct it. Jeffs reported that he must have made a mistake with Beall's name, must have just assumed it was Beall who had treated him when he was researching his back story for his book, because Beall was known for having treated a number of lost boys.

2  Subsequently, studies of Mormon genealogical data from the same period (in part because of the Mormon beliefs regarding the posthumous baptism of ancestors, the LDS's records are second to none) demonstrated very persuasively the advantage and disadvantage of polygamy among Mormons in this period. The bottom line was that polygamy, as expected, was a highly advantageous genetic strategy for the men who adopted it – they were far more likely than monogamous men to pass along their genes. However, this was only because the sheer numbers of their offspring overcame their higher infant mortality rate. It was a nice point: seen from the point of view of evolutionary fitness, the men of polygamy were better off, however,

at the expense of other men and children, who were, on average much worse off than within mainstream monogamous society.

3　In retrospect, this comment should be added to the very long list of things that I have concluded, with *l'esprit d'escalier*, was kind of a dumb thing to say. It was the height of hubris to predict victory at that early stage, and of arrogant self-regard to ignore the fact that the team's case was not "my case." And, in any event, *that* day belonged to Henrich, not me. But hindsight is 20/20, and I include this anecdote to emphasize the euphoria I recall feeling as that pivotal day drew to a close.

4　Aharon Gaimani, "Marriage and Divorce Customs in Yemen and Eretz Israel" (Spring, 5766/2006) 11, Yemenite Jewish Women, *Nashim: A Journal of Jewish Women's Studies & Gender Issues* at 43–83.

5　Indeed, most anthropologists would, I think, be reluctant to characterize First Nations' complex and rich spiritual beliefs as "religions" at all.

6　We were all very pleased that Deborah had returned to the file in time for the decision the following November.

7　In 2012, during the presidential campaign (when Mormon Mitt Romney was a candidate for the Republican nomination), the Pew Research Center's Forum on Religion and Public Life conducted a comprehensive study of Mormons in the United States and found that only 2 percent considered polygamy "morally acceptable."

8　In Texas he would express doubt, for instance, that stories about the rape of girls in the YFZ temple were true, because Mormon practice and tradition did not accommodate the use of temple beds for that purpose. In January 2012 Walsh reappeared in British Columbia as an expert witness in Winston Blackmore's tax trial. Blackmore was claiming that taxes assessed to him personally as a result of business income from his forestry companies should be spread among all the members of his religious "congregation." Walsh revealed to the court that he was being paid $250/hr for his "expert" services (including for testifying)—not a bad rate, all considered.

9　A reservation is an instrument declaring that the signatory nation claimed an emption with respect to some aspect of the treaty or convention.

10　An *infamia* was a legal designation barring an individual from some private and public rights, such as holding public office or appearing in court.

11　Jessop did go back for her daughter and still managed to get away that morning. Ironically, at eighteen her daughter decided to return to the FLDS and Jessop had been unable to speak with her for over a year. The ostracization of "apostates" like Jessop was a recurring theme in the witnesses' testimony. Don Fischer recounted how he had once found his mother walking roadside and had unsuccessfully tried to convince her to hold her new grandson, whom she'd never met. The FLDS expected its members to shun persons who had left the community.

12　The order, as far as I know the first of its kind in Canada, was worded as follows:

(a) If a witness for the [FLDS] tenders evidence by affidavit, then:

> i. the witness may elect not to include his or her name or other details which might identify the witness or others who may be engaging in what may later be determined to be criminally polygamous relationships; and

> ii. the witness may use a pseudonym.

(b) If a witness for the applicants is cross-examined on an affidavit and/or gives *viva voce* evidence in these proceedings, then:

> i. the witness shall not be asked questions of any kind that might lead to the identification of that witness or others who may be engaging in what may later be determined to be criminally polygamous relationships;

> ii. the witness may elect to give evidence from behind a screen; and

> iii. the witness may use a pseudonym.

# Part 6: The Case Against Polygamy

1   Richard S Van Wagoner, *Mormon Polygamy: A History*, 2d ed (Salt Lake City, UT: Signature Books, 1989) at 91.

2   *Ibid* at 195.

3   Prosecutor Eric Nichols, in his Affidavit #1, documented the following marriages from the prosecutions in Texas that had, by that time, led to guilty pleas or convictions:

On 5 August 2004, at age 45, Michael Emack entered a "celestial marriage" to Ruleen Johnson Jessop Emack, who was 16. Ruleen was Emack's fourth wife.

On 3 October 2005, at age 26, Lehi Jeffs entered a celestial marriage to Rachel Keate, who was 15 (born 25 July 1990). Rachel gave birth to Jeffs's son on 11 June 2007 (she was 16). Rachel was Jeffs's third wife.

On 12 August 2004, at age 33, Raymond Merril Jessop entered a celestial marriage to Janet Jeffs, who was 15 (born 16 September 1988). Janet gave birth to Jessop's child in August 2005 (she was 16).

On 5 May 2005, at age 52, Allan Keate entered a celestial marriage with Merilyn Barlow, who was 15 (born 7 January 1990). Merilyn gave birth to Keate's child in December 2006 (she was 16). This was Merilyn's second marriage.

On 18 January 2004, Allan Keate gave his daughter, Veda Lucille Keate, to Warren Jeffs in celestial marriage. Veda was 14 (born 20 April 1989).

On 27 July 2006, at age 32, Merril Leroy Jessop ("Leroy") entered a celestial marriage with LeAnn Jeffs / Nielsen, who was 15 (born 24 March 1991). He had at least two other wives at the time.

On or about 5 October 2005, at age 34, Abram Jeffs entered a celestial marriage with Suzanne Johnson/Jessop, who was 14 (born 13 November 1990). Suzanne was one of Jeffs's many wives.

4   To similar effect was the evidence of Sarah Hammon, Kathleen Mackert, and Jorjina Broadbent.

5   Most were girls from Bountiful bound for American husbands, but several were American girls headed North.

6   Mainstream Mormons do, according to one source, marry somewhat earlier than average Canadians, but there is no record or suggestion of the pattern of adolescent marriage apparent in the FLDS.

7   Except that the *amicus* suggested to Professor McDermott that there had been inadequate control of confounding variables beyond GDP—a criticism that could not be, and was not, levelled at Dr Henrich's report where many more variables *were* controlled for.

8   Quoted in Quebec Report, "Polygamy and the Rights of Women" at 67, attached to Gabay, Affidavit #1.

9   Sarah Carter, *The Importance of Being Monogamous: Marriage and Nation Building in Western Canada to 1915* (Edmonton: University of Alberta Press, 2008) at 107.

10   In that sample 40 percent of Mormon women married before age twenty, compared to about 30 percent of the entire population. The average age of marriage in Canada, by the way, is twenty-nine.

11   In fact, the data in the article are apparently based on statistics for *legal* marriage, which in Canada would not include persons in the twelve-to-fifteen-years-old range at all.

12   Steven Pinker, *How the Mind Works* (New York: Norton, 1997) at 497–98.

13   Here I was quoting to Shackelford from Pinker, *ibid* at 476–78.

14   Benjamin Bistline, *The Polygamists: A History of Colorado City, Arizona* (Phoenix, AZ: Agreka LLC, 2004) at 142–43.

15   Dr Beall reported that boys he treated had been expelled from the community on one of two grounds: reassignment of father, or the umbrella term of "rebelliousness." Dr Beall testified that young men had to be kicked out of the community to make room for older men marring younger girls, and that young boys were aware of the pressure to ostracize them. Teressa Wall testified to four of her brothers being kicked out of their home and the community, and there was similar testimony from Sarah Hammon.

16   This was reflected in the evidence of Brent Jeffs, Richard Ream, Howard Mackert, and Don Fischer, the latter who was sent to Bountiful "reform camp" in Canada to work around the clock, earning C$60 every two weeks. Truman Oler had testified that he worked full-time over the summers and

was paid $20 every two weeks, then went to work full-time at age fifteen and made $60 every two weeks.

17 Carolyn Jessop testified that it was not unusual in her community to have twelve to sixteen kids. She cited one example of twenty-one children.

18 Rena Mackert noted that it was really difficult for her mother as "her worth as a woman depended on how many faithful children that she raised for the principle and every one of her children has left."

19 Eric Nichols's affidavit quoted Dictations of President Warren Jeffs on Thursday, 5 January 2006: "I met with Allan Keate and his young wife Merilyn. She has been withdrawn from him all this time since she was married. I gave very direct training on the need to be close and how to be close. She wouldn't even hold his hand. So I said, 'Hold hands, and walk home all the way holding hands. Go have a good hour talk,' because she still hasn't hardly talked to him."

20 Bistline, above note 14 at 120.

21 "R1" we had learned, is a coded reference to an FLDS location—each was assigned a number according to how many hours' drive it was from Short Creek (thus, for instance, Yearning for Zion in Texas was "R17").

22 Howard Mackert testified that "just the ability to make a decision and stick with and see it through is just really void in that community."

23 This is not to say that the total is representative as a percentage (because the cohort was selected, in part, based on the birthplace of the mothers in known FLDS communities), but even as raw numbers the figure is striking, given a community of only a few hundred residents.

24 Pinker, *How the Mind Works*, above note 12 at 478.

25 *R v Malmo-Levine*; *R v Caine*, [2003] 3 SCR 571, 2003 SCC 74 at para 116, citing *R v Butler*, [1992] 1 SCR 452 at 498.

26 *Ibid*; *R v Murdock* (2003), 11 CR (6th) 43 at para 32 (Ont CA).

27 I won't say that it is an arrangement mandated or dictated by religious belief, because as I emphasize throughout this book, my view is that the religious endorsements of polygamy evolved to accommodate the practice, not the other way around.

28 *Syndicat Northcrest v Amselem*, [2004] 2 SCR 551, Iacobucci J had written (for the majority) at para 56.

29 The nature of the religious challenge presented by the CPAA is not quite clear. On the one hand the group seems to suggest that "conjugal poly-amory" is a deeply held matter of conscience and therefore deserving of section 2(a) protection as such. In other passages, the group suggests that it is a desire to formalize polyamorous relationships through religious ceremony that permits its members to invoke freedom of religion. Even assuming both to be true, the arguments would add no further dimension to the section 2(a) arguments advanced by the other challengers.

30 [1985] 1 SCR 295.

31 *Bruker v Marcovitz*, [2007] 3 SCR 607, 2007 SCC 54 at paras 72–73; *Multani v Commission scolaire Marguerite-Bourgeoys*, [2006] 1 SCR 256, 2006 SCC 6 at para 26.

32 *Amselem*, above note 28 at para 62.

33 *Multani*, above note 31 at paras 28–29.

34 Peter W Hogg, *Constitutional Law of Canada*, loose-leaf, vol. 2 (Toronto: Carswell, 2007) at 42–49.

35 2009 SCC 30, [2009] SCR 181 at para 155.

36 (2001), 95 BCLR (3d) 122 at para 132 (SC).

37 [2007] 2 SCR 391, 2007 SCC 27.

38 (1989), 69 OR (2d) 189 at 203–4.

39 See *Halpern v Canada (Attorney General)* (2002), 60 OR (3d) 321 (Div Ct) at paras 30–31, 33, 72, and 212; *EGALE Canada Inc v Canada (Attorney General)*, 2001 BCSC 1365 at paras 134–39; *Barbeau v British Columbia (Attorney General)*, 2003 BCCA 406 at paras 97–100.

40 [1997] 3 SCR 844 at para 68.

41 [1988] 1 SCR 30 at 56 [emphasis added].

42 The witness described the stress as resulting from apprehensions arising from the Yearning for Zion search and rescue operation and also school inspections.

43 [1994] 3 SCR 761 at 792–94.

44 *Alberta v Hutterian Brethren of Wilson Colony*, 2009 SCC 37, [2009] 2 SCR 567 at para 108.

45 *Ibid* at paras 105–8.

46 [1999] 2 SCR 203 at para 13.

47 The CPAA's s 15 argument is not developed beyond that made by the *amicus* and amounts to the same thing: that, at least in the case of *polygynous* polyamory, the law is discriminating against polyamorists on the basis that they practise polygamy. But, for the reasons articulated here, such is not an enumerated or analogous ground. The fact that some types of polyamory, such as polyandry and multiple-partner same-sex unions, fall clearly outside the scope of s 293 is demonstration that the distinction is based on the harm of polygyny, and is emphatically not a prejudice toward nonmonogamous conjugality *per se*.

48 *Malmo-Levine*, above note 25 at para 133.

49 *Reference re ss. 193 and 195.1(1)(c) of the Criminal Code (Man.)*, [1990] 1 SCR 1123; see also *Harper v Canada (Attorney General)*, [2004] 1 SCR 827 at para 29; *Sharpe*, below note 74 at para 85; and *Butler*, above note 25 at 504.

50 *Butler, ibid* at 501.

51 *Little Sisters Book and Art Emporium v Canada (Minister of Justice)*, [2000] 2 SCR 1120 at para 228.

52 Reference re *ss. 193 and 195.1(1)(c) of the Criminal Code* (Man.), [1990] 1 SCR 1123.

53 [1995] 3 SCR 1999.

54 Brigham Young Card, "Charles Ora Card and the Founding of the Mormon Settlements in Southwestern Alberta, North-West Territories" in Card et al, eds, *The Mormon Presence in Canada* (Edmonton: University of Alberta Press, 1990) at 91 [Card et al].

55 Howard Palmer, "Polygamy and Progress: The Reaction to Mormons in Canada, 1887–1923" in Card et al, *ibid* at 117.

56 Jessie L Embry, "'Two Legal Wives': Mormon Polygamy in Canada, the United States and Mexico" in Card et al, *ibid* at 174.

57 Palmer, "Polygamy and Progress," above note 55 at 117.

58 See, generally, B Carmon Hardy, "Mormon Polygamy in Mexico and Canada: A Legal and Historiographical Review" in Card et al, above note 54, describing polygamy as contrary to the "intent" of Mexico's bigamy prohibition but possibly not captured by its precise language. He writes at 189:

> Mormon polygamous unions were not formally contracted by public magistrates. Therefore, as the products of private religious ceremonies, Mormon polygamous arrangements were not, strictly speaking, in violation of Mexican law. This, unquestionably, is the reason that some have alleged that those Latter-day Saints who went to Mexico to practise plural marriage did so legally.

59 Embry, "Two Legal Wives," above note 56 at 178.

60 Hardy, "Mormon Polygamy in Mexico and Canada," above note 58 at 197.

61 Embry, "Two Legal Wives," above note 56 at 175.

62 Daphne Bramham, *The Secret Lives of Saints* (Toronto: Random House Canada, 2008) at 47.

63 Palmer, "Polygamy and Progress," above note 55 at 128.

64 Robert J McCue, "British Columbia and the Mormons in the Nineteenth Century" in Card et al, above note 54 at 50.

65 The figure of 970 was from the Utah Territory Attorney General; the LDS church itself estimated the number at 1,300: Wagoner, above note 1.

66 Dr Henrich notes that children of polygamous men tend to have a lower survival rate than those of monogamous men, but this is more than compensated for by the numbers of children a polygamous man can have.

67 It would be disingenuous to argue, however, that "serial monogamy" is the equivalent of true polygyny in terms of harm. There can be no "hyperpolygynists" under present laws; even the most successful serial monogamists will have only a handful of wives or families over their lifetime (Dr Shackelford suggested that it generally happens at twenty-year intervals), and their obligations to former spouses and their children are strictly regu-

lated by law. In polygyny, even in North America, we have seen individuals amassing sixty wives at once (Brigham Young and Warren Jeffs); even lesser polygynists (like the bishop Winston Blackmore) can have dozens. Historically, in periods of great wealth inequality, polygyny customarily reaches "ridiculous levels" (a quote from Steven Pinker, adopted by Dr Shackelford).

68 2000 (6) SCC 224, 2000 AIR 1650.

69 Coomi Kapoor, "India Diary: Dodging the anti-bigamy laws" (19 January 2009), *The Star Online*: www.thestar.com.my/news/story. asp?file=/2009/1/19/focus/3046397&sec=focus.

70 Law Commission of India, *Report No. 227, Preventing Bigamy via Conversion to Islam—a Proposal for giving Statutory Effect to Supreme Court Rulings* (August 2009), online: www.lawcommissionofindia.nic.in/reports/report227.pdf.

71 Eric Gould, Omer Moav, & Avi Simhon, "The Mystery of Monogamy" (2008) 98:1 Am Econ Rev 333–357 at 349, appended to Affidavit of Emma Lehrer Sworn 2 December 2010.

72 "What the World Thinks of Canada: Canada and the World in 2010—Immigration and Diversity," Ipsos Reid for Historica Dominica Institute, Isbister, Affidavit #1, Exhibit F, Tab 4.

73 "Polygamy and the Rights of Women," Quebec *Conseil du statut de la femme* Report, Gabay, Affidavit #1, Exhibit B.

74 [2001] 1 SCR 45.

75 *Ibid* at para 93.

76 2004 UT 76.

77 Richard A Vazquez, "The Practice of Polygamy: Legitimate Free Exercise of Religion or Legitimate Public Menace? Revisiting Reynolds in Light of Modern Constitutional Jurisprudence" (2001) 5 NYUJ Legis & Pub Pol'y 225 at 243.

78 *Butler*, above note 25 at paras 122–24.

79 [1995] 2 SCR 418.

80 Para 41, citing *Maynard v Hill*, 125 US 190 (1888) at 205 and 211.

81 Para 42, citing *inter alia Meyer v Nebraska*, 262 US 390 (1923) at 399 which asserted that the Fourteenth Amendment includes "the right of the individual . . . to marry, establish a home and bring up children."

82 Justice Gonthier wrote at para 44:

> Moving from domestic to international law, art. 16 of the *Universal Declaration of Human Rights*, G.A. Res. 217 A (III), U.N. Doc. A/810, at 71 (1948), which is binding on Canada, and art. 12 of the *European Convention on Human Rights*, 213 U.N.T.S. 221, provide individuals with "the right to marry." For example, art. 16 of the *Universal Declaration* states that "Men and women of full age, with-

out any limitation due to race, nationality or religion, have the right to marry and to found a family. They are entitled to equal rights as to marriage, during marriage and at its dissolution."

83  As it might if more persons of one gender decided not to marry than the other.

84  *Re ss. 193 and 195.1(1)(c) of the Criminal Code (Man.)*, [1990] 1 SCR 1123 at paras 11 and 106; *Butler*, above note 25 at paras 120 and 122; *Thomson Newspapers Co (cob Globe and Mail) v Canada (AG)*, [1998] 1 SCR 877 at paras 125 and 129; *Sharpe*, above note 74 at para 78; *Hutterian Brethren*, above note 44 at paras 73, 89, 95, and 102.

85  [1986] 2 SCR 713.

# Afterword: The March of the Zombies

1  Like so many other iconic phrases, there are an almost limitless number of variables of this expression. It was never written or directly recorded as uttered by Keynes, but variations of the theme have been attributed to him by a number of sources. The interesting thing about this and other enduring quotes (or possible misquotes) is that their perseverance through language and argument speaks to their Darwinian utility. In this way the expression takes on an authority of its own and no longer needs to trade the gravitas of its attributed originator.

2  The actual source transcripts of Campbell's interviews, like the identity of her participants, remain confidential. By agreement and pursuant to a 23 November 2010 Order of the Court, we were granted access to anonymized versions of these transcripts. That order provided that all copies of the transcripts should be destroyed after the trial, which they were, in January 2012. So here, when I discuss anything said by Campbell's interviewees, I am referring only to what was excerpted, quoted, or synopsized in Campbell's own articles, in her testimony, and in the Chief Justice's reasons.

3  The Rushdie affair is ongoing, but its tenor has changed. In January 2012 Rushdie was forced to cancel an in-person appearance at the Jaipur Literature Festival in India amidst death threats. In his absence, defiant festival participants read from *The Satanic Verses* (whose importation into that country remains forbidden) to express solidarity, despite the spectre of violent protest.

# Index